LEVET

THE WORLD ALMANAC FOR KIDS
1997

WORLD ALMANAC BOOKS

AN IMPRINT OF K-III REFERENCE CORPORATION

A K-III Communications Company

THE WORLD ALMANAC FOR KIDS 1997

EDITOR:
Judith S. Levey

CURRICULUM CONSULTANT:
Jean Craven
District Coordinator of Curriculum Development
Albuquerque, NM, Public Schools

CONTRIBUTORS:
Irene Gunther, Bill Gutman, Judith Leale, Alan D. Levy, Randi Metsch-Ampel,
Richard Steins, Patricia Bonder, Jerilyn Famighetti, Joan Gampert,
Robert Gampert, Bonny R. Hart, Susan R. Norton, Terry Simon
Consultants: Christina Simmons (Animals); Sammie E. Hutchison (Computers);
Mary Jo Comber (Science); Anthony T. Padovano, S.T.D., Ph.D. (Religion)

DESIGN:
Janice Edelman-Lee, Bill Smith Studio
Cover Design: Todd Cooper, Bill Smith Studio

WORLD ALMANAC BOOKS
Vice President and Publisher: Richard W. Eiger

Editor:	**Vice President of Sales:**	**Director of Marketing:**
Robert Famighetti	James R. Keenley	Joyce H. Stein

Editorial Staff: William A. McGeveran, Jr., Deputy Editor; Christina Cheddar,
Matthew Friedlander, Associate Editors; Melissa Janssens, Desktop Publishing Associate

K-III REFERENCE
Vice President and Editorial Director: Leon L. Bram
Vice President of Manufacturing: Sally McCravey
Director of Editorial Production: Andrea J. Pitluk
Director of Indexing Services: Marjorie B. Bank

THE WORLD ALMANAC FOR KIDS 1997
Copyright © 1996 by K-III Reference Corporation
A K-III Communications Company

The World Almanac is a registered trademark of K-III Reference Corporation.

ISBN (softcover) 0-88687-794-6
ISBN (hardcover) 0-88687-795-4

Printed in the United States of America

The softcover and hardcover editions are distributed to the
trade in the United States by St. Martin's Press.

WORLD ALMANAC BOOKS
An Imprint of K-III Reference Corporation
One International Boulevard
Mahwah, New Jersey 07495-0017
E-Mail: Walmanac@aol.com

CONTENTS

INTRODUCTION 7

SPECIAL FEATURES 9-17
What Kids Are Saying..9
People and Places in the News....................................13
   Anniversaries in 1996 and 1997............................13
   Stars of Today..14
   Sports Highlights...15
   In the Headlines..16

ANIMALS 18-27
The Largest and the Fastest......................................18
How Long Do Animals Live?..19
Pet Shopping...20
Endangered Species...23
Dinosaur Facts and Figures.......................................25
Museums of Natural History.......................................26

ART 28-30
Painting: Landscape, Portrait, and Still Life...................28
Modern Art...29

BOOKS 31-34
Book Awards, 1995-1996...31
Ten All-Time Best-Selling Paperbacks.............................32
Other Books You May Enjoy Reading................................33

BUILDINGS, BRIDGES, AND TUNNELS 35-36
The 7 Wonders of the Ancient World...............................35
The Longest Bridges in the World.................................36

COMPUTERS 37-43
How Computers Work...38
Computer Museums...41
The Internet and the World Wide Web..............................43

COUNTRIES 44-82
Countries of the World...44
Maps and Flags of the Countries of the World.....................65
A Quick Visit to Some Countries of the World.....................81

ENERGY AND NATURAL RESOURCES 83-87
Energy: What It Is and Where It Comes From.......................83
How Does Energy Get To You?......................................85

ENVIRONMENT 88-97
Garbage and Recycling..90
The Air We Breathe...92
Protecting Our Water...94
How Kids Can Help Protect the Environment........................97

GEOGRAPHY 98-106

The Continents and Oceans of the World 99
Famous Regions of the World 100
Volcanoes 101
Earthquakes 102
The Tallest, Longest, Highest, Deepest in the World 105
Some Famous European and American Explorers.........................106

HEALTH 107-114

Learning About What's Inside Your Body 107
Tips for Tip-Top Teeth 109
Staying Healthy With Exercise...110
Which Foods Are the Right Foods? 111
Understanding AIDS 113

HOLIDAYS 115-116

Legal or Public Holidays in the United States 115
Some Holidays Around the World 116

INVENTIONS 117-119

Inventions That Take Us From One Place to Another.....................117
Inventions That Entertain Us 118
Inventions That Make Our Lives Easier......................................119

LANGUAGE 120-125

Abbreviations...120
Writing a Letter...121
Idioms: Words That Are Not as They Seem 123
Languages of the World...124
Which Languages Are Spoken in the United States?......................124
Where in the World Do English Words Come From?.......................125

LAW 126-127

What Happens When You Break the Law? 126
Rights for Children 127

MONEY AND BUSINESS 128-137

Making Money: The U.S. Mint...130
How Much Money Is in Circulation in the United States? 131
Budgets...132
What Do Americans Buy? 134
What Kinds of Jobs Do Americans Have?....................................135

MOVIES, VIDEOS, AND TELEVISION 138-140

20 Movie Hits of 1995 139
Some Best-Selling Videos in 1995 140
Popular TV Shows in 1995-1996...140

MUSEUMS 141-143

Children's Museums...141
Ethnic Museums 142
Historic Restorations...143

MUSIC AND DANCE — 144-149

Music and Music Makers 144
Instruments of the Orchestra...146
American Musical Theater 147
Dance...148

NUMBERS — 150-153

Roman Numerals...150
The Prefix Tells the Number 151
Reading and Writing Large Numbers 151
How Many Sides and Faces Do They Have? 152

PLANETS, STARS, AND SPACE TRAVEL — 154-163

The Solar System 154
What Is an Eclipse?..157
Constellations: Pictures in the Sky 158
Traveling Into Outer Space...161

PLANTS — 164-167

Where Do Plants Grow?..166
Fascinating Plants 167

POPULATION — 168-173

The Largest and Smallest Places in the World 168
Population of the United States 169
Taking the Census: Everyone Counts 170
Counting the First Americans 171
The Many Faces of America: Immigration...............................172
Becoming an American Citizen: Naturalization.........................173
Ellis Island and The Statue of Liberty 173

PRIZES, AWARDS, AND CONTESTS — 174-178

Entertainment Awards...174
Other Prizes and Awards..176
Halls of Fame 177
Contests...178

RELIGION — 179-182

Religion Around the World 179
Religious Membership in the United States 181
Major Holy Days for Christians, Jews, and Muslims....................182

SCIENCE — 183-189

A Look at Some Common Elements.......................................184
Some Answers to Science Questions 185
Some Light and Sound Subjects..186
Rocks, Minerals, and Gems 187
Science Museums..189

SIGNS AND SYMBOLS — 190-193

Road Signs 191
Sign Language 192
Secret Messages 193

SPORTS — 194-209

Olympic Games 194
Baseball 196
Basketball 198
Football 201
Ice Hockey 205
Ice Skating 206
Soccer 207

TIME AND CALENDARS — 210-21

What Are Time Zones? 210
Birthstones 211

UNITED NATIONS — 212-213

How the UN Is Organized 212

UNITED STATES — 214-280

Facts and Figures 214
The U.S. Government and How It Works 216
Using a Voting Machine 225
Presidents and Vice Presidents of the United States 226
Presidential Facts, Families, and First Ladies 233
United States History Timeline 234
Maps of the United States 241
Facts About the States 257
Washington, D.C.: The Capital of the United States 275
How the States Got Their Names 276
National Parks 278

WEATHER — 281-283

Naming Hurricanes 281
The Speed of Wind 281

WEIGHTS AND MEASURES — 284-287

Measurements Used in the United States 284
The Metric System 286
Converting U.S. Measurements to Metrics and
    Metrics to U.S. Measurements 287

WORLD HISTORY — 288-30

Highlights of World History 288
The Middle East 288
Africa 290
Asia 292
Europe 295
The Americas 299

PUZZLES AND ANSWERS

Puzzles are on pages 20, 26, 42, 64, 97, 105, 109, 120, 122, 123, 125,
    153, 163, 193, 209, 274
Answers to Puzzles 302

INDEX — 306-319

INTRODUCTION

A Note to Kids

Do you often find yourself looking for new ideas and fascinating facts you haven't yet seen? Do you pride yourself on doing school projects that include the latest and most interesting information—the kind no one else will find? Do you enjoy solving puzzles, finding hidden words, or figuring out coded messages? If so, this book is for you.

In *The World Almanac for Kids* you will find facts on many topics—from earthquakes, sports, dinosaurs, and space travel to the Internet, books, movies, and explorers—topics kids are interested in and often study in school. All of this information is easy to read and understand. You will find yourself turning from one page to another, stopping to explore topics you didn't know you would like. If curiosity comes naturally to you, keep this book handy.

As you look through *The World Almanac for Kids*, keep your eyes open for the different kinds of puzzles. You will have fun testing your know-how as you unscramble mixed-up words, fill in crossword puzzles, or decode secret messages. Also, notice the "Did You Know?" sections tucked away on many pages. They contain bits of information that are fun and will surprise you and your friends. Share them with your parents and teachers as well—fun is for people of all ages.

A Word for Parents

How many times have you searched the house for one more reliable source of information your child could use to write a report due the next day? How often have you needed to help your youngster check one last fact for a project to be sure everything would be correct and up to date? Here's a book to meet your needs—and it's written for kids, so they can use it themselves.

The World Almanac for Kids is packed with information— not only the facts needed for reports and projects, but also information kids like to read and think about. Its friendly format and helpful illustrations attract the eye and invite the reader to keep turning pages to check out one more topic.

How did we select the subjects to include? We started with topics of interest to kids, and we put in the most recent facts and figures, which are completely revised and updated each year. We included topics kids typically study in school and ones they could use for reports and projects. Many facts are similar to those you would usually find in *The World Almanac*. This is a kid's version of that book, with information that is current, organized for easy use, and designed for the curious mind. A child who explores this book will learn how to find information about many subjects and will enjoy using it often.

Will your youngster be the only one in the family to use *The World Almanac for Kids*? I suspect not. Do you ever find that he or she is writing a report on a topic you don't fully understand? The clear explanations, explanatory diagrams, well-organized basic facts, and answers to questions will enlighten and intrigue adults as well as kids. So don't be surprised if you learn as much as your child does—and try to leave a few puzzles for the kids!

Jean Craven
District Coordinator of Curriculum Development
Albuquerque, NM, Public Schools

WHAT KIDS ARE SAYING

For the second year in a row *The World Almanac for Kids* asked fourth and fifth graders in schools all over the United States to answer a few questions. We wanted to find out more about our readers. Again, we enjoyed reading the answers and learned a lot from them.

QUESTION: If you could be president of the United States for a day, what's the first thing you would do to make the world or the country a better place?

Kids had very definite ideas about what they would do. Their top goals were to help the poor and the homeless, clean up the environment, stop crime and violence, lower taxes or get rid of them, end all wars, and get rid of drugs, alcohol, and tobacco.

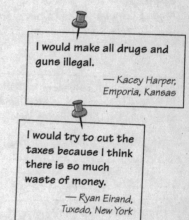

I would make all drugs and guns illegal.

— Kacey Harper, Emporia, Kansas

I would let all of the kids out of school and the grownups off of work and they could all help clean up the earth.

— Sarah Beth Kuylen, South Heart, North Dakota

I would try to cut the taxes because I think there is so much waste of money.

— Ryan Eirand, Tuxedo, New York

Many kids were interested in improving schools, protecting animals, ending racism and prejudice, or making a favorite wish come true.

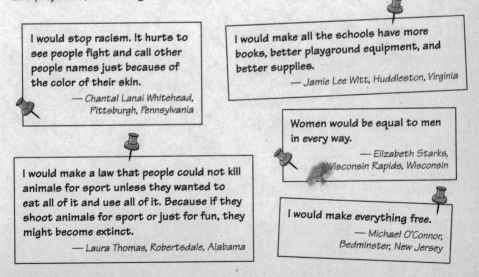

I would stop racism. It hurts to see people fight and call other people names just because of the color of their skin.

— Chantal Lanai Whitehead, Pittsburgh, Pennsylvania

I would make all the schools have more books, better playground equipment, and better supplies.

— Jamie Lee Witt, Huddleston, Virginia

Women would be equal to men in every way.

— Elizabeth Starks, Wisconsin Rapids, Wisconsin

I would make a law that people could not kill animals for sport unless they wanted to eat all of it and use all of it. Because if they shoot animals for sport or just for fun, they might become extinct.

— Laura Thomas, Robertsdale, Alabama

I would make everything free.

— Michael O'Connor, Bedminster, New Jersey

QUESTION: If you were given $25 to do anything you want with, what would you do with it?

Many of the kids who answered this question were very generous. About a third said they would give away all or part of the $25 to help people in need. A little more than a third said they would spend the money, either on themselves or others.

The kids knew that handling money means making choices. Some said they would save all the money, others would spend part of it and save part, still others would spend some and give some away, in some cases to their own families. Here are some of their answers.

Spend it
Among popular items to buy were books, comic books, magazines, clothes, toys, games, CDs, pets, and candy.

I would take my Mommy, Daddy, and brother to lunch at McDonalds. I would enjoy paying for once.
—Danielle Anderson, Thousand Oaks, California

I would buy as many books as I could before the money ran out.
— Patrick Hume, Stoneham, Massachusetts

I would save it up and then buy a computer game.
— PJ Meany, Hochessin, Delaware

I would buy myself some awesome clothes and I would get pizza and pop for my class.
— Janell Saunders, Huntington, Indiana

I would buy a big kite and fly around the world because I think it would be fun.
— Taylor McDonald, Woods Cross, Utah

SALE

Save it

Many kids would put the money away for college. Others would save up to buy something special, such as sports equipment, computer games or programs, a bicycle, a car, or a vacation.

I would save my money and put it into my college fund. My money is usually not spent unless it is for a good cause. I work for all my money, so $25 is not something I would waste.

— Cindy Ruzicka, Marble Rock, Iowa

I would save it for a new saddle for my horse, or put it in the bank for college.

— Lisa Ashley Derzay, Deer Lodge, Montana

Give all or part of it away

Some would use the money to buy food or clothing for the poor or homeless. Others would give the money to an organization that helped others, such as a church, hospital, orphanage, or nursing home.

I would take a homeless person and buy him or her a big dinner.

— Travis Overstreet, Moneta, Virginia

I would give half of it to the poor and use half of it to buy tickets to a UConn Huskies basketball game.

— Willie Zaleha III, Derby, Connecticut

I would give the money to the poor. It won't be a lot but it is money. It is so sad to know people do not have that much money.

— Tanika Benjamin, Broadway, North Carolina

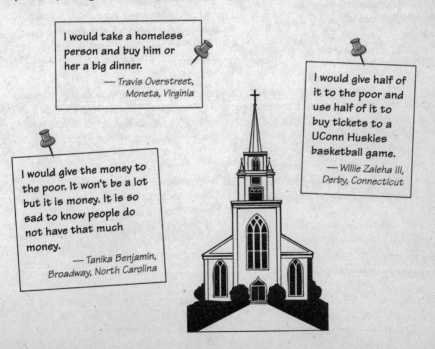

QUESTION: If you could be any character (not a real person) from a book, movie, or TV show, who would you be? Why?

Cartoon characters and animated movie characters were the most popular, with Bugs Bunny heading the list. Kids also admired brave or adventurous characters with superhuman or magical powers, like Superman, Batman, or Luke Skywalker from *Star Wars*. Some kids chose independent, spunky characters like Jo March from *Little Women* or characters who seemed kind and caring.

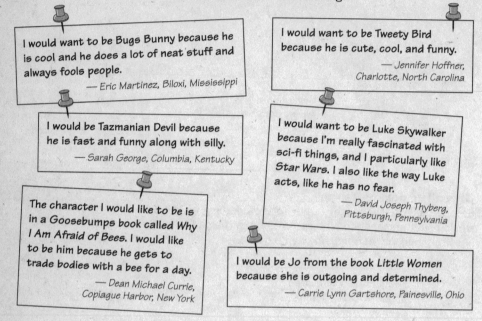

I would want to be Bugs Bunny because he is cool and he does a lot of neat stuff and always fools people.
— Eric Martinez, Biloxi, Mississippi

I would want to be Tweety Bird because he is cute, cool, and funny.
— Jennifer Hoffner, Charlotte, North Carolina

I would be Tazmanian Devil because he is fast and funny along with silly.
— Sarah George, Columbia, Kentucky

I would want to be Luke Skywalker because I'm really fascinated with sci-fi things, and I particularly like *Star Wars*. I also like the way Luke acts, like he has no fear.
— David Joseph Thyberg, Pittsburgh, Pennsylvania

The character I would like to be is in a Goosebumps book called *Why I Am Afraid of Bees*. I would like to be him because he gets to trade bodies with a bee for a day.
— Dean Michael Currie, Copiague Harbor, New York

I would be Jo from the book *Little Women* because she is outgoing and determined.
— Carrie Lynn Gartshore, Painesville, Ohio

Many kids were drawn to characters who reminded them in some way of themselves. They would like to be cool like Bart Simpson, who "gets into trouble like me," or run fast like Road Runner, or be pretty and get the prince like Sleeping Beauty or Snow White, or popular like Rachel and Phoebe from the TV show *Friends,* or rich like Richie Rich.

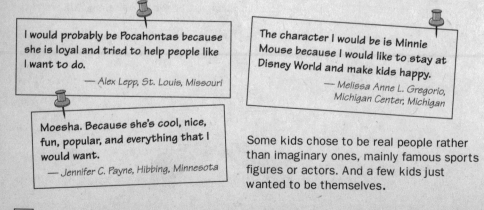

I would probably be Pocahontas because she is loyal and tried to help people like I want to do.
— Alex Lepp, St. Louis, Missouri

The character I would be is Minnie Mouse because I would like to stay at Disney World and make kids happy.
— Melissa Anne L. Gregorio, Michigan Center, Michigan

Moesha. Because she's cool, nice, fun, popular, and everything that I would want.
— Jennifer C. Payne, Hibbing, Minnesota

Some kids chose to be real people rather than imaginary ones, mainly famous sports figures or actors. And a few kids just wanted to be themselves.

ANNIVERSARIES IN 1996

100 YEARS AGO—1896

- ☑ The first motion picture was shown to the public, on April 23 in New York City.
- ☑ Rural free postal delivery started on October 1.
- ☑ The first motor cars in the United States were offered for sale.
- ☑ The first color comic strip came out. It was called "The Yellow Kid."
- ☑ The first modern Olympic Games were held, in Athens, Greece. A total of 311 athletes from 13 nations competed in 9 sports.
- ☑ The first Tootsie Rolls were made by candyman Leo Hirschfield. He named them after his six-year-old daughter, whom he called "Tootsie."

ANNIVERSARIES IN 1997

100 YEARS AGO—1897

- ☑ The first subway line in the United States opened in Boston, September 1.
- ☑ The first Boston Marathon was run, on April 19.
- ☑ John Philip Sousa's marching song "Stars and Stripes Forever" was performed for the first time.
- ☑ Jell-O dessert was introduced.

▲ Chuck Yeager

50 YEARS AGO—1947

- ☑ On October 14, Chuck Yeager became the first pilot to fly faster than the speed of sound. He was flying the X-1 rocket plane.
- ☑ Jackie Robinson became the first African-American to play for a major league baseball team, the Brooklyn Dodgers.
- ☑ The World Series was shown on television for the first time, as the New York Yankees beat the Brooklyn Dodgers, 4 games to 3.
- ☑ The first Little League Baseball World Series was played, in Williamsport, Pennsylvania.

25 YEARS AGO—1972

- ☑ American swimmer Mark Spitz won a record seven gold medals at the summer Olympics in Munich, Germany.
- ☑ President Richard Nixon became the first president of the United States to visit China.

STARS OF TODAY

DO NICE GUYS ALWAYS FINISH LAST?

Not in the case of **Hootie and the Blowfish.** This folk-rock band from South Carolina won two Grammy Awards in 1996 for the album *Cracked Rear View.* It sold over 13 million copies, making it one of the best-selling recordings ever. The band named itself after a couple of friends—one who wore owlish glasses and another with large, puffy cheeks. The name may seem odd, but the band members are famous for being regular guys. They like burgers, basketball, malls, movies, golf—and perhaps most of all, their fans.

POP SINGER BECOMES TV TEEN

Brandy Norwood has been singing since she was a baby. She and her brother sang together in their church choir, and by the time she was 15, Brandy's first hit song ("I Wanna Be Down") topped the music charts. While she still makes records, Brandy also plays the starring role on TV's popular sitcom *Moesha.* A lot like Brandy herself, Moesha is a smart, spunky teenager who has fun and hard times alike as she grows up dealing with her parents, brother, friends, and school.

▲ *Brandy Norwood*

GOOD NEWS FOR JONATHAN TAYLOR THOMAS FANS

In 1996 popular teen actor **Jonathan Taylor Thomas** (Randy from TV's *Home Improvement*) starred in two more movies. Both are based on classic tales. Early in the year J.T.T. appeared as Tom Sawyer, with Brad Renfro as Huck Finn, in *Tom and Huck,* which is based on Mark Twain's writings. In *The Adventures of Pinocchio,* which was in movie theaters in the summer of 1996, J.T.T. played Pinocchio, the wooden puppet that turns into a real boy.

▲ *Jonathan Taylor Thomas*

AND THE WINNER IS . . . A TALKING PIG?

Well, almost. The movie *Babe,* about a talking pig of the same name, won an Oscar in 1996 for Best Visual Effects and a Golden Globe Award for Best Comedy Film. *Babe* is about a pig who saves himself from becoming the farmer's dinner by learning to be a sheep dog, or rather a "sheep pig." The filmmakers used computers and a process called animatronics to make the animals look as if they are really talking to one another.

SPORTS HIGHLIGHTS

BASEBALL'S NEW IRON MAN

On September 6, 1995, Baltimore Orioles shortstop **Cal Ripken, Jr.,** broke one of baseball's greatest records. He played in his 2,131st straight game, beating the mark set by Yankee legend Lou Gehrig in 1939. It was truly an amazing feat. Ripken had not missed a single game since May 30, 1982.

NCAA CHAMPS: THE LADY VOLS AND THE WILDCATS

By defeating Georgia, 83-65, college basketball's **Lady Volunteers** of the University of Tennessee became NCAA women's champs in 1996. It was the Lady Vols' fourth championship in 15 years. That's twice as many titles as any other women's team. The **Kentucky Wildcats** won NCAA men's title number six with a 76-67 victory over Syracuse in the 1996 championship game. Only UCLA, with 11 national titles, has won more.

THE COWBOYS, SUPER ONCE MORE

It wasn't easy, but the **Dallas Cowboys** beat the Pittsburgh Steelers, 27-17, at Sun Devil Stadium in Tempe, Arizona, on January 28, 1996, to become football's Super Bowl champions for the third time in four years. Not only did the Cowboys become the first team to win three titles in four years. They were also the second team (San Francisco was the first) to win five Super Bowls all together. Defensive back **Larry Brown** was the game's Most Valuable Player, with a pair of key interceptions. And Cowboys quarterback **Troy Aikman** became the first signal caller to lead his team to three Super Bowl triumphs by the age of 30.

▲ *Michael Jordan (Number 23)*

JORDAN AND THE BULLS STAMPEDE

The 1995-1996 season was a record-breaking one for the National Basketball Association's **Chicago Bulls** and their superstar guard **Michael Jordan**. The unstoppable Bulls won 72 regular-season games, breaking the record of 69 set by the Los Angeles Lakers in 1971-1972. Chicago went on to win its fourth NBA championship in six years! Jordan set NBA records by winning his eighth scoring title and by being named Most Valuable Player in the NBA Finals for a fourth time. He was also named regular-season MVP for a fourth time.

QUEEN OF THE ICE

Gliding over the ice at Canada's Edmonton Coliseum, **Michelle Kwan,** from Torrance, California, won the women's world figure skating championship in 1996. Kwan, who was 15 years old, landed seven difficult triple jumps and dazzled the crowd with her style and grace.

IN THE HEADLINES

NEW PLANETS FOUND

During late 1995 and early 1996, scientists reported finding five new planets circling stars outside the solar system. One of the planets is nicknamed **Goldilocks.** While the other new planets are either too hot or too cold, Goldilocks may be just the right temperature to have rain, and maybe even oceans. This means it might also have some kind of life. All of these planets are too far away to be seen from Earth. Scientists can tell they exist by the light from the stars they orbit.

YITZHAK RABIN ASSASSINATED

On November 4, 1995, Israeli Prime Minister Yitzhak Rabin was assassinated. He had just finished speaking at a peace rally in Tel Aviv when he was shot by an Israeli who was against a recent peace agreement made between Palestinians and Israelis. At his funeral, Rabin's 18-year-old granddaughter, Noa Ben Artzi-Pelossof, honored her grandfather's memory in a moving speech that touched mourners in Israel and around the world. In 1996, Noa published a book about her grandfather, called In the Name of Sorrow and Hope.

MILLION MAN MARCH

Hundreds of thousands of African-American men and boys gathered in Washington, D.C., on October 16, 1995, to join in the Million Man March. The idea of the march was to encourage black men to strengthen their communities by taking good care of their children, treating women with respect, and ending violence and drug abuse. This peaceful rally was the largest ever held by African-Americans in Washington, D.C. It was the idea of Louis Farrakhan, a controversial minister who is the leader of the Nation of Islam.

FIRST AMERICAN WOMAN ON MIR

High above Earth on March 24, 1996, the American space shuttle *Atlantis* linked up with the Russian space station *Mir*. Dr. Shannon Lucid, a 53-year-old NASA scientist, went aboard *Mir* and began a planned five-month stay, the longest by an American astronaut. Dr. Lucid became the first American woman to live on *Mir*. She conducted experiments and studied the effects of long periods of weightlessness.

▲ *Dr. Shannon Lucid*

O.J. SIMPSON FOUND "NOT GUILTY"

For eight months, O.J. Simpson, the actor and former football star, had been on trial for the murder of his ex-wife, Nicole Brown Simpson, and her friend Ronald Goldman. When the verdict was announced on October 3, 1995, just about the entire country came to a halt. Kids and adults alike gathered around TVs and radios at home, at school and work, and in stores and restaurants to hear the that O.J. Simpson was found "not guilty" of the murders. When the verdict was read, some people cheered and others booed, but all had stopped what they were doing to hear the news.

▲ *Skull of the Carcharodontosaurus*

BATTLE OF THE DINOSAURS

Fossil experts have found more and more evidence that Tyrannosaurus Rex may not be "king" of the meat-eating dinosaurs after all. In Africa's Sahara Desert they uncovered the 5-foot, 4-inch skull of a dinosaur called Carcharodontosaurus ("shark-toothed reptile"). It was bigger than any T. Rex skull ever found. In the same area, fossil hunters found the remains of Deltadromeus, a very long but thin meat-eating dinosaur that had not been known before. Both dinosaurs probably lived about 90 million years ago.

DAYTON ACCORDS BRING HOPES FOR PEACE IN BOSNIA

After four years of fighting that killed thousands of people, the presidents of Bosnia, Croatia, and Serbia agreed to end the war in Bosnia and set up a new government there. The United States had brought the leaders together at an air force base in Dayton, Ohio, where they talked for three weeks before agreeing. The peace agreement was signed on December 14, 1995, in Paris. Later in December, 20,000 American troops were sent to Bosnia as part of an international peacekeeping force.

KASPAROV BEATS DEEP BLUE AT CHESS

In February 1996, Gary Kasparov, who most experts think is the world's best chess player, faced an opponent that wasn't even human–a computer named Deep Blue. Its powerful "brain" could analyze more than 100 million chess moves per second. Kasparov thought he could beat Deep Blue easily, but he lost the first game of the match. In the end, Kasparov rebounded and won with a score of 4 to 2. But he admitted that Deep Blue was as clever as some of his toughest human challengers.

ROCK AND ROLL HALL OF FAME AND MUSEUM

A gala celebration marked the opening of The Rock and Roll Hall of Fame and Museum in Cleveland, Ohio, on September 1, 1995. There was a parade with a giant Elvis Presley puppet, and a six-hour rock concert. The huge building, which sits on the shore of Lake Erie, was designed by a well-known architect, I.M. Pei. Rock artists who recorded their first song at least 25 years ago are honored in the Hall of Fame, while current rockers are featured in the museum.

▲ *Elvis Presley*

The LARGEST and the FASTEST

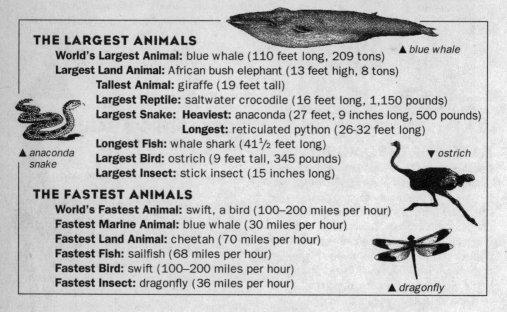

THE LARGEST ANIMALS

▲ blue whale

World's Largest Animal: blue whale (110 feet long, 209 tons)
Largest Land Animal: African bush elephant (13 feet high, 8 tons)
    Tallest Animal: giraffe (19 feet tall)
    Largest Reptile: saltwater crocodile (16 feet long, 1,150 pounds)
    Largest Snake: Heaviest: anaconda (27 feet, 9 inches long, 500 pounds)
        Longest: reticulated python (26-32 feet long)
    Longest Fish: whale shark ($41\frac{1}{2}$ feet long)

▲ anaconda snake

    Largest Bird: ostrich (9 feet tall, 345 pounds)

▼ ostrich

    Largest Insect: stick insect (15 inches long)

THE FASTEST ANIMALS

World's Fastest Animal: swift, a bird (100–200 miles per hour)
Fastest Marine Animal: blue whale (30 miles per hour)
Fastest Land Animal: cheetah (70 miles per hour)
Fastest Fish: sailfish (68 miles per hour)
Fastest Bird: swift (100–200 miles per hour)
Fastest Insect: dragonfly (36 miles per hour)

▲ dragonfly

How Fast Do Animals Run?

Did you know that some animals can run as fast as a car can move or that a snail would need more than 30 hours just to go one mile? If you look at this table, you will see how fast some common land animals can move.

	MILES PER HOUR
Cheetah	70
Lion	50
Cape hunting dog	45
Zebra	40
Rabbit	35
Grizzly bear	30
Cat (domestic)	30
Human	28
Elephant	25
Squirrel	12
Pig (domestic)	11
Chicken	9
Snail	0.03

▲ cheetah

▲ rabbit

◄ snail

Box turtle	100 years
Asian elephant	40 years
Grizzly bear	25 years
Horse	20 years
Gorilla	20 years
Polar bear	20 years
Rhinoceros (white)	20 years
Black bear	18 years
Lion	15 years
Rhesus monkey	15 years
Rhinoceros (black)	15 years
Camel	12 years
Cat (domestic)	12 years
Dog (domestic)	12 years
Leopard	12 years
Giraffe	10 years
Pig	10 years
Squirrel	10 years
Red fox	7 years
Kangaroo	7 years
Chipmunk	6 years
Rabbit	5 years
Guinea pig	4 years
Mouse	3 years
Opossum	1 year

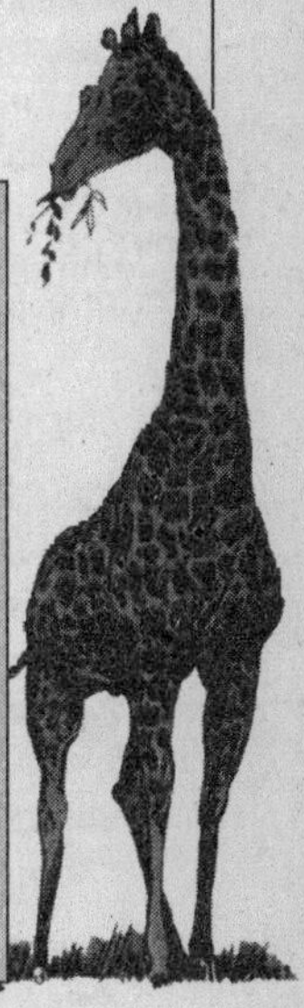

How Long Do Animals Live?

Most animals do not live as long as human beings. A monkey that is 14 years old is thought to be old. A person who is 14 is considered young. In 1996, the average life span of a human being is 70 to 80 years. The average life spans of some animals are shown here. Only one lives longer than human beings.

What to Call ANIMALS and THEIR YOUNG

ANIMAL	MALE	FEMALE	YOUNG
bear	boar	sow	cub
pig	boar	sow	piglet
cattle, elephant, hippopotamus, giraffe, whale	bull	cow	calf
deer	buck	doe	fawn
goat	buck, billy goat	doe, nanny goat	kid
rabbit	buck	doe	bunny, kit
duck	drake	duck	duckling
goose	gander	goose	gosling
horse	stallion	mare	foal
lion	lion	lioness	cub
sheep	ram	ewe	lamb
tiger	tiger	tigress	cub

PET SHOPPING

Pets can be lots of fun. If you already have one, you also know that a pet may need a lot of care. And proper care takes time, effort, and money. If you are thinking of getting a pet, the questions below will help you choose one that will be a good match for you and your family. Look for information on pets at a public library, a local pet shelter, or a veterinarian's office.

QUESTIONS TO ANSWER BEFORE CHOOSING A PET

- ☑ Why do you want a pet? Do you want an animal to cuddle or keep you company? Do you want to teach a bird to talk? Or watch fish swim?
- ☑ How much space does the animal need? Do you have enough space?
- ☑ What kind of shelter should it live in?
- ☑ Does the animal you want like to be held or left alone?
- ☑ What kind of food is best for the animal? How often and how much food does it eat? How much does the food cost?
- ☑ What kind of exercise should the pet get? How often?
- ☑ What kind of grooming does the animal need?
- ☑ Is there a veterinarian nearby to meet your pet's health needs?
- ☑ Does the animal need regular care from a veterinarian? How much does this cost?
- ☑ Are you or anyone in your family allergic to any animals?

PET PUZZLE

If you can unscramble the words below, you will know which animals are the most popular pets in the United States. (Answers are on page 302.)

TACS	SOGD	SHIF	DIRBS	STIBBAR
STAMREHS	SEKANS	STEFERR	SLURETT	NUIGEA GIPS

What Are GROUPS OF ANIMALS Called?

The next time you see a group of these animals, rather than saying that you saw a bunch of fish, sheep, or ants, use the expressions below.

▲ *gaggle of geese*

ants: *colony* of ants
bees: *swarm* of bees
chicks: *clutch* of chicks
clams: *bed* of clams
ducks: *brace* of ducks
elks: *gang* of elks
fish: *school* of fish
geese: *flock* or *gaggle*
gorillas: *band* of gorillas
hares: *down* of hares

hens: *brood* of hens
kangaroos: *troop* of kangaroos
leopards: *leap* of leopards
lions: *pride* of lions
monkeys: *troop* of monkeys
oxen: *yoke* of oxen
seals: *pod* of seals
sheep: *flock* of sheep
swans: *bevy* of swans
whales: *pod* of whales

CLASSIFYING ANIMALS

There are so many different types of animals in the world that scientists had to find a way to organize them into groups. A man named Carolus Linnaeus, who lived in the 1700s, worked out a system for classifying both animals and plants. We still use that system today. All animals together are called the **animal kingdom**. Below is a simplified chart showing how a few animals in the animal kingdom are classified.

ANIMAL KINGDOM

The animal kingdom includes all the animals in the world. The animal kingdom is separated into two large groups—animals with backbones, called **vertebrates**, and animals without backbones, called **invertebrates**. These large groups are divided into smaller groups called *phyla*. And phyla are divided into even smaller groups called *classes*. The animals in each group are classified together when their bodies are similar in certain ways. Below are examples of some of the animals in these groups.

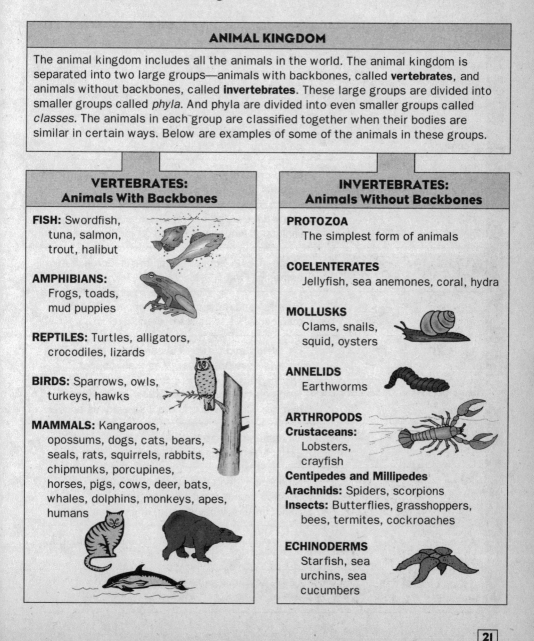

VERTEBRATES: Animals With Backbones

FISH: Swordfish, tuna, salmon, trout, halibut

AMPHIBIANS: Frogs, toads, mud puppies

REPTILES: Turtles, alligators, crocodiles, lizards

BIRDS: Sparrows, owls, turkeys, hawks

MAMMALS: Kangaroos, opossums, dogs, cats, bears, seals, rats, squirrels, rabbits, chipmunks, porcupines, horses, pigs, cows, deer, bats, whales, dolphins, monkeys, apes, humans

INVERTEBRATES: Animals Without Backbones

PROTOZOA
The simplest form of animals

COELENTERATES
Jellyfish, sea anemones, coral, hydra

MOLLUSKS
Clams, snails, squid, oysters

ANNELIDS
Earthworms

ARTHROPODS
Crustaceans: Lobsters, crayfish
Centipedes and Millipedes
Arachnids: Spiders, scorpions
Insects: Butterflies, grasshoppers, bees, termites, cockroaches

ECHINODERMS
Starfish, sea urchins, sea cucumbers

ANIMAL LIFE on Earth

This time line shows how animal life developed on earth and when land plants developed. The earliest animals are at the top of the chart. The most recent are at the bottom of the chart.

	YEARS AGO		ANIMAL LIFE ON EARTH
PRECAMBRIAN	4.5 billion		Formation of the earth. No signs of life.
PRECAMBRIAN	2.5 billion		First evidence of life in the form of bacteria and algae. All life is in water.
PALEOZOIC	570-500 million		Animals with shells (called trilobites) and some mollusks. Some fossils begin to form.
PALEOZOIC	500-430 million		Jawless fish appear, oldest known animals with backbones (vertebrates).
PALEOZOIC	430-395 million		Many coral reefs, jawed fishes, and scorpion-like animals. First land plants.
PALEOZOIC	395-345 million		Many fishes. Earliest known insect. Amphibians (animals living in water and on land) appear.
PALEOZOIC	345-280 million		Large insects appear. Amphibians increase in numbers. First trees appear.
PALEOZOIC	280-225 million		Reptiles and modern insects appear. Trilobites, many corals and fishes become extinct.
MESOZOIC	225-195 million		Dinosaurs and turtles appear. Many reptiles and insects develop further. Mammals appear.
MESOZOIC	195-135 million		Many giant dinosaurs. Reptiles increase in number. First birds and crablike animals appear.
MESOZOIC	135-65 million		Dinosaurs develop further and then become extinct. Flowering plants begin to appear.
CENOZOIC	65-2.5 million		Modern-day land and sea animals begin to develop, including such mammals as rhinoceroses, whales, cats, dogs, apes, seals.
CENOZOIC	2.5 million-10,000		Earliest humans appear. Mastodon, mammoths, and other huge animals become extinct.
CENOZOIC	10,000-present		Modern human beings and animals.

ENDANGERED SPECIES

When an animal becomes less and less plentiful on one part of the earth or in the entire world, the animal is said to be **endangered** or **threatened**. The U.S. Department of the Interior keeps track of endangered and threatened species. Throughout the world today, 995 species of animals are endangered or threatened. These include:

- ☑ 335 species of mammals
- ☑ 275 species of birds
- ☑ 116 species of fish
- ☑ 112 species of reptiles
- ☑ 59 species of clams
- ☑ 33 species of insects
- ☑ 65 other species

A FEW ENDANGERED SPECIES
Mammals: *Giant panda* in China; *Gray whale* in North Pacific Ocean
Fish: *Sockeye (red) salmon* in North Pacific from the United States to Russia
Bird: *American peregrine falcon* from Alaska to Mexico
Reptile: *American alligator* in the southeastern United States

HOW DO ANIMALS BECOME ENDANGERED?
Over very long periods of time, many kinds of animals and plants have disappeared from the earth (become extinct). This happens for several reasons:

☑ **Changes in Climate.** Animals are threatened when the climate of their habitat (where they live) changes in a major way. For example, if an area becomes very hot and dry and a river dries up, the fish and other plant and animal life in the river will die.

☑ **Habitat Destruction.** Sometimes animal habitats are destroyed when people need the land. Wetlands, for example, where many types of waterfowl, fish, and insects live, might be drained for new houses or a mall. The animals that lived there would either have to find a new home or else die out.

☑ **Over-hunting.** Bison or buffalo once ranged over the entire Great Plains of the United States, but they were hunted almost to extinction in the 19th century. Since then, they have been protected by laws, and their numbers are increasing. Sometimes, when an animal population is too large, controlled hunting may reduce the number of animals enough so that the surviving animals can live comfortably with the food available to them.

HABITATS: Where Animals Live

The area in nature where an animal lives is called its **habitat**. The table below lists some large habitats and some of the animals that live in them.

HABITAT	SOME ANIMALS THAT LIVE THERE
Deserts (hot, dry regions)	camels, bobcats, coyotes, kangaroos, mice, gila monsters, scorpions, rattlesnakes
Tropical Forests (warm, humid climate)	orangutans, gibbons, leopards, tamandua anteaters, tapirs, iguanas, parrots, tarantulas
Grasslands (flat, open lands)	African elephants, kangaroos, Indian rhinoceroses, giraffes, zebras, prairie dogs, ostriches
Mountains (highlands)	yaks, snow leopards, vicunas, bighorn sheep, chinchillas, pikas, eagles, mountain goats
Polar Regions (cold climate)	polar bears, musk oxen, caribous, ermines, arctic foxes, walruses, penguins, Siberian huskies
Oceans (sea water)	whales, dolphins, seals, manatees, octopuses, stingrays, coral, starfish, lobsters, and many kinds of fish

FOSSILS: Clues to Ancient Animals

A fossil is the remains of an animal or plant that lived long ago. Most fossils are formed from the hard parts of an animal's body, such as bones, shells, or teeth. Some are large, like dinosaur footprints. Some are so tiny that you need a microscope to see them. Most fossils are found in rocks formed from the mud or sand that collects at the bottom of oceans, rivers, and lakes. Fossils offer scientists clues to ancient animals.

WHAT DO FOSSILS TELL US?

Scientists study fossils to help them understand plant and animal life in ancient periods of the world's history. The age and structure of the rocks in which fossils are found can help scientists tell how long ago certain kinds of animals or plants lived. For example, dinosaurs lived millions of years ago, but people have known about dinosaurs only since the first dinosaur fossils were uncovered, less than 200 years ago.

WHERE ARE FOSSILS FOUND?

Fossils, including dinosaur fossils, are found on every continent on the earth. In eastern and southern Africa, people have found fossils that are ancestors of early humans. Insects that lived millions of years ago are sometimes found preserved in amber. Amber is hardened tree sap. Fossils have also been found in ice and tar. In 1991 a frozen corpse of a man believed to have lived over 5,000 years ago was found in the Austrian Alps.

Dinosaur FACTS and FIGURES

From dinosaur fossils found throughout the world, scientists have gained evidence about when dinosaurs lived, what they ate, and how large they grew. Dinosaurs lived during the Mesozoic era, from 225 to 65 million years ago. The Mesozoic era is divided into the three periods shown below.

TRIASSIC PERIOD, from 225 to 195 million years ago
- ☑ **First dinosaurs** appeared during the **Triassic period.** Most early dinosaurs were small, rarely longer than 15 feet.
- ☑ **Early meat-eating dinosaurs** were called **Theropods.**
- ☑ **Earliest-known dinosaurs** were meat-eaters, found in Argentina: **Eoraptor** (the most primitive dinosaur, only about 40 inches long) and **Herrerasaurus.**
- ☑ **Early plant-eating dinosaurs** were called **Prosauropods. Plateosaurus** and **Anchisaurus** were two early plant-eating dinosaurs.

JURASSIC PERIOD, from 195 to 135 million years ago
- ☑ Dinosaurs that lived during the **Jurassc period** were gigantic.
- ☑ Jurassic dinosaurs included the **Sauropods,** giant long-necked plant-eaters, the **largest land animals** ever. **Apatosaurus** and **Brachiosaurus** (70-80 feet) and **Diplodocus** (over 80 feet) were Sauropods.
- ☑ **Stegosaurus** (30 feet), a large plant-eater, had sharp, bony plates along its back.
- ☑ **Allosaurus** and **Megalosaurus,** two giant meat-eaters, fed on large plant-eating dinosaurs like the Apatosaurus and Stegosaurus. Megalosaurus grew to 30 feet in length; Allosaurus, 30-36 feet.

? DID YOU KNOW? Some Sauropods' teeth were not good for chewing, so they ate stones, which ground up the food in their stomachs. The Stegosaurus had the smallest brain of any dinosaur. Its brain weighed only 2½ ounces.

CRETACEOUS PERIOD, from 135 to 65 million years ago
- ☑ New dinosaurs appeared during the **Cretaceous period,** but by the end of the Cretaceous period, all dinosaurs had died out.
- ☑ New plant-eaters: **Triceratops** and other horned dinosaurs, **Anatosaurus** and other duckbilled dinosaurs, **Ankylosaurus** and other armored dinosaurs.
- ☑ New meat-eater: **Tyrannosaurus Rex**, the largest and one of the fiercest meat-eaters, growing to 20 feet high and 40 feet long.

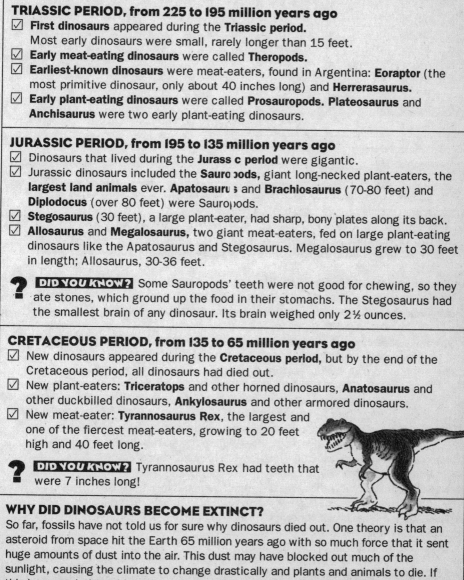

? DID YOU KNOW? Tyrannosaurus Rex had teeth that were 7 inches long!

WHY DID DINOSAURS BECOME EXTINCT?
So far, fossils have not told us for sure why dinosaurs died out. One theory is that an asteroid from space hit the Earth 65 million years ago with so much force that it sent huge amounts of dust into the air. This dust may have blocked out much of the sunlight, causing the climate to change drastically and plants and animals to die. If this happened, the cold, stormy weather and the death of plants and other animals may have led to the extinction of dinosaurs.

SEARCHING FOR DINOSAURS PUZZLE

Can you find the eight dinosaurs hidden in this puzzle? ALLOSAURUS, APATOSAURUS, DIPLODOCUS, EORAPTOR, SAUROPOD, STEGOSAURUS, TRICERATOPS, TYRANNOSAURUS. (Answers are on page 302.)

```
K S A U R O P O D W T Y U I D S A F G
A T G C B X N H I C O R V B O T P O B
S E N D V A S A P A T O S A U R U S T
D G C Z X C V B L L P L K J H I F G H
F O M N B V C X O L S A D F G C V B N
G S T R E W Q U D O V C X Z A E M H G
K A T Y R A N N O S A U R U S R U Y T
L U H G F D S A C A N N O B X A W E U
I R K J H G F D U U I U Y T R T R E W
P U Q W E R T Y S R S D F G H O K J H
H S V B N M J K L U G E O R A P T O R
Q L T K Y R G F R S X D S W G S J K L
```

Museums of NATURAL HISTORY

Museums of natural history contain exhibits of things found in nature. These include animals, plants, rocks, and fossils of prehistoric animals and plants. Below are a few natural history museums.

Academy of Natural Sciences, 1900 Benjamin Franklin Parkway, Philadelphia, Pennsylvania 19103. Phone: (215) 299-1000

American Museum of Natural History, Central Park West at 79th Street, New York, New York 10024. Phone: (212) 769-5100

Carnegie Museum of Natural History, 4400 Forbes Avenue, Pittsburgh, Pennsylvania 15213. Phone: (412) 622-3131

Denver Museum of Natural History, City Park, Denver, Colorado 80205. Phone: (303) 370-6387

Field Museum of Natural History, Roosevelt Road at Lake Shore Drive, Chicago, Illinois 60605. Phone: (312) 922-9410

Museum of Comparative Zoology, Harvard University, 26 Oxford Street, Cambridge, Massachusetts 02138. Phone: (617) 495-3045

Museum of the Rockies, 600 West Kagy, Bozeman, Montana 59715. Phone: (406) 994-5283

National Museum of Natural History, Smithsonian Institution, 10th Street & Constitution Avenue, N.W., Washington, D.C. 20560. Phone: (202) 357-1300

New Mexico Museum of Natural History and Science, 1801 Mountain Road NW, Albuquerque, NM 87104. Phone: (505) 841-8837

Royal Tyrrell Museum of Palaeontology, Drumheller, Alberta, Canada. Phone: (403) 823-7707

University of Nebraska State Museum, 307 Morrill Hall, 14th and U Streets, Lincoln, Nebraska 68588. Phone: (402) 472-6302

Which U.S. Zoos Have the LARGEST NUMBERS of Species?

San Diego Zoo
2920 Zoo Drive
San Diego,
California 92103
Phone:
  (619) 231-1515
Number of
  Species: 900
Popular Exhibits:
  Tiger River,
  Komodo dragons,
  koalas,
  Hippo Beach

Cleveland Metroparks Zoo
3900 Brookside Drive
Cleveland, Ohio 44109
Phone: (216) 661-6500
Number of Species: 794
Popular Exhibits: Rain Forest with 600
  animals and 7,000 plants

Cincinnati Zoo
3400 Vine Street
Cincinnati, Ohio 45220
Phone: (513) 281-4701
Number of Species: 750
Popular Exhibits: Gorilla World, white
  Bengal tigers, Jungle Trails

Houston Zoological Gardens
1513 North MacGregor
Houston, Texas 77030
Phone: (713) 525-3300
Number of Species: 718
Popular Exhibits: Wortham World
  of Primates, Mexican wolves,
  cheetahs

St. Louis Zoological Park
Forest Park
St. Louis, Missouri 63110
Phone: (314) 781-0900
Number of Species: 699
Popular Exhibits: Living World, Bear
  Pits, Jungle of the Apes

Bronx Zoo/Wildlife Conservation Park
Fordham Road and Bronx River Pkwy.
Bronx, New York 10460
Phone: (718) 367-1010
Number of Species: 650
Popular Exhibits: Himalayan Highlands,
  Jungle World, endangered species

**San Antonio Zoological Gardens
and Aquarium**
3903 N. St. Mary's Street
San Antonio, Texas 78212
Phone: (210) 734-7184
Number of Species: 650
Popular Exhibits: Australian Walkabout,
  Amazonia, children's zoo

Denver Zoological Gardens
City Park
Denver, Colorado 80205
Phone:
  (303) 331-4100
Number of Species:
  630
Popular Exhibits:
  Tropical
    Discovery,
  Northern
    Shores,
  Primate
    Panorama

Columbus Zoo
9990 Riverside Drive
Powell, Ohio 43065-0400
Phone: (614) 645-3550
Number of Species: 607
Popular Exhibits: Discovery Reef, Ohio
  Wetlands, Tidepool Touch Tank

Omaha/Henry Doorly Zoo
3701 South 10th Street
Omaha, Nebraska 68107
Phone: (402) 733-8401
Number of Species: 590
Popular Exhibits: indoor rain forest,
  aquarium, cat complex

PAINTING:
Landscape, Portrait, and Still Life

Art can be real or imaginary, funny or sad, beautiful or disturbing. Before photography was invented, most artists tried to show things as they saw them or as they imagined them to look. Throughout history, artists have painted pictures of nature (called **landscapes**); or pictures of people (called **portraits**); or pictures of flowers in vases, food, and other objects (known as **still lifes**). When artists paint people and things to look as they do in real life, their art is called **realistic**, or **representational**.

SOME FAMOUS PAINTERS AND LANDSCAPES

A drawing or painting of nature is called a **landscape**. A picture of the sea is called a **seascape**. A picture of city buildings is called a **cityscape**. Below are a few famous painters, when they lived, their nationality, and the name of one of their landscapes.

▲ *A landscape*

El Greco (1541-1614), Spanish painter: "View of Toledo" (cityscape)
Jan Vermeer (1632-1675), Dutch painter: "View of Delft" (cityscape)
Katsushika Hokusai (1760-1849), Japanese painter: "Views of Mount Fuji" (landscape)
John Constable (1776-1837), English painter: "The Cornfield" (landscape)
Winslow Homer (1836-1910), American painter: "Northeaster" (seascape)
Georgia O'Keeffe (1887-1986), American painter: "Grey Hills" (landscape)

SOME FAMOUS PAINTERS AND PORTRAITS

A painting of a person (or more than one person) is called a **portrait**. When a person paints a picture of himself or herself, it is called a **self-portrait**. Below are a few famous painters, when they lived, their nationality, and the name of one of their portraits.

Leonardo da Vinci (1452-1519), Italian painter: "The Mona Lisa"
Rembrandt (1606-1669), Dutch painter: "Self Portrait"
John Singleton Copley (1737-1815), American painter: "Paul Revere"
Edouard Manet (1832-1883), French painter: "The Fifer"
Pierre Auguste Renoir (1841-1919), French painter: "Madame Charpentier and Her Children"
Mary Cassatt (1844-1926), American painter: "The Bath"

▲ *A portrait*

SOME FAMOUS PAINTERS AND STILL LIFES

A picture of small objects—like flowers, bottles, books, food, and other things—is called a **still life**. Below are a few famous painters, when they lived, their nationality, and the name of one of their still-life paintings.

▲ *A still life*

Henri Fantin-Latour (1836-1904), French painter: "Still Life with Flowers and Fruit"
Paul Cezanne (1839-1906), French painter: "Apples and Pears"
William Michael Harnett (1848-1892), American painter: "Still Life—Violin and Music"
Vincent van Gogh (1853-1890), Dutch painter: "Sunflowers"

? **DID YOU KNOW?** Thousands of years ago, people painted pictures on the walls of caves. In December 1994, prehistoric paintings from about 30,000 years ago were discovered in an underground cave in France by three French explorers. These works of art are the oldest cave paintings ever found.

Modern Art

Many artists still paint pictures that can be recognized as landscapes and portraits. But many artists today create pictures using shapes or colors or textures in interesting ways that do not look like anything in the real world. These paintings are called **abstract**, or **nonrepresentational**. Abstract art is also called **modern art**.

SOME FAMOUS MODERN ARTISTS AND ABSTRACT PAINTINGS

Below are a few famous painters known for their abstract paintings, along with the years they lived, their nationality, and the name of one of their paintings. Sometimes an abstract painting has a name that sounds realistic—like Picasso's "Three Musicians"—even though the painting is abstract.

Pablo Picasso (1881-1973), Spanish painter: "Three Musicians"
Joan Miró (1893-1983), Spanish painter: "Composition"
Helen Frankenthaler (born 1928), American painter: "Blue Territory"
Wassily Kandinsky (1866-1944), Russian painter: "Impression No. 30"
Piet Mondrian (1872-1944), Dutch painter: "Composition"
Jackson Pollock (1912-1956), American painter: "Number 1"

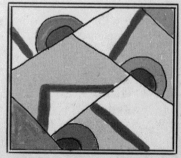
▲ *Abstract art*

SCULPTURE

Sculpture is a three-dimensional form made from clay, stone, metal, or other material. Many sculptures stand freely so that you can walk around them. Some are mobiles that hang from the ceiling. Sculptures can be large, like the Statue of Liberty or the statue of Abraham Lincoln in the Lincoln Memorial, or they can be small. Some sculpture is representational (looks like the person or animal it represents). Some modern sculpture is abstract and has no form that can be recognized.

SOME FAMOUS SCULPTORS AND SCULPTURE

Below is a list of a few sculptors, when they lived, their nationality, and the name of one of their sculptures.

Michelangelo Buonarroti (1475-1564), Italian sculptor and painter: "Pieta" (representational)

Edgar Degas (1834-1917), French painter and sculptor: "Little Fourteen-Year-Old Dancer" (representational)

Auguste Rodin (1840-1917), French sculptor: "The Thinker" (representational)

Henry Moore (born 1898), English sculptor: "Family Group" (abstract)

Louise Nevelson (1899-1988), American sculptor: "Royal Tide II" (abstract)

Isamu Noguchi (born 1904), American sculptor, "Unidentified Object" (abstract)

WHERE TO LOOK AT ART

There are art museums in many cities in the United States. Some of them are general art museums, where you can see art from many different countries and from many different time periods—sometimes from early Egyptian art to modern art. Many cities also have museums of American art, museums of modern art, and other special collections. For museums that focus on ethnic art, culture, and history, such as African or Asian culture, see the section called ETHNIC MUSEUMS, page 142. A few general art museums are listed below.

Art Institute of Chicago
Baltimore Museum of Art
Boston Museum of Fine Arts
Cleveland Museum of Art
Dallas Museum of Art
Denver Art Museum
Detroit Institute of Arts
Houston Museum of Fine Arts
Los Angeles County Museum of Art
Kansas City Art Institute

Metropolitan Museum of Art
  (New York City)
Minneapolis Institute of Arts
National Gallery of Art
  (Washington, D.C.)
North Carolina Museum of Art (Raleigh, NC)
Philadelphia Museum of Art
San Antonio Museum of Art
San Francisco Museum of Art
Seattle Art Museum

BOOK AWARDS, 1995-1996

Here are some awards that are given each year for children's books. You may want to look for some of these books in your library.

Boston Globe-Horn Book Award—Given every year for outstanding fiction, nonfiction, and illustration.
   1995 winners:
      Fiction: *Some of the Kinder Planets*, by Tim Wynne-Jones
      Nonfiction: *Abigail Adams: Witness to a Revolution*, by Natalie S. Bober
      Picture Book: *John Henry*, illustrated by Jerry Pinkney, retold by Julius Lester

Caldecott Medal—Given for the most distinguished American illustrated book.
   1996 winner: *Officer Buckle and Gloria*, by Peggy Rathmann

Coretta Scott King Awards—Given to artists and authors who promote the cause of peace and world brotherhood.
   1996 winners:
      Author Award: *Her Stories*, by Virginia Hamilton
      Illustrator Award: *The Middle Passage*, by Tom Feelings

Golden Kite Awards—Given every year for the best children's fiction, nonfiction, and illustration.
   1995 winners:
      Fiction: *The Watsons Go to Birmingham—1963,* by Christopher Paul Curtis
      Nonfiction: *Abigail Adams,* by Natalie S. Bober
      Picture Illustration: *Fairy Wings,* by Dennis Nolan and Lauren Mills

Newbery Award—Given for the most distinguished contribution to children's literature in the United States.
   1996 winner: *The Midwife's Apprentice,* by Karen Cushman

Hans Christian Andersen Awards—Given every two years to an author and an illustrator whose complete works have made an important contribution to children's literature.
   Author: Michio Mado (Japan) for *The Animals* and other books
   Illustrator: Jörg Müller (Switzerland) for *The Changing City* and others

Ten of the BEST BOOKS of 1995

(Recommended by the American Library Association)

The Boy Who Lived With the Bears and Other Iroquois Stories, by Joseph Bruchac

Dog Friday, by Hilary McKay

Ezra Jack Keats: A Biography, by Dean Engel and Florence B. Freedman

Fig Pudding, by Ralph Fletcher

The Midwife's Apprentice, by Karen Cushman

Poppy, by Avi

Star of Fear, Star of Hope, by Jo Hoestlandt

Sweet Corn, by James Stevenson

The Watsons Go to Birmingham —1963, by Christopher Paul Curtis

You Want Women to Vote, Lizzie Stanton?, by Jean Fritz

Ten ALL-TIME BEST-SELLING Paperbacks

Charlotte's Web, by E. B. White, illustrated by Garth Williams

Tales of a Fourth Grade Nothing, by Judy Blume

Shane, by Jack Schaeffer

Are You There, God? It's Me, Margaret, by Judy Blume

Where the Red Fern Grows, by Wilson Rawls

A Wrinkle in Time, by Madeleine L'Engle

Island of the Blue Dolphins, by Scott O'Dell

Little House on the Prairie, by Laura Ingalls Wilder

The Incredible Journey, by Sheila Burnford

The Little Prince, by Antoine de Saint-Exupéry

? DID YOU KNOW? Would you guess that, in 1995, 8 of the 10 best-selling paperback books for children were Goosebumps books, by R. L. Stine? By now, about 100 million Goosebumps books have been printed! The most popular ones in 1995 were *The Horror at Camp Jellyjam,* *The Barking Ghost,* and *Night of the Living Dummy II.*

◄ *The Horror at Camp Jellyjam,* by R. L. Stine

Some Other ALL-TIME FAVORITES

Anne of Green Gables, by Lucy Maud Montgomery

The Black Stallion, by Walter Farley

Charlie and the Chocolate Factory, by Roald Dahl

The Chronicles of Narnia, by C. S. Lewis

The Giving Tree, by Shel Silverstein

The Pinballs, by Betsy Byers

Sarah, Plain and Tall, by Patricia MacLachlan

Tuck Everlasting, by Natalie Babbitt

Other BOOKS YOU MAY ENJOY Reading

The books that are listed and described on this page and on the next one have won awards for excellence.

FICTION

Fiction books are stories that come out of the writer's imagination. Some of these stories are realistic and could really happen, even if they never did happen. Others, such as stories about talking animals or mysterious kingdoms, are fantasy.

Abel's Island, by William Steig. A spoiled mouse is swept away in a violent storm while picnicking with his wife and finds himself marooned on an island.

Across Five Aprils, by Irene Hunt. A story of a nine-year-old boy whose brothers are fighting on opposite sides of the Civil War.

Bridge to Terabithia, by Katherine Paterson. In a rural community, two new friends, a boy and a girl, build a secret kingdom of wooden boards and call it Terabithia.

The Dark-Thirty: Southern Tales of the Supernatural, by Patricia McKissack. Ten hair-raising stories rooted in the history of African-Americans.

Dear Mr. Henshaw, by Beverly Cleary. A lonely 12-year-old boy writes letters about himself to his favorite author.

Dragonwings, by Lawrence Yep. Set in a Chinese community of San Francisco, this story is about a boy's love for a father who has dreams about flying.

The Friendship, by Mildred Taylor. What happens when, in Mississippi in the 1930s, a black man refuses to call his white friend "Mister."

Maniac Magee, by Jerry Spinelli. An unhappy orphaned boy runs away from home at age eight and tries to survive on his own.

Missing May, by Cynthia Rylant. A 12-year-old girl learns to accept the death of her beloved aunt.

Morning Girl, by Michael Dorris. The story of a brother and sister who grow up on an island.

Mrs. Frisby and the Rats of NIMH, by Robert C. O'Brien. When Mrs. Frisby, the mother of a family of field mice, sees her home threatened by the farmer's plow, she seeks help from some super-bright rats who have escaped from a laboratory.

Number the Stars, by Lois Lowry. In World War II in Denmark, AnneMarie Johansen bravely hides her Jewish friend Ellen Rosen to keep her from being taken away by the Germans.

Scooter, by Vera B. Williams. Elana Rose Rosen moves to a big apartment building in New York City and discovers an amazingly varied new world.

Shiloh, by Phyllis Reynolds Naylor. When a beagle who is being mistreated by his owner follows him home, Marty, a West Virginia boy, wants to keep the dog. His parents help him understand that it isn't an easy decision.

Sign of the Beaver, by Elizabeth Speare. Set in the backwoods of Maine in the 18th century, this is the story of the friendship that develops between a 12-year-old boy and the chief of the Beaver clan.

Toning the Sweep, by Angela Johnson. When Emily, a 14-year-old African-American, finds out that her Grandmama Ola is very sick, she begins to videotape the people and places in the California desert that Ola loved.

NONFICTION

Nonfiction books are factual books that provide information about what is real, from aardvarks to zithers. Many are about science or history or are biographies (books that tell the story of a real person, either living or dead). Reference books, like almanacs and encyclopedias, are also nonfiction. Below are some outstanding nonfiction books you might enjoy reading.

The Big Beast Book: Dinosaurs and How They Got That Way, by Jerry Booth. How did scientists find out about these huge beasts who lived so long ago? The story of dinosaurs and their fossil remains.

The Book of Eagles, by Helen Roney Sattler. All about eagles in words and pictures and about the attempts to save them from dying out.

Christopher Columbus: Voyage to the Unknown, by Nancy Smiler Levinson. An account of the explorer's childhood and his voyages to the New World, with excerpts from his letters and diaries.

Good Queen Bess: The Story of Elizabeth I of England, by Diane Stanley and Peter Vennema. This biography describes how the first Queen Elizabeth grew up and tells of the times in which she lived.

Inspirations: Stories About Women Artists, by Leslie Sills. The lives of four very different women artists, Georgia O'Keeffe, Frida Kahlo, Alice Neel, and Faith Ringold, and how they found their inspiration.

Lincoln: A Photobiography, by Russell Freedman. This profile reveals the many sides of President Abraham Lincoln and describes both his successes and his failures.

Maggie by My Side, by Beverly Butler. The author is a blind teacher, and Maggie is the German shepherd who becomes her Seeing Eye dog and her friend.

The Origin of Life on Earth: An African Creation Myth, retold by David Anderson, illustrated by Kathleen Atkins. An African myth about how the world began.

REFERENCE BOOKS: Where the Answers Are

Would you know where to find answers to the following questions? Which is the correct spelling, *receive* or *recieve*? In what part of Africa is Egypt? Which team won the Super Bowl in 1995? How much can the blue whale, the largest animal in the world, weigh? When did North Dakota become a state? Can you figure out which type of reference book below would have the answer? In some cases, the answer can be found in more than one book.

Almanac: A one-volume book of facts and statistics. Almanacs cover sports, the government, countries of the world, the planets, states, prize winners, and many other subjects.

Atlas: A collection of maps. Political maps help us locate towns and cities and roads and show borders between countries or states. Physical maps show features like mountains, rivers, and forests.

Dictionary: A book of words in alphabetical order. A dictionary gives the meanings and spelling of words and shows how they are pronounced.

Encyclopedia: The place to go for information on almost every subject you can think of. Encyclopedias cover the past and the present, the arts and sciences, and the countries of the world, either in one volume or several.

The 7 WONDERS of the Ancient World

These were considered the most remarkable structures of ancient times. Only one of them—the pyramids in Egypt—has survived and can be visited today.

Pyramids of Egypt
At Giza, Egypt, built as royal tombs from 3000 to 1800 B.C. The largest is the **Great Pyramid of Khufu** (or Cheops).

Hanging Gardens of Babylon
Terraced gardens built by King Nebuchadnezzar II around 600 B.C. for his wife.

Temple of Artemis
At Ephesus (now part of Turkey), built mostly of marble around 550 B.C. in honor of the Greek goddess Artemis.

Statue of Zeus
At Olympia, Greece. The statue, made about 462 B.C. by the ancient Greek sculptor Phidias from ivory and gold, showed the king of the gods sitting on a throne.

Mausoleum of Halicarnassus
(Now part of Turkey), built about 353 B.C. in honor of King Mausolus, a ruler of ancient Caria.

Colossus of Rhodes
Overlooking the harbor on the island of Rhodes (Greece), a bronze statue of the sun god Helios, built about 280 B.C. Probably 120 feet high.

Lighthouse of Alexandria, Egypt
Built about 270 B.C. during the reign of King Ptolemy II. It may have been around 500 feet tall.

TALLEST BUILDINGS in the United States

Sears Tower, Chicago, IL (built 1974).........................1,454 feet
World Trade Center, New York, NY (built 1973)...........1,368 feet
Empire State Building, New York, NY (built 1931)......1,250 feet
Amoco, Chicago, IL (built 1973) ....1,136 feet
John Hancock Center, Chicago, IL (built 1969) ....1,127 feet
First Interstate World Center, Los Angeles (built 1989)...1,107 feet
Chrysler Building, New York, NY (built 1930).............1,046 feet

? **DID YOU KNOW?** The tallest free-standing structure in the world is the CN Tower in Toronto, Canada, built in 1975 as a communications and observation tower. It is 1,821 feet high.

The LONGEST BRIDGES in the World

The **span** of a bridge is the distance between its supports. The three bridges below, as measured by their main spans, were the longest bridges in the world when this book was published. But bridges seem to be getting longer and longer. Bridges now under construction in Denmark and Japan will be longer than any of these when they are completed.

NAME OF BRIDGE	LOCATION	MAIN SPAN
Humber	England	4,626 feet
Verrazano-Narrows	United States (New York)	4,260 feet
Golden Gate	United States (California)	4,200 feet

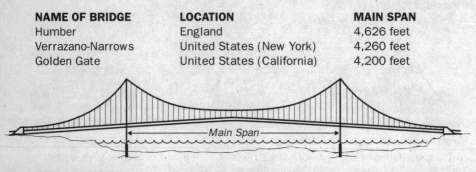

Main Span

? **DID YOU KNOW?** The oldest covered bridge in continuous use in the United States spans the Ammonoosuc River in New Hampshire. The bridge was completed in 1827. It is a wooden bridge, 278 feet long.

The LONGEST TUNNELS in the World

A **tunnel** is a long underground passageway, dug through rock or earth or built underwater. Vehicular tunnels (on land and under water) are for automobiles, trucks, and the like. Railroad tunnels are for trains and subway traffic. Water tunnels are for water mains, drainage, sewage, mining, and storage. These are the longest tunnels of each type:

TYPE OF TUNNEL	NAME	LOCATION	LENGTH
Land Vehicular	St. Gotthard	Switzerland	10.1 miles
Underwater Vehicular	Brooklyn-Battery	New York, USA	1.7 miles
Railroad	Seikan	Japan	33.5 miles
Water	Delaware Aqueduct	New York, USA	85.0 miles

How COMPUTERS Are USED

Today's high-powered computers can do things in a few seconds that would take a person working by hand days, or even years, to do.

Computers Help People Learn.

☑ Educational programs teach subjects like math, spelling, and geography. ☑ The computer can keep track of a student's progress. ☑ Pilots and astronauts practice their skills with computer flight simulators.

Computers Help People Communicate.

☑ Computers are used to write reports for school, to write letters to friends and family, or to write stories.
☑ Computers are also used to create newspapers, magazines, and books.
☑ People use computers to send electronic mail (e-mail), sometimes across the continent or to other countries. ☑ People who cannot speak can keyboard messages that the computer translates into speech, and people who cannot type can speak into a computer, which translates their speech into text.

Computers Help People Create.

☑ People are using computers to create artwork and music or to design buildings.
☑ Special effects that appear in movies and television are often created with the use of computers.

Computers Keep Information Organized.

☑ Computers keep track of information in files called databases. For example, from an FBI database, police departments can get information about criminals or stolen goods from all around the United States.

Computers Help Make Predictions.

☑ Companies use computer programs to predict how the business decisions they make will affect them in the future. ☑ Special computer programs use data collected from satellites to help forecast the weather.

Computers Are Used to Manufacture Products.

☑ Engineers use Computer-Aided Design (CAD) software to create detailed drawings of an object and then test it to see how to make it stronger or cheaper.
☑ Computers can then be used to control machinery used to make parts or to control robots that assemble the parts.

Computers Aren't Just Found on Desks.

☑ Computers are used in automatic teller machines at the bank and with the price scanner at the supermarket checkout. ☑ Automobiles, microwave ovens, VCRs, and digital watches all have built-in computers.

HOW COMPUTERS WORK

For a computer to work, three things are necessary:
1. **hardware**, the pieces of equipment that make up the computer;
2. **software** or **programs**, the instructions that tell the computer how to perform its tasks; and
3. **you**, the **user,** the person who tells the computer what tasks it should perform.

First, you enter **data,** or **information,** into the computer. This is called **input**. The computer then **processes** the data to perform the required task. When it is finished, the computer gives you the results. The results are called **output**. A computer also **stores** your work for you, so you can use it again or make changes to it at another time. If you want to write a story, here's how the computer can help.

INPUT:

Selecting the Right Software.

To write a story (or letter or school report) you need to use a type of software called a word-processing program. This can be selected by using the **keyboard** or a **mouse**.

Entering Data.

Once you are in the right program, you can begin to input the story by typing on the **keyboard**. The backspace and delete keys are like electronic erasers. In addition to letters and numbers, the keyboard has special keys (called **function keys**) for centering or underlining words, moving sentences around, checking spelling, printing out a page, and doing other tasks. When you hit one of these keys, the word-processing program tells the computer what to do.

PROCESSING:

Inside the Computer.

The instructions from the word-processing program are carried out inside the computer by the **central processing unit**, or **CPU**. The CPU is the computer's brain.

STORAGE:

Keeping Data To Use It Later.

A computer also stores information that you want to use later. Suppose you want to stop working on your story and eat lunch. You can save the work you've done so far and then go back to it later.

Floppy Disk.

Information can be saved on a small plastic **"floppy" disk** (many of these are not floppy anymore). The floppy disk goes into a slot in the computer called the **floppy drive**. If you use a floppy disk for your story, it can be moved and used on other computers.

Hard Disk.

Inside most computers is a **hard drive.** The hard drive contains a **hard disk** made of metal that cannot be removed. This disk holds much more information than a floppy disk and works faster. The hard disk stores the programs you need and also stores the information you want to save.

OUTPUT:
Getting the Results.

The **monitor** and **printer** are the most commonly used output devices. As you type your story, the words appear on a **monitor,** which is similar to a television screen. Your story can then be printed on paper by using a **printer.**

COMMUNICATIONS:
Computers Talk to Each Other.

When you finish writing your story, if you want to send it to a friend you can print it out and mail it. But if your computer has a **modem** and your friend's does too, the story can be sent from your computer directly to your friend's computer. A **modem** allows information from a computer to travel over telephone lines. With a modem, your friend can send you back a note, telling you how he or she liked the story.

SOFTWARE:
There Are Many Kinds.

Besides word-processing programs, there are many other types of software that people can use in their computers at home, in school, or at work. Some common types of software are programs for doing mathematics, keeping records, playing games, and creating pictures.

CD-ROMS

Many newer computers have a third type of drive (besides the floppy drive and the hard drive), called a CD-ROM drive. This allows you to play special disks called **CD-ROMs,** which are similar to music CDs. A CD-ROM can hold a huge amount of information, including pictures and sound. Almanacs, games, encyclopedias, dictionaries, and many other types of information and entertainment are on CD-ROMs.

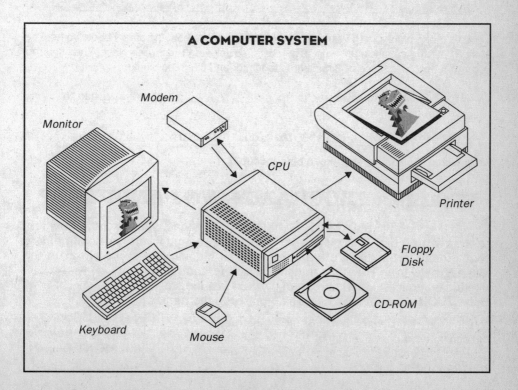

A COMPUTER SYSTEM

Modem

Monitor

CPU

Printer

Floppy Disk

CD-ROM

Keyboard

Mouse

The BINARY SYSTEM

A computer can do many impressive things, but one thing it cannot do is understand English. For a computer to do its work, every piece of information given to it must be translated into binary code. You are probably used to using ten digits, 0 through 9, when you do arithmetic. When the computer uses the **binary code**, it uses only two digits, 0 and 1. Think of it as sending messages to the computer by switching a light on and off.

Each 0 or 1 digit is called a **bit,** and most computers use a sequence of 8 bits (called a **byte**) for each piece of data. Almost all computers use the same code, called ASCII (pronounced "askey"), to stand for letters of the alphabet, number digits, punctuation, and other special characters that control the computer's operation. Below is a list of ASCII bytes for the alphabet.

A	01000001	J	01001010	S	01010011
B	01000010	K	01001011	T	01010100
C	01000011	L	01001100	U	01010101
D	01000100	M	01001101	V	01010110
E	01000101	N	01001110	W	01010111
F	01000110	O	01001111	X	01011000
G	01000111	P	01010000	Y	01011001
H	01001000	Q	01010001	Z	01011010
I	01001001	R	01010010		

If you fill in the blanks in the sentence below, you can see how the binary code works. Start by putting a mark after every 8 numbers, so you won't lose your place. Then find the letter that each sequence of 8 numbers stands for and fill in the blanks.

You don't have to set a trap for a ___ ___ ___ ___ ___ that's attached to your computer.

01001101010011110101010101001101000101

What would your name look like in binary code?

What Is a PROGRAMMING LANGUAGE?

If you decoded the binary code for the sentence above, you saw how slow it is to work with binary code. The first computer programs were written in binary code. Today, programs are written in special languages that are closer to the language we use. They are translated by the computer into binary code. A simple program, written in a language called **BASIC,** might look like what you see to the right.

```
LET A=1
LET B=2
LET C=A+B
PRINT C
```

This is a very simple program in BASIC. It instructs the computer to print the sum of 1 + 2, or 3. Some other programming languages you might hear about are FORTRAN, COBOL, and C++.

SMILEYS

When you send e-mail to a friend, do you ever use smileys? Smileys are small pictures made up of typed letters and symbols that look like faces when you turn them sideways. They are used to express feelings in messages you send by computer. "Emoticon" is another name for "smiley." It comes from the words "emotion" and "icon."

SMILEY PUZZLE

Look at each smiley sideways and see if you can match each one with one of the words written below. (Answers are on page 302.)

:-)	:-(	:-D	:'(
:-o	:-x	;-)	:-&
Unhappy	Smile	Tongue-tied	Wink
Crying	Kiss	Laughing	Shouting

? DID YOU KNOW?

- ☑ In ancient times people did computing with a device called an **abacus,** which is made up of rods and beads. A modern version of the abacus is still used today in Japan. A person who is skilled with an abacus can *add more than 15 numbers in one minute.*

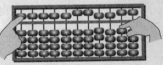

- ☑ The first electronic computer was introduced in 1946. It was called ENIAC (short for Electronic Numerical Integrator and Computer) and could *multiply around 3,000 numbers in one second.*
- ☑ The high-powered computers of today can do in a few seconds calculations that would take a person working by hand days, or even years, to do. A modern personal computer can *perform more than 10,000,000 mathematical operations in one second.*

COMPUTER MUSEUMS

Some museums have sections where you can learn about computers and use them to do many fascinating things. A few museums are devoted entirely to the computer. Here are three:

THE COMPUTER
MUSEUM, INC.
300 Congress Street
Boston, MA 02210
Phone: (617) 426-2800
Internet:
http://www.net.org

AMERICAN COMPUTER
MUSEUM
234 East Babcock Street
Bozeman, MT 59715
Phone: (406) 587-7545
Internet:
http://www.compustory.com
e-mail: bitenbyte@aol.com

TECH MUSEUM OF
INNOVATION
145 West San Carlos Street
San Jose, CA 95113
Phone: (408) 279-7150
Internet:
http://www.thetech.org
e-mail: info@thetech.org

COMPUTER TALK

artificial intelligence or AI
The ability of computers and robots to imitate human intelligence by learning and making decisions.

boot
To turn a computer on.

bug or glitch
An error in a program or in the computer.

database
A large collection of information organized electronically, so that the information can be easily retrieved and used in different ways. A list of names and addresses of everyone eligible to vote is an example of a database.

desktop publishing
The use of computers for combining text and pictures to design and produce magazines, newspapers, and books.

e-mail or electronic mail
Messages sent from one computer to another over a network, such as telephone lines.

hard copy
Computer output printed on paper or similar material.

mainframe
The largest type of computer. A mainframe stores large amounts of information and can be used by many people at the same time.

multimedia
Software that includes pictures, video, and sound, often on CD-ROMs. In multimedia books and encyclopedias, you can see pictures move and hear music and other sounds.

network
A group of computers linked together so that they can share information.

notebook or laptop
A portable personal computer that runs on batteries. It has a built-in keyboard and display screen.

password
A secret code that keeps unwanted people from using a computer or software.

program
A set of instructions for a computer to follow. Programs are written in languages called programming languages.

PC
Short for personal computer. PC is another name for a microcomputer, which is a small computer often used in homes, schools, offices, and small businesses.

RAM
One of the kinds of memory inside a computer, RAM is short for Random Access Memory. The person using a computer can use and change the programs and other information in RAM. The information in RAM disappears when the computer is turned off.

ROM
One of the kinds of memory inside a computer, ROM is short for Read Only Memory. ROM contains permanent instructions for the computer and cannot be changed. The information in ROM stays in the computer after it is turned off.

scanner
A device that can read words and pictures from a printed page into the computer without using a mouse or the keyboard.

spreadsheet
Software used for doing many calculations quickly. Spreadsheet programs are used in accounting and bookkeeping.

user-friendly
Easy for the person using the computer to figure out without a lot of reading.

virtual reality
Three-dimensional images on a screen that are viewed using special equipment (like gloves and goggles). With virtual reality, the user feels as if he or she is part of the image and can interact with everything around.

virus
A program that causes damage to other computer programs and data. A virus can get into a computer through shared disks or telephone lines without the user's knowledge.

The INTERNET and the WORLD WIDE WEB

People all around the world can communicate with one another through the world's largest computer network, called the **Internet.** The Internet connects government agencies and offices, colleges, science laboratories, businesses, individuals, and schools. When computers are connected to the Internet, people can send and receive e-mail, copy software, and get many kinds of information. They can get news about world events, about sports, or about movies and TV shows, information to help with homework or reports, and recipes and cooking tips. The **World Wide Web** is the part of the Internet that can send pictures and sound as well as words.

What's on the Internet for Kids?

Below are some sites for kids on the Internet's World Wide Web where you can do many different things. When you enter an address on the Internet, you must keyboard it *exactly* the way it is written. Every capital and lowercase letter and every symbol and space must be correct.

INTERNATIONAL KIDS' SPACE (Write stories, share music, and find places that are fun with other kids): **http://www.interport.net/kids-space**

KIDSCOM (Connect with kids in English, Spanish, French, German): **http://www.kids.com**

KIDS ON THE WEB (Educational information and activities for fun): **http://www.vividus.com:80/ucis.html**

STEVE AND RUTH BENNETT'S FAMILY SURFBOARD (An Internet scavenger hunt, creative projects, and links for kids): **http://www.familysurf.com**

UNCLE BOB'S KIDS' PAGE (Links for kids): **http://gagme.wwa.com/~boba/kids.html**

Writing to the President

If you want to write to the president of the United States, here is his Internet e-mail address: **president@whitehouse.gov**

USING THE INTERNET SAFELY

Remember the safety rule about NOT getting into a car with a stranger? Below are safety rules to follow when using the Internet.

- ☑ **Don't give out** your address, telephone number, the name or location of your school, or your computer password.
- ☑ **Don't agree** to really get together with someone you "meet" on the Internet.
- ☑ **Don't send** anyone your picture or any personal possession.
- ☑ **Don't answer** messages that are mean or make you feel uneasy.

Writing to The World Almanac for Kids: If you want to use the Internet to write to *The World Almanac for Kids*, the e-mail address is: **Walmanac@aol.com**

COUNTRIES of the World

There are 192 countries in the world. The information for each country goes across two pages. The left-hand page gives the **name** and **capital** of each country, where the country is **located**, and its **area** in both square miles (sq. mi.) and square kilometers (sq. km.). On the right-hand page, the **population** column tells approximately how many people lived in each country (as of 1995). The **currency** column tells you what the money is called and approximately how much it was worth in United States dollars or cents as of March 1, 1996 (if the information was available). If a country belongs to the **United Nations,** the column called "Joined UN" gives the date the country became a member of the UN.

COUNTRY	CAPITAL	LOCATION OF COUNTRY	AREA
Afghanistan	Kabul	Southern Asia, between Iran and Pakistan	251,825 sq. mi. (652,224 sq. km.)
Albania	Tiranë	Eastern Europe, north of Greece	11,100 sq. mi. (28,749 sq. km.)
Algeria	Algiers	North Africa on the Mediterranean Sea, between Libya and Morocco	919,595 sq. mi. (2,381,740 sq. km.)
Andorra	Andorra la Vella	Europe, in the mountains between France and Spain	181 sq. mi. (469 sq. km.)
Angola	Luanda	Southern Africa on the Atlantic Ocean, south of Zaire	481,354 sq. mi. (1,246,701 sq. km.)
Antigua and Barbuda	St. John's	Islands on eastern edge of the Caribbean Sea	171 sq. mi. (443 sq. km.)
Argentina	Buenos Aires	Fills up most of the southern part of South America	1,073,518 sq. mi. (2,780,399 sq. km.)
Armenia	Yerevan	Western Asia, north of Turkey and Iran	11,500 sq. mi. (29,784 sq. km.)
Australia	Canberra	Island south of Asia, between Indian and Pacific Oceans	2,966,200 sq. mi. (7,682,423 sq. km.)
Austria	Vienna	Central Europe, north of Italy	32,378 sq. mi. (83,859 sq. km.)
Azerbaijan	Baku	Western Asia, north of Iran	33,400 sq. mi. (86,506 sq. km.)

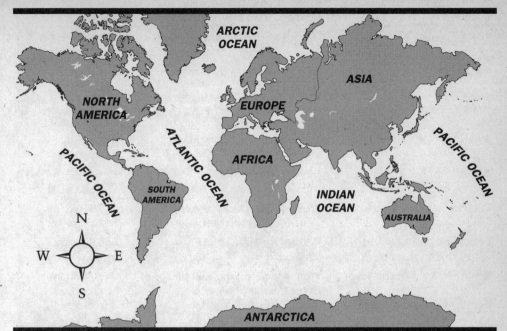

POPULATION	CURRENCY	JOINED UN	COUNTRY
21,251,821	Afghani 1 afghani = $\frac{1}{48}$ of a cent	1946	**Afghanistan**
3,413,904	Lek 1 lek = 1 cent	1955	**Albania**
28,539,321	Dinar 1 dinar = 2 cents	1962	**Algeria**
65,780	French franc or Spanish peseta	1993	**Andorra**
10,069,501	New kwanza 1 new kwanza = $\frac{1}{57}$ of a cent	1976	**Angola**
65,176	East Caribbean dollar 1 EC dollar = 37 cents	1981	**Antigua and Barbuda**
34,292,742	Peso 1 peso = $1.00	1945	**Argentina**
3,557,284	Dram 1 dram = $\frac{1}{4}$ of a cent	1992	**Armenia**
18,322,231	Australian dollar 1 Australian dollar = 76 cents	1945	**Australia**
7,986,664	Schilling 1 schilling = 10 cents	1955	**Austria**
7,789,886	Manat 1 manat = $\frac{1}{44}$ of a cent	1992	**Azerbaijan**

COUNTRY	CAPITAL	LOCATION OF COUNTRY	AREA
The Bahamas	Nassau	Islands in the Atlantic Ocean, east of Florida	5,382 sq. mi. (13,939 sq. km.)
Bahrain	Manama	In the Persian Gulf, near the coast of Qatar	268 sq. mi. (694 sq. km.)
Bangladesh	Dhaka	Southern Asia, nearly surrounded by India	57,295 sq. mi. (148,393 sq. km.)
Barbados	Bridgetown	Island in the Atlantic Ocean, north of Trinidad	166 sq. mi. (430 sq. km.)
Belarus	Minsk	Eastern Europe, east of Poland	80,134 sq. mi. (207,546 sq. km.)
Belgium	Brussels	Western Europe, on the North Sea, south of the Netherlands	11,787 sq. mi. (30,528 sq. km.)
Belize	Belmopan	Central America, next to Mexico	8,867 sq. mi. (22,965 sq. km.)
Benin	Porto-Novo	West Africa, on the Gulf of Guinea, west of Nigeria	43,500 sq. mi. (112,665 sq. km.)
Bhutan	Thimphu	Asia, in the Himalaya Mountains, between China and India	18,147 sq. mi. (47,001 sq. km.)
Bolivia	La Paz	South America, in the Andes Mountains, next to Brazil	424,164 sq. mi. (1,098,580 sq. km.)
Bosnia and Herzegovina	Sarajevo	Southern Europe, on the Balkan Peninsula, west of Yugoslavia	19,741 sq. mi. (51,129 sq. km.)
Botswana	Gaborone	Southern Africa, between South Africa and Zambia	224,607 sq. mi. (581,730 sq. km.)
Brazil	Brasília	Occupies most of the eastern part of South America	3,286,470 sq. mi. (8,511,918 sq. km.)
Brunei	Bandar Seri Begawan	On the island of Borneo, northwest of Australia in the Pacific Ocean	2,226 sq. mi. (5,765 sq. km.)
Bulgaria	Sofia	Eastern Europe, on the Balkan Peninsula, bordering the Black Sea	42,855 sq. mi. (110,994 sq. km.)
Burkina Faso	Ouagadougou	West Africa, between Mali and Ghana	105,946 sq. mi. (274,399 sq. km.)
Burundi	Bujumbura	Central Africa, between Tanzania and Zaire	10,740 sq. mi. (27,816 sq. km.)
Cambodia	Phnom Penh	Southeast Asia, between Vietnam and Thailand	70,238 sq. mi. (181,916 sq. km.)
Cameroon	Yaoundé	Central Africa, between Nigeria and Congo	183,569 sq. mi. (475,442 sq. km.)
Canada	Ottawa	Occupies the northern part of North America, north of the United States	3,849,674 sq. mi. (9,970,610 sq. km.)
Cape Verde	Praia	Islands off the western tip of Africa	1,557 sq. mi. (4,033 sq. km.)

POPULATION	CURRENCY	JOINED UN	COUNTRY
256,616	Bahamas dollar Same value as U.S. dollar	1973	**The Bahamas**
575,925	Dinar 1 dinar = $2.65	1971	**Bahrain**
128,094,948	Taka 1 taka = $2\frac{1}{2}$ cents	1974	**Bangladesh**
256,395	Barbados dollar 1 Barbados dollar = 50 cents	1966	**Barbados**
10,437,418	Belarusian ruble 1 Belarusian ruble = $\frac{1}{115}$ of a cent	1945	**Belarus**
10,081,880	Franc 1 franc = $3\frac{1}{3}$ cents	1945	**Belgium**
214,061	Belize dollar 1 Belize dollar = 50 cents	1981	**Belize**
5,522,677	CFA franc 1 CFA franc = $\frac{1}{5}$ of a cent	1960	**Benin**
1,780,638	Ngultrum 1 ngultrum = 3 cents	1971	**Bhutan**
7,896,254	Boliviano 1 Boliviano = 20 cents	1945	**Bolivia**
3,201,823	Yugoslav new dinar 1 dinar = 20 cents	1992	**Bosnia and Herzegovina**
1,392,414	Pula 1 pula = 34 cents	1966	**Botswana**
160,737,489	Real 1 real = $1.02	1945	**Brazil**
292,266	Brunei dollar 1 Brunei dollar = 71 cents	1984	**Brunei**
8,775,198	Lev 1 lev = $1\frac{1}{3}$ cents	1955	**Bulgaria**
10,422,828	CFA franc 1 CFA franc = $\frac{1}{5}$ of a cent	1960	**Burkina Faso**
6,262,429	Franc 1 franc = $\frac{2}{5}$ of a cent	1962	**Burundi**
10,561,373	Riel 1 riel = $\frac{1}{23}$ of a cent	1955	**Cambodia**
13,521,000	CFA franc 1 CFA franc = $\frac{1}{5}$ of a cent	1960	**Cameroon**
28,434,545	Canadian dollar 1 Canadian dollar = 73 cents	1945	**Canada**
435,983	Escudo 1 escudo = 1 cent	1975	**Cape Verde**

COUNTRY	CAPITAL	LOCATION OF COUNTRY	AREA
Central African Republic	Bangui	Central Africa, north of Zaire	240,324 sq. mi. (622,436 sq. km.)
Chad	N'Djamena	North Africa, south of Libya	495,755 sq. mi. (1,284,000 sq. km.)
Chile	Santiago	Along the western coast of South America	292,135 sq. mi. (756,626 sq. km.)
China	Beijing	Occupies most of the mainland of eastern Asia	3,696,100 sq. mi. (9,572,855 sq. km.)
Colombia	Bogotá	Northwestern South America, southeast of Panama	440,831 sq. mi. (1,141,747 sq. km.)
Comoros	Moroni	Islands between Madagascar and the east coast of Africa	719 sq. mi. (1,862 sq. km.)
Congo	Brazzaville	Central Africa, west of Zaire	132,047 sq. mi. (342,000 sq. km.)
Costa Rica	San José	Central America, south of Nicaragua	19,730 sq. mi (51,100 sq. km.)
Côte d'Ivoire (Ivory Coast)	Yamoussoukro	West Africa, on the Gulf of Guinea, west of Ghana	124,504 sq. mi. (322,464 sq. km.)
Croatia	Zagreb	Southern Europe, south of Hungary	21,829 sq. mi. (56,537 sq. km.)
Cuba	Havana	In the Caribbean Sea, south of Florida	42,804 sq. mi. (110,862 sq. km.)
Cyprus	Nicosia	Island in the Mediterranean Sea, off the coast of Turkey	3,572 sq. mi. (9,251 sq. km.)
Czech Republic	Prague	Central Europe, south of Poland, east of Germany	30,449 sq. mi. (78,863 sq. km.)
Denmark	Copenhagen	Northern Europe, between the Baltic Sea and North Sea	16,639 sq. mi. (43,095 sq. km.)
Djibouti	Djibouti	North Africa, on the Gulf of Aden, across from Saudi Arabia	8,950 sq. mi. (23,180 sq. km.)
Dominica	Roseau	Island in the Caribbean Sea	290 sq. mi. (751 sq. km.)
Dominican Republic	Santo Domingo	On an island, along with Haiti, in the Caribbean Sea	18,704 sq. mi. (48,443 sq. km.)
Ecuador	Quito	South America, on the equator, bordering the Pacific Ocean	105,037 sq. mi. (272,045 sq. km.)
Egypt	Cairo	Northeastern Africa, on the Red Sea and Mediterranean Sea	385,229 sq. mi. (997,739 sq. km.)
El Salvador	San Salvador	Central America, southwest of Honduras	8,124 sq. mi. (21,041 sq. km.)
Equatorial Guinea	Malabo	West Africa, on the Gulf of Guinea, off the west coast of Cameroon	10,831 sq. mi. (28,052 sq. km.)

POPULATION	CURRENCY	JOINED UN	COUNTRY
3,209,759	CFA franc 1 CFA franc = $\frac{1}{5}$ of a cent	1960	**Central African Republic**
5,586,505	CFA franc 1 CFA franc = $\frac{1}{5}$ of a cent	1960	**Chad**
14,161,216	Peso 1 peso = $\frac{1}{4}$ of a cent	1945	**Chile**
1,203,097,268	Yuan 1 yuan = 12 cents	1945	**China**
36,200,251	Peso 1 peso = $\frac{1}{10}$ of a cent	1945	**Colombia**
549,338	Franc 1 franc = $\frac{1}{4}$ of a cent	1975	**Comoros**
2,504,996	CFA franc 1 CFA franc = $\frac{1}{5}$ of a cent	1960	**Congo**
3,419,114	Colon 1 colon = $\frac{1}{2}$ of a cent	1945	**Costa Rica**
14,296,000	CFA franc 1 CFA franc = $\frac{1}{5}$ of a cent	1960	**Côte d'Ivoire (Ivory Coast)**
4,665,821	Kuna 1 Kuna = 18 $\frac{1}{2}$ cents	1992	**Croatia**
10,937,635	Peso 1 peso = $1	1945	**Cuba**
736,636	Pound 1 pound = $2.14	1960	**Cyprus**
10,432,774	Koruna 1 koruna = 3 $\frac{3}{4}$ cents	1993	**Czech Republic**
5,199,437	Krone 1 krone = 18 cents	1945	**Denmark**
421,320	Franc 1 franc = $\frac{3}{5}$ of a cent	1977	**Djibouti**
82,608	East Caribbean dollar 1 EC dollar = 37 cents	1978	**Dominica**
7,948,223	Peso 1 peso = 7 cents	1945	**Dominican Republic**
10,890,950	Sucre 1 sucre = $\frac{1}{29}$ of a cent	1945	**Ecuador**
62,359,623	Pound 1 pound = 29 cents	1945	**Egypt**
5,870,481	Colon 1 colon = 11 cents	1945	**El Salvador**
420,293	CFA franc 1 CFA franc = $\frac{1}{5}$ of a cent	1968	**Equatorial Guinea**

COUNTRY	CAPITAL	LOCATION OF COUNTRY	AREA
Eritrea	Asmara	Northeast Africa, north of Ethiopia	45,300 sq. mi. (117,327 sq. km.)
Estonia	Tallinn	Northern Europe, on the Baltic Sea, north of Latvia	17,413 sq. mi. (45,099 sq. km.)
Ethiopia	Addis Ababa	East Africa, east of Sudan	437,794 sq. mi. (1,133,881 sq. km.)
Fiji	Suva	Islands in the South Pacific Ocean, east of Australia	7,056 sq. mi. (18,275 sq. km.)
Finland	Helsinki	Northern Europe, between Sweden and Russia	130,559 sq. mi. (338,146 sq. km.)
France	Paris	Western Europe, extending from the Atlantic Ocean to the Mediterranean Sea	210,026 sq. mi. (543,965 sq. km.)
Gabon	Libreville	Central Africa, on the Atlantic coast, west of the Congo	103,347 sq. mi. (267,668 sq. km.)
The Gambia	Banjul	West Africa, on the Atlantic Ocean, surrounded by Senegal	4,127 sq. mi. (10,689 sq. km.)
Georgia	Tbilisi	Western Asia, south of Russia, on the Black Sea	26,900 sq. mi. (69,671 sq. km.)
Germany	Berlin	Central Europe, northeast of France	137,735 sq. mi. (356,732 sq. km.)
Ghana	Accra	West Africa, on the southern coast	92,098 sq. mi. (238,533 sq. km.)
Great Britain (United Kingdom)	London	Off the northwest coast of Europe	94,251 sq. mi. (244,109 sq. km.)
Greece	Athens	Southern Europe, in the southern part of the Balkan Peninsula	50,949 sq. mi. (131,957 sq. km.)
Grenada	Saint George's	Island on the eastern edge of the Caribbean Sea	133 sq. mi. (344 sq. km.)
Guatemala	Guatemala City	Central America, southeast of Mexico	42,042 sq. mi. (108,888 sq. km.)
Guinea	Conakry	West Africa, on the Atlantic Ocean, north of Sierra Leone	94,926 sq. mi. (245,857 sq. km.)
Guinea-Bissau	Bissau	West Africa, on the Atlantic Ocean, south of Senegal	13,948 sq. mi. (36,125 sq. km.)
Guyana	Georgetown	South America, on the northern coast, east of Venezuela	83,044 sq. mi. (215,083 sq. km.)
Haiti	Port-au-Prince	On an island, along with Dominican Republic, in the Caribbean Sea	10,695 sq. mi. (27,700 sq. km.)
Honduras	Tegucigalpa	Central America, between Guatemala and Nicaragua	43,277 sq. mi. (112,087 sq. km.)

POPULATION	CURRENCY	JOINED UN	COUNTRY
3,578,709	Ethiopian Birr 1 birr = 16 cents	1993	**Eritrea**
1,625,399	Kroon 1 kroon = $8\frac{1}{2}$ cents	1991	**Estonia**
55,979,018	Birr 1 birr = 16 cents	1945	**Ethiopia**
772,891	Fiji dollar 1 Fiji dollar = 71 cents	1970	**Fiji**
5,085,206	Markka 1 markka = 22 cents	1955	**Finland**
58,109,160	Franc 1 franc = 20 cents	1945	**France**
1,155,749	CFA franc 1 CFA franc = $\frac{1}{5}$ of a cent	1960	**Gabon**
989,273	Dalasi 1 dalasi = 10 cents	1965	**The Gambia**
5,725,972	Lari 1 lari = 83 cents	1992	**Georgia**
81,337,541	Mark 1 mark = 68 cents	1973	**Germany**
17,763,138	Cedi 1 cedi = $\frac{1}{15}$ of a cent	1957	**Ghana**
58,295,119	Pound 1 pound = $1.53	1945	**Great Britain** (United Kingdom)
10,647,511	Drachma 1 drachma = $\frac{2}{5}$ of a cent	1945	**Greece**
94,468	East Caribbean dollar 1 EC dollar = 37 cents	1974	**Grenada**
10,998,602	Quetzal 1 quetzal = 16 cents	1945	**Guatemala**
6,549,336	Franc 1 franc = $\frac{1}{10}$ of a cent	1958	**Guinea**
1,124,537	Peso 1 peso = $\frac{1}{180}$ of a cent	1974	**Guinea-Bissau**
723,774	Guyana dollar 1 Guyana dollar = $\frac{3}{4}$ of a cent	1966	**Guyana**
6,518,159	Gourde 1 gourde = 6 cents	1945	**Haiti**
5,459,743	Lempira 1 lempira = $9\frac{1}{2}$ cents	1945	**Honduras**

COUNTRY	CAPITAL	LOCATION OF COUNTRY	AREA
Hungary	Budapest	Central Europe, north of Yugoslavia	35,919 sq. mi. (93,030 sq. km.)
Iceland	Reykjavik	Island off the coast of Europe, in the North Atlantic Ocean, near Greenland	36,699 sq. mi. (95,050 sq. km.)
India	New Delhi	Southern Asia, on a large peninsula on the Indian Ocean	1,222,559 sq. mi. (3,166,413 sq. km.)
Indonesia	Jakarta	Islands south of Southeast Asia, along the equator	741,052 sq. mi. (1,919,316 sq. km.)
Iran	Tehran	Southern Asia, between Iraq and Pakistan	632,457 sq. mi. (1,638,056 sq. km.)
Iraq	Baghdad	In the Middle East, between Syria and Iran	167,975 sq. mi. (435,053 sq. km.)
Ireland	Dublin	Off the coast of Europe, in the Atlantic Ocean, west of Great Britain	27,137 sq. mi. (70,285 sq. km.)
Israel	Jerusalem	In the Middle East, between Jordan and the Mediterranean Sea	7,992 sq. mi. (20,699 sq. km.)
Italy	Rome	Southern Europe, jutting out into the Mediterranean Sea	116,333 sq. mi. (301,301 sq. km.)
Jamaica	Kingston	Island in the Caribbean Sea, south of Cuba	4,244 sq. mi. (10,992 sq. km.)
Japan	Tokyo	Four big islands and many small ones, off the east coast of Asia	145,850 sq. mi. (377,750 sq. km.)
Jordan	Amman	In the Middle East, south of Syria, east of Israel	34,342 sq. mi. (88,945 sq. km.)
Kazakstan	Almaty (Alma-Ata)	Central Asia, south of Russia	1,049,200 sq. mi. (2,717,416 sq. km.)
Kenya	Nairobi	East Africa, on the Indian Ocean, south of Ethiopia	224,961 sq. mi. (582,646 sq. km.)
Kiribati	Tarawa	Islands in the middle of the Pacific Ocean, near the equator	313 sq. mi. (811 sq. km.)
Korea, North	Pyongyang	Eastern Asia, in the northern part of the Korean Peninsula; China is to the north	47,399 sq. mi. (122,763 sq. km.)
Korea, South	Seoul	Eastern Asia, south of North Korea, on the Korean Peninsula	38,330 sq. mi. (99,274 sq. km.)
Kuwait	Kuwait City	In the Middle East, on the northern end of the Persian Gulf	6,880 sq. mi. (17,819 sq. km.)
Kyrgyzstan	Bishkek	Western Asia, between Kazakstan and Tajikistan	76,642 sq. mi. (198,502 sq. km.)
Laos	Vientiane	Southeast Asia, between Vietnam and Thailand	91,429 sq. mi. (236,800 sq. km.)

POPULATION	CURRENCY	JOINED UN	COUNTRY
10,318,838	Forint 1 forint = $^{7}/_{10}$ of a cent	1955	**Hungary**
265,998	Krona 1 krona = $1^{1}/_{2}$ cents	1946	**Iceland**
936,545,814	Rupee 1 rupee = 3 cents	1945	**India**
203,583,886	Rupiah 1 rupiah = $^{1}/_{23}$ of a cent	1950	**Indonesia**
64,625,455	Rial 1 rial = $^{1}/_{30}$ of cent	1945	**Iran**
20,643,769	Dinar 1 dinar = $^{1}/_{10}$ of a cent	1945	**Iraq**
3,550,448	Pound 1 pound = $1.57	1955	**Ireland**
5,142,834	New shekel 1 new shekel = 32 cents	1949	**Israel**
58,261,971	Lira 1 lira = $^{1}/_{16}$ of a cent	1955	**Italy**
2,574,291	Jamaican dollar 1 Jamaican dollar = 3 cents	1962	**Jamaica**
125,506,492	Yen 1 yen = 1 cent	1956	**Japan**
4,100,709	Dinar 1 dinar = $1.41	1955	**Jordan**
17,376,615	Tenge 1 tenge = $1^{1}/_{2}$ cents	1992	**Kazakstan**
28,817,227	Shilling 1 shilling = $1^{3}/_{4}$ cents	1963	**Kenya**
79,386	Australian dollar 1 Australian dollar = 76 cents	not in UN	**Kiribati**
23,486,550	Won 1 won = $46^{1}/_{2}$ cents	1991	**Korea, North**
45,553,882	Won 1 won = $^{1}/_{8}$ of a cent	1991	**Korea, South**
1,817,397	Dinar 1 dinar = $3.35	1963	**Kuwait**
4,769,877	Som 1 som = $8^{3}/_{4}$ cents	1992	**Kyrgyzstan**
4,837,237	New kip 1 new kip = $^{1}/_{9}$ of a cent	1955	**Laos**

COUNTRY	CAPITAL	LOCATION OF COUNTRY	AREA
Latvia	Riga	On the Baltic Sea, between Lithuania and Estonia	24,900 sq. mi. (64,491 sq. km.)
Lebanon	Beirut	In the Middle East, between the Mediterranean Sea and Syria	3,950 sq. mi. (10,230 sq. km.)
Lesotho	Maseru	Southern Africa, surrounded by the nation of South Africa	11,716 sq. mi. (30,344 sq. km.)
Liberia	Monrovia	Western Africa, on the Atlantic Ocean, southeast of Sierra Leone	38,250 sq. mi. (99,067 sq. km.)
Libya	Tripoli	North Africa, on the Mediterranean Sea, to the west of Egypt	679,359 sq. mi. (1,759,532 sq. km.)
Liechtenstein	Vaduz	Southern Europe, in the Alps between Austria and Switzerland	62 sq. mi. (161 sq. km.)
Lithuania	Vilnius	Northern Europe, on the Baltic Sea, north of Poland	25,213 sq. mi. (65,301 sq. km.)
Luxembourg	Luxembourg	Western Europe, between France and Germany	999 sq. mi. (2,587 sq. km.)
Macedonia	Skopje	Southern Europe, north of Greece	9,928 sq. mi. (25,713 sq. km.)
Madagascar	Antananarivo	Island in the Indian Ocean, off the east coast of Africa	226,658 sq. mi. (587,042 sq. km.)
Malawi	Lilongwe	Southern Africa, south of Tanzania and Zaire	45,747 sq. mi. (118,484 sq. km.)
Malaysia	Kuala Lumpur	Southeast Asia, on the island of Borneo	127,584 sq. mi. (330,441 sq. km.)
Maldives	Male	Islands in the Indian Ocean, south of India	115 sq. mi. (298 sq. km.)
Mali	Bamako	West Africa, between Algeria and Mauritania	482,077 sq. mi. (1,248,574 sq. km.)
Malta	Valletta	Island in the Mediterranean Sea, south of Italy	122 sq. mi. (316 sq. km.)
Marshall Islands	Majuro	Chain of small islands in the middle of the Pacific Ocean	70 sq. mi. (181 sq. km.)
Mauritania	Nouakchott	West Africa, on the Atlantic Ocean, north of Senegal	398,000 sq. mi. (1,030,815 sq. km.)
Mauritius	Port Louis	Islands in the Indian Ocean, east of Madagascar	788 sq. mi. (2,041 sq. km.)
Mexico	Mexico City	North America, south of the United States	756,066 sq. mi. (1,958,202 sq. km.)
Micronesia	Palikir	Islands in the Western Pacific Ocean	271 sq. mi. (702 sq. km.)
Moldova	Chisinau	Eastern Europe, between Ukraine and Romania	13,012 sq. mi. (33,701 sq. km.)

POPULATION	CURRENCY	JOINED UN	COUNTRY
2,762,899	Lat 1 lat = 1.82	1991	**Latvia**
3,695,921	Pound 1 pound = $^1/_{16}$ of a cent	1945	**Lebanon**
1,992,960	Maloti 1 maloti = 26 cents	1966	**Lesotho**
3,073,245	Liberian dollar Same as U.S. dollar	1945	**Liberia**
5,248,401	Dinar 1 dinar = $2.81	1955	**Libya**
30,654	Swiss franc 1 Swiss franc = 83 cents	1990	**Liechtenstein**
3,876,396	Litas 1 litas = 25 cents	1991	**Lithuania**
404,660	Franc 1 franc = $3^1/_3$ cents	1945	**Luxembourg**
2,159,503	Denar 1 denar = $2^1/_2$ cents	1993	**Macedonia**
13,862,325	Franc 1 franc = $^1/_{39}$ of a cent	1960	**Madagascar**
9,808,384	Kwacha 1 kwacha = $6^1/_2$ cents	1964	**Malawi**
19,723,587	Ringgit 1 ringgit = 39 cents	1957	**Malaysia**
261,310	Rufiyaa 1 rufiyaa = $8^1/_2$ cents	1965	**Maldives**
9,375,132	CFA franc 1 CFA franc = $^1/_5$ of a cent	1960	**Mali**
369,609	Maltese lira 1 Maltese lira = $2.76	1964	**Malta**
56,157	U.S. dollar	1991	**Marshall Islands**
2,263,202	Ouguiya 1 ouguiya = $^3/_4$ of a cent	1961	**Mauritania**
1,127,068	Mauritian rupee 1 Mauritian rupee = $5^1/_3$ cents	1968	**Mauritius**
93,985,848	New peso 1 new peso = 13 cents	1945	**Mexico**
122,950	U.S. dollar	1991	**Micronesia**
4,489,657	Leu 1 leu = 22 cents	1992	**Moldova**

COUNTRY	CAPITAL	LOCATION OF COUNTRY	AREA
Monaco	Monaco	Europe, on the Mediterranean Sea, surrounded by France	3/4 of a sq. mi. (1.9 sq. km.)
Mongolia	Ulaanbaatar	Central Asia between Russia and China	604,800 sq. mi. (1,566,425 sq. km.)
Morocco	Rabat	Northwest Africa, on the Atlantic Ocean and Mediterranean Sea	177,117 sq. mi. (458,731 sq. km.)
Mozambique	Maputo	Southeastern Africa, on the Indian Ocean	313,661 sq. mi. (812,378 sq. km.)
Myanmar (Burma)	Yangôn (Rangoon)	Southern Asia, to the east of India and Bangladesh	261,228 sq. mi. (676,577 sq. km.)
Namibia	Windhoek	Southwestern Africa, on the Atlantic Ocean, west of Botswana	318,146 sq. mi. (823,994 sq. km.)
Nauru	Yaren	Island in the western Pacific Ocean, just below the equator	8 sq. mi. (21 sq. km.)
Nepal	Kathmandu	Asia, in the Himalaya Mountains, between China and India	56,827 sq. mi. (147,181 sq. km.)
The Netherlands	Amsterdam	Northern Europe, on the North Sea, to the west of Germany	16,033 sq. mi. (41,525 sq. km.)
New Zealand	Wellington	Islands in the Pacific Ocean east of Australia	104,454 sq. mi. (270,535 sq. km.)
Nicaragua	Managua	Central America, between Honduras and Costa Rica	50,880 sq. mi. (131,779 sq. km.)
Niger	Niamey	North Africa, south of Algeria and Libya	497,000 sq. mi. (1,287,224 sq. km.)
Nigeria	Abuja	West Africa, on the southern coast between Benin and Cameroon	356,669 sq. mi. (923,769 sq. km.)
Norway	Oslo	Northern Europe, on the Scandinavian Peninsula, west of Sweden	125,050 sq. mi. (323,878 sq. km.)
Oman	Muscat	On the Arabian Peninsula, southeast of Saudi Arabia	118,150 sq. mi. (306,007 sq. km.)
Pakistan	Islamabad	South Asia, between Iran and India	339,697 sq. mi. (879,811 sq. km.)
Palau	Koror	Islands in North Pacific Ocean, southeast of Philippines	179 sq. mi. (464 sq. km.)
Panama	Panama City	Central America, between Costa Rica and Colombia	29,157 sq. mi. (75,516 sq. km.)
Papua New Guinea	Port Moresby	Part of the island of New Guinea, north of Australia	178,704 sq. mi. (462,841 sq. km.)
Paraguay	Asunción	South America, between Argentina and Brazil	157,048 sq. mi. (406,753 sq. km.)

POPULATION	CURRENCY	JOINED UN	COUNTRY
31,515	French franc 1 franc = 20 cents	1993	**Monaco**
2,493,615	Tugrik 1 tugrik = $^1/_5$ of a cent	1961	**Mongolia**
29,168,848	Dirham 1 dirham = 12 cents	1956	**Morocco**
18,115,250	Metical 1 metical = $^1/_{99}$ of a cent	1975	**Mozambique**
45,103,809	Kyat 1 kyat = 17 cents	1948	**Myanmar (Burma)**
1,651,545	Namibian dollar 1 Namibian dollar = 26 cents	1990	**Namibia**
10,149	Australian dollar 1 Australian dollar = 76 cents	not in UN	**Nauru**
21,560,869	Rupee 1 rupee = $1^3/_4$ cents	1955	**Nepal**
15,452,903	Guilder 1 guilder = 60 cents	1945	**The Netherlands**
3,407,277	New Zealand dollar 1 NZ dollar = 67 cents	1945	**New Zealand**
4,206,353	Gold cordoba 1 gold cordoba = 12 cents	1945	**Nicaragua**
9,280,208	CFA franc 1 CFA franc = $^1/_5$ of a cent	1960	**Niger**
101,232,251	Naira 1 naira = $1^1/_4$ cents	1960	**Nigeria**
4,330,951	Krone 1 krone = 16 cents	1945	**Norway**
2,125,089	Rial Omani 1 rial Omani = $2.60	1971	**Oman**
131,541,920	Rupee 1 rupee = 3 cents	1947	**Pakistan**
16,661	U.S. dollar	1994	**Palau**
2,680,903	Balboa Same value as U.S. dollar	1945	**Panama**
4,294,750	Kina 1 kina = 74 cents	1975	**Papua New Guinea**
5,358,198	Guarani 1 guarani = $^1/_{20}$ of a cent	1945	**Paraguay**

COUNTRY	CAPITAL	LOCATION OF COUNTRY	AREA
Peru	Lima	South America, along the Pacific coast, north of Chile	496,225 sq. mi. (1,285,217 sq. km.)
Philippines	Manila	Islands in the Pacific Ocean, off the coast of Southeast Asia	115,860 sq. mi. (300,076 sq. km.)
Poland	Warsaw	Central Europe, on the Baltic Sea, east of Germany	120,727 sq. mi. (312,682 sq. km.)
Portugal	Lisbon	Southern Europe, on the Iberian Peninsula, west of Spain	35,672 sq. mi. (92,390 sq. km.)
Qatar	Doha	Arabian Peninsula, on the Persian Gulf	4,412 sq. mi. (11,427 sq. km.)
Romania	Bucharest	Southern Europe, on the Black Sea, north of Bulgaria	91,699 sq. mi. (237,499 sq. km.)
Russia	Moscow	Stretches from Eastern Europe across northern Asia to the Pacific Ocean	6,592,800 sq. mi. (17,075,274 sq. km.)
Rwanda	Kigali	Central Africa, between Zaire and Tanzania	10,169 sq. mi. (26,338 sq. km.)
Saint Kitts and Nevis	Basseterre	Islands in the Caribbean Sea, near Puerto Rico	104 sq. mi. (269 sq. km.)
Saint Lucia	Castries	Island on eastern edge of the Caribbean Sea	238 sq. mi. (616 sq. km.)
Saint Vincent and the Grenadines	Kingstown	Islands on eastern edge of the Caribbean Sea, north of Grenada	150 sq. mi. (388 sq. km.)
San Marino	San Marino	Southern Europe, surrounded by Italy	24 sq. mi. (62 sq. km.)
São Tomé and Príncipe	São Tomé	In the Gulf of Guinea, off the coast of West Africa	386 sq. mi. (1,000 sq. km.)
Saudi Arabia	Riyadh	Western Asia, occupying most of the Arabian Peninsula	865,000 sq. mi. (2,240,340 sq. km.)
Senegal	Dakar	West Africa, on the Atlantic Ocean, south of Mauritania	75,951 sq. mi. (196,712 sq. km.)
Seychelles	Victoria	Islands off the coast of Africa, in the Indian Ocean, north of Madagascar	176 sq. mi. (456 sq. km.)
Sierra Leone	Freetown	West Africa, on the Atlantic Ocean, south of Guinea	27,699 sq. mi. (71,740 sq. km.)
Singapore	Singapore	Mostly on one island, off the tip of Southeast Asia	247 sq. mi. (640 sq. km.)
Slovakia	Bratislava	Eastern Europe, between Poland and Hungary	18,933 sq. mi. (49,036 sq. km.)

POPULATION	CURRENCY	JOINED UN	COUNTRY
24,087,372	New sol 1 new sol = 42 cents	1945	Peru
73,265,584	Peso 1 peso = 4 cents	1945	Philippines
38,792,442	Zloty 1 zloty = 39 cents	1945	Poland
10,562,388	Escudo 1 escudo = $\frac{2}{3}$ of a cent	1955	Portugal
533,916	Riyal 1 riyal = 27 cents	1971	Qatar
23,198,330	Leu 1 leu = $\frac{1}{29}$ of a cent	1955	Romania
149,909,089	Ruble 1 ruble = $\frac{1}{48}$ of a cent	1945	Russia
8,605,307	Franc 1 franc = $\frac{1}{2}$ of a cent	1962	Rwanda
40,992	East Caribbean dollar 1 EC dollar = 37 cents	1983	Saint Kitts and Nevis
156,050	East Caribbean dollar 1 EC dollar = 37 cents	1979	Saint Lucia
117,580	East Caribbean dollar 1 EC dollar = 37 cents	1980	Saint Vincent and the Grenadines
24,313	Italian lira 1 lira = $\frac{1}{16}$ of a cent	1992	San Marino
140,423	Dobra 1 dobra = $\frac{1}{19}$ of a cent	1975	São Tomé and Príncipe
18,729,576	Riyal 1 riyal = 27 cents	1945	Saudi Arabia
9,007,080	CFA franc 1 CFA franc = $\frac{1}{5}$ of a cent	1960	Senegal
72,709	Rupee 1 rupee = 20 cents	1976	Seychelles
4,753,120	Leone 1 leone = $\frac{1}{9}$ of a cent	1961	Sierra Leone
2,890,468	Singapore dollar 1 Singapore dollar = 71 cents	1965	Singapore
5,432,383	Koruna 1 koruna = $3\frac{1}{3}$ cents	1993	Slovakia

COUNTRY	CAPITAL	LOCATION OF COUNTRY	AREA
Slovenia	Ljubljana	Eastern Europe, between Austria and Croatia	7,821 sq. mi. (20,256 sq. km.)
Solomon Islands	Honiara	Western Pacific Ocean	10,954 sq. mi. (28,371 sq. km.)
Somalia	Mogadishu	East Africa, east of Ethiopia	246,300 sq. mi. (637,914 sq. km.)
South Africa	Pretoria	At the southern tip of Africa	473,290 sq. mi. (1,225,815 sq. km.)
Spain	Madrid	Europe, south of France, on the Iberian Peninsula	194,898 sq. mi. (504,784 sq. km.)
Sri Lanka	Colombo	Island in the Indian Ocean, southeast of India	25,332 sq. mi. (65,610 sq. km.)
Sudan	Khartoum	North Africa, south of Egypt, on the Red Sea	966,757 sq. mi. (2,503,889 sq. km.)
Suriname	Paramaribo	South America, on the northern shore, east of Guyana	63,251 sq. mi. (163,819 sq. km.)
Swaziland	Mbabane	Southern Africa, almost surrounded by South Africa	6,704 sq. mi. (17,363 sq. km.)
Sweden	Stockholm	Northern Europe, on the Scandinavian Peninsula, east of Norway	173,732 sq. mi. (449,964 sq. km.)
Switzerland	Bern	Central Europe, in the Alps, north of Italy	15,943 sq. mi. (41,292 sq. km.)
Syria	Damascus	In the Middle East, on the Mediterranean Sea, north of Jordan and Iraq	71,498 sq. mi. (185,179 sq. km.)
Taiwan	Taipei	Island off southeast coast of China	13,969 sq. mi. (36,180 sq. km.)
Tajikistan	Dushanbe	Asia, west of China, south of Kyrgyzstan	55,300 sq. mi. (143,226 sq. km.)
Tanzania	Dar-es-Salaam	East Africa, on the Indian Ocean, south of Kenya	364,017 sq. mi. (942,800 sq. km.)
Thailand	Bangkok	Southeast Asia, west of Laos	198,115 sq. mi. (513,116 sq. km.)
Togo	Lomé	West Africa, between Ghana and Benin	21,925 sq. mi. (56,785 sq. km.)
Tonga	Nuku'alofa	Islands in the South Pacific Ocean	301 sq. mi. (780 sq. km.)
Trinidad and Tobago	Port-of-Spain	Islands off the north coast of South America	1,980 sq. mi. (5,128 sq. km.)
Tunisia	Tunis	North Africa, on the Mediterranean, between Algeria and Libya	63,378 sq. mi. (164,148 sq. km.)

POPULATION	CURRENCY	JOINED UN	COUNTRY
2,051,522	Tolar 1 tolar = $^3/_4$ of a cent	1992	Slovenia
399,206	Solomon Islands dollar 1 Solomon dollar = 29 cents	1978	Solomon Islands
7,347,554	Shilling 1 shilling = $^1/_{26}$ of a cent	1960	Somalia
45,095,459	Rand 1 rand = 26 cents	1945	South Africa
39,404,348	Peseta 1 peseta = $^4/_5$ of a cent	1955	Spain
18,342,660	Rupee 1 rupee = 2 cents	1955	Sri Lanka
30,120,420	Dinar 1 dinar = 1 cent	1956	Sudan
429,544	Guilder 1 guilder = $^1/_3$ of a cent	1975	Suriname
966,977	Lilangeni 1 lilangeni = 26 cents	1968	Swaziland
8,821,759	Krona 1 krona = 15 cents	1946	Sweden
7,084,984	Franc 1 franc = 83 cents	participant, not a member	Switzerland
15,451,917	Pound 1 pound = $2^1/_3$ cents	1945	Syria
21,500,583	New Taiwan dollar 1 new Taiwan dollar = $3^2/_3$ cents	not in UN	Taiwan
6,155,474	Tajik ruble 1 Tajik ruble = $^1/_3$ of a cent	1992	Tajikistan
28,701,077	Shilling 1 shilling = $^1/_6$ of a cent	1961	Tanzania
60,271,300	Baht 1 baht = 4 cents	1946	Thailand
4,410,370	CFA franc 1 CFA franc = $^1/_5$ of a cent	1960	Togo
105,600	Pa'anga 1 pa'anga = 80 cents	not in UN	Tonga
1,271,159	Trinidad and Tobago dollar 1 Trinidad dollar = 17 cents	1962	Trinidad and Tobago
8,879,845	Dinar 1 dinar = $1.04	1956	Tunisia

COUNTRY	CAPITAL	LOCATION OF COUNTRY	AREA
Turkey	Ankara	On the southern shore of the Black Sea, partly in Europe and partly in Asia	300,948 sq. mi. (779,452 sq. km.)
Turkmenistan	Ashgabat	Western Asia, north of Afghanistan and Iran	188,417 sq. mi. (487,998 sq. km.)
Tuvalu	Fongafale	Chain of islands in the South Pacific Ocean	9 sq. mi. (24 sq. km.)
Uganda	Kampala	East Africa, south of Sudan	93,070 sq. mi. (241,050 sq. km.)
Ukraine	Kiev	Eastern Europe, south of Belarus and Russia	233,100 sq. mi. (603,726 sq. km.)
United Arab Emirates	Abu Dhabi	Arabian Peninsula, on the Persian Gulf	30,000 sq. mi. (77,700 sq. km.)
United States	Washington, D.C.	48 (of 50) states in North America, between Canada and Mexico	3,787,319 sq. mi. (9,809,109 sq. km.)
Uruguay	Montevideo	South America, on the Atlantic Ocean, south of Brazil	68,037 sq. mi. (176,215 sq. km.)
Uzbekistan	Tashkent	Central Asia, south of Kazakstan	172,700 sq. mi. (447,291 sq. km.)
Vanuatu	Vila	Islands in the South Pacific Ocean	4,707 sq. mi. (12,191 sq. km.)
Vatican City		Surrounded by the city of Rome, Italy	1/5 sq. mi. (2/5 sq. km.)
Venezuela	Caracas	On the northern coast of South America, east of Colombia	352,144 sq. mi. (912,049 sq. km.)
Vietnam	Hanoi	Southeast Asia, south of China, on the eastern coast	127,246 sq. mi. (329,566 sq. km.)
Western Samoa	Apia	Islands in the South Pacific Ocean	1,093 sq. mi. (2,831 sq. km.)
Yemen	Sanaa	Asia, on the southern coast of the Arabian Peninsula	205,356 sq. mi. (531,870 sq. km.)
Yugoslavia	Belgrade	Southern Europe, on the Balkan Peninsula, west of Romania and Bulgaria	39,449 sq. mi. (102,172 sq. km.)
Zaire	Kinshasa	Central Africa, north of Angola and Zambia	905,446 sq. mi. (2,345,094 sq. km.)
Zambia	Lusaka	Southern Africa, south of Zaire	290,586 sq. mi. (752,614 sq. km.)
Zimbabwe	Harare	Southern Africa, south of Zambia	150,872 sq. mi. (390,757 sq. km.)

POPULATION	CURRENCY	JOINED UN	COUNTRY
63,405,526	Turkish lira 1 Turkish lira = $\frac{1}{665}$ of a cent	1945	**Turkey**
4,075,316	Manat 1 manat = $\frac{1}{25}$ of a cent	1992	**Turkmenistan**
9,991	Tuvaluan (Australian) dollar 1 Tuvaluan (Australian) dollar = 76 cents	not in UN	**Tuvalu**
19,573,262	Shilling 1 shilling = $\frac{1}{10}$ of a cent	1962	**Uganda**
51,867,828	Karbovanet 1 karbovanet = $\frac{1}{1900}$ of a cent	1945	**Ukraine**
2,924,594	Dirham 1 dirham = 27 cents	1971	**United Arab Emirates**
263,814,032	U.S. dollar	1945	**United States**
3,222,716	Peso 1 peso = 14 cents	1945	**Uruguay**
23,089,261	Sum 1 sum = $2\frac{3}{4}$ cents	1992	**Uzbekistan**
173,648	Vatu 1 vatu = $\frac{9}{10}$ of a cent	1981	**Vanuatu**
811	Vatican lira, Italian lira 1 lira = $\frac{1}{16}$ of a cent	not in UN	**Vatican City**
21,004,773	Bolivar 1 bolivar = $\frac{1}{3}$ of a cent	1945	**Venezuela**
74,393,324	Dong 1 dong = $\frac{1}{110}$ of a cent	1977	**Vietnam**
209,360	Tala 1 tala = 40 cents	1976	**Western Samoa**
14,728,474	Rial 1 rial = $\frac{3}{4}$ of a cent	1947	**Yemen**
11,101,833	New dinar 1 new dinar = 20 cents	1945 (suspended in 1992)	**Yugoslavia**
44,060,636	New Zaire 1 new zaire = $\frac{1}{200}$ of a cent	1960	**Zaire**
9,445,723	Kwacha 1 kwacha = $\frac{1}{11}$ of a cent	1964	**Zambia**
11,139,961	Zimbabwe dollar 1 Zimbabwe dollar = 11 cents	1980	**Zimbabwe**

COUNTRY PUZZLE

There are 48 countries in Asia. The names of 25 of them are hidden below. How many of the countries listed can you find? AFGHANISTAN, CAMBODIA, CHINA, INDIA, IRAN, IRAQ, ISRAEL, JAPAN, JORDAN, KUWAIT, LAOS, MALAYSIA, MONGOLIA, MYANMAR, NEPAL, OMAN, PAKISTAN, PHILIPPINES, QATAR, SINGAPORE, SYRIA, TAIWAN, THAILAND, VIETNAM, YEMEN. (Answers are on page 302.)

```
T H A I L A N D F T U J D F R E S T B V C D A
K A L A H F Z X C V N M I S R A E L P O L Y M
E J I K L G A D S F G N K I F D S A L K J U G
T Y P W E H S W E R Y T H N J Y J O R D A N T
R E W Y A A Q U Y T H G F G A S L S O U P A Y
L O R Y I N A S D J F E Q A T A R G Y H A J S
K I T R S I N D I A Z A C P V B N M U R K G A
M U W D A S L W E P Q W E O R T Y U L P I T Y
G E S A S T J O M A N A S R P O L J H G S A T
F R D Y D A H Y T N E N T E A M T R E N T W E
J V I E T N A M Q Z A S D F G Y T E P R A Y T
D Y A U F Y G A W A I L P H I L I P P I N E S
R H S I G U F L E S R Y U P R T R Y W E B M A
T N D O H M Y A N M A R L K A J H G A C S E D
S F E P J I D Y R A N N B V Q C X Z R H A N K
Y D H P K P A S T P O I L U H K U W A I T O F
W L J L A L T I Y T R E W S H I B C E N L H A
M O N G O L I A P M H N C A M B O D I A S A L
```

CAPITAL CITY PUZZLE

All the cities listed are capitals of countries in South America. Can you match each capital city with its country? (Answers are on page 303.)

Cities	Countries
Bogotá	Argentina (1)
Brasília	Bolivia (2)
Buenos Aires	Brazil (3)
Caracas	Chile (4)
La Paz	Colombia (5)
Lima	Ecuador (6)
Montevideo	Peru (7)
Paramaribo	Suriname (8)
Quito	Uruguay (9)
Santiago	Venezuela (10)

MAPS and FLAGS of the COUNTRIES of the WORLD

Maps showing the continents and countries of the world appear on pages 65 through 76. Flags of the countries appear on pages 77 through 80.

Australia............................65

North America.................66

South America................68

Europe.............................70

Asia....................................72

Africa 74

Pacific Islands..................76

Flags of the countries.......77

Maps of the United States appear on pages 241-256

Australia

National Capital
State Capital
Other City
1:40,886,000

0   250   500 mi
0   250   500 km
Two-Point Equidistant Projection

North America

⊛ National Capital
★ Territorial Capital
• Other City

1:39,978,000

0   350   700 mi
0   350   700 km

Azimuthal Equal Area Projection

ATLANTIC OCEAN

PACIFIC OCEAN

UNITED STATES

MEXICO

VENEZUELA

BRAZIL

COLOMBIA

Caribbean Sea

Gulf of Mexico

CUBA

THE BAHAMAS

Bermuda (Brit.)

NOVA SCOTIA

Bangor John Portland
Montréal N.Y. N.H. Boston
Sherbrooke VT. MASS.
Ottawa N.J. CONN. R.I.
N.Y. PENN. New York City
Buffalo Philadelphia
Rochester Baltimore NEW JERSEY
Toronto Cleveland DELAWARE
Detroit Pittsburgh MARYLAND
Sudbury MICH. OHIO Washington, D.C.
Columbus W. VA. Richmond
Cincinnati VA. N.C. Raleigh
Indianapolis Charlotte
IND. Louisville KY. S.C. Columbia
ILL. Nashville TENN. Atlanta
Chicago St. Louis Birmingham GA.
Milwaukee MO. ARK. ALA. Savannah
WIS. IOWA Memphis MISS. Jacksonville
Duluth Omaha Little Rock Jackson Mobile FLA.
MINN. NEB. Oklahoma New Orleans Tampa
Minneapolis KANSAS City LA. St. Petersburg Miami
Fargo Wichita OKLA. Shreveport Baton Rouge
Bismarck Kansas City Dallas Houston
N. DAK. S. DAK. Rapid City Austin
MONT. WYO. Cheyenne NEB. TEXAS San Antonio
Missoula Billings Casper COLORADO Denver
Helena Pocatello Salt Lake City UTAH
IDAHO Boise Colorado Plateau NEW MEXICO
Las Vegas Albuquerque Santa Fe
NEVADA Reno ARIZONA Phoenix El Paso
Sacramento CALIF. Fresno Ciudad Juárez
San Francisco Mt. Whitney Chihuahua
Eugene Eureka SIERRA NEVADA Los Angeles
COAST RANGES San Diego Tijuana Mexicali Hermosillo
Santa Barbara Nogales Ciudad Obregón
BAJA CALIFORNIA Durango
Gulf of California Mazatlán
Monterrey Torreón
SIERRA MADRE OCCIDENTAL
SIERRA MADRE ORIENTAL
San Luis Potosí
Guadalajara León
Mexico City Puebla
Orizaba Pk. (18,405 ft) 5,610 m
Acapulco Oaxaca
Veracruz Villahermosa
Campeche Tuxtla Gutiérrez
YUCATÁN PENINSULA
Bay of Campeche
Mérida
BELIZE Belmopan
GUATEMALA Guatemala City
HONDURAS Tegucigalpa
San Salvador EL SALVADOR
NICARAGUA Managua
COSTA RICA San José
PANAMA Panama City
GREAT PLAINS
ROCKY MOUNTAINS
Columbia Plateau
CASCADE RANGE
Appalachian
Straits of Florida
Havana Santiago de Cuba
Nassau
CAYMAN IS. (Brit.)
JAMAICA Kingston
HAITI Port-au-Prince
DOMINICAN REPUBLIC Santo Domingo
PUERTO RICO (U.S.) San Juan
TURKS & CAICOS IS. (Brit.)
VIRGIN IS. (U.S., Brit.)
ST. KITTS & NEVIS
ANTIGUA & BARBUDA
GUADELOUPE (Fr.)
DOMINICA
MARTINIQUE (Fr.)
ST. LUCIA
ST. VINCENT & THE GRENADINES
BARBADOS
GRENADA
TRINIDAD & TOBAGO Port-of-Spain
BONAIRE (Neth.)
CURAÇAO (Neth.)
ARUBA (Neth.)

Mt. Rainier 4,392 m (14,410 ft)
Mt. Whitney 4,418 m (14,494 ft)

Lake Superior
Lake Michigan
Lake Huron

Rio Grande
Missouri R.
Platte R.
Snake R.
Columbia R.

Tropic of Cancer

67

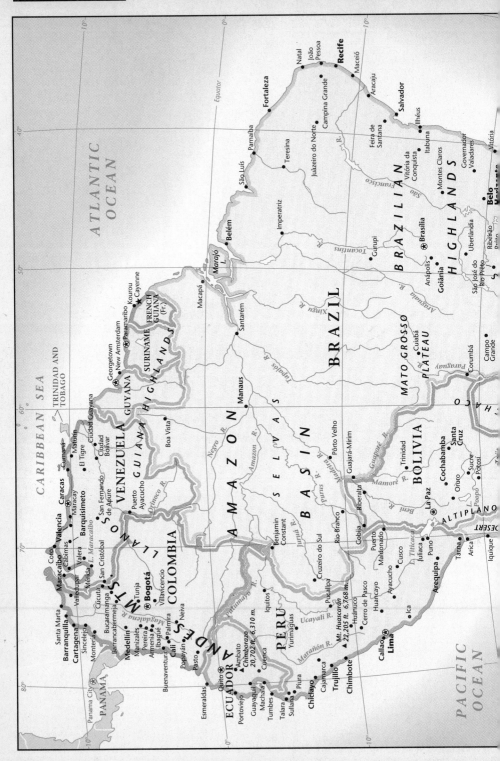

ATLANTIC OCEAN

CARIBBEAN SEA

TRINIDAD AND TOBAGO

PACIFIC OCEAN

Equator

Recife
Natal
João Pessoa
Fortaleza
Campina Grande
Maceió
Aracaju
Parnaíba
Salvador
Ilhéus
Feira de Santana
Teresina
Vitória da Conquista
Itabuna
São Luís
Montes Claros
Imperatriz
Governador Valadares
Vitória
B R A Z I L I A N   H I G H L A N D S
Belo
Anápolis
Uberlândia
Belém
São José do Rio Prêto
Ribeirão
Gurupi
Brasília
Goiânia
São Francisco
Tocantins R.
Marajó I.
Macapá
B R A Z I L
Cuiabá
Campo Grande
Corumbá
M A T O   G R O S S O   P L A T E A U
Paraguay R.
Kourou
Cayenne
FRENCH GUIANA (Fr.)
Paramaribo
New Amsterdam
SURINAME
Santarém
Xingu R.
Tapajós R.
Georgetown
GUYANA
G U I A N A   H I G H L A N D S
Manaus
Negro R.
Amazon R.
A M A Z O N   B A S I N
Boa Vista
S E L V A S
Pôrto Velho
Madeira R.
Guaporé R.
Trinidad
Santa Cruz
Cochabamba
BOLIVIA
Sucre
Potosí
Oruro
La Paz
Mamoré R.
Beni R.
Guajará-Mirim
Riberalta
Cobija
A L T I P L A N O
DESERT
L. Poopó
Ciudad Guayana
Ciudad Bolívar
El Tigre
Maturín
Cumaná
Caracas
Valencia
Maracay
Barquisimeto
San Fernando de Apure
V E N E Z U E L A
L L A N O S
Orinoco R.
Puerto Ayacucho
Coro
Cabimas
Maracaibo
Valera
Mérida
L. Maracaibo
San Cristóbal
Cúcuta
Bucaramanga
Barrancabermeja
Medellín
Manizales
Pereira
Armenia
Ibagué
Bogotá
Tunja
Villavicencio
Neiva
COLOMBIA
Magdalena R.
Santa Marta
Barranquilla
Cartagena
Sincelejo
Montería
Cali
Buenaventura
Palmira
Popayán
Pasto
A N D E S
Putumayo R.
Esmeraldas
Quito
Guayaquil
Portoviejo
Machala
Tumbes
ECUADOR
Ambato
Chimborazo 20,702 ft. 6,310 m.
Cuenca
Talara
Sullana
Piura
Chiclayo
Cajamarca
Trujillo
Chimbote
Mt. Huascarán 22,205 ft. 6,768 m.
Marañón R.
Yurimaguas
Iquitos
P E R U
Huánuco
Cerro de Pasco
Huancayo
Ayacucho
Ica
Pucallpa
Cruzeiro do Sul
Benjamin Constant
Juruá R.
Purus R.
Ucayali R.
Callao
Lima
Cusco
Arequipa
Juliaca
Puno
L. Titicaca
Tacna
Arica
Iquique
Puerto Maldonado
Rio Branco
Panama City
PANAMA
SIERRA MTS.
Valledupar

10°
0°
10°
20°
30°
40°
50°
60°
70°
80°

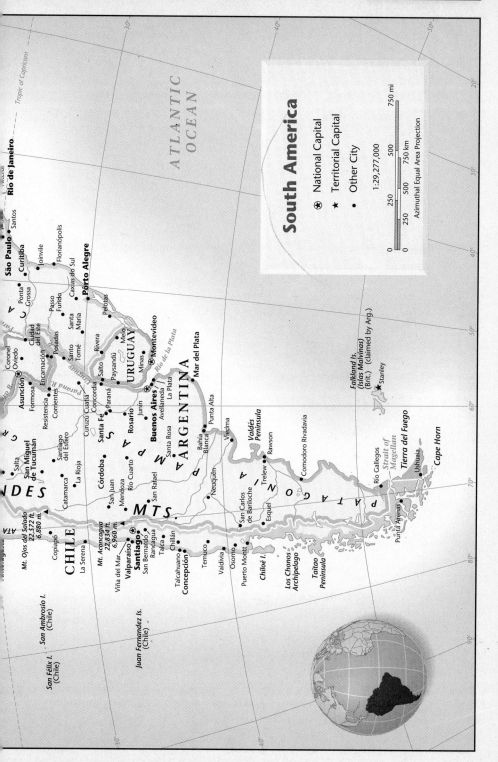

South America

- ⊛ National Capital
- ★ Territorial Capital
- • Other City

1:29,277,000

```
0      250    500    750 mi
0  250   500   750 km
```

Azimuthal Equal Area Projection

Tropic of Capricorn

ATLANTIC OCEAN

São Paulo
Santos
Rio de Janeiro
Curitiba
Joinvile
Ponta Grossa
Florianópolis
Passo Fundo
Caxias do Sul
Porto Alegre
Santa Maria
Pelotas
Coronel Oviedo
Ciudad del Este
Posadas
Santo Tomé
Rivera
Melo
Asunción
Formosa
Encarnación
Salto
Paysandú
Minas
Montevideo
URUGUAY
Resistencia
Corrientes
Curuzú Cuatiá
Concordia
Paraná
La Plata
Mar del Plata
Santa Fe
Paraná
Rosario
Buenos Aires
Avellaneda
Río de la Plata
Salta
Santiago del Estero
Córdoba
Junín
Punta Alta
ARGENTINA
San Miguel de Tucumán
Catamarca
La Rioja
San Juan
Santa Rosa
Bahía Blanca
Viedma
Valdés Peninsula
Falkland Is.
(Islas Malvinas)
(Brit.) (claimed by Arg.)
Stanley
ANDES
Mt. Ojos del Salado
22,572 ft.
6,880 m.
Copiapó
La Serena
CHILE
Mt. Aconcagua
22,834 ft.
6,960 m.
Viña del Mar
Valparaíso
San Bernardo
Santiago
Rancagua
Mendoza
San Rafael
Río Cuarto
Rawson
Comodoro Rivadavia
Strait of Magellan
Tierra del Fuego
San Ambrosio I.
(Chile)
San Félix I.
(Chile)
Juan Fernández Is.
(Chile)
MTS.
Talca
Chillán
Concepción
Talcahuano
Temuco
Valdivia
Osorno
Puerto Montt
Chiloé I.
San Carlos de Bariloche
Esquel
Neuquén
Trelew
Río Gallegos
Punta Arenas
Ushuaia
Cape Horn
PATAGONIA
Los Chonos Archipelago
Taitao Peninsula
```

69
```

Europe

⍟ National Capital

• Other City

1:22,107,000

| 0 | 250 | 500 mi |
| 0 | 250 | 500 km |

Azimuthal Equal Area Projection

North
Cape
Hammerfest

*Barents
Sea*

Nar'yan-Mar

Ob

LAPLAND

Murmansk

KOLA
PENINSULA
Apatity

Arctic Circle

Pechora

Pechora

Irtysh

na

uleå

Oulu

Gulf of Bothnia

White Sea

Belomorsk

Arkhangel'sk

R U S S I A

Serov

U R A L

Ukhta

Petropavl

FINLAND

Vaasa

Divina

Kotlas

Syktyvkar

Berezniki

Yekaterinburg

Tampere
Lahti

*Lake
Onega*

Petrozavodsk

P L A I N

Kirov

Perm'

M
O
U
N
T
A
I
N
S

Chelyabinsk

Qostanay

Helsinki

*Lake
Ladoga*

Vologda

Izhevsk

Kama

Magnitogorsk

St.
Petersburg

Cherepovets

Naberezhnyye
Chelny

Ufa

Gulf of Finland

Novgorod

Yaroslavl'

Kazan

ESTONIA

Tallinn

Ivanovo

Nizhniy
Novgorod

Tartu

E U R O P E A N

Tver'

Ul'yanovsk

Tol'yatti

Orenburg

Orsk

Riga

Pskov

Moscow

Ryazan'

Saransk

Samara

KAZAKSTAN

LATVIA

Daugavpils

Volga

Oral

LITHUANIA

Vitsyebsk

Smolensk

Tula

Penza

Aqtöbe

Kaunas
SSIA
ngrad

Vilnius

Mahilyow

Lipetsk

Tambov

Ural

Atyraū

*Aral
Sea*

THERN

Hrodna

Minsk

Bryansk

Saratov

UZBEKISTAN

BELARUS

Homyel'

Kursk

Voronezh

Brest

Volgograd

Warsaw

Kiev

Kharkiv

Aqtaū

 POLAND

L'viv

UKRAINE

Dnieper

Luhans'k

Astrakhan

Caspian

TURKMENISTAN

w

CARPATHIAN

Chernivtsi

Dnipropetrovs'k

Donets'k

Don

Dniester

Zaporizhzhya

Rostov na Donu

MOLDOVA

Kryvyy Rih

Mariupol'

Grozznyy

Makhachkala

Sea

Debrecen

Iaşi

Chişinău

Mykolaiv

*Sea of
Azov*

Stavropol'

Türkmenbashi

Košice

Odesa

Krasnodar

C A U C A S U S

ROMANIA

Timişoara

Ploieşti

CRIMEA

Simferopol'

GEORGIA

40°

Sad

Constanţa

Sevastopol'

T'bilisi

AZERBAIJAN

Baku

Belgrade

Bucharest

Danube

Black   Sea

ARMENIA

YUGOSLAVIA

BULGARIA

Varna

Yerevan

Tabriz

Burgas

Trabzon

Tehran

Sofia

Skopje

Plovdiv

MACEDONIA

Thessaloníki

Istanbul

Ankara

T U R K E Y

IRAN

BALKAN
PENINSULA

Lárisa

Izmir

GREECE

*Aegean
Sea*

Adana

IRAQ

Athens

PELOPONNESUS

Cyclades

Rhodes

Nicosia

SYRIA

Baghdad

Euphrates

Crete

Iráklion

Sea of Crete

CYPRUS

LEBANON
Beirut

Damascus

*Persian
Gulf*

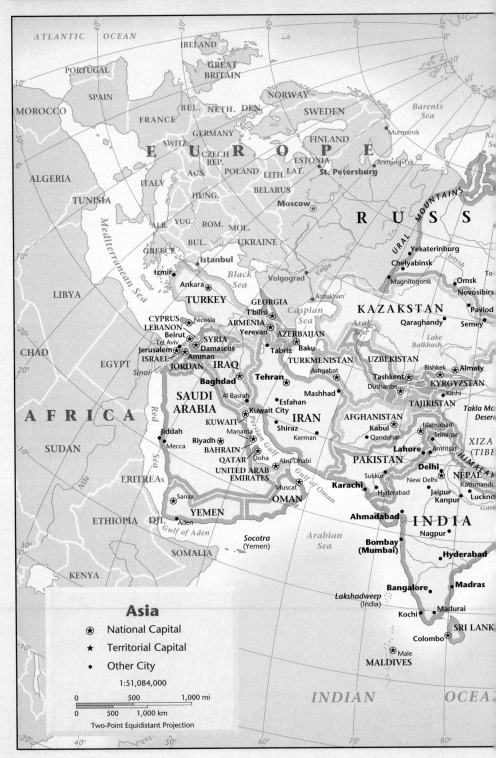

ATLANTIC OCEAN

IRELAND
GREAT
BRITAIN
PORTUGAL
SPAIN
NORWAY
SWEDEN
Barents
Sea
MOROCCO
FRANCE
BEL. NETH. DEN.
GERMANY
FINLAND
Murmansk
Arkhangel'sk
ALGERIA
SWITZ.
CZECH
REP.
AUS.
POLAND
LITH. LAT.
ESTONIA
St. Petersburg
E U R O P E
ITALY
HUNG.
BELARUS
Moscow
R U S S
TUNISIA
ALB. YUG. ROM.
MOL.
UKRAINE
LIBYA
GREECE
BUL.
Izmir
Istanbul
Yekaterinburg
Chelyabinsk
Magnitogorsk
URAL MOUNTAINS
Omsk
Novosibirs
To
Ankara
Black
Sea
Volgograd
Volga
Pavlod
CHAD
CYPRUS
Nicosia
LEBANON
Beirut
Tel Aviv
Jerusalem
ISRAEL
Amman
JORDAN
TURKEY
GEORGIA
T'bilisi
ARMENIA
Yerevan
AZERBAIJAN
Baku
Tabriz
Astrakhan'
Caspian
Sea
KAZAKSTAN
Aral
Sea
Qaraghandy
Lake
Balkhash
Semey
SYRIA
Damascus
IRAQ
Baghdad
Tehran
TURKMENISTAN
Ashgabat
UZBEKISTAN
Tashkent
Dushanbe
Bishkek
Almaty
KYRGYZSTAN
Kashi
Takla Ma
Deser
EGYPT
Sinai
AFRICA
SAUDI
ARABIA
Al Basrah
Esfahan
Mashhad
TAJIKISTAN
KUWAIT
Kuwait City
IRAN
Shiraz
Kerman
AFGHANISTAN
Kabul
Qandahar
Islamabad
Srinagar
XIZA
(TIBE
SUDAN
Red
Sea
Jiddah
Mecca
Manama
Riyadh
BAHRAIN
QATAR
Doha
UNITED ARAB
EMIRATES
Abu Dhabi
Lahore
Amritsar
PAKISTAN
Delhi
New Delhi
NEPAL
Kathmandu
HIMALAY
ERITREA
Persian Gulf
Muscat
Gulf of Oman
Sukkur
Karachi
Hyderabad
Jaipur
Kanpur
Luckno
Gan
Nile
OMAN
Ahmadabad
INDIA
Nagpur
ETHIOPIA
DJI.
Sanaa
Aden
Gulf of Aden
YEMEN
Arabian
Sea
Bombay
(Mumbai)
Hyderabad
Socotra
(Yemen)
SOMALIA
KENYA
Lakshadweep
(India)
Bangalore
Madras
Madurai
Kochi
Colombo
SRI LANK
INDIAN OCEA
Male
MALDIVES

Mediterranean Sea

Ka

20°

Asia

⊛ National Capital

★ Territorial Capital

• Other City

1:51,084,000

| 0 | 500 | 1,000 mi |

| 0 | 500 | 1,000 km |

Two-Point Equidistant Projection

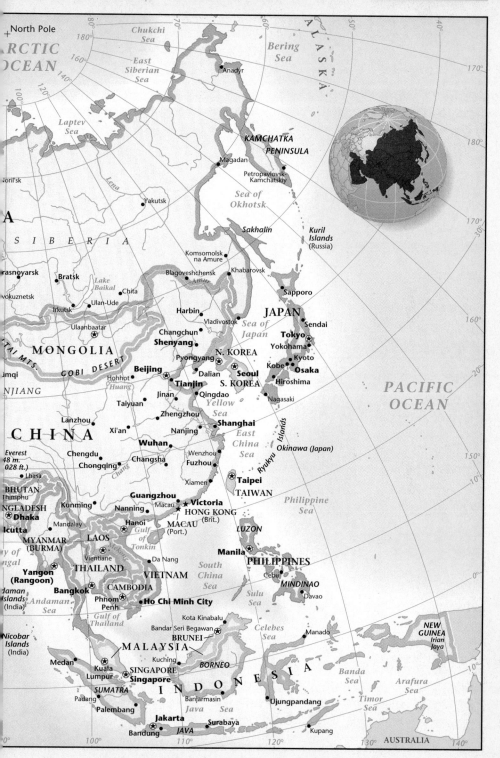

North Pole

ARCTIC OCEAN

Chukchi Sea

ALASKA

Bering Sea

Laptev Sea

East Siberian Sea

Anadyr

Noril'sk

Lena

KAMCHATKA PENINSULA

Magadan

Petropavlovsk-Kamchatskly

Sea of Okhotsk

Sakhalin

Kuril Islands (Russia)

SIBERIA

Komsomolsk na Amure

Khabarovsk

Blagoveshchensk

Amur

Sapporo

rasnoyarsk   Bratsk   *Lake Baikal*   Chita

vokuznetsk   Irkutsk   Ulan-Ude

Ulaanbaatar

Harbin

Vladivostok   *Sea of Japan*

JAPAN

Sendai

Changchun

Shenyang

Tokyo

Yokohama

Kyoto

TAI MTS.

MONGOLIA   GOBI DESERT

Pyongyang

N. KOREA

Kobe   Osaka

umqi   Hohhot

Beijing   Dalian

Seoul

Tianjin

S. KOREA

Hiroshima

NJIANG   *Huang*

Jinan   Qingdao

Nagasaki

Taiyuan

Yellow Sea

Lanzhou   Xi'an   Zhengzhou

Nanjing

Shanghai

Islands

PACIFIC OCEAN

CHINA

Everest
48 m.
028 ft.)

Lhasa

Chengdu

Chongqing

Changsha

Wuhan

Wenzhou

Fuzhou

East China Sea

Okinawa (Japan)

Ryukyu

Xiamen

Taipei

TAIWAN

BHUTAN
Thimphu

Kunming

Nanning

Macau

Victoria

HONG KONG (Brit.)

Philippine Sea

NGLADESH
Dhaka

Guangzhou

lcutta

Mandalay

Hanoi

Gulf of Tonkin

MACAU (Port.)

LUZON

MYANMAR
(BURMA)

LAOS

Vientiane

Da Nang

South China Sea

Manila

PHILIPPINES

y of
ngal

Yangon
(Rangoon)

THAILAND

VIETNAM

Cebu

MINDINAO

Bangkok

CAMBODIA

Phnom
Penh

Ho Chi Minh City

Sulu Sea

Davao

daman
slands
(India)

Andaman Sea

Gulf of Thailand

Kota Kinabalu

Bandar Seri Begawan

Celebes Sea

Manado

NEW GUINEA
Irian Jaya

Nicobar
Islands
(India)

MALAYSIA

BRUNEI

BORNEO

Banda Sea

Arafura Sea

Medan

Kuala
Lumpur

Kuching

SINGAPORE

Singapore

INDONESIA

SUMATRA

Banjarmasin

Ujungpandang

Timor Sea

AUSTRALIA

Padang

Palembang

Java Sea

Jakarta

Bandung

JAVA

Surabaya

Kupang

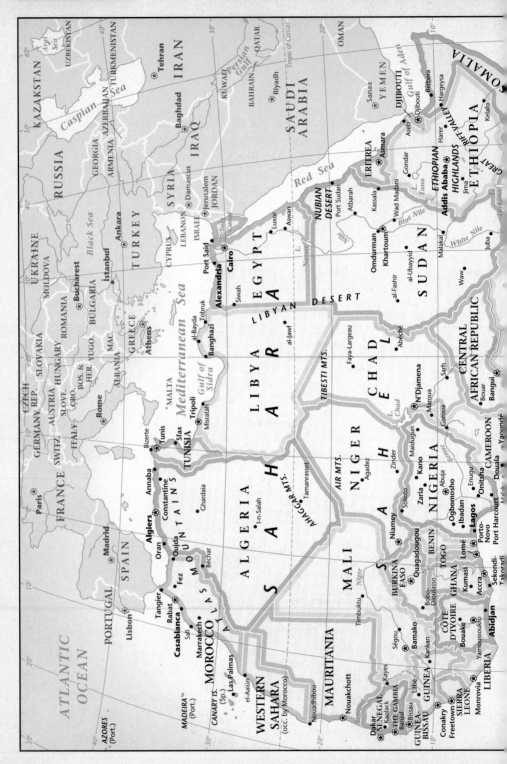

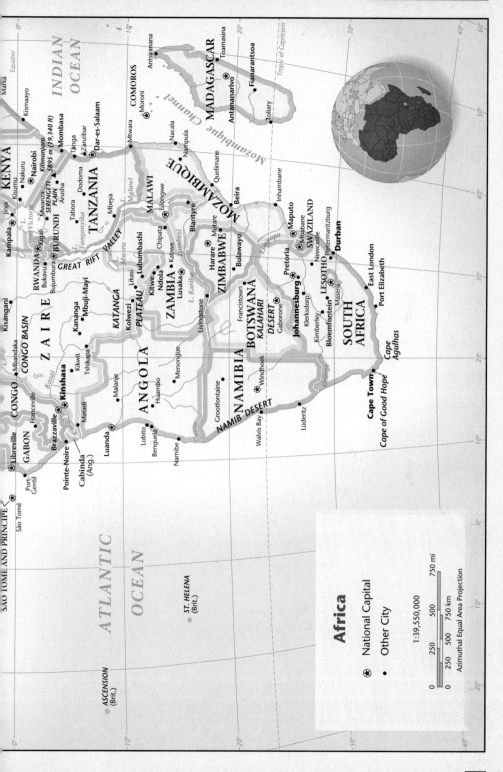

MarKa
Equator
INDIAN OCEAN
Kismaayo
Tropic of Capricorn

MADAGASCAR
Antsiranana
Toamasina
Antananarivo
Fianarantsoa
Toliary
COMOROS
Moroni

KENYA
Mombasa
Kisumu
Nakuru
Nairobi
Kilimanjaro
5895 m (19,340 ft)
Mwanza
Tanga
Zanzibar
Dar-es-Salaam
Mtwara
Nampula
Nacala
Quelimane
Inhambane

Kampala
Jinja
L. Victoria
SERENGETI PLAIN
Arusha
Dodoma
TANZANIA
Tabora
Mbeya
Lake Malawi

MOZAMBIQUE
Mozambique Channel

RWANDA
Kigali
BURUNDI
Bujumbura
Bukavu

GREAT RIFT VALLEY

Kisangani

ZAIRE
CONGO BASIN
Mbandaka

Lake Tanganyika

Lilongwe
MALAWI
Blantyre

Beira

Mutare
Harare
ZIMBABWE
Bulawayo

Maputo
MOZAMBIQUE
Pietermaritzburg
SWAZILAND
Mbabane
Newcastle
Durban

Kananga
Mbuji-Mayi
Likasi
Lubumbashi
KATANGA
PLATEAU
Kolwezi
Kitwe
Ndola
Kabwe
ZAMBIA
Lusaka
L. Kariba
Livingstone
Chipata
Kasai

Kikwit
Tshikapa

Kinshasa
Brazzaville
CONGO
Pointe-Noire
Matadi
Cabinda (Ang.)

GABON
Libreville
Franceville
Port-Gentil

SAO TOME AND PRINCIPE
São Tomé

Luanda
Lobito
Benguela
Namibe

ANGOLA
Malanje
Huambo
Menongue

NAMIBIA
NAMIB DESERT
Walvis Bay
Windhoek
Grootfontaine

Lüderitz

Francistown
BOTSWANA
KALAHARI DESERT
Gaborone

Pretoria
Johannesburg
Klerksdorp
Kimberley
Bloemfontein
LESOTHO
Maseru

SOUTH AFRICA
East London
Port Elizabeth

Cape Town
Cape of Good Hope
Cape Agulhas

ATLANTIC OCEAN

ST. HELENA (Brit.)

ASCENSION (Brit.)

Africa

⊛ National Capital
• Other City

1:39,550,000

0   250   500   750 mi
0   250   500   750 km

Azimuthal Equal Area Projection

75

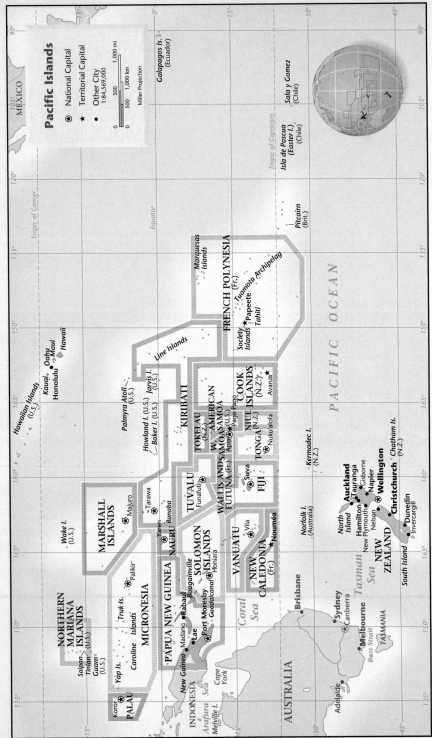

Pacific Islands

⊗ National Capital
★ Territorial Capital
• Other City

1:84,569,000

Miller Projection

MEXICO

PACIFIC OCEAN

Galapagos Is.
(Ecuador)

Sala y Gomez
(Chile)

Isla de Pascua
(Easter I.)
(Chile)

Pitcairn
(Brit.)

Equator

Tropic of Cancer

Tropic of Capricorn

Marquesas
Islands

FRENCH POLYNESIA

Tuamotu Archipelag
(Fr.)

Society *Papeete*
Island *Tahiti*

Line Islands

Hawaiian Islands
(U.S.)

Kauai *Oahu*
Honolulu *Maui*
Hawaii

Palmyra Atoll (U.S.)

Jarvis I.
(U.S.)

Howland I. (U.S.)
Baker I. (U.S.)

KIRIBATI

COOK
ISLANDS
(N.Z.)

★ *Avarua*

TOKELAU
(N.Z.)

W. AMERICAN
SAMOA SAMOA
Apia (U.S.)

Pago Pago

NIUE (N.Z.)

Wake I.
(U.S.)

MARSHALL
ISLANDS

Majuro

Tarawa

TUVALU

Funafuti

WALLIS AND
FUTUNA (Fr.)

TONGA

Nuku'alofa

FIJI

Suva

Vila

NAURU
Yaren *Banaba*

NORTHERN
MARIANA
ISLANDS

Saipan
Tinian (U.S.)
Guam (U.S.)

Truk Is.

Caroline Islands

MICRONESIA

Palikir

Yap Is.

Koror
PALAU

PAPUA NEW GUINEA

New Guinea
Rabaul
Madang *Bougainville*
Lae
Port Moresby

SOLOMON
ISLANDS
Honiara
Guadalcanal

VANUATU

NEW
CALEDONIA
(Fr.)
★ *Nouméa*

Coral
Sea

INDONESIA

Arafura
Sea
Melville I.

Cape
York

AUSTRALIA

Brisbane

⊗ *Sydney*
Canberra

⊗ *Melbourne*

Adelaide

Bass Strait

TASMANIA

Tasman
Sea

Norfolk I.
(Australia)

Kermadec I.
(N.Z.)

North
Island

Auckland *Tauranga*
Hamilton *Gisborne*
New Plymouth *Napier*
Nelson **Wellington**

Chatham Is.
(N.Z.)

NEW
ZEALAND

South Island

Christchurch
Dunedin

Invercargill

FLAGS of the
COUNTRIES of the WORLD

(Afghanistan-Ecuador)

 AFGHANISTAN

ALBANIA

 ALGERIA

 ANDORRA

 ANGOLA

 ANTIGUA AND BARBUDA

ARGENTINA

ARMENIA

 AUSTRALIA

 AUSTRIA

 AZERBAIJAN

THE BAHAMAS

BAHRAIN

BANGLADESH

 BARBADOS

 BELARUS

BELGIUM

 BELIZE

BENIN

 BHUTAN

BOLIVIA

 BOSNIA AND HERZEGOVINA

 BOTSWANA

 BRAZIL

 BRUNEI

BULGARIA

 BURKINA FASO

 BURUNDI

 CAMBODIA

CAMEROON

CANADA

 CAPE VERDE

 CENTRAL AFRICAN REPUBLIC

CHAD

 CHILE

CHINA

COLOMBIA

 COMOROS

 CONGO

 COSTA RICA

COTE D'IVOIRE

 CROATIA

 CUBA

 CYPRUS

 CZECH REPUBLIC

DENMARK

 DJIBOUTI

 DOMINICA

 DOMINICAN REPUBLIC

 ECUADOR

FLAGS of the COUNTRIES of the WORLD
(Egypt-Luxembourg)

EGYPT	EL SALVADOR	EQUATORIAL GUINEA	ERITREA	ESTONIA
ETHIOPIA	FIJI	FINLAND	FRANCE	GABON
THE GAMBIA	GEORGIA	GERMANY	GHANA	GREECE
GRENADA	GUATEMALA	GUINEA	GUINEA-BISSAU	GUYANA
HAITI	HONDURAS	HUNGARY	ICELAND	INDIA
INDONESIA	IRAN	IRAQ	IRELAND	ISRAEL
ITALY	JAMAICA	JAPAN	JORDAN	KAZAKSTAN
KENYA	KIRIBATI	NORTH KOREA	SOUTH KOREA	KUWAIT
KYRGYZSTAN	LAOS	LATVIA	LEBANON	LESOTHO
LIBERIA	LIBYA	LIECHTENSTEIN	LITHUANIA	LUXEMBOURG

FLAGS of the COUNTRIES of the WORLD

(Macedonia-Sierra Leone)

 MACEDONIA

 MADAGASCAR

 MALAWI

 MALAYSIA

 MALDIVES

MALI

 MALTA

 MARSHALL ISLANDS

 MAURITANIA

 MAURITIUS

 MEXICO

 MICRONESIA

 MOLDOVA

 MONACO

 MONGOLIA

 MOROCCO

 MOZAMBIQUE

 MYANMAR (BURMA)

 NAMIBIA

 NAURU

 NEPAL

 NETHERLANDS

 NEW ZEALAND

 NICARAGUA

 NIGER

 NIGERIA

 NORWAY

 OMAN

 PAKISTAN

 PALAU

 PANAMA

 PAPUA NEW GUINEA

 PARAGUAY

 PERU

 PHILIPPINES

 POLAND

 PORTUGAL

 QATAR

 ROMANIA

 RUSSIA

 RWANDA

 ST. KITTS AND NEVIS

 ST. LUCIA

 ST. VINCENT AND THE GRENADINES

 SAN MARINO

 SÃO TOMÉ AND PRÍNCIPE

 SAUDI ARABIA

 SENEGAL

 SEYCHELLES

 SIERRA LEONE

 79

FLAGS of the COUNTRIES of the WORLD
(Singapore-Zimbabwe)

 SINGAPORE

 SLOVAKIA

 SLOVENIA

 SOLOMON ISLANDS

 SOMALIA

 SOUTH AFRICA

 SPAIN

 SRI LANKA

 SUDAN

 SURINAME

 SWAZILAND

 SWEDEN

 SWITZERLAND

 SYRIA

 TAIWAN

 TAJIKISTAN

 TANZANIA

 THAILAND

 TOGO

 TONGA

 TRINIDAD AND TOBAGO

 TUNISIA

 TURKEY

    TURKMENISTAN

 TUVALU

 UGANDA

 UKRAINE

 UNITED ARAB EMIRATES

 UNITED KINGDOM (GREAT BRITAIN)

UNITED STATES

 URUGUAY

 UZBEKISTAN

 VANUATU

VATICAN CITY

VENEZUELA

VIETNAM

WESTERN SAMOA

YEMEN

YUGOSLAVIA

ZAIRE

ZAMBIA

ZIMBABWE

A QUICK VISIT to Some COUNTRIES of the WORLD

Suppose you got a free round-trip ticket to visit any spot in the whole world. Where would you like to go? Here are a few sights you might want to see.

AUSTRALIA

In Australia is **Ayers Rock,** the biggest exposed rock in the world. Located in a remote desert, it is about 1 ½ miles long and shines bright red when the sun sets. Australia's first people, the Aborigines, thought it was sacred.

CANADA

Want to feel like you're in France without leaving North America? Visit **Quebec City.** You'll see a high, walled fortress (the Citadel), a hotel that looks like a French castle (Château Frontenac), and people who speak French. In **Toronto,** however, English is the main language. You can get a view of that fast-growing city by going to the top of the **CN Tower,** the tallest free-standing structure in the world.

CANADA—UNITED STATES

On the border between Canada and the United States is the famous waterfall **Niagara Falls.** About 20,000 bathtubs of water pour over the falls every second. You can put on a slicker and look at the falls from an observation deck—or ride by in a boat.

CHINA

Some 2,400 years ago, workers started putting up the **Great Wall.** It became the world's longest structure, with a main section 2,150 miles long. It was built to keep out invaders, but it didn't stop Genghis Khan from conquering much of China in the 1200s.

DENMARK

One of the world's oldest and most charming amusement parks is Denmark's **Tivoli Gardens.** There you will find everything from a mouse circus to the world's oldest roller coaster.

ECUADOR

The **Galapagos Islands**, which belong to Ecuador, are remote islands in the Pacific Ocean, about 600 miles off South America. They are filled with wildlife (such as cormorants and penguins, giant tortoises and lizards) and odd plants.

EGYPT

In Egypt you can see the **Great Sphinx,** a stone figure with a man's head and a lion's body. Carved in the desert 4,500 years ago, it's still there, despite wear and tear. Nearby, at Giza, are the great **pyramids** of ancient Egyptian pharaohs.

FRANCE

A high point of a trip to France would be the **Eiffel Tower.** You get to the top of this open, cast-iron tower in four elevators, one after another. Then you can look down 1,000 feet on the beautiful city of Paris below.

GERMANY

Though it was built in the 1800s, the mad King Ludwig II planned **Neuschwanstein Castle** to look just like a fairy-tale castle from the Middle Ages, complete with turrets and drawbridges.

Eiffel Tower ▶

GREECE

On the **Acropolis**, you will find the ruins of the Parthenon and other public buildings from ancient Athens. The remains of the buildings, some partly rebuilt, stand high on a hill overlooking the city.

GREAT BRITAIN

The regular London home of the queen of England is **Buckingham Palace**. When she's there a royal flag is flying. Outside you can see the Changing of the Guard. Another attraction is the **Tower of London**, where many famous people were jailed, tortured, and killed. The crown jewels are shown there.

INDIA

One of the world's biggest and richest tombs is the **Taj Mahal**, which took about 20,000 workers to build. A ruler of India had it built for his wife after her death in 1631.

IRELAND

If you kiss the **Blarney Stone**, which is in the tower of Blarney Castle, legends say you'll be able to throw words around and get people to agree with you—even if what you say is nonsense.

ISRAEL

In Israel you can visit **Jerusalem**—a Holy City for three faiths. You can see the **Dome of the Rock**, built over the rock where Muhammad, founder of Islam, is said to have risen to heaven. You can stop at the **Western Wall**, where Jews pray; it is said to contain stones from Solomon's Temple. And you can see the **Church of the Holy Sepulcher**, built where it is believed that Jesus was crucified and buried.

ITALY

The **Leaning Tower of Pisa** is proof that kids aren't the only ones who make mistakes. Long before it was finished, the bell tower began sinking into the soft ground and leaning to one side. Every year, it leans $\frac{1}{20}$ of an inch more.

KENYA

Here and in other countries of East Africa, you can visit **National Parks**. You can go on safaris to see lions, zebras, giraffes, elephants, and other animals in their natural home.

MEXICO

On the Yucatán peninsula, you can visit remains of the city of **Chichén Itzá**, where the Mayan people settled in the sixth century. Abandoned before the Spanish came, it's now partly rebuilt. You can see stone pyramids and temples and a Mayan ballfield.

▲ *Kremlin in Moscow, Russia*

RUSSIA

A famous place to visit here is the **Kremlin**, a walled fortress in Moscow, with old churches, palaces, and towers with onion-shaped gold domes, dating back to the Middle Ages. Today the Kremlin is the headquarters for the Russian government.

UNITED STATES

Yellowstone National Park was the world's first natural park and is one of the best. (See U.S. NATIONAL PARKS section of this book for more details.) There are many other places to visit in Washington, D.C., and the 50 states (see U.S. STATES section for more information).

ENERGY: What It Is and Where It Comes From

You can't touch or smell or taste energy, but you can observe what energy can *do*. You can feel that sunlight warms objects, and you can see that electricity lights up a light bulb, even if you can't see the heat or the electricity.

What Is Energy? Things that you see and touch every day use some form of energy to work: your body, a bike, a basketball, a car. Energy enables things to move. Scientists define **energy** as the ability to do work.

Why Do We Need Energy To Do Work? Scientists define **work** as a force moving an object. Scientifically speaking, throwing a ball is work, but studying for a test isn't! When you throw a ball, you use energy from the food you eat to do work on the ball. The engine in a car uses energy from gasoline to make the car move.

Are There Different Kinds of Energy? Yes, there are. When we rest or sleep we still have the ability to move. We do not lose our energy. We simply store it for another time. Stored energy is called **potential energy**. When we get up and begin to move around, we are using stored energy. As we move around and walk, our stored (potential) energy changes into **kinetic energy**, which is the energy of moving things. A parked car has potential energy. A moving car has kinetic energy. A sled stopped at the top of the hill has potential energy. As the sled goes down the hill, its potential energy changes to kinetic energy.

potential energy

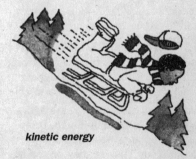

kinetic energy

How Is Energy Created? Energy cannot be created or destroyed, but it can be changed or converted into different forms. **Heat**, **light**, and **electricity** are forms of energy. Other forms of energy are **sound**, **chemical energy**, **mechanical energy**, and **nuclear energy**.

Where Does Energy Come From? All of the forms of energy we use come from the energy stored in **natural resources**. Sunlight, water, wind, petroleum, coal, and natural gas are natural resources. From these resources, we get heat and electricity.

Turning NATURAL RESOURCES Into Energy

THE SUN AND ITS ENERGY

Most of our energy comes from the sun. The sun is a big ball of glowing gases, made up mostly of hydrogen. Inside the sun, hydrogen atoms join together (through a process called nuclear fusion) and become helium. During the fusion process, large amounts of energy are released. This energy works its way to the sun's surface and then radiates out into space in the form of waves. These waves give us heat and light. The energy from the sun is stored in our food, which provides fuel for our bodies.

1. Plants absorb energy from the sun (solar energy) and convert absorbed energy to chemical energy for storage.

2. Animals eat plants and gain the stored chemical energy.

3. People eat plants and meat.

4. Food provides the body with energy to work and play.

THE SUN STORES ITS ENERGY IN FOSSIL FUELS

The sun also provides the energy stored in fossil fuels. Coal, petroleum, and natural gas are **fossil fuels**. Fossil fuels come from the remains of ancient plants and animals over millions and millions of years. This is how it happened:

1. Hundreds of millions of years ago, before people lived on Earth, trees and other plants absorbed energy from the sun, just as they do today.

2. Animals ate plants and smaller animals.

3. After the plants and animals died, they slowly became buried deeper and deeper underground.

4. After millions of years, they eventually turned into coal and petroleum.

Although the buried prehistoric plants and animals changed form over time, they still contained stored energy.

When we burn fossil fuels today, the stored energy from the sun is released in the form of heat. The heat is used to warm our homes and other buildings and produce electricity for our lights and appliances.

How Does ENERGY GET TO YOU?

ENERGY FROM FOSSIL FUELS

Most of our energy comes from fossil fuels. Your home may be heated with oil or natural gas. You may have a kitchen stove that uses natural gas. Cars need gasoline to run. The diagram below shows how energy goes from a primary source (like coal or other fossil fuels) to a form of energy that you can use (like electricity).

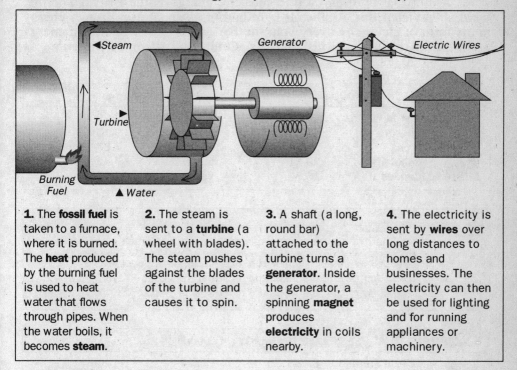

1. The **fossil fuel** is taken to a furnace, where it is burned. The **heat** produced by the burning fuel is used to heat water that flows through pipes. When the water boils, it becomes **steam**.

2. The steam is sent to a **turbine** (a wheel with blades). The steam pushes against the blades of the turbine and causes it to spin.

3. A shaft (a long, round bar) attached to the turbine turns a **generator**. Inside the generator, a spinning **magnet** produces **electricity** in coils nearby.

4. The electricity is sent by **wires** over long distances to homes and businesses. The electricity can then be used for lighting and for running appliances or machinery.

ENERGY FROM WATER

For centuries, people have been getting energy from rushing water. In a **hydroelectric plant**, water from rivers or dams is used to drive machinery like a turbine. The turbine is connected to a generator, which produces electricity.

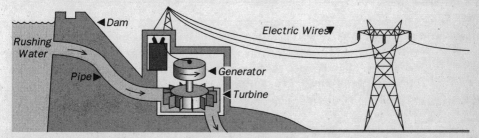

NUCLEAR ENERGY

In **nuclear reactors**, uranium atoms are split into smaller atoms to produce heat. The heat is then used to produce electricity, just as the heat from burning coal is used.

Who PRODUCES and USES the Most Energy?

Do you know that the United States produces more energy and uses more energy than any other country in the world? Below you can see which countries produced the most energy in 1993 and which countries used the most. A unit that is often used to measure energy is the British Thermal Unit, abbreviated Btu. A 60-watt light bulb uses about 205 Btus of energy in the form of electricity every hour. In these charts, the amounts of energy are written in quadrillions of Btus. One quadrillion is the same as 1,000,000,000,000,000.

COUNTRIES THAT PRODUCE THE MOST ENERGY (in quadrillion Btus)

United States	65.31	Great Britain	9.29
Russia	43.30	Iran	9.15
China	31.69	Mexico	7.84
Saudi Arabia	20.11	India	7.42
Canada	15.37	Venezuela	7.27

DID YOU KNOW?

☑ Do you know which countries produce the most fossil fuels?

The country that produces the most crude oil is Saudi Arabia.
The country that produces the most natural gas is Russia.
The country that produces the most coal is China.

COUNTRIES THAT USE THE MOST ENERGY (in quadrillion Btus)

United States	83.88	Canada	11.39
China	31.67	France	9.42
Russia	30.94	Great Britain	9.29
Japan	19.05	India	9.11
Germany	13.91	Ukraine	7.71

DID YOU KNOW?

☑ The United States uses more energy than it produces. To meet its energy needs, the United States must import large amounts of fossil fuels from other countries. The United States gets crude oil mainly from Saudi Arabia, Venezuela, Canada, Mexico, and West Africa. It also gets natural gas from Canada.

☑ Alaska used more energy per person than any other state in the United States in 1993. The ten other states that used the greatest amount of energy per person were Wyoming, Louisiana, Texas, North Dakota, West Virginia, Indiana, Montana, Oklahoma, Kansas, and Kentucky.

WILL WE HAVE ENOUGH ENERGY?

SOME ENERGY SOURCES ARE LIMITED

In 1994, 85% of the energy used in the United States came from fossil fuels (39% from petroleum, 24% from natural gas, and 22% from coal). The rest came mostly from hydropower (water power) and nuclear energy.

Fossil fuels are **nonrenewable** sources of energy. That means the amount of fossil fuel available for use is limited and might get used up after many years.

Petroleum
39%

Natural Gas
24%

Coal
22%

Hydropower and
Nuclear Power
11%

Other
4%

LOOKING FOR RENEWABLE RESOURCES

Scientists are trying to find more sources of energy that will reduce pollution and save some of the fossil fuels. People are using several types of **renewable resources**. Some of these forms of energy exist in an unlimited supply.

☑ **Solar power.** Solar power uses energy from sunlight. Solar panels can collect the sun's rays for heating. Solar cells can convert light energy directly into electricity.

☑ **Water from the ocean.** Ocean waves and tides can be used to drive generators to produce electricity.

☑ **The wind.** Old-fashioned windmills were used to drive machinery. Today, some people are using wind turbines to generate electricity.

☑ **Geothermal energy.** Geothermal energy is energy that comes from the hot, molten rock inside Earth. In certain parts of the world, people use this kind of energy for electricity and to heat buildings.

☑ **Biomass energy.** Biomass includes wood from trees and other plants, animal wastes, and garbage. When these are burned or allowed to decay, they produce natural gas. Biomass energy is widely available and used in some parts of the world, although it is not unlimited.

SAVING ENERGY FOR TOMORROW

☑ Many businesses are trying to find ways to reuse heat from steam turbine generators.
☑ Recycling reduces the energy that would be used for making new products.
☑ Riding buses and trains, car pooling, and driving fuel-efficient cars reduces fossil fuel usage (and also air pollution).
☑ Using less heat, less hot water, and less air conditioning also helps save energy.

What Is the ENVIRONMENT?

Everything that surrounds us is part of the environment. Not just living things like plants and animals, but also the air we breathe, the sunlight that provides warmth and energy, the water we use in our homes, schools, and businesses, and even rocks.

People and the Environment. People have been a part of the environment for thousands and thousands of years. For a long time people thought the Earth was so huge that it would always absorb any kind of pollution. And they thought that its natural resources would never be used up.

Even prehistoric life affected the environment. People killed animals for food and built fires to cook food and keep themselves warm. They cut down trees for fuel, and their fires released gases into the air. In prehistoric times, though, there were so few people that their activities had little impact on the environment.

Today, there are an enormous number of people in the world—we've had a population explosion. The world's population has been growing very fast. In 1850 there were around 1 billion people in the world. In 1950 there were around 2.5 billion, and by 1995 there were over 5.7 billion. Because there are so many people on the planet Earth, the things we do can affect the environment dramatically.

Sharing the Earth. People share the planet with trees, flowers, insects, fish, whales, dogs, and many other plants and animals. Each type (species) of animal or plant has its place on Earth, and each one is dependent on the others. Plants give off oxygen that animals need to breathe. Animals pollinate plants and spread their seeds. Animals eat plants and are in turn eaten by larger animals. When plants and animals die, they become part of the soil in which new plants, in their turn, take root and grow.

The Earth Belongs to Everyone. Many people are becoming aware that some of the things people do could seriously damage the planet and the animals and plants that live on it. Sometimes this damage can be fixed over a long period of time. But sometimes it is permanent. On the following pages there are facts about some of the parts of the environment, how they are being affected, and what can be done to clean up and protect the environment. People are an important part of the environment because they have the unique ability to change it.

What Is BIODIVERSITY?

Our planet, Earth, is shared by more than 5 million species. Human beings of all colors, races, and nationalities make up just one species, *Homo sapiens*. All of the species together form the variety of life we call *biodiversity* (*bio* means "life" and *diversity* means "variety").

How Many Species Are There? The list of species below is a small sampling of how diverse Earth is.

BEETLES: 290,000 species
> **Fascinating Fact ▶**
> There are more kinds of beetles than any other animal on Earth.

FLOWERING PLANTS: 250,000 species
> **Fascinating Fact ▶** The 750,000 species of insects and the 250,000 species of flowering plants depend on one another. The insects need the plants for food, the plants need the insects for pollination.

EDIBLE PLANTS: 30,000 species
> **Fascinating Fact ▶** Although 30,000 are edible, 90% of the world's food comes from only 20 species.

ANTS: 20,000 species
> **Fascinating Fact ▶**
> If you were to weigh all the insects on earth, ants would make up almost half of the total.

BIRDS: 9,040 species
> **Fascinating Fact ▶** More than 1,000 of these species are in danger of becoming extinct.

BATS: 1,000 species
> **Fascinating Fact ▶**There are more species of bats than of any other mammal.

PET DOGS: 1 species
> **Fascinating Fact ▶** Even though they can look very different, all dogs belong to the same species.

HUMAN BEINGS: 1 species
> **Fascinating Fact ▶** This one species holds the fate of all the others in its hands. People can affect the environment more than any other type of living thing.

? DID YOU KNOW? Did you know that rain forests contain more species of plants and animals than all the other parts of the world combined? About half of all plant and animal species on Earth live there, and some of them could not survive anywhere else. Also, many of the plants are unique and have been used by scientists to develop drugs for fighting diseases, including cancer.

Some Threats to Biodiversity. Plants and animals are harmed by air, water, and land pollution, and their habitats are often destroyed by deforestation. For example, in recent years, large areas of rain forests have been cleared for wood, farmland, and cattle ranches, and people have become concerned that rain forests may be disappearing. Another threat is overharvesting, or the use of too many animals for food or other products. For example, the number of whales has been steadily declining, and some species of whales could eventually be wiped out entirely.

Protecting Biodiversity. Efforts to reduce pollutants in air, water, and soil, to preserve rain forests, and to limit deforestation and overharvesting help to preserve biodiversity. A few species that were endangered have increased sufficiently in number, so that they are no longer in danger of becoming extinct.

GARBAGE and RECYCLING

Look around. Everything you see will probably be replaced or thrown away someday. Skates, clothes, the toaster, the refrigerator, furniture—they may break or wear out, or you may get tired of them and want new ones sooner or later. Where will they go when they are thrown out? What kinds of waste will they create, and how will it affect the environment? The average person in the United States today produces more than 4 pounds of trash every day, and only 1 pound of that is recycled or composted.

What HAPPENS to the THINGS We THROW AWAY?

LANDFILLS

Most of our trash goes to places called landfills. A **landfill** (or dump) is a low area of land that is filled with garbage. Most modern landfills are lined with a layer of plastic or clay to try to keep dangerous liquids from seeping out. The garbage is spread in layers and packed down by a bulldozer so that it takes up less space.

The Problem with Landfills

There is so much trash that we are quickly running out of room for it. In less than ten years, all the landfills in more than half of the states of the United States will be full.

INCINERATORS

Another way to get rid of trash is to burn it. Trash is burned in a device like a furnace called an **incinerator**. Because incinerators can get rid of almost all of the bulk of the trash, some communities would rather use incinerators than landfills.

The Problem with Incinerators

Leftover ash and smoke from burning trash may contain harmful chemicals, called **pollutants**. These pollutants can harm plants, animals, and people.

Look at what is now in U.S. landfills

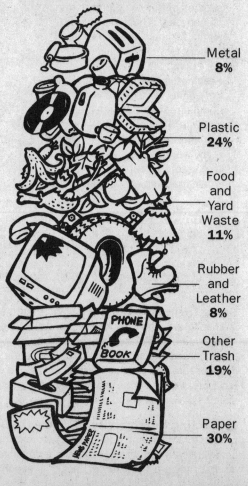

Metal **8%**

Plastic **24%**

Food and Yard Waste **11%**

Rubber and Leather **8%**

Other Trash **19%**

Paper **30%**

REUSE, RECYCLE, REDUCE

When we reuse containers, batteries, paper, and other things, we can reduce the amount of garbage we create. When we recycle things like newspaper, glass, and plastics, we reduce the amount of garbage and provide materials for making other products. Here are some of the things we can do.

PAPER
Use both sides of a piece of paper. Recycle newspapers, magazines, comic books, catalogs, and cardboard. Use cloth towels instead of paper towels.

PLASTIC
Recycle soda bottles by returning them to the store. Refill or recycle detergent bottles and milk jugs. Wash food containers and use them to store leftovers or to store your collections or hobby things. Reuse plastic bags.

GLASS
Reuse or recycle glass bottles and jars.

CLOTHES
Give clothes to younger relatives, or donate used clothes to thrift shops. Cut torn, unwearable old clothes into rags to use instead of paper towels.

METAL
Recycle aluminum cans and foil trays. Give the dry cleaner any wire clothes hangers you don't need.

FOOD AND YARD WASTE
If you have a yard, make a compost heap for food scraps and grass clippings and leaves. A **compost heap** is a pile of food scraps, leaves, and other natural materials that decompose (rot) with the help of earthworms and tiny organisms. **Compost** can be used to fertilize soil and help plants grow.

BATTERIES
Use rechargeable batteries for toys and games, radios, tape players, and flashlights. There are special rules for disposing of batteries, paints, and other harmful materials. Find out how your community wants people to dispose of them.

What Is Made From RECYCLED MATERIALS

☑ From **RECYCLED PAPER** we get newspapers, cereal boxes, wrapping paper, cardboard containers, insulation, and many other things.

☑ From **RECYCLED PLASTIC** we get soda bottles, tables, benches, bicycle racks, cameras, backpacks, carpeting, shoes, clothes, and many other things.

☑ From **RECYCLED STEEL** we get steel cans, cars, bicycles, nails, refrigerators and many other things.

☑ From **RECYCLED GLASS** we get glass jars, tiles, and many other things.

☑ From **RECYCLED RUBBER** we get bulletin boards, floor tiles, playground equipment, speed bumps, and many other things.

THE AIR WE BREATHE

All human beings and animals need air to survive. Without air we would all die. Plants also need air to live. Plants use sunlight and the carbon dioxide in air to make food, and then give off oxygen.

We all breathe the air that surrounds Earth. The air is composed mainly of gases: around 78% nitrogen, 21% oxygen, and 1% carbon dioxide, other gases, and water vapor. Human beings breathe more than 6 quarts of air every minute. Because air is so basic to life, it is very important to keep the air clean by reducing or preventing air pollution. Today, air pollution causes problems worldwide, such as **acid rain, global warming,** and the **breakdown of the ozone layer.**

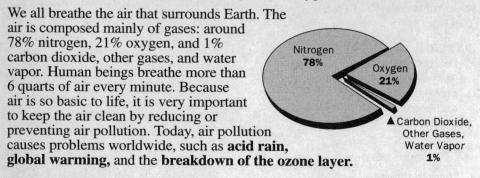

Nitrogen 78%

Oxygen 21%

▲ Carbon Dioxide, Other Gases, Water Vapor 1%

What Is Air Pollution and Where Does It Come From? **Air pollution** is dirtying the air with chemicals or other materials that can injure health, the enjoyment of life, or the working of ecosystems. The major sources of air pollution are cars, trucks and buses, waste incinerators, factories, and some electric power plants, especially those that burn fossil fuels.

What Is Acid Rain and Where Does It Come From? **Acid rain** is a kind of air pollution. It is caused by chemicals that are released into the air and cause rain, snow, and fog to be more acidic than usual. The main sources of these chemicals are power plants that burn coal to create the electricity we use. When these chemicals mix with moisture and other particles in the air, they create sulfuric acid and nitric acid. The wind often carries these acids many miles before they fall to the ground in rain, snow, and fog, or even as dry particles.

Why Worry About Air Pollution and Acid Rain? Air pollution and acid rain can harm people, animals, and plants. Air pollution can cause our eyes to sting and can make some people sick. It can also damage crops and trees.

Air pollution (especially acid rain) is also harmful to water in lakes, often killing plants and fish that live there. Hundreds of lakes in the northeastern United States and 14,000 lakes in Canada are so acidic that fish can no longer live there. Acid rain has affected trees in U.S. national parks. In the Appalachian Mountains, for example, it has harmed spruce trees growing in the Shenandoah and Great Smoky Mountain National Parks. And it can turn buildings and statues black and damage them by eating away at metal, stone, and paint. Monuments and statues that have survived hundreds of years are suddenly disintegrating.

Global Warming and the Greenhouse Effect

Many scientists believe that gases in the air are causing Earth's climate to become warmer. This is called **global warming.** If the climate becomes so warm that a great deal of ice near the north and south poles melts and more water goes into the oceans, many areas along the coasts may be flooded.

In Earth's atmosphere there are tiny amounts of gases called **greenhouse gases.** These gases let the rays of the sun pass through to the planet, but they hold in the heat that comes up from the sun-warmed Earth—just as the glass of a greenhouse holds in the warmth of the sun.

As cities increased in size and population, factories and businesses also grew. People needed more and more electricity, cars, and other things that had to be manufactured. As industries in the world have increased, greenhouse gases have been added to the atmosphere. These gases increase the thickness of the greenhouse "glass," causing too much heat to be trapped. This is called **the greenhouse effect.**

? **DID YOU KNOW?** Americans contribute 21% of the greenhouse gases that enter the atmosphere. That is more than any other country.

Good and Bad Ozone

Good Ozone. Another problem caused by air pollution involves a layer in the atmosphere high above Earth, called the **ozone layer.** The ozone layer protects us from the harsh rays of the sun. When refrigerators, air conditioners, and similar items are thrown away, gases from them (called chlorofluorocarbons or CFCs) rise into the air and destroy some of the ozone in this layer.
Bad Ozone. There is also ozone near the ground that forms when sunlight hits air pollutants from cars and smokestacks, causing smog. This ozone near the ground can be harmful.

What Are We Doing To Reduce Air Pollution?

Many countries, including the United States, are trying to reduce air pollution. Today's cars can go farther on a gallon of gasoline than cars of 20 or 30 years ago, so that less gasoline has to be burned to get people where they want to go. In the United States, cars must have a special device to remove harmful chemicals from their smoke before it comes out of the tailpipe. More and more power plants and factories are putting devices on their smokestacks to catch harmful chemicals before they can enter the air. Many people are trying not to use more electricity than they really need, so that less coal will have to be burned to produce electricity. And in some places, power companies are using windmills or other equipment that does not pollute the air to make some of their electricity.

PROTECTING OUR WATER

Every plant and animal needs water for its body to work. Fish, frogs, and many other animals depend on water as a place to live. Besides drinking, people use water to cook, to clean, to cool machinery in factories, to produce power, to irrigate farmland, and for swimming and boating.

Around two thirds of the earth's surface is water. About 97% of that is seawater, and 2% is frozen in glaciers and the ice around the north and south poles. Only 1% is fresh water, and only part of that is close enough to the earth's surface for us to use. If all of the water on earth fit in a two-gallon bucket, just over two tablespoons would be available as fresh water.

A DROP IN THE BUCKET?

How Do Americans Use Fresh Water?

People in the United States use 338 billion gallons of fresh water every day.

Gallons Used Every Day	How Fresh Water Is Used in the United States
137 billion	To water crops on farms
131 billion	To produce electricity
28 billion	In factories
24 billion	In homes, for drinking, cooking, flushing toilets, etc.
7 billion	In hotels, restaurants, offices
4 billion	For farm animals
4 billion	Public use in parks, firefighting, street washing
3 billion	For mining
Total water used every day: 338 billion gallons	

What Is Threatening Our Water and What Are We Doing About It?

Water pollution and overuse of water are the major threats to our water.

Water Pollution. Water is said to be polluted when it is not fit for its intended uses, such as drinking, swimming, watering crops, or serving as a habitat. Polluted water can cause disease and kill fish and other animals. Some major water pollutants include sewage, chemicals from factories, fertilizers and weed killers, and leaking landfills. But water pollution is also being reduced in some areas. Some lakes are being cleaned up enough to restore plants and fish to them. Companies continue to look for better ways to get rid of wastes, and many farmers are trying new ways to grow crops without using fertilizers or chemicals that kill weeds or bugs.

Overuse of Water. Another major threat to our water supply is overuse—using up so much water that not enough is left. It is important to try to conserve as much water as possible. Some modern plumbing supplies (like toilets and shower heads) are now designed to use less water. Many people take shorter showers, and they don't let the water run when they brush their teeth or wash dishes by hand. People concerned about water are also running dishwashers or washing machines only when they have a full load. They fix faucets that drip and don't water the lawn unless it really needs it.

The IMPORTANCE of FORESTS

Trees and forests are very important to the environment. In addition to holding water, trees hold the soil in place. Trees use carbon dioxide and give off oxygen, which animals and plants need for survival. And they provide homes and food for millions of types of animals.

Why Do We Cut Down Trees? People cut down trees for many reasons. When the population grows, people cut down trees to clear space to build houses, schools, factories, and other buildings. People may clear land to plant crops and graze livestock. Sometimes all the trees in an area are cut and sold for lumber and paper.

What Happens When Trees Are Cut Down? Cutting down trees—usually to use the land for something besides a forest—is called **deforestation.** Although people often have good reasons for cutting down trees, deforestation can have serious effects. If animal habitats are destroyed, many species will become extinct. Because of deforestation, thousands of species in the Amazon rain forest in South America are being lost before scientists can even learn about them.

Cutting down trees can also affect the climate. After rain falls on a forest, mist starts rising and new rain clouds are created. When forests are cut down, this cycle is disrupted, and the area eventually grows drier, causing a change in the local climate.

If huge areas of trees are cut down, the carbon dioxide they would have used builds up in the atmosphere and contributes to the greenhouse effect. And without trees to hold the soil and absorb water, rain washes topsoil away into rivers and reservoirs, a process called **soil erosion.** Farming on the poorer soil that is left can be very hard.

What Are We Doing To Save Forests? In 24 European countries, trees are being planted faster than they are being cut down. Also, trees are being planted to restock woodland areas and to create forests in some countries where timber is scarce. In addition, communities and individuals are helping to save forests by recycling paper.

? **DID YOU KNOW?**

☑ Because changes in climate affect how much a tree grows each year, scientists can tell what the climate was like in years past (in some cases 4,000 years!) by examining a tree's annual rings.

☑ Some trees, such as the northern red oak and the junipers, resist pollution better than others.

☑ Of the forests in the lower 48 states that were standing before Europeans came to America, only 5% still stand. Most of this old growth forest is in the Pacific Northwest—in Washington, Oregon, and northern California.

☑ Each year, the average American uses enough wood and wood products to add up to one tree 100 feet tall.

☑ By the mid-1990s, more paper in the United States was being recycled than was being sent to landfills.

ENVIRONMENT GLOSSARY

climate
The average weather in a region of the world.

compost heap
A pile of food scraps and yard waste that is broken down by worms and tiny insects. The result looks like dirt. It can be used to enrich the soil.

conservation
The planned and wise use of water, forests, and other natural resources so they will not be wasted.

deforestation
The cutting down of most of the trees from forested land, usually so that the land can be used for something besides a forest.

ecosystem
A community of living things and the place where they live, such as a forest or pond.

environment
All living and non-living things in an area at a given time. The environment affects the growth of living things.

extinction
The disappearance of a type (species) of plant or animal from Earth. Some species become extinct because of natural forces, but many others are becoming endangered or threatened with extinction because of the activities of people.

fossil fuel
Anything that comes from once-living matter deep in the earth, such as oil, gas, and coal.

global warming
An increase in Earth's temperature due to a buildup of certain gases in the atmosphere.

greenhouse effect
Warming of Earth caused by certain gases (called **greenhouse gases**) that form a blanket in the atmosphere high over Earth. Small amounts of these gases keep Earth warm so we can live here, but the larger amounts produced by factories, cars, and burning trees may hold in too much heat and cause global warming.

groundwater
Water in the ground that flows in the spaces between soil particles and rocks. Groundwater supplies water for wells and springs.

habitat
The natural home of an animal or a plant.

pollution
Contamination of air, water, or soil by materials that can injure health, the quality of life, or the working of ecosystems.

recycling
Using something more than once, either just the way it is, or treated and made into something else.

reforestation
Planting new trees where other trees have been cut down.

soil erosion
The washing away or blowing away of topsoil. Trees and other plants hold the soil in place and help reduce the force of the wind. Soil erosion can happen when trees and plants are removed from the ground.

How KIDS Can Help PROTECT the ENVIRONMENT

☑ *Recycle* as many things as possible: plastic, glass, papers, and clothes.

☑ *Save electricity* by turning off lights when you leave the room. Close the refrigerator door as quickly as possible. Don't stand with it open.

☑ *Save water* by not letting the water run when you brush your teeth. Take shorter showers. Don't leave water running when you're not using it.

☑ *Take care of things made from wood.* Remember that they come from trees. When you're finished with them, give them to someone else.

☑ *Buy products that have only a small amount of packaging.* And try to buy products made from recycled products.

? **DID YOU KNOW?** Every year on April 22, people throughout the world celebrate Earth Day. They have ecology fairs, tree plantings, parades, rallies, and demonstrations to educate people about the environment and to show them ways to conserve natural resources.

ENVIRONMENT CROSSWORD PUZZLE

The words in the crossword puzzle can be found in the Environment Glossary or in **heavy black type** on pages 90–95. (Answers are on page 303.)

1. Wise use of water, forests, and other resources.
2. Planting new trees after other trees have been cut down.
3. Low area of land that has been filled with garbage.
4. To use things over and over again.
5. Food scraps and leaves that rot and are used as fertilizer.
6. An animal or plant's natural home.
7. Dirt in the air or water.
8. Water in the ground that supplies wells and springs.

1. CONSERVATION

WHAT IS A GLOBE?

Did you ever travel on a spaceship? Whether you know it or not, you're traveling right now on the spaceship called Planet Earth. Earth is always zooming through space and around the sun at very fast speeds.

A tiny model of Earth is called a **globe**. Like Earth, a globe is shaped like a ball or **sphere**. Although Earth isn't exactly a sphere because it gets flat at the top and bottom and bulges a little in the middle, a globe gives us the best idea of what Earth looks like. Because Earth is round, most flat maps do not show the shapes of the land masses exactly right. The shapes at the top and bottom usually look too big. For example, on a flat map the island of Greenland, which is next to North America, looks bigger than Australia, but it is really much smaller.

When you look at a ball or sphere, you can see only the half of it that is facing toward you. The drawing here shows half of a globe.

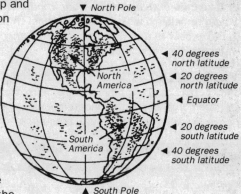

Which Hemisphere Do You Live In?
You can draw an imaginary line around the middle of Earth, like a belt. This is called the **equator**. The closer you get to the equator, the hotter it gets. The equator splits Earth into two halves called **hemispheres**. The part that's north of the equator is called the **northern hemisphere**. The part that's south of the equator is called the **southern hemisphere**. You can also divide Earth into the **western hemisphere** and the **eastern hemisphere**. The western hemisphere is the part shown on the globe above.

Lines of LATITUDE and LONGITUDE

Imaginary lines that run east and west around Earth, parallel to the equator, are called **parallels**. They tell you the **latitude** of a place, or how far it is from the equator. The equator is at 0 degrees latitude. As you go farther north or south, the latitude increases. The North Pole is at 90 degrees **north latitude**. The South Pole is at 90 degrees **south latitude**.

Imaginary lines that run north and south around the globe, from one pole to the other, are called **meridians**. These meridians tell you the degree of **longitude**, or how far east or west a place is from an imaginary line called the **Greenwich meridian** or **prime meridian**. That line runs through the city of Greenwich in England.

The CONTINENTS and OCEANS of the World

Almost two thirds of Earth's surface is made up of water. The rest is land. The largest areas of water are called **oceans**, and the largest pieces of land are called **continents**. The Earth has seven continents and four oceans. There are also many islands in the Pacific Ocean that are not counted as part of the continents. In the table below, the highest point of each continent is the top of the highest mountain, and the lowest point is the place that is the farthest below sea level. See pages 65-75 for maps of the continents.

CONTINENTS

NORTH AMERICA
Area: 9,400,000 square miles
Population: 455,000,000
(including Central America and
  Caribbean islands)
Highest Point: Mount McKinley (Alaska),
  20,320 feet
Lowest Point: Death Valley (California),
  282 feet below sea level

SOUTH AMERICA
Area: 6,900,000 square miles
Population: 319,000,000
Highest Point: Mount Aconcagua
  (Argentina), 22,834 feet
Lowest Point: Valdes Peninsula
  (Argentina), 131 feet below sea level

EUROPE
Area: 3,800,000 square miles
Population: 729,000,000
Highest Point: Mount Elbrus (Russia),
  18,510 feet
Lowest Point: Caspian Sea (Russia,
  Azerbaijan; eastern Europe and
  western Asia), 92 feet below sea level

ASIA
Area: 17,200,000 square miles
Population (1994): 3,451,000,000
Highest Point: Mount Everest (Nepal,
  Tibet), 29,028 feet
Lowest Point: Dead Sea (Israel, Jordan),
  1,312 feet below sea level

AFRICA
Area: 11,700,000 square miles
Population: 720,000,000
Highest Point: Mount Kilimanjaro
  (Tanzania), 19,340 feet
Lowest Point: Lake Assal (Djibouti),
  512 feet below sea level

AUSTRALIA
(including Australia and New Zealand)
Area: 3,070,000 square miles
Population: 21,500,000
Highest Point: Mount Kosciusko (New
  South Wales), 7,310 feet
Lowest Point: Lake Eyre (South
  Australia), 52 feet below sea level

ANTARCTICA
Area: 5,400,000 square miles
Population: Zero
Highest Point: Vinson Massif, 16,864 feet
Lowest Point: Not known

OCEANS

The facts about the oceans include their
size and average depth.

Pacific Ocean: 64,186,300 square miles;
  12,925 feet deep
Atlantic Ocean: 33,420,000 square
  miles; 11,730 feet deep
Indian Ocean: 28,350,500 square miles;
  12,598 feet deep
Arctic Ocean: 5,105,700 square miles;
  3,407 feet deep

FAMOUS REGIONS
of the World

When you watch the news on television or read the newspaper, you will see the names of many different regions of the world. Do you know where the Middle East is? Can you name the countries that make up the region known as the Balkans? Below are some of the major regions of the world.

BALKANS. A region often in the news is the Balkans, in southeastern Europe. This region consists of Yugoslavia, Slovenia, Croatia, Bosnia and Herzegovina, Macedonia, and Albania. Bulgaria, southeastern Romania, northern Greece, and the portion of Turkey in Europe are also part of the Balkans. All the Balkan states were once part of the Ottoman Empire.

CARIBBEAN. The Caribbean region is centered on the Caribbean Sea, an arm of the Atlantic Ocean that lies south of the United States, east of Central America, and north of South America. The Caribbean has thousands of islands. The largest groups are the Greater Antilles and the Lesser Antilles. Among the countries in the Greater Antilles are Cuba, Haiti, the Dominican Republic, Jamaica, and the U.S. Commonwealth of Puerto Rico. The Lesser Antilles include Dominica, Barbados, Grenada, and Trinidad and Tobago.

CENTRAL AMERICA. Central America is the region between Mexico and South America. It consists of Belize, Guatemala, Honduras, El Salvador, Nicaragua, Costa Rica, and Panama.

EASTERN EUROPE. Countries of Eastern Europe include Poland, the Czech Republic, Slovakia, Hungary, Romania, and Bulgaria. Three other Eastern European countries (Estonia, Latvia, and Lithuania) form a region known as the Baltic States.

MIDDLE EAST. One of the most famous regions in the news is the Middle East. The Middle East refers to Egypt and Libya (in northeast Africa), to Israel, Jordan, Lebanon, Syria, and Iraq, and to countries of the Arabian Peninsula: Saudi Arabia, Kuwait, Bahrain, Qatar, United Arab Emirates, Oman, and Yemen (all in southwestern Asia). The term "Middle East" sometimes also includes the other Islamic countries of North Africa: Morocco, Algeria, and Tunisia.

POLYNESIA. Polynesia is a region in the central and southern Pacific Ocean. It consists of a number of large island groups. The Hawaiian Islands make up the 50th state of the United States. Western Samoa and Tonga are independent countries. American Samoa is a territory of the United States administered by the U.S. Department of the Interior. French Polynesia, which includes Tahiti, is an overseas territory of France.

SCANDINAVIA. Scandinavia is in northern Europe. Its countries are Norway, Sweden, Denmark, and Finland. Iceland, in the north Atlantic Ocean, is also considered a Scandinavian country.

SOUTHEAST ASIA. The region of Southeast Asia lies east of India and south of China. It consists of 10 independent countries: Myanmar (Burma), Thailand, Vietnam, Laos, Cambodia, Malaysia, Singapore, the Philippines, Indonesia, and Brunei.

VOLCANOES

A **volcano** is a mountain or hill with an opening on top known as a **crater**. Every once in a while, hot melted rock (**magma**), gases, ash, and other material from inside the earth may blast out, or erupt, through the opening. The magma is called **lava** when it reaches the air. This red-hot lava may have a temperature of more than 2,000 degrees Fahrenheit. The hill or mountain is made out of lava and other materials that come out of the opening, and then cool off and harden. Some islands are really the tops of volcanoes. The Hawaiian islands developed when volcanoes erupted under the Pacific Ocean.

Why Do Volcanoes Erupt?

There are about 540 active volcanoes in the world. Some have erupted many times. Volcanic eruptions come from pools of magma and other materials a few miles underground. The pools come from rock far below. After the rock melts and mixes with gases, it rises up through cracks and weak spots in the mountain.

SOME FAMOUS VOLCANIC ERUPTIONS

YEAR	VOLCANO (PLACE)	DEATHS (Approximate)
79	Mount Vesuvius (Italy)	16,000
1169	Mount Etna (Sicily)	15,000
1669	Mount Etna (Sicily)	20,000
1792	Mount Unzen-Dake (Japan)	10,400
1815	Tambora (Indonesia)	10,000
1883	Krakatau or Krakatoa (Indonesia)	36,000
1902	Mount Pelee (Martinique)	28,000
1980	Mount St. Helens (U.S.)	57
1985	Nevada del Ruiz (Colombia)	23,000
1994	Merapi (Indonesia)	60

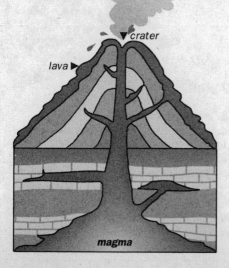

ash and gas ▶

▼ crater

lava ▶

magma

Where Is the Ring of Fire?

There are volcanoes on the bottom of the ocean and on every continent. Many of the active volcanoes are found on land along the edges of the Pacific Ocean. These volcanoes are often called the **Ring of Fire.**

The Ring of Fire marks the boundary between the plates under the Pacific Ocean and the plates under the continents around the Pacific Ocean (North America, South America, Asia). The plates of Earth are explained on page 102 and can be seen on a map on page 103, under the section on Earthquakes.

EARTHQUAKES

Earthquakes may be so weak that they are hardly felt, or they may be strong enough to do tremendous damage. There are thousands of earthquakes each year, but most of them are too small to be felt. About 1 in 5 can be felt, and about 1 in 500 causes damage.

What Causes Earthquakes?

The Earth's outer layer, called the **crust**, is divided into huge pieces called **plates**. These plates, which are made of rock, are constantly moving in different directions—away from each other, toward each other, or past each other. A crack in Earth's crust

between two plates is called a **fault**. Many earthquakes occur along faults where two plates collide as they move toward each other or grind together as they move past each other. Earthquakes along the famous **San Andreas Fault** in California are caused by the grinding of two plates moving past each other.

How Are Earthquakes Measured?

The strength of an earthquake is called its **magnitude**. The magnitude of an earthquake is registered on an instrument called a **seismograph** and is given a number on a scale called the **Richter scale**.

RICHTER SCALE

The Richter scale goes from zero to more than 9. These numbers are used to describe the strength of an earthquake. Each number on the Richter scale is 10 times greater than the one before it. An earthquake measuring 6 on the Richter scale is 10 times stronger than an earthquake measuring 5 and 100 times stronger than one measuring 4. Earthquakes that register below 4 on the Richter scale are considered minor. Those of 4 or above are considered major.

A seismograph ▶

MAGNITUDE	EFFECTS
0-2	Earthquake is recorded by instruments but is not felt by people.
2-3	Earthquake is felt slightly by a few people.
3-4	People feel tremors. Hanging objects like ceiling lights swing.
4-5	Earthquake causes some damage; walls crack; dishes and windows may break.
5-6	Furniture moves; earthquake seriously damages weak buildings.
6-7	Furniture may overturn; strong buildings are damaged; walls and buildings may collapse.
7-8	Many buildings are destroyed; underground pipes break; wide cracks appear in the ground.
Above 8	Total devastation, including buildings and bridges; ground wavy.

MAJOR EARTHQUAKES
of the 20th Century

The earthquakes listed below are among the largest and most destructive recorded in the 20th century. The list begins with the most recent earthquakes.

YEAR	LOCATION	MAGNITUDE	DEATHS
1995	Sakhalin Island (Russia)	7.6	2,000+
1995	Japan (Kobe)	7.2	5,000+
1994	United States (Los Angeles area)	6.6	61
1992	Indonesia (Flores)	7.5	2,500
1990	Iran (northwestern)	7.7	40,000+
1989	United States (San Francisco area)	6.9	62
1988	Armenia (northwestern)	6.8	55,000+
1985	Mexico (Mexico City)	8.1	4,200+
1976	China (Tangshan)	8.2	242,000
1976	Guatemala	7.5	22,778
1970	Peru (northern)	7.7	66,794
1960	Chile (southern)	8.3	5,000
1950	India (Assam)	8.7	1,530
1946	Japan (Honshu)	8.4	2,000
1939	Chile (Chillan)	8.3	28,000
1934	India (Bihar) - Nepal	8.4	10,700
1933	Japan	8.9	2,990
1927	China (Nanshan)	8.3	200,000
1923	Japan (Yokohama)	8.3	200,000
1920	China (Gansu)	8.6	100,000
1906	Chile (Valparaiso)	8.6	20,000
1906	United States (San Francisco)	8.3	503

? **DID YOU KNOW?** Between December 16, 1811, and February 7, 1812, a series of earthquakes near New Madrid, Missouri, caused enormous damage to much of the Midwest. These earthquakes (estimated at about 8.7 on the Richter scale) were so powerful that they caused the Mississippi River to change its course.

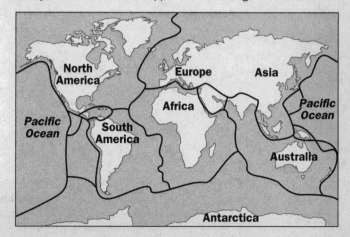

The Earth's surface is divided into huge pieces called plates that are constantly moving.

How To READ a MAP

There are many different kinds of maps. **Physical maps** mainly show features that are part of nature, such as mountains, deserts, jungles, and grasslands. **Political** maps show features such as states and countries and the **boundaries** between them.

DISTANCE
Of course the distances on a map are much smaller than the distances in the real world. The **scale** shows you how much smaller they are. In the map below, every inch on paper means a real distance of 10 miles.

DIRECTION
Maps usually have a compass rose that shows you which way is north. On most maps, north is toward the top. On the map below, north is straight up. If you went from Westwood to Lake City you would be going almost exactly north. When north is straight up, east is to the right, and west is to the left.

LOCATING PLACES
To help you locate places on a map, there often is a list, giving you a letter and number for each city or town. In the map below, you can find the first city on the list, Centerville, by drawing a straight line down from the letter E on top, and another line going across from the number 3 on the side. Centerville should be near the area where these two lines meet.

SYMBOLS
Maps usually have different **symbols** in them. If you look along the side or bottom, you can find out what these symbols mean. At the bottom of this map, you can see the symbols for towns, roads, railroads tracks, and airports. Can you tell which are the two biggest cities or towns on the map? Can you find the airport and railroad? How would you get from the airport to Centerville by car?

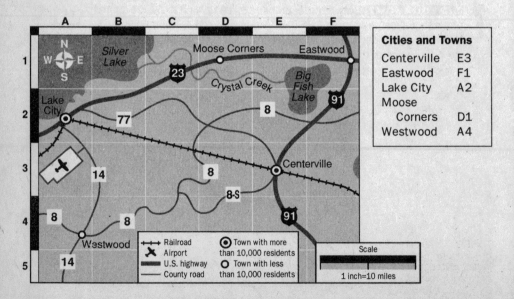

Cities and Towns	
Centerville	E3
Eastwood	F1
Lake City	A2
Moose Corners	D1
Westwood	A4

Railroad
Airport
U.S. highway
County road

Town with more than 10,000 residents
Town with less than 10,000 residents

Scale
1 inch=10 miles

The TALLEST, LONGEST, HIGHEST, DEEPEST in the World

Tallest Mountain: Mount Everest, in Tibet and Nepal (29,028 feet)

Longest River: Nile, in Egypt and Sudan (4,160 miles)

Highest Waterfall: Angel Falls, in Venezuela (3,212 feet)

Deepest Lake: Lake Baikal, in Asia (5,315 feet)

Biggest Lake: Caspian Sea, in Europe and Asia (143,244 square miles)

Biggest Desert: The Sahara, in Africa (3,500,000 square miles)

Biggest Island: Greenland, in the Atlantic Ocean (840,000 square miles)

Biggest Swamp: Grand Pantanal, in Brazil (42,000 square miles)

A's IN GEOGRAPHY PUZZLE

Did you know that there are many continents, countries, and U.S. states that start and end with the letter "A"? Can you fill in the blanks below? To help out, the A's and one other letter have been filled in for each name. If you are stumped, look for the names under **Geography, Countries,** and Facts About the States under **United States.** (Answers are on page 303.)

CONTINENTS:

1. A __ I A

2. A F __ __ __ __ A

3. A __ __ __ __ __ A L __ A

4. A __ __ __ A R __ __ __ __ __ A

COUNTRIES:

1. A __ __ A N __ A

2. A __ G __ __ __ __ A

3. A __ __ __ __ __ R A

4. A __ __ __ __ L A

5. A __ __ __ __ __ T __ __ A

6. A __ M __ __ __ __ A

7. A __ S __ __ A __ __ A

8. A __ __ __ R __ A

STATES:

1. A __ A __ A M A

2. A __ A __ K A

3. A __ __ Z __ __ A

105

Some FAMOUS European and American EXPLORERS

EXPLORERS OF THE AMERICAS

around 1000	**Leif Ericson,** from Iceland, explored "Vinland," which may have been the coasts of northeast Canada and New England.
1492 to 1504	**Christopher Columbus,** from Italy, sailed four times to America and started colonies there.
1513	**Juan Ponce de León,** from Spain, explored and named Florida.
1513	**Vasco Núñez de Balboa,** from Spain, explored Panama and reached the Pacific Ocean.
1519-36	**Hernan Cortés,** from Spain, conquered Mexico and traveled as far as Baja California.
1527-42	**Alvar Núñez Cabeza de Vaca,** from Spain, explored the southwestern United States, Brazil, and Paraguay.
1532-35	**Francisco Pizarro,** from Spain, explored the west coast of South America and conquered Peru.
1534-36	**Jacques Cartier,** from France, sailed up the St. Lawrence River to the site of present-day Montreal.
1539-42	**Hernando de Soto,** from Spain, explored the southeastern United States and the lower Mississippi Valley.
1603-13	**Samuel de Champlain,** from France, traced the course of the St. Lawrence River and explored the northeastern United States.
1609-10	**Henry Hudson,** from England, explored the Hudson River, Hudson Bay, and Hudson Strait.
1682	**Robert Cavelier, sieur de La Salle,** from France, traced the Mississippi River to its mouth in the Gulf of Mexico.
1804-6	**Meriwether Lewis** and **William Clark,** from the United States, traveled overland from St. Louis along the Missouri and Columbia rivers to the Pacific Ocean and back.

EXPLORERS OF ASIA AND THE PACIFIC

1271-95	**Marco Polo,** from Venice, Italy, traveled through Central Asia, India, China, and Indonesia.
1519-21	**Ferdinand Magellan,** from Portugal, sailed around the tip of South America and across the Pacific Ocean to the Philippines, where he died. His expedition continued around the world.
1768-78	**James Cook,** from England, charted the world's major bodies of water and explored Hawaii and Antarctica.

EXPLORERS OF AFRICA

1488	**Bartolomeu Dias,** from Portugal, explored the Cape of Good Hope in southern Africa.
1497-98	**Vasco da Gama,** from Portugal, sailed farther than Dias, around the Cape of Good Hope to east Africa and India.
1849-59	**David Livingstone,** from Scotland, explored southern Africa, including the Zambezi River and Victoria Falls.

Learning About
WHAT'S INSIDE YOUR BODY

Your body is made up of many different parts that work together every minute of every day and night. It is more amazing than any machine or computer. Machines don't eat, run, have feelings, read and learn, or do other things that you do. Even though everyone's body looks different outside, people have the same parts inside.

? DID YOU KNOW?

- ☑ Your body is made up of billions of tiny living units called **cells.** Different kinds of cells have different tasks to do in the body.

- ☑ Cells that do similar work form **tissue,** like nerve tissue or bone tissue.

- ☑ Tissues that work together form **organs,** like the heart, lungs, and kidneys.

- ☑ The **skin** is the body's largest organ. It protects the internal organs from infection, injury, and harmful sunlight. It also helps control body temperature.

- ☑ Organs work together as **systems,** and each system has a separate job to do.

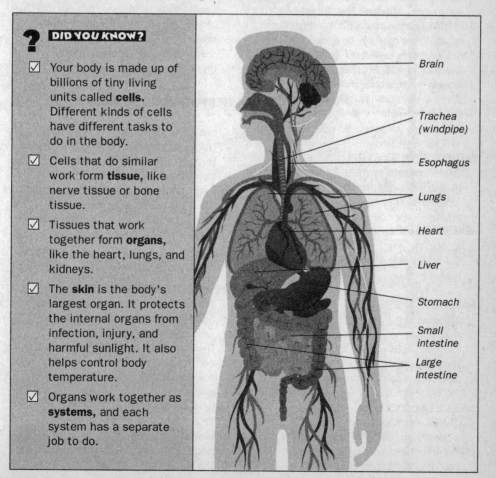

Brain

Trachea (windpipe)

Esophagus

Lungs

Heart

Liver

Stomach

Small intestine

Large intestine

What Do the BODY'S SYSTEMS Do?

Each system of the body has its own job to do. Some of the systems also work together in teams to keep you healthy and strong.

CIRCULATORY SYSTEM

In the circulatory system, the **heart** pumps **blood**, which then travels through tubes, called **arteries**, to all parts of the body. The blood carries the oxygen and food that the body needs to stay alive. **Veins** carry the blood back to the heart.

DIGESTIVE SYSTEM

The digestive system moves food through parts of the body called the **esophagus**, **stomach**, and **intestines**. As the food passes through the digestive system, some of it is broken down into tiny particles called nutrients, which the body needs. Nutrients enter the bloodstream, which carries them to all parts of the body. The digestive system then changes the remaining food into waste that is eliminated from the body.

ENDOCRINE SYSTEM

The endocrine system includes **glands** that are needed for some body functions. There are two kinds of glands. Exocrine glands produce liquids such as sweat and saliva. Endocrine glands produce chemicals called **hormones**. Hormones control body functions, such as growth.

MUSCULAR SYSTEM

Muscles are made up of elastic fibers that help the body move. We use large muscles to walk and run, and small muscles to smile. Muscles also help protect organs.

SKELETAL SYSTEM

The skeletal system is made up of the **bones** that hold your body upright. Some bones protect organs, such as the ribs that cover the lungs.

NERVOUS SYSTEM

The nervous system enables us to think, feel, move, hear, and see. It includes the **brain**, the **spinal cord**, and **nerves** in all parts of the body. Nerves in the spinal cord carry signals back and forth between the brain and the rest of the body. The brain tells us what to do and how to respond. The brain has three major parts. The **cerebrum** controls our thinking, speech, and vision. The **cerebellum** is responsible for physical coordination. The **brain stem** controls the body's respiratory, circulatory, and digestive systems.

RESPIRATORY SYSTEM

The respiratory system allows us to breathe. Air comes into the body through the nose and mouth. It goes through the windpipe (or trachea) to two tubes (called bronchi), which carry air to the **lungs**. Oxygen from the air is taken in by tiny blood vessels in the lungs. The blood then carries oxygen to the cells of the body.

REPRODUCTIVE SYSTEM

Through the reproductive system, adult human beings are able to create new human beings. Reproduction begins when a sperm cell from a man fertilizes an egg cell from a woman.

URINARY SYSTEM

This system, which includes the **kidneys**, cleans waste from the blood and regulates the amount of water in the body.

Tips for TIP-TOP TEETH

If you want to chew food properly and speak clearly, it is important to keep your teeth healthy. Here are some tips for keeping your teeth in tip-top shape.

◄ **Brush your teeth at least twice a day.** If possible, brush after every meal.

◄ **Floss.** Clean between your teeth regularly with dental floss.

◄ **Eat healthful foods.** Don't eat too many sweets or sugary foods and sodas. They cause cavities.

◄ **Visit your dentist** to have your teeth checked and cleaned every six months.

What Causes a Cavity in Your Tooth?

Cavities are caused by tiny pieces of food left on or between the teeth after eating. These pieces of food combine with the natural bacteria in your mouth to form an acid. The acid slowly eats away the tooth's enamel and causes tooth decay, or cavities.

TOOTHACHE PUZZLE

Unlike a real toothache, a toothache puzzle is fun. Using the letters in the word "toothache," see how many words you can make that have at least three letters. Plurals don't count. (Answers are on page 303.)

Which DOCTOR Does What?

A doctor who takes general care of your teeth is called a **dentist.**
A doctor who straightens teeth is called an **orthodontist.**
A doctor who takes care of children is called a **pediatrician.**
A doctor who fixes broken bones is called an **orthopedist.**
A doctor who treats people who have allergies is called an **allergist.**
A doctor who treats skin problems and diseases is called a **dermatologist.**
A doctor whose machines can see inside your body is called a **radiologist.**
A doctor who treats people who have cancer is called an **oncologist.**
A doctor who treats people with heart problems is called a **cardiologist.**
A doctor who helps people with emotional problems is called a **psychiatrist.**

FACTS AND FIGURES About the Body

- ☑ **A newborn baby has more bones than an adult.** A baby's body has 350 bones, but an adult's body has 206 bones. That's because bones grow together to make fewer, larger bones as the baby grows up.
- ☑ **The largest bone in your body is your thigh bone** (or femur). The smallest bone in your body is the stirrup (or stapes), a tiny bone in your middle ear.
- ☑ **Children have 20 first teeth.** Adults have 32 teeth.
- ☑ **The human body has more than 650 muscles.**
- ☑ **The heart weighs less than one pound.** It beats about 100,000 times a day, and it pumps 2,000 gallons of blood in a day.
- ☑ **An adult's large intestine is about 5 feet long.** The small intestine, which is much narrower than the large one, is about 25 feet long.
- ☑ **Red blood cells live for about 120 days.** Then they are replaced by new ones. The bone cells in your body live for 25 to 30 years. Your brain cells live for a lifetime.
- ☑ **About 70% of the average-sized adult body is made up of water.**
- ☑ **It takes around 17 muscles to smile and around 43 to frown.**

Staying Healthy With EXERCISE

Daily exercise is important for your good health, fitness, and appearance. Exercise makes you feel good. It helps you think better. And, believe it or not, it helps you sleep better and feel less tired and more relaxed. Once you start exercising regularly, you will feel stronger and get better and better at physical activities.

What Happens When You Exercise? When you exercise, you breathe more deeply and get more oxygen into your lungs with each breath. Your heart pumps more oxygen-filled blood to all parts of your body with each beat. Your muscles and joints feel more flexible. Exercise also helps you to stay at a healthy weight.

What About People Who Don't Exercise? People who don't exercise may have less strength and energy. They may not sleep well and may feel tired. And they may gain more weight than would be healthy.

What Kind of Exercise Is Good? Almost all kinds of activity that move the body around. Bicycling, dancing, skating, swimming, running, roller-blading, and playing soccer are a few ways to exercise and have fun at the same time.

Which Foods Are the RIGHT FOODS?

To stay healthy, it is important to eat the right foods and to exercise. To help people choose the right foods for good health and fitness, the U.S. government developed the food pyramid shown below. The food pyramid shows the groups of foods that should be eaten every day.

The foods shown at the bottom (or largest part) of the pyramid are the foods to be eaten in the largest amounts. At the top are the foods to be eaten in the smallest amounts. The number of servings a person should eat depends on the person's age and body size. Younger, smaller people may eat fewer servings. Older, larger people may eat more. The meaning of "serving" is explained below the pyramid.

FOOD GUIDE PYRAMID: A GUIDE TO DAILY FOOD CHOICES

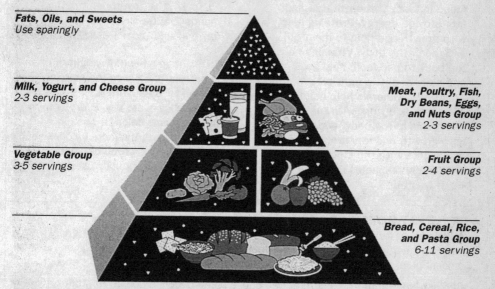

Fats, Oils, and Sweets
Use sparingly

Milk, Yogurt, and Cheese Group
2-3 servings

Meat, Poultry, Fish, Dry Beans, Eggs, and Nuts Group
2-3 servings

Vegetable Group
3-5 servings

Fruit Group
2-4 servings

Bread, Cereal, Rice, and Pasta Group
6-11 servings

HOW MUCH FOOD IS IN A SERVING?

☑ **Milk, Yogurt, and Cheese Group**
1 serving = 1 cup of milk or yogurt; or $1^1/_2$ to 2 ounces of cheese

☑ **Meat, Poultry, Fish Group**
1 serving = 2 to 3 ounces of cooked lean meat, fish, or poultry; 1 to $1^1/_2$ cups of cooked dry beans; 2 eggs; or 4 to 6 tablespoons of peanut butter

☑ **Vegetable Group**
1 serving = 1 cup of raw, leafy vegetables; $^1/_2$ cup of other vegetables (cooked or chopped raw); or $^3/_4$ cup vegetable juice

☑ **Fruit Group**
1 serving = 1 medium apple, banana, or orange; $^1/_2$ cup of cooked, chopped, or canned fruit; or $^3/_4$ cup of fruit juice

☑ **Bread, Cereal, Rice and Pasta Group**
1 serving = 1 slice of bread; 1 ounce of ready-to-eat cereal; or $^1/_2$ cup of cooked cereal, rice, or pasta

HEALTH TALK

Have you ever noticed the labels on the packages of food you and your family buy? The labels give information to help people make healthy choices about the foods they eat. Below are some words that will help you understand what the labels mean.

NUTRIENTS ARE NECESSARY

Nutrients are the parts of food that the body can use. The body needs nutrients for growth, for energy, and to repair itself when something goes wrong. Carbohydrates, fats, proteins, vitamins, minerals, and water are different kinds of nutrients that are found in food. **Carbohydrates** and **fats** provide energy. **Proteins** help with growth and help to maintain and repair the body. **Vitamins** help the body to use food, help eyesight and skin, and help fight off infections. **Minerals** help build bones and teeth and work with the chemicals in the body. **Water** helps with growth and repair of the body. It also works with the blood and chemicals, and helps the body get rid of wastes.

CALORIES COUNT

A **calorie** is a measure of the amount of energy we get from food. The government recommends the number of calories that should be taken in for different age groups. The number of calories recommended for children ages 7 to 10 is 2,400 a day. For ages 11 to 14, the government recommends 2,400 calories for girls every day and 2,800 calories for boys.

To maintain a **healthy weight**, it is important to balance the calories in the food you eat with the calories used by the body every day. Every activity uses up some calories. The more active you are, the more calories your body is burning. If you eat more calories than your body uses, you will gain weight.

A LITTLE FAT GOES A LONG WAY

A little bit of fat is important for your body. It keeps your body warm. It gives the muscles energy. It helps keep the skin soft and healthy. But the body needs only a small amount of fat to do all these things—just one tablespoon of fat each day is enough.

Cholesterol. Eating too much fat can cause some people's bodies to produce too much of a chemical called **cholesterol** (ko-LESS-ter-all). This is a waxy substance that can build up over the years on the inside of arteries. Too much cholesterol keeps blood from flowing freely through the arteries and can cause serious health problems like heart attacks.

To eat less fat, try eating lower-fat foods instead of fatty foods:

Some lower-fat foods:
chicken or turkey hot dog
broiled chicken breast
tuna fish canned in water
pretzels
low-fat or nonfat frozen yogurt
plain popcorn (with no butter)
skim milk or 1% or 2% milk

Some fatty foods:
beef or pork hot dog
fried hamburger
tuna fish canned in oil
potato chips
ice cream
buttered popcorn
whole milk

Learning to Say NO to Harmful Substances

It's no secret that drugs, alcohol, and cigarettes can do serious damage to people's bodies and minds. Some kids try these harmful substances, but a lot of kids don't want to try them. And some kids don't know how to say "no" when someone wants them to say "yes." DARE, a program developed by the U.S. government to help young people say "no" to drugs, suggests some ways to refuse drugs, alcohol, and cigarettes:

☑ **Say "No thanks."** (Show that you mean it by saying it again and again if you have to.)

☑ **Give reasons.** ("I don't like beer" or "I'm going to soccer practice" or "I have asthma.")

☑ **Change the subject** or offer a better suggestion.

☑ **Walk away.** (Don't argue, don't discuss it. Just leave.)

☑ **Avoid the situation.** (If you are asked to a party where kids will be drinking, smoking, or using drugs, don't go. Make plans to do something else instead.)

☑ **Find strength in numbers.** (Do things with friends who don't use harmful substances.)

Understanding AIDS

What Is AIDS? AIDS is a disease that is caused by a virus called HIV. AIDS attacks the body's immune system. The immune system is made up of cells that usually help the body fight off infections and diseases, but it doesn't destroy the AIDS virus.

How Do Kids Get AIDS? A mother with AIDS may give it to her baby before the baby is born. Sometimes children (and adults, too) have gotten AIDS from blood transfusions. But this happens less and less, because blood banks now test all donations of blood for the AIDS virus.

How Do Adults Get AIDS? There are two main ways people get AIDS: Having sex with a person who has AIDS, or sharing a needle used for drugs with a person who has AIDS.

How Kids and Adults *Don't* Get AIDS. People *don't* get AIDS from everyday contact with infected people at school, at home, or other places. People *don't* get AIDS from clothes, telephones, or toilet seats, or from food prepared by someone with AIDS. Children *don't* get AIDS from sitting near AIDS victims or from shaking hands with them.

Is There a Cure for AIDS? Not yet. But researchers are hard at work trying to develop a vaccine to prevent AIDS or a drug to cure it.

Keeping SAFE and PREVENTING ACCIDENTS

When you are careful and use common sense, you're off to a good start at preventing accidents. Most accidents happen at home. Although no one can prevent every accident, there are some steps you can take to prevent many of them from happening.

☑ **Safety in the Kitchen.** Sharp knives should be handled very carefully. Always cut away from your body. Be sure the knife is in a safe place when you put it down. To avoid fire, don't leave paper or cloth (like napkins or towels) near the stove. Keep sharp knives and matches away from babies and little children.

☑ **Safety in the Bathroom.** A rubber mat or other non-slip surface can keep you from slipping in the bathtub. Also, the soap should be kept in a soap dish, so that no one will slip on it. Don't use hair dryers or other electrical appliances near water.

☑ **Other Safety Tips at Home.** Everyone in your family should know all the ways of getting out of your house or apartment in case there is a fire. If an accident happens, get an adult to help. Don't let strangers into your house or apartment. Don't give your name or address to strangers over the phone. Don't tell a stranger if you are home alone.

☑ **Riding Your Bike Safely.** Wear a helmet when riding your bike. Use reflectors and lights on your bike. Be alert—watch for traffic, other bikes, roller bladers, and people who are walking. Learn the safety laws for cars—bikes must obey the same laws.

☑ **Safety in the Car.** In the car always wear a seat belt. Don't distract the driver by making loud noise or jumping around.

☑ **Crossing the Street Safely.** When crossing a street, watch for traffic. Look both ways before crossing the street. Cross only at corners. Stay on the curb until the light turns green and the "Walk" sign is on. Don't fool around near traffic.

If There Is an Emergency

With your family, make a list of emergency telephone numbers and keep the list near the telephone or taped to the refrigerator. Here are some numbers to put on the list: your parent's or guardian's telephone numbers at work, the telephone number of a friend who lives nearby or a neighbor, your family doctor, hospital, fire department, police department. Phone numbers for emergencies can often be found inside the front cover of your telephone book.

Remember 911. The number 911 is a special phone number for emergencies. When a person who needs help calls 911, the 911 operator asks the caller for his or her name and address and what the emergency is. Then the 911 operator will quickly send the police, an ambulance, or the fire department. If your town doesn't have 911, dial 0 (operator) and ask the operator for help.

EMERGENCY DIAL 911

LEGAL or PUBLIC HOLIDAYS
in the United States

There are no legal holidays for the whole United States. The federal government decides which days will be holidays for its workers and for Washington, D.C. Each state picks its own holidays, but most states celebrate most of those listed below. On legal holidays, banks and schools are usually closed, and so are many offices. Since 1971, Washington's Birthday (now Presidents' Day), Memorial Day, Columbus Day, and Veterans Day have been celebrated on a Monday so that many people can have a three-day weekend.

New Year's Day. Countries the world over celebrate the new year, although not always on January 1. The Chinese New Year falls between January 10 and February 19. In ancient Egypt, the New Year began around mid-June, when the Nile river overflowed and watered the crops.

Martin Luther King, Jr., Day. Observed on the third Monday in January, this holiday marks the birth (January 15, 1929) of the African-American civil rights leader Martin Luther King, Jr.

Presidents' Day or Washington's Birthday. On the third Monday in February, Americans celebrate the births of both George Washington (born on February 22, 1732) and Abraham Lincoln (born on February 12, 1809).

Memorial Day or Decoration Day. Memorial Day, observed on the last Monday in May, is set aside to remember all those who died in United States wars.

Fourth of July or Independence Day. July 4 is the anniversary of the day in 1776 when the American colonies declared their independence from England. Kids and grownups celebrate with bands and parades, picnics, barbecues, and fireworks.

Labor Day. Labor Day, the first Monday in September, honors the workers of America. It was first celebrated in 1882.

Columbus Day. Celebrated on the second Monday in October, Columbus Day is the anniversary of October 12, 1492, the day when Christopher Columbus was traditionally thought to have discovered America.

Election Day. Election Day, the first Tuesday after the first Monday in November, is a legal holiday in some states.

Veterans Day. Veterans Day, November 11, honors the veterans of United States wars. First called Armistice Day, it marked the armistice (agreement) that ended World War I. This was signed on the 11th hour (11 A.M.) of the 11th day of the 11th month of 1918.

Thanksgiving. Celebrated on the fourth Thursday in November, Thanksgiving Day was first observed by the Pilgrims in 1621 as a harvest festival and a day for thanks and feasting.

Christmas. Christmas is both a religious holiday and a legal holiday. (See p. 182.)

HOLIDAYS in 1997		
Holiday	**Date in 1997**	**Day**
New Year's Day	January 1	Wednesday
Martin Luther King, Jr., Day	January 20	Monday
Presidents' Day	February 17	Monday
Memorial Day	May 26	Monday
Independence Day	July 4	Friday
Labor Day	September 1	Monday
Columbus Day	October 13	Monday
Election Day	November 4	Tuesday
Veterans Day	November 11	Tuesday
Thanksgiving	November 27	Thursday
Christmas	December 25	Thursday

SOME OTHER SPECIAL HOLIDAYS

Valentine's Day. February 14 is a day for sending cards to people you love.

Arbor Day. Trees are planted on Arbor Day, reminding us of the importance of protecting the environment. Each state observes the day at different times in the spring, depending on the state's climate.

Mother's Day and Father's Day. Mothers are honored on the second Sunday in May. Fathers are honored on the third Sunday in June.

Halloween. In ancient Britain, Druids lit fires and wore grotesque costumes on October 31 to scare off evil spirits. Today, "trick or treating" children collect candy and other sweets. Some also collect money for UNICEF, the United Nations Children's Fund.

Kwanza. Originally an African harvest festival, Kwanza is a week-long African-American celebration beginning on December 26. Candles are lit every night.

SOME HOLIDAYS AROUND THE WORLD

Children's Day. In Japan, May 5 is set aside to honor children.

Canada Day. Canada's national holiday, July 1, commemorates the union of Canadian provinces under one government in 1867.

Bastille Day. July 14 is France's national holiday. It commemorates the storming of the Bastille prison in 1789 at the beginning of the French Revolution.

Boxing Day. December 26 is a holiday in Britain, and also in Australia, Canada, and New Zealand. On this day, at one time, Christmas gifts were distributed in boxes to servants, tradespeople, and the poor.

Independence Day. Mexico celebrates September 16 as its national holiday, commemorating a revolt in 1810 against rule by Spain.

Some Major INVENTIONS

Some of the world's most important inventions were developed before history was ever written. These include the invention of tools and the wheel, the ability to make and control fire, and the ability to make pottery. And these inventions led to others, which in turn helped create new and better and cheaper ways of doing things. For example, light bulbs replaced candles and oil lamps, and rocket engines made it possible to go to the moon.

INVENTIONS THAT TAKE US FROM ONE PLACE TO ANOTHER

Automobiles made travel easier, and jet planes allowed ordinary people to see the world.

Year	Invention	Inventor	Country
1785	parachute	Jean Pierre Blanchard	France
1807	steamboat	Robert Fulton	U.S.
1829	steam locomotive	George Stephenson	England
1852	safety elevator	Elisha G. Otis	U.S.
1885	bicycle	James Starley	England
1885	motorcycle	Gottlieb Daimler	Germany
1892	automobile (gasoline)	Charles E. Duryea & J. Frank Duryea	U.S.
1891	escalator	Jesse W. Reno	U.S.
1894	submarine	Simon Lake	U.S.
1895	diesel engine	Rudolf Diesel	Germany
1903	propeller airplane	Orville & Wilbur Wright	U.S.
1939	helicopter	Igor Sikorsky	U.S.
1939	turbojet airplane	Hans von Ohain	Germany

INVENTIONS THAT HELP US LIVE HEALTHIER AND LONGER LIVES

Penicillin and other drugs known as antibiotics help fight some illnesses. CAT scanners and X-rays let doctors look inside our bodies to see what's wrong.

Year	Invention	Inventor	Country
1780	bifocal lenses for glasses	Benjamin Franklin	U.S.
1819	stethoscope	René T.M.H. Laënnec	France
1842	anesthesia (ether)	Crawford W. Long	U.S.
1895	X-ray	Wilhelm Roentgen	Germany
1922	insulin	Sir Frederick G. Banting	Canada
1929	penicillin	Alexander Fleming	Scotland
1954	antibiotic for fungal diseases	Rachel F. Brown & Elizabeth L. Hazen	U.S.
1955	polio vaccine	Jonas E. Salk	U.S.
1973	CAT scanner	Godfrey N. Hounsfield	England

INVENTIONS THAT HELP US COMMUNICATE WITH ONE ANOTHER

The pen and pencil and printing press, fax and phone and computer are all ways of exchanging messages, information, and ideas. Today, we use older inventions like the pencil along with newer ones like the computer.

Year	Invention	Inventor	Country
A.D. 105	paper	Ts'ai Lun	China
1447	movable type	Johann Gutenberg	Germany
1795	modern pencil	Nicolas Jacques Conté	France
1837	telegraph	Samuel F.B. Morse	U.S.
1845	rotary printing press	Richard M. Hoe	U.S.
1867	typewriter	Christopher L. Sholes, Carlos Glidden, & Samuel W. Soulé	U.S.
1876	telephone	Alexander G. Bell	U.S.
1913	modern radio receiver	Reginald A. Fessenden	U.S.
1937	xerography copies	Chester Carlson	U.S.
1943	ballpoint pen	Laszlo Biro	Argentina
1944	auto sequence computer	Howard H. Aiken	U.S.
1945	electronic computer	J. Presper Eckert & John W. Mauchly	U.S.
1947	transistor	William Shockley, Walter H. Brattain, & John Bardeen	U.S.
1955	fiber optics	Narinder S. Kapany	England
1965	word processor	IBM	U.S.

INVENTIONS THAT ENTERTAIN US

Books and games, the radio and television have entertained people in their homes for many years and continue to do so. Newer inventions like VCRs and CD players have brought more movies and concerts into homes.

Year	Invention	Inventor	Country
1709	piano	Bartolomeo Cristofori	Italy
1877	phonograph	Thomas A. Edison	U.S.
1877	microphone	Emile Berliner	U.S.
1888	portable camera	George Eastman	U.S.
1893	moving picture viewer	Thomas A. Edison	U.S.
1894	motion picture projector	Charles F. Jenkins	U.S.
1899	tape recorder	Valdemar Poulsen	Denmark
1924	television	Vladimir K. Zworykin	U.S.
1951	flexible kite	Gertrude Rogallo & Francis Rogallo	U.S.
1963	audiocassette	Phillips Corporation	Netherlands
1969	videotape cassette	Sony	Japan
1972	compact disc (CD)	RCA	U.S.
1972	video game (Pong)	Norman Buschnel	U.S.

INVENTIONS THAT MAKE OUR LIVES EASIER

Year	Invention	Inventor	Country
1800	electric battery	Alessandro Volta	Italy
1827	matches	John Walker	England
1831	lawn mower	Edwin Budding &	
		John Ferrabee	England
1834	refrigeration	Jacob Perkins	England
1846	sewing machine	Elias Howe	U.S.
1851	cylinder (door) lock	Linus Yale	U.S.
1879	electric light bulb	Thomas A. Edison	U.S.
1886	dishwasher	Josephine Cochran	U.S.
1801	zipper	Whitcomb L. Judson	U.S.
1901	washing machine	Langmuir Fisher	U.S.
1903	windshield wipers	Mary Anderson	U.S.
1907	vacuum cleaner	J. Murray Spangler	U.S.
1911	air conditioning	Willis H. Carrier	U.S.
1924	frozen packaged food	Clarence Birdseye	U.S.
1938	Teflon	DuPont Corporation	U.S.
1947	microwave oven	Percy L. Spencer	U.S.
1948	Velcro	Georges de Mestral	Switzerland
1971	food processor	Pierre Verdon	France

INVENTIONS THAT HELP US EXPLORE AND UNDERSTAND THE WORLD AND THE UNIVERSE

Year	Invention	Inventor	Country
1250	magnifying glass	Roger Bacon	England
1590	microscope using two lenses	Zacharias Janssen	Netherlands
1608	telescope	Hans Lippershey	Netherlands
1714	mercury thermometer	Gabriel D. Fahrenheit	Germany
1926	rocket engine	Robert H. Goddard	U.S.
1930	cyclotron (atom smasher)	Ernest O. Lawrence	U.S.
1931	electron microscope	Max Knoll & Ernst Ruska	Germany
1943	Aqua Lung	Jacques-Yves Cousteau & Emile Gagnan	France
1953	bathyscaphe	August Piccard	France
1977	space shuttle	NASA	U.S.

NATIONAL INVENTORS HALL OF FAME

If you would like to learn more about inventions and the people who created them, or if you would like to try to make your own invention, you can do both at Inventure Place, National Inventors Hall of Fame, 221 S. Broadway St., Akron, Ohio, 44308. Phone: (216) 762-4463. A few of the inventors honored in the Hall of Fame are Rachel F. Brown and Elizabeth L. Hazen (antibiotics for fungal diseases), George Washington Carver (process for organic dyes), Thomas Edison (electric light bulb), Henry Ford (automobile transmission), Elisha Otis (elevator), Orville and Wilbur Wright (flying machine), An Wang (computer control device). Another part of Inventure Place has hands-on exhibits and workshops where you can learn about inventions and experiment with building your own.

ABBREVIATIONS

Abbreviations are short forms of words or phrases. We use abbreviations all the time because they save us time in both writing and speaking. Acronyms are abbreviations made out of the first letters of several words. An acronym can be pronounced as a word. NASA is an acronym for National Aeronautics and Space Administration.

TITLES
We almost always use abbreviations before and after people's names. For example, Mr., Mrs., Ms., Miss, Jr., and Sr.

TECHNICAL TALK
Special fields have their own abbreviations.

> Another run scores! His third RBI of the day!

Sports. Baseball players brag about their RBIs (runs batted in) or ERA (earned run average).

> Whoops! It says 2 tsp. of red peppers, not 2 tbs.!

Cooking. Cooks measure their ingredients by the tsp. (teaspoon), tbs. or tbsp. (tablespoon), oz. (ounce), or lb. (pound).

Computers. Computer users talk about their PCs (personal computers), a CD-ROM (Compact Disk-Read Only Memory), and DOS (Disk Operating System), and some communicate electronically through a BBS (Bulletin Board Service).

Navigation. Navigators use N, S, E, and W to refer to compass directions.

POSTAL ABBREVIATIONS
When addressing an envelope, we use two-letter postal abbreviations for the U.S. states. When writing to a friend in Kentucky, you would write KY instead of the whole state name, and follow it with the ZIP code.

HIDDEN STATE ABBREVIATIONS PUZZLE

Hidden in the two sentences above are postal abbreviations for the 10 states listed on the right. See how many you can find and underline. The first state you will find, IN, is underlined for you. Some states appear more than once. (Answers are on page 303.)

CO (Colorado)	ND (North Dakota)
DE (Delaware)	OR (Oregon)
IN (Indiana)	RI (Rhode Island)
KY (Kentucky)	VI (Virginia)
ME (Maine)	WI (Wisconsin)

The postal abbreviation for each state is listed in Facts About the States on pages 257-273.

Writing a LETTER

Did you know there are different kinds of letters? A letter or note to a friend or family member is informal, and you can write it any way you like. But a letter to an official person—say, your mayor or the head of a company—is a formal letter and should include your name and address, the date, the address of the person you're writing to, and an ending such as "Sincerely yours" or "Yours truly." Below are examples of a formal letter to a company and two informal letters, one written on a computer for e-mail.

193 South Street
Downtown, MI 54321

May 1, 1996

The President
The Thousand-And-One Puzzles Company
10 Riddle Square
Alltown, TN 87654

Dear Sir or Madam:

Last week I got a jigsaw puzzle of a triceratops as a birthday present. But when I finished it, I realized that some of the pieces were missing. My dinosaur was missing two of its three horns!

I'm writing to ask you to please replace the puzzle with a new one with all the pieces. Enclosed is the picture of the puzzle that came in the box. Thank you for your help.

Sincerely,

Leslie Lee

Leslie Lee

Hi, Grandpa!
I'm having a great time in Florida. We went out on a boat today and Dad caught a fish! See you soon!

Love,
Jack

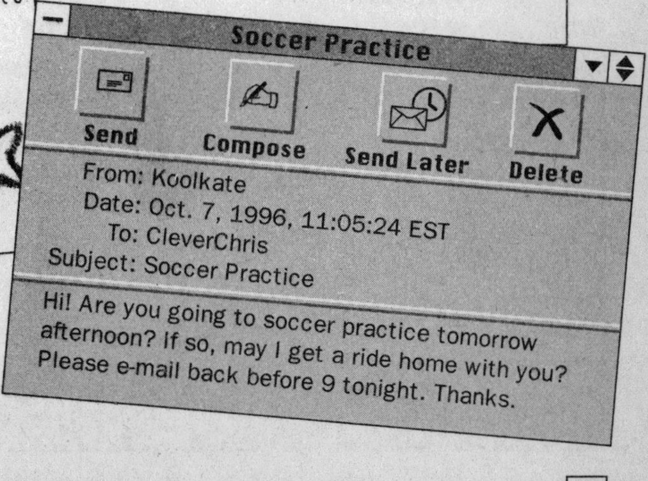

Soccer Practice

Send   Compose   Send Later   Delete

From: Koolkate
Date: Oct. 7, 1996, 11:05:24 EST
To: CleverChris
Subject: Soccer Practice

Hi! Are you going to soccer practice tomorrow afternoon? If so, may I get a ride home with you? Please e-mail back before 9 tonight. Thanks.

Words That Sound Alike or Almost Alike

When words sound similar, sometimes their spellings and meanings are confusing.

brake or break
A **brake** is a device for slowing or stopping a vehicle. A **break** is a brief rest period (a lunch break).

capital or capitol
A **capital** is the city where a country or state government is located. The **capitol** is the building where a legislative body meets.

desert or dessert

A **desert** is a hot, sandy area where few plants can grow. **Dessert** is fruit, ice cream, or something else eaten at the end of a meal.

emigrate or immigrate
To **emigrate** means to move away from a country. To **immigrate** means to move to another country. (Ana emigrated from Brazil. She immigrated to the United States.)

fair or fare
A **fair** is an exhibition or show. **Fair** also means better than poor, but less than good. **Fare** is the cost of a ride on a public vehicle like a bus, train, plane, or taxi.

its or it's
Its is the possessive form of "it" (the bird flapped its wings). **It's** is a contraction of "it is."

principal or principle
A **principal** is the person in charge of a school. **Principal** also means first in importance. A **principle** is a basic idea that a person believes in deeply.

stationary or stationery
Stationary means fixed in one place. When you have **stationery,** you have paper and envelopes to write on.

their, they're, or there
Their is the possessive form of "they." **They're** is a contraction of "they are." **There** means at or in that place. (They're going to put their packages there on the table.)

AHA! IT'S A PALINDROME

Can you see anything special about the following words?

aha, eye, kayak, level, noon, redder, toot, Dad, Mom, Sis, Anna, Otto

All of these words read the same forward and backward. They are called **palindromes.** A palindrome may be a single word or a group of words—for example, "Madam I'm Adam." Can you read "Madam I'm Adam" backward?

PALINDROME PUZZLE

See if you can make some palindromes by filling in the blanks below. The boxed letter (or letters) is the center. **Hint:** Start by using the first letter for the last letter, or the last letter for the first letter. Then just keep on going. (Answers are on page 303.)

Rac e c____ ____

Was it a c at I ____ ____ ____?

Step o n n ____   ____ ____ ____ ____

No lemon s , ____ ____   ____ ____ ____ ____

____ ____ ____ ____   ____ ____ ____ E dna dine.

IDIOMS: Words That Are Not as They Seem

Idioms are groups of words (phrases) that cannot be understood just by knowing the meaning of each of the words. This often makes them particularly puzzling to people learning a new language. Some idioms are hard to understand even in your own language. Here are some common idioms, with their meanings.

COLORFUL EXPRESSIONS

in the black: making a profit, not in debt
out of the blue: unexpectedly, without warning
to be green with envy: to be extremely envious
to see red: to become very angry
to wave a white flag: to indicate, in battle, that you wish to surrender

IT'S ALL IN THE GAME

to play games: to fool someone or keep the truth from someone
to be on the ball: to be alert or quick to catch on or understand
get the ball rolling: get something started
to be off base: to be wrong
right off the bat: immediately, first thing
skate on thin ice: be in a dangerous or risky situation

THE ANIMAL KINGDOM

straight from the horse's mouth: from the original, or most reliable, source
let the cat out of the bag: reveal a secret, usually by mistake
like a fish out of water: ill at ease or in unfamiliar surroundings
rain cats and dogs: rain very hard
the lion's share: the greatest amount, the largest portion
take the bull by the horns: to deal courageously with a situation

BODY LANGUAGE PUZZLE

Look at the definitions in the left column. See if you can match each one with the correct idiom in the right column. (Answers are on page 304.)

1. to tease or play a trick on someone
2. to get someone's attention
3. to refuse to listen or to show interest
4. easily seen or within plain view
5. dead even, like two horses in a race

a. to catch someone's eye
b. right under your nose
c. neck and neck
d. to pull someone's leg
e. to turn a deaf ear

LANGUAGES of the WORLD

Would you have guessed that Mandarin, the principal language of China, is the world's most spoken language? You may find more surprises in the chart below, which lists languages spoken by at least 50,000,000 native speakers (those for whom the language is their first language, or mother tongue).

PRINCIPAL LANGUAGES OF THE WORLD

LANGUAGE	NUMBER OF NATIVE SPEAKERS (as of 1995)
Mandarin	844,000,000
Hindi*	340,000,000
Spanish	339,000,000
English	326,000,000
Bengali*	193,000,000
Arabic	190,000,000
Portuguese	172,000,000
Russian	169,000,000
Japanese	125,000,000
German	98,000,000
French	73,000,000
Malay-Indonesian	52,000,000

*Hindi and Bengali are spoken in different parts of India.

Are you surprised to see that English ranks only fourth?

Which Languages Are Spoken in the United States?

Since the beginning of American history, immigrants have come to the United States from all over the world and brought their native languages with them. That's why so many Americans speak a language other than English at home. Here are some of the languages other than English that are spoken by 200,000 or more Americans.

Hello! I'm Carmen!

¡Buenos días! ¡Soy Carmen!

LANGUAGE USED AT HOME	SPEAKERS OVER 5 YEARS OLD	LANGUAGE USED AT HOME	SPEAKERS OVER 5 YEARS OLD
1. Spanish	17,339,000	11. Japanese	428,000
2. French	1,703,000	12. Greek	388,000
3. German	1,547,000	13. Arabic	355,000
4. Italian	1,309,000	14. Hindu, Urdu,	
5. Chinese	1,249,000	& related	
6. Tagalog	843,000	languages	331,000
7. Polish	723,000	15. Russian	242,000
8. Korean	626,000	16. Yiddish	213,000
9. Vietnamese	507,000	17. Thai	206,000
10. Portuguese	430,000	18. Persian	202,000

Where in the WORLD Do ENGLISH WORDS Come From?

In addition to its language, each new ethnic group that immigrated to the United States brought its own traditions and customs. Immigrants brought their music, art, folk dances, style of dress, and special foods. Many of their foods and customs were adopted by Americans, and so were the words that described them.

Food from many cultures has become part of the American diet. Even words for typically American foods such as hamburgers and frankfurters have foreign origins. Here are some foods and food-related words and the languages from which they came.

from Arabic:
apricot, candy, coffee, couscous, lime, sherbet, spinach, sugar, syrup, tuna

from Chinese:
chopsticks, chow, chow mein, soy, tea, wok, wonton

from French:
bouillon, casserole, chowder, crepe, croissant, croutons, mayonnaise, menu, mousse, omelette, quiche, tart

from German:
delicatessen, frankfurter, hamburger, pretzel, pumpernickel, sauerkraut, seltzer

from Italian:
bologna, broccoli, lasagna, minestrone, pasta, pizza, salami, spaghetti

from Japanese:
sukiyaki, sushi, tempura, teriyaki, tofu

from Spanish:
avocado, burrito, chili, chocolate, cocoa, garbanzo, maize, tomato, tamale, tortilla

from Yiddish:
bagel, blintze, knish, nosh

"C" FOOD SEARCH PUZZLE

The names of foods and food-related words beginning with the letter "C" are hidden in the puzzle below. How many can you find? CASSEROLE, CHILI, CHOCOLATE, CHOWDER, CHOW MEIN, COCOA, COUSCOUS, CROISSANT, CREPE, CROUTONS (Answers are on page 304.)

```
Q  U  I  N  R  E  W  C  H  O  W  D  E  R  D  C  B  N  C
A  S  D  F  C  H  O  H  I  U  C  Y  T  R  E  A  W  E  R
Z  X  C  V  R  G  F  I  S  A  W  R  G  H  J  S  M  N  B
Y  T  C  H  O  C  O  L  A  T  E  F  O  L  K  S  J  U  Y
S  D  F  G  I  L  K  I  H  J  V  C  X  U  M  E  C  V  N
P  O  I  U  S  Y  T  R  E  W  Q  S  D  F  T  R  H  G  F
B  C  O  U  S  C  O  U  S  V  X  Z  A  S  W  O  Q  R  T
L  O  K  J  A  G  H  F  D  S  T  R  E  W  Y  L  N  I  Y
Z  C  X  C  N  V  B  O  N  M  L  C  R  E  P  E  T  S  H
J  O  I  S  T  B  V  F  W  R  E  W  Q  P  O  I  U  L  K
M  A  V  F  G  H  U  Y  T  D  R  T  Y  U  I  P  L  J  H
O  G  F  R  T  C  H  O  W  M  E  I  N  S  A  D  F  G  Y
```

WHY DO WE NEED LAWS?

Did you ever wonder what your day would be like if there weren't any rules to follow? What if you could go to school any time you wanted? What if your teacher could also get to school any time he or she wanted? And what if there were no rules on the playground, or no traffic lights or stop signs for crossing the street?

Life would be difficult and confusing without rules. We all need them. Governments, businesses, organizations, and families make rules so that people don't get hurt and are not treated unfairly. The rules that a government makes are called laws. The government has the power to punish people who break a law.

Laws are made to:
- ☑ Protect people from getting hurt
- ☑ Help people to be treated fairly
- ☑ Help people do their jobs properly
- ☑ Help people know how to act in public

WHAT HAPPENS WHEN YOU BREAK THE LAW?

Kids. When children under 18 years old are caught breaking the law, they are arrested by the police and sometimes have to appear in a court called **juvenile court.** In this court, there is no jury. There is a judge who first decides whether or not there is strong enough evidence that the child has broken the law.

If there is enough evidence, the judge then decides what kind of help or punishment the child needs to get back on the right track. Sometimes the judge sends the child home, instructing him or her to follow certain rules. This is called **probation.** Sometimes the child is sent to a **foster home** or to another place where the judge thinks the child can more easily stay out of trouble or benefit from some training. In very serious cases, the child may be sent to a jail for kids, or a **reformatory**.

Adults. When an adult breaks the law, the offense may be minor or it may be serious. If the adult parks a car in a no-parking zone, this is considered a minor offense. The grown-up would be given a parking ticket, which may offer the choice of paying a fine by mail or going to court to argue against the ticket.

An adult who commits a serious crime would be arrested and have to appear in court. If there is strong evidence against him or her, there would be a trial. At the trial, a government lawyer, called a **prosecutor,** would present the case against the accused person (called the **defendant**). At the end of the trial, if the accused person is **acquitted,** or found "not guilty," he or she is free to go home. When the defendant is **convicted,** or found "guilty," he or she will get a punishment, or a **sentence,** such as having to go to jail for a specific length of time.

LAWS YOU CAN NO LONGER BREAK

Here are some state laws that people were supposed to follow a long time ago. You can see why these laws are no longer on the books.

☑ In California, a permit was needed to set a trap for a mouse.

☑ In Louisiana, it was illegal to lead a bear around with a rope.

☑ In Massachusetts, a dachshund could not be kept as a pet dog.

☑ In Michigan, it was illegal to hitch a crocodile to a fire hydrant.

☑ In West Virginia, it was illegal to sneeze on a train.

GROWN-UPS HAVE RIGHTS AND SO DO KIDS

All people have rights. This means that no one should be treated unfairly. It means that everyone should be free to do certain things. In the United States many years ago, the government made a list of these rights. This list is part of the U.S. Constitution and is called the **Bill of Rights**.

The Bill of Rights says that all the people in the United States should have the right to belong to any religion they choose and to say and write whatever they believe, even if it is against the government. It also says that the police cannot search people or go into their houses, unless they have a good reason and get special permission. And any person who is arrested has the right to a lawyer and a fair trial.

RIGHTS FOR CHILDREN

Under the laws in the United States, children do not have all the rights that grown-ups do. Children cannot drive a car or vote until they reach a certain age. They must go to school and live with their parents or legal guardian. Children have some special rights. They have the right to be taken care of by their parents.

Today, most countries in the world have laws to help children be taken care of properly and treated fairly. The United Nations has a **Declaration of the Rights of the Child,** which affirms, among other things, that:

☑ All children in the world have the same rights.

☑ All children should be protected by laws, so they can grow up normally.

☑ All children should have a name and a country to belong to.

☑ All children should have a decent place to live, enough food to eat, and whatever health care they need.

☑ Children who are handicapped should have the help they need.

☑ All children should have love and security.

☑ All children should be able to get an education.

☑ Children should be among the first to get help and protection in emergencies.

☑ Children should be protected against abuse and should learn to respect and help others.

☑ Children should be protected against unfair treatment because of race or religion.

HISTORY of MONEY

Why Did People Start Using Money? People first started using money in order to trade. A farmer who had cattle might want to have salt to preserve meat or cloth to make clothing. For this farmer, a cow became a "medium of exchange"—a way of getting things that the farmer did not make or grow. Cattle became a form of money. Whatever people agreed to use for trade became the earliest kinds of money.

What Objects Have Been Used as Money Throughout History? You may be surprised by some of the items that people have used every day as money. What does the form of money tell you about a society and its people?

- ☑ knives, rice, and spades in China around 3000 B.C.
- ☑ cattle and clay tablets in Babylonia around 2500 B.C.
- ☑ wampum (beads) and beaver fur by American Indians of the northeast around A.D. 1500
- ☑ tobacco by early American colonists around 1650
- ☑ whales' teeth by the Pacific peoples on the island of Fiji, until the early 1900s

The First Paper Money. By the time of the Middle Ages in Europe (A.D. 800-1100), gold had become a popular medium for trade. But gold was heavy and difficult to carry, and European cities and the roads of Europe at that time were dangerous places to carry large amounts of gold. So merchants and goldsmiths began issuing notes promising to pay gold to the person carrying the note. These "promissory notes" were the beginning of paper money in Europe. Paper money was probably also invented in China, where the explorer Marco Polo saw it in the 1280s.

Why Did Governments Get Interested in Issuing Money? The first government to make coins that looked alike and use them as money is thought to be the Greek city-state of Lydia in the 7th century B.C. These Lydian coins were actually bean-shaped lumps made from a mixture of gold and silver.

The first government in Europe to issue paper money that looked alike was France in the early 18th century. Governments were interested in issuing money because the money itself had value. If a government could gain control over the manufacture of money, it could increase its own wealth—often simply by making more money.

Today, money throughout the world is issued only by governments. In the United States, the Department of the Treasury and the U.S. Mint make all the paper money and coins we use. Nowadays, we also use credit cards and checks to pay for things we buy. These are not thought of as real money but more as "promises to pay."

MONEY TALK:
AN ECONOMICS GLOSSARY

ATM or automated teller machine
An electronic machine in a public place where customers of a bank can withdraw cash from their accounts or make deposits by using a special plastic card.

bank
A business establishment in which people and businesses keep money in savings accounts or checking accounts.

bond
A certificate issued by a government or a business to a person or business from whom it has borrowed money. A bond promises to pay back the borrowed money with interest.

CD or certificate of deposit
A kind of bank savings account that earns a fixed rate of interest over a specific period of time.

cost of living
The average cost of the basic needs of life, including food, clothing, housing, medical care, and other services.

debt
Something that is owed.

depression
A period of severe decline. During a depression, many people are unemployed, many businesses fail, and people buy less. The last depression in the United States came in the 1930s.

FDIC or Federal Deposit Insurance Corporation
A government agency created in 1933 to protect deposits when a bank fails. The FDIC guarantees to insure deposits up to $100,000 if they are in a bank that is a member of the FDIC.

GDP or Gross Domestic Product
The total value of all goods and services in the United States in one year, including government spending as well as spending by private individuals and companies.

goods and services
Goods refer to real items such as cars, TVs, VCRs, wristwatches, clothes, and so on. **Services** refer to work that is done for other people. Firefighters, nurses, waiters, actors, lawyers all perform services.

inflation
An increase in the level of prices.

1990
$5.95

1996
$6.95

interest
The amount of money a borrower pays to borrow money. A bank pays interest on a savings account.

money
Paper and coins that are issued by the government and are used in exchange for all goods and services.

recession
A period of economic decline. During a recession, more people become unemployed, some businesses fail, and people buy less than usual. A recession is not as severe as a depression.

stock
A share in a corporation. A corporation sells shares to individuals or other companies to raise money for investment. When the company makes money, it pays the stockholder a "dividend," or a portion of the profit.

Making Money: THE U.S. MINT

What Is the U.S. Mint? The U.S. Mint is a federal government organization responsible for making all U.S. coins. It also safeguards the Treasury Department's stored gold and silver. The U.S. Mint was founded in 1792 and is today a part of the U.S. Treasury Department.

The U.S. Mint's headquarters are in Washington, D.C. Local branches that produce coins are located in Philadelphia, PA; Denver, CO; San Francisco, CA; and West Point, NY. Treasury Department gold and silver is stored at Fort Knox, KY.

Another division of the Treasury Department—the Bureau of Engraving and Printing, also in Washington, D.C —designs, engraves, and prints all U.S. paper money.

What Kinds of Coins Does the Mint Make? The U.S. Mint makes all the pennies, nickels, dimes, quarters, half dollars, and dollar coins that Americans use each day. These coins are made of a mixture of metals. For example, dimes, quarters, half dollars, and dollar coins look like silver but are a mixture of copper, nickel, and silver. The U.S. Mint also makes special coins honoring famous people and special events.

Where Can I Get Information About the Mint? You can get information about the Mint and the coins it sells from the United States Mint, Customer Service Center, 10001 Aerospace Road, Lanham, MD 20706. Telephone: (202) 223-COIN. The Mint also offers free public tours at some of its facilities.

Whose Portraits Are on Our Money? On the front of all U.S. paper money are portraits of presidents and other famous people in American history. Presidents also appear on the most commonly used coins. How many of them do you recognize?

Denomination	Portrait
1¢	Abraham Lincoln, 16th U.S. President
5¢	Thomas Jefferson, 3rd U.S. President
10¢	Franklin Delano Roosevelt, 32nd U.S. President
25¢	George Washington, 1st U.S. President
$1	George Washington, 1st U.S. President
$2	Thomas Jefferson, 3rd U.S. President
$5	Abraham Lincoln, 16th U.S. President
$10	Alexander Hamilton, 1st U.S. Treasury Secretary
$20	Andrew Jackson, 7th U.S. President
$50	Ulysses S. Grant, 18th U.S. President
$100	Benjamin Franklin, colonial inventor and U.S. patriot

Bills larger than $100 stopped being made in 1969. Up until then, $500, $1,000, $5,000, $10,000, and even $100,000 bills were produced.

? DID YOU KNOW? In 1996 the United States printed a new $100 bill with many features to help prevent counterfeiting. For example, the new bill has ink that changes color when you hold it up at different angles, plus a special mark and thin "security threads" that cannot be copied on color copiers or by computer. The government also plans to make new designs for each of the other denominations.

How Much MONEY Is in CIRCULATION in the United States?

As of March 31, 1995, the total amount of money in circulation was $401,609,609,449 (more than 400 billion dollars). About 22 billion dollars was in coins, the rest in paper money. The following chart shows the number of bills in circulation in each denomination.

Denomination	Value of Money in Circulation	Number of Bills in Circulation	
$1 bills	$5,845,268,648	5,845,268,648	
$2 bills	$1,003,940,584	501,970,292	
$5 bills	$6,948,740,110	1,389,748,022	
$10 bills	$13,013,456,290	1,301,345,629	
$20 bills	$76,265,781,080	3,813,289,054	
$50 bills	$42,906,224,700	858,124,494	
$100 bills	$233,423,525,300	2,334,235,253	

CURRENCY in Other Countries

The money that a country uses is called its *currency*. The currency of the United States is based on the U.S. dollar. All money used in the United States is a fraction of the dollar (a quarter, dime, nickel, cent) or a multiple of the dollar (such as $5, $10, and $20 bills). Listed below are names of some of the currencies used throughout the world. Although many countries have currency with the same name, each of the currencies is different and may have a different value.

Name of Currency	Country	Name of Currency	Country
bolivar	Venezuela	krone	Denmark, Norway
real	Brazil	lira	Italy, Turkey, and others
dinar	Algeria, Jordan, Kuwait, and others	mark	Germany
		peseta	Spain
dirham	Morocco, United Arab Emirates	peso	Argentina, Chile, Colombia, Mexico, Philippines, Uruguay, and others
dollar	Australia, Canada, Hong Kong, New Zealand, Singapore, United States, and others	pound	Egypt, Great Britain, Lebanon, and others
		rand	South Africa, Namibia
drachma	Greece	riyal	Saudi Arabia, Qatar
franc	Belgium, France, Switzerland, and others	ruble	Russia
		rupee	India, Pakistan, and others
guilder	Netherlands, Suriname	schilling	Austria and others
koruna	Czech Republic, Slovak Republic	yen	Japan
		yuan	China
krona	Iceland, Sweden	zloty	Poland

BUDGETS

A budget is a plan that estimates how much money a person, a business, or a government will receive during a particular period of time, how much money will be spent and what it will be spent on, and how much money will be left over (if any).

A FAMILY BUDGET

Does your family have a budget? Do you know what your family spends money on? Do you know where your family's income comes from? The chart below shows some sources of income and typical yearly expenses for a family's budget.

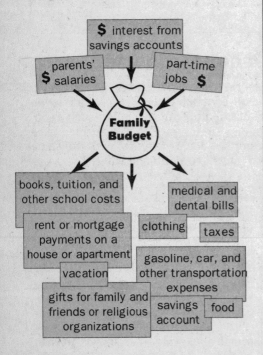

A Balanced Budget

A budget is **balanced** when the amount of money you receive equals the amount of money you spend. A budget is **unbalanced** when the amount of money you spend is greater than the amount of money you have.

MAKING YOUR OWN BUDGET

Imagine that you have been given a special allowance of $10. You may do anything you wish with the money, but you must make a budget showing how you plan to spend it. Here are some of the things you may want to include in your budget:

Possible Purchases and Cost
Rental of a video movie: $1.99
A candy bar: $.89
A poster of your favorite TV star: $4.99
A ballpoint pen: $.99
An audiocassette of your favorite music: $8.99
A visit to a museum: $4.00
A paperback book: $5.99

On the lines below, list the items you want along with their price. You may also add any other items that interest you— and their prices. And don't forget to include any money you want to save.

Item	Amount
_____	_____
_____	_____
_____	_____
_____	_____
_____	_____
Savings	_____

Now total all your purchases and savings: _____

Is your budget balanced? Is the amount you plan to spend and save equal to the amount of your "income" ($10)?

The U.S. BUDGET

Not only do families and individuals have budgets, but businesses and governments have them too. Businesses take in money by making and selling products or by providing services. But what about the government? Where does the government's income come from? And what are the government's major expenses?

WHERE DOES THE U.S. GOVERNMENT GET MONEY?

The government gets much of its money from the taxes that Americans pay.

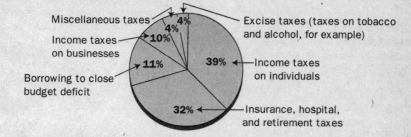

Miscellaneous taxes — 4%
Excise taxes (taxes on tobacco and alcohol, for example)
Income taxes on businesses — 10%
4%
Borrowing to close budget deficit — 11%
39% — Income taxes on individuals
32% — Insurance, hospital, and retirement taxes

WHERE DOES THE U.S. GOVERNMENT SPEND MONEY?

Most of the money the government spends is for programs of government departments (listed in the chart on page 218, under "Cabinet Departments") or independent government agencies. The chart below shows some of the major ways the U.S. government spent money during the 1995 budget year.

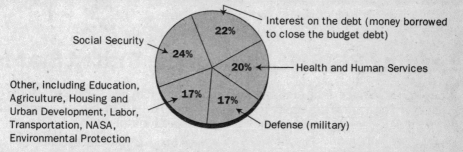

Social Security — 24%
22% — Interest on the debt (money borrowed to close the budget debt)
20% — Health and Human Services
Other, including Education, Agriculture, Housing and Urban Development, Labor, Transportation, NASA, Environmental Protection — 17%
17% — Defense (military)

THE GOVERNMENT'S UNBALANCED BUDGET

The U.S. government has not balanced its budget since 1969. Every year since then, the government has spent more money than it has taken in through taxes. The difference between the higher amount spent and the amount taken in each year is called the **budget deficit.** The budget deficit has been going down since 1993, but it remains high. Most economists believe that paying interest on such a large debt hurts the economy. But cutting the debt is also difficult, because that would mean cutting programs that many citizens now depend on.

YEAR	$ TAKEN IN	$ SPENT	DEFICIT
1992	$1.092 trillion	$1.382 trillion	$–290 billion
1993	$1.153 trillion	$1.408 trillion	$–255 billion
1994	$1.257 trillion	$1.460 trillion	$–203 billion
1995	$1.350 trillion	$1.514 trillion	$–164 billion

What Do AMERICANS BUY?

What do Americans spend their money on? The U.S. Department of Commerce publishes statistics each year that answer this question. The following chart shows how Americans spent their money in 1994.

CATEGORY	AMOUNT SPENT
Medical and dental care, (including health insurance, drugs, hospital care)	$833,700,000,000
Food	$763,300,000,000
Rent for housing	$706,600,000,000
Transportation expenses (such as cars, gasoline, and train, bus, and plane tickets)	$536,600,000,000
Household expenses (such as telephone, furniture, electricity, kitchen supplies)	$528,100,000,000
Recreation (such as books, magazines, toys, videos, sports events, amusement parks)	$374,800,000,000
Personal expenses (such as baby sitters, lawn care, house cleaning, lawyers)	$361,900,000,000
Clothing	$310,500,000,000
Religious and charitable contributions	$131,200,000,000
School tuition and other educational expenses	$105,400,000,000
Personal care (such as haircuts, health clubs)	$67,700,000,000

Leading BUSINESSES in the United States

The United States is a leading manufacturer of many different kinds of products. The following chart lists the leading American business in many different categories and the money the company took in during 1994.

Airplanes
Boeing, $21,924,000,000

Beverages
Coca-Cola, $16,172,000,000

Cars and Other Motor Vehicles
General Motors,
$154,951,000,000

Chemicals
E. I. du Pont de Nemours, $34,968,000,000

Clothing
Levi Strauss, $6,074,000,000

Computers and Office Equipment
IBM, $64,052,000,000

Electronics
General Electric, $64,682,000,000

Industrial and Farm Equipment
Caterpillar, $14,328,000,000

Medicines and Drugs
Johnson & Johnson, $15,734,000,000

Petroleum Refining
Exxon, $101,459,000,000

Retail Stores
Wal-Mart Stores, $83,412,000,000

Rubber and Plastic Products
Goodyear Tire, $12,288,000,000

Supermarkets
Kroger, $22,959,000,000

Telecommunications
AT&T, $75,094,000,000

What Kinds of JOBS Do Americans Have?

How are Americans employed? Each year the U.S. Department of Labor publishes information on employment in the United States. The following chart shows the number of men and women who worked in different kinds of jobs during 1994. The column with yearly earnings shows the mid-range of earnings for that year. This means that many people in each kind of job earned more than this amount and many earned less.

JOBS	NUMBER OF WORKERS	YEARLY EARNINGS
Managers and professionals (for example, business executives and supervisors, doctors, lawyers, teachers, nurses)		
Men	13,021,000	$41,750
Women	12,187,000	$31,000
Sales people, technicians, administrative workers (including clerical workers)		
Men	9,764,000	$28,500
Women	15,954,000	$19,500
People who repair things, precision workers, crafts people		
Men	9,824,000	$27,000
Women	970,000	$19,000
Machine operators and drivers of transportation equipment		
Men	11,333,000	$21,000
Women	3,412,000	$15,000
Service jobs (for example, waiters, guards, janitors, maids)		
Men	4,784,000	$18,000
Women	4,702,000	$13,500
Farming, forestry, and fishing		
Men	1,266,000	$15,000
Women	161,000	$12,000

OCCUPATIONS THAT ARE GROWING

Below is a list of some of the fastest-growing occupations in the United States:

Health and medical field: medical assistants and secretaries, physicians, technicians, licensed practical nurses, home health aides

Computer science field: computer programmers and scientists, systems analysts

Human services: social workers, child care workers, chefs and cooks, gardeners and groundskeepers

Corrections officers

Teaching: elementary, secondary, and adult-education teachers

Travel: travel agents and flight attendants

TRADE

When companies or countries buy and sell their products or services to other companies or countries, we call this **trade. Exports** are goods that one country *sells* to another country. **Imports** are goods that one country *buys* from another country. The United States trades with many other countries. It exports and imports goods.

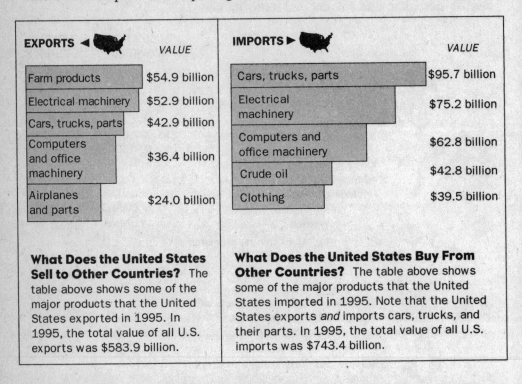

EXPORTS ◄	VALUE
Farm products	$54.9 billion
Electrical machinery	$52.9 billion
Cars, trucks, parts	$42.9 billion
Computers and office machinery	$36.4 billion
Airplanes and parts	$24.0 billion

IMPORTS ►	VALUE
Cars, trucks, parts	$95.7 billion
Electrical machinery	$75.2 billion
Computers and office machinery	$62.8 billion
Crude oil	$42.8 billion
Clothing	$39.5 billion

What Does the United States Sell to Other Countries? The table above shows some of the major products that the United States exported in 1995. In 1995, the total value of all U.S. exports was $583.9 billion.

What Does the United States Buy From Other Countries? The table above shows some of the major products that the United States imported in 1995. Note that the United States exports *and* imports cars, trucks, and their parts. In 1995, the total value of all U.S. imports was $743.4 billion.

Who Are America's Leading Trading Partners? In 1995, the countries with which the United States traded most were: Canada, Japan, Mexico, Germany, China, and Great Britain.

Why Do Americans Buy Foreign-made Products? Americans buy products from abroad that (1) they do not make for themselves or (2) that are less expensive or better-made than products made in the United States. For example, the United States imports most of its clothing because foreign-made products are less expensive.

What Happens If a Country Imports More Than It Exports? When the United States sells to other countries (or exports), other countries pay the United States for the goods. When the United States buys from other countries (or imports), it makes payments to them. It is best for a country to export more than it imports, or to export and import an equal amount. When a country imports more than it exports, it has what is called a **trade deficit.** The United States imports more than it exports and has a trade deficit. That means it is spending more money abroad for foreign-made products than it is getting from selling American-made products overseas.

The BUSIEST PORTS in the United States

Can you guess where the busiest ports in the United States are? Most products that are imported into the United States and exported to other countries from the United States travel by ship over oceans and other bodies of water. The busiest U.S. ports are on the east coast (near the Atlantic Ocean), on the west coast (near the Pacific Ocean), and in the south (near the Gulf of Mexico). The table below lists the five busiest ports and the tons of cargo they handled in 1993.

Port	Tons of cargo in 1993
Port of South Louisiana	193.8 million tons
Houston, Texas	141.5 million tons
New York, New York (and New Jersey)	116.7 million tons
Valdez, Alaska	85.7 million tons
Baton Rouge, Louisiana	85.1 million tons

Some ports specialize in certain goods. Valdez, Alaska, for example, is known for oil from the Alaska pipeline. Long Beach, California, is noted as the arrival port for many Japanese cars being imported into the United States.

What Are EXCHANGE RATES?

When one country exports goods to another, the payment from the country buying the goods must be changed into the currency of the country selling the goods. An **exchange rate** is the price of one national currency in terms of another. For example, 1 U.S. dollar was equivalent to (or could buy) 5.1 French francs in 1996. The ratio of 1 to 5.1 is the exchange rate between the U.S. dollar and the French franc.

Exchange rates are not the same all the time. As a nation's economy becomes stronger or weaker, the exchange rates also change. The following chart compares the exchange rates in 1970 and 1996 between the U.S. dollar and five of the country's most important trading partners. The more foreign currency the dollar can buy, the better the exchange rate for Americans.

		$1 BOUGHT:	
COUNTRY	**IN 1970**		**IN 1996**
France	5.5 francs		5.1 francs
Germany	3.6 marks		1.5 marks
Great Britain	.42 pounds		.66 pounds
Japan	358 yen		106 yen
Italy	623 lira		1,561 lira

$4 — U.S.

about 20 francs — France

In 1996, products from France cost the United States a little more than they did in 1970. Products from Germany and Japan cost the United States much more than they did in 1970, and products from Great Britain and Italy cost less.

Some MOVIES Popular With KIDS

Snow White and the Seven Dwarfs (1937). This Disney classic was the first movie-length cartoon ever released. Since the late 1980s, Disney's new animated movies, such as *Beauty and the Beast, Aladdin, The Lion King,* and *Pocahontas* have been popular with adults almost as much as with kids.

The Wizard of Oz (1939). This movie made Judy Garland a star and "Over the Rainbow" a popular hit song. During the movie's filming, however, some people wanted to cut the song, thinking that it slowed down the action.

National Velvet (1944). This is the story of two kids and their beloved racehorse.

The Sound of Music (1965). Winner of five Academy Awards, including Best Picture, this musical tells the story of Maria Von Trapp, whose plans to become a nun change when she becomes the governess to seven children and falls in love with their father.

E.T. The Extra-Terrestrial (1982). A heartwarming tale about a boy and a space alien whose deep relationship helps them both to grow. "E.T., phone home" became the catchphrase for the year.

Anne of Green Gables (1985). This movie is based on the novel by L. M. Montgomery about the experience of a young girl who is adopted by a family living on Canada's isolated Prince Edward Island.

Some MOVIES Popular With Older KIDS

The movies below, which are rated PG or PG-13, have been popular with some of the older kids.

Star Wars (1977). Luke Skywalker, Princess Leia, and others battle Darth Vader and the forces of evil in a thriller set in outer space. Two sequels to *Star Wars, The Empire Strikes Back* (1980) and *The Return of the Jedi* (1983), were also huge hits. (PG)

Home Alone (1990). An 8-year-old kid left home alone by accident outwits the bad guys all by himself but decides that, in the end, he'd rather have his family back anyway. (PG)

Wayne's World (1992). Based on a *Saturday Night Live* skit about two wacky teenagers obsessed with rock 'n' roll and TV. Wayne and Garth match wits (as best they can) with a sleazy guy, who wants to get rich off their public-access cable TV show. (PG-13)

Jurassic Park (1993). A thriller about dinosaurs created in a lab from DNA found in fossils and put on a Caribbean island as the attraction in what is supposed to be a secure park. It's not. (PG-13)

20 MOVIE HITS OF 1995

Apollo 13 (PG)
Toy Story (G)
Pocahontas (G)
Casper (PG)
While You Were Sleeping (PG)
Babe (G)
Father of the Bride Part II (PG)
Man of the House (PG)
Mighty Morphin Power
    Rangers (PG)
The Indian in the Cupboard (PG)
A Goofy Movie (G)
Little Women (PG)
Free Willy 2 (PG)
Sabrina (PG)
The Jungle Book (PG)
Operation Dumbo Drop (PG)
Richie Rich (PG)
The Big Green (PG)
Heavyweights (PG)
I.Q. (PG)

▲ Toy Story

MOVIE-MAKING TALK

cameo
A brief appearance in a movie by a major star, usually in a small, rather unimportant role. Sometimes the star doing the cameo doesn't even receive billing (or listing) in the movie credits.

dubbing
Adding sound to a scene or a movie that has already been shot. Films are often dubbed when they are shown in countries where the language is different from the language in which the movie was originally shot. Another word for dubbing is *looping*.

editing
The process of choosing which of the scenes filmed will actually make it into the final movie and deciding on the order they should take. Editing also involves combining the finished movie with the sound track.

extra
An actor who is hired by the day to play a small non-speaking part, such as someone in a crowd or someone sitting in a park.

freeze-frame
A camera shot that seems to stop in an instant all the action on the screen.

outtake
A shot filmed by the camera operator but not used in the final movie, either because it just doesn't fit in or because one of the actors flubbed a line.

rushes
The first prints of a day's shooting. The prints are developed in a rush and given to the director, so that he or she can see how well the movie is coming along. Rushes are also called *dailies*.

Some BEST-SELLING VIDEOS in 1995

The Lion King (G)
Jurassic Park (PG-13)
The Mask (PG)
Snow White and the Seven
  Dwarfs (G)
The Land Before Time II (G)

The Little Rascals (PG)
The Flintstones (PG)
Star Wars Trilogy (PG)
Angels in the Outfield (PG)
The Nightmare Before
  Christmas (PG)

Popular VIDEO GAMES in 1995

Super Nintendo Donkey Kong
  Country
Genesis Donkey Kong Country 2
Super Nintendo Super Mario World 2:
  Yoshi's Island
Genesis Madden NFL '96
Genesis NBA Jam Tournament
  Edition

Super Nintendo NBA Jam Tournament
  Edition
Super Nintendo Lion King
Genesis NBA Live '96
Genesis NHL '96
Genesis Lion King
Genesis Toy Story

Popular TV SHOWS in 1995-1996

▲ *The Cast of Friends.*
©1996 Warner Bros. All Rights Reserved.

AGES 6-11
1. Step by Step
2. Boy Meets World
3. Hangin' With Mr. Cooper
4. Aliens in the Family
5. Family Matters
6. Muppets Tonight
7. Home Improvement
8. Simpsons
9. America's Funniest Home Videos
10. Lois & Clark

AGES 12-17
1. Friends
2. Home Improvement
3. Simpsons
4. In the House
5. Boy Meets World
6. Step by Step
7. Seinfeld
8. Fresh Prince of Bel Air
9. Hangin' With Mr. Cooper
10. Single Guy

(SOURCE: *Nielsen Media Research*)

Visiting the PAST and the FUTURE

If you like to learn new things and have fun at the same time, museums are the places to go. Some museums, like children's museums, have exhibits on many subjects. Some museums have exhibits in which you can learn a lot about one subject, such as people who share the same customs. In another kind of museum, you can walk in a village from an earlier time in history and watch people from another century work and go about their daily lives. This type of museum is called an historic restoration.

The ancient Greeks were the first people to have public museums open to everyone. The oldest museum in the United States in continuous existence is the Charleston Museum, founded in South Carolina in 1773 to gather material on the natural history of that colony. The United States now has more than 7,000 museums. A few children's museums, ethnic museums, museums of entertainment, and historic restorations are listed below. Look in the INDEX for museums of art, computers, natural history, and science.

CHILDREN'S MUSEUMS

Children's museums often have many different types of hands-on exhibits.

Children's Museum, Inc., Boston, Massachusetts
Has a full-size Japanese house, a Latino market, plus displays on Native Americans.
Visitors (1995), 395,000

Children's Museum of Indianapolis, Indianapolis, Indiana
Has natural science exhibits, including a walk-through limestone cave; computer center; old-fashioned railway depot with a 19th-century locomotive and caboose; exhibits about people around the world, including interactive videos.
Visitors (1995), 920,554

Children's Museum of Manhattan, New York, New York
Displays on natural history, science, and art. Visitors (1995), 250,000

Children's Museum, Portland, Oregon
Hands-on displays on transportation, natural history, and toys.
Visitors (1995), 86,000

Los Angeles Children's Museum, Los Angeles, California
Exhibits on health and city life; has a TV studio. Visitors (1995), 250,000

MUSEUMS OF ENTERTAINMENT

Country Music Hall of Fame and Museum, Nashville, Tennessee
Celebrates country music's history and stars, displaying costumes and instruments connected with country music. Visitors (1995), 230,000

Graceland, Memphis, Tennessee
The 14-acre estate of the King of Rock 'n' Roll, Elvis Presley. Visitors (1995), 700,000

Museum of Television and Radio, New York, New York
Contains 15,000 radio and 35,000 TV tapes from the 1920s to the present. Visitors (1995), 127,927

ETHNIC MUSEUMS

Below are some museums that show the culture or the history of groups of people who share traditions and customs.

Arthur M. Sackler Gallery and the **Freer Gallery of Art,** Washington, D.C.
Displays paintings and other art objects from China, Japan, Korea, India, Iran, and other Asian countries.
Visitors (1995), 612,254

California Afro-American Museum, Los Angeles, California
Displays art, books, and photographs on African-American culture. Visitors (1995), 250,541

Gilcrease Museum, Tulsa, Oklahoma
Exhibits on the Five Civilized Tribes (Cherokee, Choctaw, Chickasaw, Creek, and Seminole). Visitors (1995), 136,318

▲ *Chinese jar*

▲ *Native American bowl*

Heard Museum, Phoenix, Arizona
Displays art by Native Americans and artists from Africa, Asia, Oceania, and the Upper Amazon. Visitors (1995), 250,000

University of Texas Institute of Texan Cultures, San Antonio, Texas
Exhibits on 24 ethnic groups showing historical and cultural contributions. Visitors (1995), 359,915

Jewish Museum, New York, New York
Exhibits covering 40 centuries of Jewish history and culture. Visitors (1995), 180,000

National Museum of African Art, Washington, D.C.
Displays African art made of many materials—wood, ivory, metal, and ceramic. Visitors (1995), 317,000

National Museum of the American Indian,
New York, New York
A branch of the Smithsonian Institution, this new museum features displays on the way of life and the history of Native Americans. Visitors (1995), 250,000

▲ *African sculpture*

HISTORIC RESTORATIONS

Historic restorations are often houses or parts of villages that have been restored to look the way they did many years ago. People in the village dress in costumes of an earlier time and show what daily life was like then.

Boot Hill Museum, Inc., Dodge City, Kansas
Historic buildings in this famous Western town, including the Fort Dodge jail. Visitors (1995), 123,821

Colonial Williamsburg, Williamsburg, Virginia
Restoration of the colonial capital of Virginia to its 18th-century appearance, with 88 original buildings. Visitors (1995), 942,000

Henry Ford Museum and Greenfield Village, Dearborn, Michigan
More than 80 historic buildings and more than 1 million artifacts on American history. Visitors (1995), 1,094,168

Mystic Seaport, Mystic, Connecticut
Re-creation of a 19th-century New England whaling village, including ships and a museum. Visitors (1995), 464,367

Old Sturbridge Village, Sturbridge, Massachusetts
Re-creation of a New England farming community of the 1830s, with more than 40 buildings. Visitors (1995), 447,429

Pioneer Arizona Living History Museum, Phoenix, Arizona
Twenty houses show pioneer life in a 19th-century rural town. Visitors (1995), 47,103

Plimoth Plantation, Inc., Plymouth, Massachusetts
Re-creation of the Pilgrims' first settlement in the New World. Visitors (1995), 450,000

Shelburne Museum, Inc., Shelburne, Vermont
Re-created New England village with 37 buildings and the *S.S. Ticonderoga*. Visitors (1995), 155,000

St. Augustine Historic District, St. Augustine, Florida
Includes the Oldest House (Gonzalez-Alvarez House), showing life in St. Augustine over 400 years. Visitors (1995), 60,000

Scene from a historic restoration ▶

MUSIC and MUSIC MAKERS

CLASSICAL MUSIC

People often think of classical music as serious music. Often more complex than other types of music, classical music is usually written to be listened to closely, as at a concert, rather than as background for another activity. Common forms of classical music include the symphony, chamber music, opera, and ballet music. **Famous early classical composers:** Johann Sebastian Bach, Ludwig van Beethoven, Johannes Brahms, Franz Joseph Haydn, Wolfgang Amadeus Mozart, Franz Schubert, Peter Ilyich Tchaikovsky, Richard Wagner. **Famous modern classical composers:** Aaron Copland, Virgil Thomson, Charles Ives, Igor Stravinsky.

CHAMBER MUSIC

Chamber music is written for a small group of musicians, often only three or four, to play together. In chamber music, each instrument plays a separate part. A string quartet (music written for two violins, viola, and cello) is an example of chamber music.

SYMPHONY

A symphony is music written for an orchestra. Symphonies usually have four parts called *movements*. The first movement is usually fast; the second is usually slow, and the last two are fast.

OPERA

An opera is a play whose words are sung to music. The music is played by an orchestra. The words of an opera are called the **libretto**, and a long song sung by one character (like a speech in a play) is called an **aria**. **Famous operas:** *Madama Butterfly* (Giacomo Puccini); *Aida* (Guiseppe Verdi).

VOICE

There are six common types of voices, three for men and three for women. Women's voices usually range from *soprano* (highest) to *mezzo-soprano* (middle) to *alto* (lowest). Men's voices range from *tenor* (highest) to *baritone* (middle) to *bass* (lowest).

MUSICAL NOTATION

These are some of the symbols composers use when they write music.

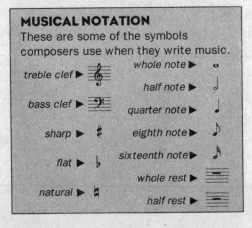

treble clef ▶

bass clef ▶

sharp ▶

flat ▶

natural ▶

whole note ▶

half note ▶

quarter note ▶

eighth note ▶

sixteenth note ▶

whole rest ▶

half rest ▶

? DID YOU KNOW? **Ludwig van Beethoven** started to go deaf in his twenties. By the end of his life, he had completely lost his hearing, yet he continued to compose and play music. **Wolfgang Amadeus Mozart** was eight years old when he wrote his first symphony. **Johann Sebastian Bach** came from a well-known musical family. Over the course of about 300 years, more than 30 of his relatives made their living as musicians.

More MUSIC and MUSIC MAKERS

BLUES

The music called "the blues" developed from work songs and religious folk songs (called spirituals) sung by African-Americans. It was introduced early in the 1900s by African-American musicians, especially the composer W. C. Handy. Blues songs are usually sad.

Famous blues performers: Ma Rainey, Bessie Smith, Buddy Guy, B. B. King, Muddy Waters. (A type of jazz is also called "the blues.")

JAZZ

Jazz is a type of American music that emphasizes rhythm and improvisation. Improvising means creating music as you play it, rather than performing written music. Jazz was created in the 1900s by African-Americans, mostly in large cities.

Famous jazz performers: Louis Armstrong, Fats Waller, Jelly Roll Morton, Duke Ellington, Benny Goodman, Billie Holiday, Sarah Vaughan, Ella Fitzgerald, Dizzy Gillespie, Charlie Parker, Miles Davis, Thelonious Monk, Wynton Marsalis.

COUNTRY MUSIC

Country music is American music based on southern mountain music. It has also been influenced by blues, jazz, and other popular musical styles. Country music became well known through the *Grand Ole Opry* radio show in Nashville, Tennessee.

Famous country performers: Johnny Cash, Dolly Parton, Willie Nelson, Garth Brooks, Travis Tritt, Vince Gill, Reba McEntire.

POP MUSIC

Pop music (short for popular music) puts more emphasis on melody (tune) than does rock and has a softer beat. It is often called "lite" music.

Famous pop singers: Frank Sinatra, Barbra Streisand, Whitney Houston, Madonna, Michael Jackson, Mariah Carey, Boyz II Men, Brandy.

ROCK (also known as rock 'n' roll)

Rock music, which started in the 1950s, has a strong, rhythmic beat. It is based on black rhythm and blues and country music. It often uses electronic instruments and equipment. Folk rock, punk, heavy metal, and alternative music are types of rock music.

Famous rock musicians: Elvis Presley, Bob Dylan, the Beatles, Janis Joplin, the Rolling Stones, Bruce Springsteen, Aerosmith, R.E.M., Pearl Jam, Joni Mitchell, Melissa Etheridge.

RAP MUSIC

Spoken, rhymed words backed by strong rhythm and music, rap was created by African-Americans in inner cities. Rap artists say their music describes what they see, hear, and experience, including the dreams, fears, anger, and violence in their communities.

Famous rappers: Arrested Development, Coolio, TLC.

▼ *Hootie and the Blowfish*

TOP ALBUM ARTISTS FOR 1995
(Including rank, artist, title, and label)
1. Hootie and the Blowfish, *Cracked Rear View*, Atlanta
2. Garth Brooks, *The Hits*, Capitol Nashville
3. Boyz II Men, *II*, Motown
4. Pearl Jam, *Vitalogy*, Epic
5. Eagles, *Hell Freezes Over*, Geffen

INSTRUMENTS of the ORCHESTRA

The instruments of an orchestra are divided into four groups, or sections: string, woodwind, brass, and percussion. In an orchestra with 100 musicians, usually more than 60 play string instruments. The rest play woodwinds, brasses, or percussion instruments.

STRINGS

Stringed instruments make sounds when the strings are either stroked with a bow or plucked with the fingers. The violin, viola, cello, bass, and harp are stringed instruments used in an orchestra. The guitar, banjo, balalaika, mandolin, koto, and dulcimer are other examples of stringed instruments.

WOODWINDS

Woodwind instruments are long and round and hollow inside. They make sounds when air is blown into them through a mouth hole or a reed. The clarinet, flute, oboe, bassoon, and piccolo are woodwinds.

BRASSES

Brass instruments are also hollow inside. They make sounds when air is blown into a mouthpiece shaped like a cup or a funnel. The trumpet, French horn, trombone, and tuba are brasses.

PERCUSSION INSTRUMENTS

Percussion instruments make sounds when they are struck. The most common percussion instrument is the drum, which comes in many forms. Other percussion instruments include cymbals, triangles, gongs, bells, and xylophone. Keyboard instruments, like the piano, are sometimes thought of as percussion instruments.

A TYPICAL ORCHESTRA

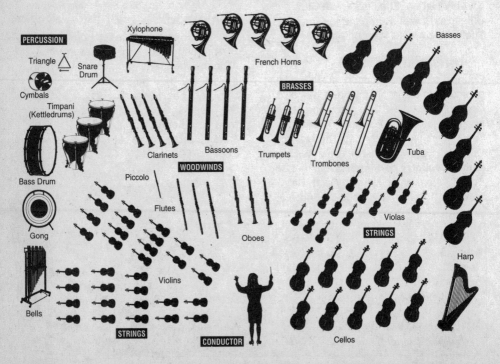

PERCUSSION

Triangle

Cymbals

Timpani (Kettledrums)

Snare Drum

Bass Drum

Gong

Bells

Xylophone

Piccolo

Flutes

Clarinets

WOODWINDS

Bassoons

Oboes

French Horns

BRASSES

Trumpets

Trombones

Tuba

Violas

STRINGS

Violins

STRINGS

CONDUCTOR

Cellos

Basses

Harp

AMERICAN MUSICAL THEATER

American musicals are plays known for their lively music and songs, comedy routines, dancing, colorful costumes, and elaborate stage sets. In the early 1900s, most musicals did not tell a story. They were simply a series of songs, dances, and comedy skits and were called musical revues. These were written by George M. Cohan, Irving Berlin, Oscar Hammerstein II, Richard Rodgers, and others. By the 1930s and 1940s, it was more common for musicals to have plots, with songs and dances used to help tell the story and to express the characters' feelings.

> **Longest running American musical:** *The Fantasticks,* by Tom Jones and Harvey Schmidt. Opened May 3, 1960. By mid-1996, there had been nearly 15,000 performances.
>
> **Tony (Antoinette Perry) Awards:** Tony Awards are given every year to outstanding Broadway plays. **1996 Tony Award winner for best musical:** *Rent,* with music and lyrics by Jonathan Larson

SOME OTHER FAMOUS MUSICALS

In the list below, the date after the name of the play is the year the play opened on Broadway, the theater district of New York City. Broadway is actually a very long street that runs through the city. The theater district is made up of part of the street and several surrounding blocks where many theaters are located.

Annie (1977), by Charles Strouse and Martin Charnin. Tony Award 1977.

Annie Get Your Gun (1946), by Irving Berlin.

Anything Goes (1930), by Cole Porter.

Beauty and the Beast (1994), by Alan Menken, Howard Ashman, and Tim Rice.

Brigadoon (1947), by Alan Jay Lerner and Frederick Loewe.

Cabaret (1966), by John Kander and Fred Ebb. Tony Award 1967.

Carousel (1945), by Richard Rodgers and Oscar Hammerstein II.

Cats (1982), by Andrew Lloyd Webber. Tony Award 1983.

A Chorus Line (1975), by Marvin Hamlisch and Edward Kleban. Tony Award 1976.

Evita (1979), by Andrew Lloyd Webber and Tim Rice. Tony Award 1980.

Fiddler on the Roof (1964), by Jerry Bock and Sheldon Harnick. Tony Award 1964.

Grease (1972), by Jim Jacobs and Warren Casey.

Guys and Dolls (1950), by Frank Loesser. Tony Award 1951.

Hello, Dolly! (1964), by Jerry Herman. Tony Award 1964.

The King and I (1952), by Richard Rodgers and Oscar Hammerstein II. Tony Award 1952.

Kiss Me Kate (1948), by Cole Porter. Tony Award 1949.

Kiss of the Spider Woman (1993), by John Kander and Fred Ebb. Tony Award 1993.

My Fair Lady (1956), by Alan Jay Lerner and Frederick Loewe. Tony Award 1957.

The Music Man (1957), by Meredith Willson. Tony Award 1958.

Of Thee I Sing (1931), by George and Ira Gershwin.

Oklahoma! (1943), by Richard Rodgers and Oscar Hammerstein II.

The Pajama Game (1954), by Richard Adler and Jerry Ross. Tony Award 1955.

Porgy and Bess (1935), by George Gershwin.

Show Boat (1927), by Jerome Kern and Oscar Hammerstein II.

The Sound of Music (1959), by Richard Rodgers and Oscar Hammerstein II.

South Pacific (1949), by Richard Rodgers and Oscar Hammerstein II. Tony Award 1950.

West Side Story (1957), by Leonard Bernstein and Stephen Sondheim.

DANCE

In dance, the body performs patterns of movement, usually to music or rhythm. Dance may be a form of art, or it may be part of a religious ceremony. Dance may express feelings and ideas, or it may be done just for fun. Ballet, modern dance, folk dance, and social dance are major forms of dance.

BALLET

Dances in ballet are based on formal steps performed in graceful, flowing movements. Ballets are performed for an audience and often tell a story. In the 15th century, ballet was part of the elaborate entertainment that was performed for the rulers of Europe. In the 1600s, professional dance companies existed, but without women. Women's parts were danced by men wearing masks. In the 1700s dancers wore bulky costumes and shoes with high heels. Women danced in hoopskirts—and so did men! In the 1800s ballet steps and costumes began to look the way they do now. In fact, many of the most popular ballets today date back to the middle or late 1800s.

SOME FAMOUS BALLETS

Swan Lake. First danced in St. Petersburg, Russia, in 1895. Perhaps the most popular ballet ever, *Swan Lake* is the story of a prince and his love for a maiden who was turned into a swan by an evil magician.

The Nutcracker. When this ballet was first performed in St. Petersburg, Russia, in 1892, it was a colossal flop. It has since become so popular that it is danced in many places every year at Christmastime.

The Sleeping Beauty is based on the fairy tale *The Sleeping Beauty.* The ballet was first danced in St. Petersburg in 1890.

Jewels. This ballet by the American choreographer George Balanchine was first performed in New York City in 1967. In *Jewels,* the dancers do not dance to a story. They explore patterns and movement of the human body.

The River. This 1970 ballet by Alvin Ailey is danced to music by the famous jazz musician Duke Ellington. It has been described as a ballet of imaginative movement and a celebration of life.

NOTED BALLET DANCERS
Anna Pavlova (1885-1931)
Vaslav Nijinsky (1890-1950)
Margot Fonteyn (1919-1991)
Arthur Mitchell (born 1934)
Rudolph Nureyev (1938-1993)
Mikhail Baryshnikov (born 1948)

NOTED CHOREOGRAPHERS
Marius Petipa (1818-1910)
Michel Fokine (1880-1942)
George Balanchine (1904-1983)
Agnes de Mille (1908-1993)
Jerome Robbins (born 1918)
Kenneth MacMillan (1929-1992)

MODERN DANCE

Modern dance differs from classical ballet in many ways. It is less concerned with graceful, flowing movement and the appearance of weightlessness. Modern dance steps are often not ballet steps or positions. Dancers may put their bodies into awkward, angular positions and turn their backs on the audience. Many modern dances are based on ancient art, such as Greek sculpture, or on dance styles found in Africa and Asia.

Noted Modern Dancers and Choreographers. Many of the most important modern dance choreographers, including those on this list, are also dancers.

Alvin Ailey (1931-1989)
Trisha Brown (born 1936)
Merce Cunningham (born 1919)
Isadora Duncan (1878-1927)

Martha Graham (1894-1991)
Mark Morris (born 1956)
Paul Taylor (born 1930)
Twyla Tharp (born 1941)

FOLK DANCE. Folk dance is the term for a dance that is passed on from generation to generation and that in some way is part of the culture or way of life of people from a particular country or ethnic group. Virginia reel (American), czardas (Hungarian), jig, and the Israeli hora are some folk dances.

SOCIAL DANCE. Social dance is the name for dances done just for fun by ordinary people. They are not made up by professionals or danced by trained dancers for an audience. Instead, they are danced at parties and clubs. Social dancing has been around since at least the Middle Ages, when it was popular at fairs and festivals. In the 1400s social dance was part of fancy court pageants. It developed into dainty dances like the minuet and the waltz during the 1700s and eventually, in the 20th century, into such dances as the Charleston, the lindy, the twist, disco, and break dancing, as well as line dances such as the achy-breaky.

DANCE TALK

arabesque (ar-a-BESK)
A ballet pose in which the dancer balances on one leg, puts the other behind, toes pointed, and extends one arm in front and the other behind, creating the illusion of a straight line from fingertip in front to toe in back.

choreographer (core-e-OG-ra-fer)
The person who makes up the steps to be danced.

corps de ballet (core de bal-LAY)
The group of dancers, usually less experienced, who dance together, with or without the stars of the ballet.

position
The way that dancers place their arms and feet. In ballet there are five standard positions for the arms and five for the feet.

prima ballerina (PREE-ma)
In ballet, a woman who is one of the star dancers in her company and who takes on leading roles.

pas de deux (pa de DU)
A part of a ballet in which a man and a woman dance a duet together.

Numerals in ANCIENT CIVILIZATIONS

People have been counting since the earliest of times. This is what some early numerals looked like.

Modern	1	2	3	4	5	6	7	8	9	10	20	50	100
Egyptian	I	II	III	IIII	III III	III III	IIII III	IIII IIII	IIII IIIII	∩	∩∩	∩∩∩∩∩	𐤒
Baby-lonian	𒁹	𒁹𒁹	𒁹𒁹𒁹	𒐬	𒐮	𒐯	𒐰	𒐱	𒐲	𒌋	𒌍	𒐏	𒐕
Greek	A	B	Γ	Δ	E	F	Z	H	θ	I	K	N	P
Mayan	•	••	•••	••••	—	•̲	••̲	•••̲	••••̲	≡	⊙	⊡	◉
Chinese	一	二	三	四	五	六	七	八	九	十	二十	五十	百
Hindu	I	२	३	৪	५	६	७	८	९	10	20	40	100
Arabic	I	٢	٣	٤	٥	٦	٧	٨	٩	1٠	2٠	8٠	10٠

ROMAN NUMERALS

Roman numerals are still used today. The symbols used to represent different numbers are the letters I (1), V (5), X (10), L (50), C (100), D (500), and M (1,000). If one Roman numeral is followed by a larger one, the first is subtracted from the second. For example, the numeral IX means 10 − 1 = 9. Think of it as "one less than ten." On the other hand, if one Roman numeral is followed by another that is equal or smaller, add them together. Therefore, VII means 5 + 1 + 1 = 7.

1	I	11	XI	30	XXX	400	CD
2	II	12	XII	40	XL	500	D
3	III	13	XIII	50	L	600	DC
4	IV	14	XIV	60	LX	700	DCC
5	V	15	XV	70	LXX	800	DCCC
6	VI	16	XVI	80	LXXX	900	CM
7	VII	17	XVII	90	XC	1,000	M
8	VIII	18	XVIII	100	C		
9	IX	19	XIX	200	CC		
10	X	20	XX	300	CCC		

Can you write the year on the front cover of this book in Roman numerals? The answer is on page 304.

The PREFIX Tells the Number

Each number listed below has one or more prefixes used to form words that include that number. Knowing which number the prefix stands for helps you to understand the meaning of the word. For example, a unicycle has 1 wheel. A triangle has 3 sides. An octopus has 8 tentacles. Next to the prefixes are some examples of words that use these prefixes.

1	uni-, mon-, mono-	unicycle, unicorn, monarch, monotone
2	bi-, di-	bicycle, binary, binoculars, bifocals, disect
3	tri-	tricycle, triangle, trilogy, triplet
4	quadr-, tetr-	quadrangle, quadruplet, tetrahedron
5	pent-, penta-	pentagon, pentathlon
6	hex-, hexa-	hexagon
7	hepta-	heptathlon
8	oct-, octa-, octo-	octave, octet, octopus, octagon
9	nona-	nonagon
10	dec-, deca-	decade, decibel, decimal
100	cent-	centipede, century
1000	kilo-	kilogram, kilometer
million	mega-	megabyte, megahertz
billion	giga-	gigabyte, gigawatt

Reading and Writing LARGE NUMBERS

Below is the name of a number and the number of zeros that would follow it when the number is written out.

ten:	1 zero	10
hundred:	2 zeros	100
thousand:	3 zeros	1,000
ten thousand:	4 zeros	10,000
hundred thousand:	5 zeros	100,000
million:	6 zeros	1,000,000
ten million:	7 zeros	10,000,000
hundred million:	8 zeros	100,000,000
billion:	9 zeros	1,000,000,000
trillion:	12 zeros	1,000,000,000,000
quadrillion:	15 zeros	1,000,000,000,000,000
quintillion:	18 zeros	1,000,000,000,000,000,000
sextillion:	21 zeros	1,000,000,000,000,000,000,000
septillion:	24 zeros	1,000,000,000,000,000,000,000,000

A googol! What's a googol?!

Look below to see how numbers larger than these would be written:

octillion has 27 zeros	decillion has 33 zeros
nonillion has 30 zeros	googol has 100 zeros

How Many SIDES and FACES Do They Have?

When a figure is flat (two-dimensional), it is a **plane figure**. When a figure takes up space (three-dimensional), it is a **solid figure**. The flat surface of a solid figure is called a **face**. Plane and solid figures come in many different shapes.

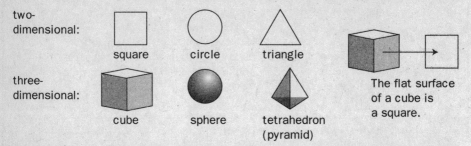

two-dimensional: square   circle   triangle

three-dimensional: cube   sphere   tetrahedron (pyramid)

The flat surface of a cube is a square.

WHAT ARE POLYGONS? A polygon is a two-dimensional figure that has three or more straight sides (called line segments). A square is a polygon. Polygons have different numbers of sides—and each has a different name. If the sides of a polygon are all the same length and all the angles between the sides are equal, the polygon is called regular. If the sides are of different lengths or the angles are not equal, the polygon is called irregular. Below are some regular and irregular polygons.

NAME AND NUMBER OF SIDES	REGULAR	IRREGULAR	NAME AND NUMBER OF SIDES	REGULAR	IRREGULAR
triangle - 3			heptagon - 7		
quadrilateral or tetragon - 4			octagon - 8		
pentagon - 5			nonagon - 9		
hexagon - 6			decagon - 10		

WHAT ARE POLYHEDRONS? A polyhedron is a three-dimensional figure with four or more faces. Each face on a polyhedron is a polygon. Below are some polyhedrons with many faces.

tetrahedron 4 faces   hexahedron 6 faces   octahedron 8 faces   dodecahedron 12 faces   icosahedron 20 faces

NUMBERS PUZZLES

HOW HIGH IS THE HIGHEST MOUNTAIN IN THE WORLD?

If you fill in the numbers below and add or subtract (whichever is asked for), you will learn the height of the highest mountain in the world. Hints: The first two numbers are given to help you out. If you use a calculator, the puzzle will be much easier. (Answers are on page 304.)

Write down the number of miles from the Earth to the moon   238,900

Divide the number by 10, OR cross off the last zero   23,890

Add the number of feet in a mile (5,280)   + [   ]

= [   ]

Subtract the number of countries in the United Nations (see page 212)   − [   ]

= [   ]

Add the number of states in the United States   + [   ]

= [   ]

Subtract the number of days in a week   − [   ]

The answer is the height of the tallest mountain in the world in feet   = [   ] feet

WHAT IS THE NAME OF THE HIGHEST MOUNTAIN?

Can you decode the name of the highest mountain? (Answer is on page 304.)
A=1, B=2, C=3, D=4, E=5, F=6, G=7, H=8, I=9, J=10, K=11, L=12, M=13, N=14, O=15, P=16, Q=17, R=18, S=19, T=20, U=21, V=22, W=23, X=24, Y=25, Z=26

The name of the highest mountain in the world is

__ __ __ __ __   __ __ __ __ __ __ __
13 15 21 14 20   5 22 5 18 5 19 20

MAGIC SQUARE

Can you place the numbers 5 through 13 (using each number only once) in the boxes at the right so that any three numbers in a row across, down, or diagonally will add up to 27? The number 9 has been placed to help you get started. (One possible answer is given on page 304.)

	9	

? DID YOU KNOW? Did you know that calculators can spell? Well, they can. To get the words shown below, take a calculator, press the sets of numbers after each word, and then turn the calculator upside-down.

BELL 7738   HOBBIES 5318804
HELLO 0.7734   SHELL 77345
HIGH 4614   OIL 710
BOIL 7108   BIG LIE 317.618

The SOLAR SYSTEM

Nine planets, including Earth, travel around the sun. These planets, together with the sun, form the **solar system**.

THE SUN IS A STAR

Did you know that the sun is a star, like all the other stars you see at night? Although the sun is the brightest object in the sky, astronomers have found that as a star it is average in size, temperature, and brightness. The diameter of the sun is 864,000 miles. The gravity of the sun is nearly 28 times the gravity of Earth.

How Hot Is the Sun? The temperature of the sun's surface is close to 10,000°F, and the inner core may reach temperatures near 35 million degrees! The sun provides enough light and heat energy to support all forms of life on our planet.

THE PLANETS ARE IN MOTION

The planets move around the sun along oval-shaped paths called **orbits**. Each planet travels in its own orbit. One complete path around the sun is called a **revolution**. Earth takes one year, or 365 days, to make one revolution around the sun. Planets that are farther away from the sun take longer. Some planets have one or more **moons**. A moon orbits a planet in much the same way that the planets orbit the sun.

Each planet also spins (or rotates) on its axis. An **axis** is an imaginary line running through the center of a planet. The time it takes for one rotation of the planet Earth on its axis equals one day. Below are some facts about the planets and the symbol for each planet.

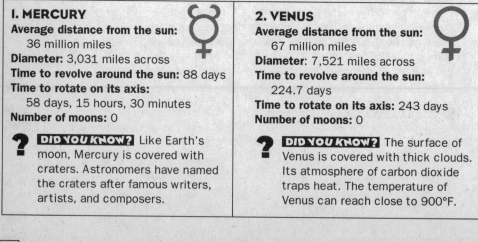

I. MERCURY
Average distance from the sun:
   36 million miles
Diameter: 3,031 miles across
Time to revolve around the sun: 88 days
Time to rotate on its axis:
   58 days, 15 hours, 30 minutes
Number of moons: 0

? **DID YOU KNOW?** Like Earth's moon, Mercury is covered with craters. Astronomers have named the craters after famous writers, artists, and composers.

2. VENUS
Average distance from the sun:
   67 million miles
Diameter: 7,521 miles across
Time to revolve around the sun:
   224.7 days
Time to rotate on its axis: 243 days
Number of moons: 0

? **DID YOU KNOW?** The surface of Venus is covered with thick clouds. Its atmosphere of carbon dioxide traps heat. The temperature of Venus can reach close to 900°F.

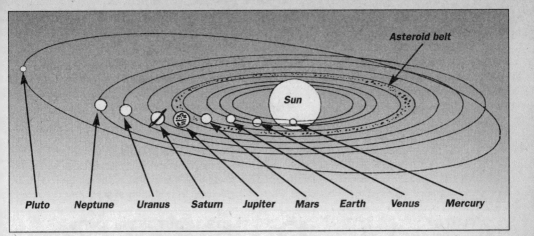

Asteroid belt

Sun

Pluto   Neptune   Uranus   Saturn   Jupiter   Mars   Earth   Venus   Mercury

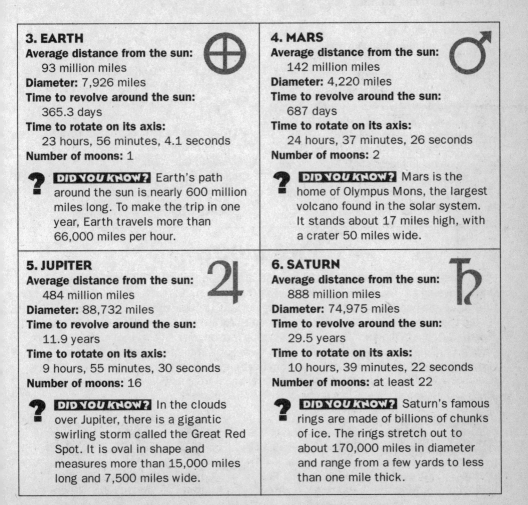

3. EARTH
Average distance from the sun:
 93 million miles
Diameter: 7,926 miles
Time to revolve around the sun:
 365.3 days
Time to rotate on its axis:
 23 hours, 56 minutes, 4.1 seconds
Number of moons: 1

? DID YOU KNOW? Earth's path around the sun is nearly 600 million miles long. To make the trip in one year, Earth travels more than 66,000 miles per hour.

4. MARS
Average distance from the sun:
 142 million miles
Diameter: 4,220 miles
Time to revolve around the sun:
 687 days
Time to rotate on its axis:
 24 hours, 37 minutes, 26 seconds
Number of moons: 2

? DID YOU KNOW? Mars is the home of Olympus Mons, the largest volcano found in the solar system. It stands about 17 miles high, with a crater 50 miles wide.

5. JUPITER
Average distance from the sun:
 484 million miles
Diameter: 88,732 miles
Time to revolve around the sun:
 11.9 years
Time to rotate on its axis:
 9 hours, 55 minutes, 30 seconds
Number of moons: 16

? DID YOU KNOW? In the clouds over Jupiter, there is a gigantic swirling storm called the Great Red Spot. It is oval in shape and measures more than 15,000 miles long and 7,500 miles wide.

6. SATURN
Average distance from the sun:
 888 million miles
Diameter: 74,975 miles
Time to revolve around the sun:
 29.5 years
Time to rotate on its axis:
 10 hours, 39 minutes, 22 seconds
Number of moons: at least 22

? DID YOU KNOW? Saturn's famous rings are made of billions of chunks of ice. The rings stretch out to about 170,000 miles in diameter and range from a few yards to less than one mile thick.

7. URANUS

Average distance from the sun:
  1.8 billion miles
Diameter: 31,763 miles
Time to revolve around the sun: 84 years
Time to rotate on its axis:
  17 hours, 14 minutes
Number of moons: 15

? DID YOU KNOW? Uranus was the first planet discovered with a telescope, by William Herschel in 1781. Its surface is covered with greenish clouds of methane gas.

8. NEPTUNE

Average distance from the sun:
  2.8 billion miles
Diameter: 30,775 miles
Time to revolve around the sun:
  164.8 years
Time to rotate on its axis:
  16 hours, 6 minutes
Number of moons: 8

? DID YOU KNOW? Neptune's largest moon is called Triton. At −393°F, Triton is the coldest place in the solar system.

9. PLUTO

Average distance from the sun:
  3.6 billion miles
Diameter: 1,429 miles
Time to revolve around the sun:
  247.7 years
Time to rotate on its axis:
  6 days, 9 hours, 17 minutes
Number of moons: 1

? DID YOU KNOW? Pluto's orbit is so strangely shaped that, since 1977, Pluto has been closer to the sun than Neptune. In March of 1999, Pluto will move beyond Neptune. So for the next few years, Pluto is actually the eighth planet from the sun.

FACTS ABOUT THE PLANETS

Largest planet: Jupiter
Smallest planet: Pluto
Planet closest to the sun: Mercury
Planet that comes closest to Earth:
  Venus (Every 19 months, Venus gets closer to Earth than any other planet.)
Fastest-moving planet: Mercury
  (107,000 miles per hour)
Slowest-moving planet: Pluto (10,600 miles per hour)
Warmest planet: Venus
Coldest planet: Pluto
Planet with the most moons: Saturn
  (At least 22 have been seen.)

THE MOON

Earth's satellite—the moon—is the only other body in the solar system that people have traveled to. The moon is about 238,900 miles from Earth. It is 2,160 miles in diameter and has no atmosphere. Its dusty surface is covered with deep craters. It takes the same amount of time for the moon to rotate on its axis as it does to orbit Earth (27 days, 7 hours, 43 minutes). For this reason, one side of the moon is always facing Earth. The moon has no light of its own, but it reflects light from the sun. The lighted part of the moon we can see from Earth is called a phase of the moon. It takes the moon 27 days to pass through all of its phases, from new moon to full moon and back to new moon. Below are some of these phases.

New Moon | Crescent Moon | First Quarter | Full Moon | Last Quarter | Crescent Moon | New Moon

COMETS, ASTEROIDS, and SATELLITES

Besides the planets and their moons, there are thousands of other objects in space that travel around the sun. These include comets, asteroids, and satellites.

Comets are fast-moving chunks of ice, dust, and rock that form long tails of gas as they move nearer to the sun. One of the most well-known is **Halley's Comet**. It can be seen every 76 years and will appear again in the year 2062.

Asteroids (or minor planets) are solid chunks of rock or metal that range in size from very small, like grains of sand, to very large. **Ceres**, the largest, is about 600 miles across. Thousands of asteroids orbit the sun between the planets Mars and Jupiter.

Satellites are objects that move in an orbit around a planet. Moons are natural satellites. Satellites made by humans are used to photograph Earth's surface and to transmit communications signals.

What Is an ECLIPSE?

An eclipse takes place when one heavenly body (like Earth or the moon) passes another heavenly body and blocks out the light.

SOLAR ECLIPSE. A **solar eclipse** occurs when the moon moves between the sun and Earth, casting a shadow over part of Earth. When the moon completely blocks out the sun, it is called a **total solar eclipse**. When this happens, a halo of gas can be seen around the sun. This halo of gas is called the **corona**.

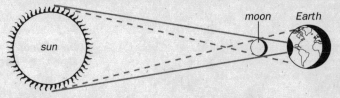

LUNAR ECLIPSE. Sometimes Earth casts a shadow on the moon. This is called a **lunar eclipse**. Usually, a lunar eclipse lasts longer than a solar eclipse. The moon remains visible, but becomes dark, often with a reddish tinge (from sunlight that is bent through Earth's atmosphere).

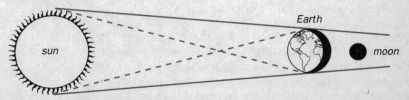

Some 1996-1997 Eclipses and Where They Can Be Seen

September 27, 1996: Total lunar eclipse. All of this eclipse will be visible from eastern North America. The end of it can be seen from the rest of North America.

March 9, 1997: Total solar eclipse. Visible in eastern Asia, Japan, and northwestern North America.

September 2, 1997: Partial solar eclipse. Visible mainly in southern Australia, New Zealand, and the South Pacific Ocean.

CONSTELLATIONS: Pictures in the Sky

Thousands of years ago, ancient astronomers grouped stars together to form pictures. These groupings are called **constellations**. Astronomers all over the world named the constellations after animals or mythological figures or tools. Many of the constellations we know today were named by the people living in ancient Greece and Rome. But many constellations could not be seen from that part of the world. Some constellations were named later, when Europeans began traveling to different parts of the world and saw many other constellations. Also, cultures in different parts of the world sometimes grouped the same stars into different constellations.

In 1930, the International Astronomical Union established a standard set of 88 constellations, which cover the entire sky that is visible from Earth. Astronomers use constellations as a quick way to locate other objects. For example, from Earth, the other planets moving around the sun appear in different constellations at different times.

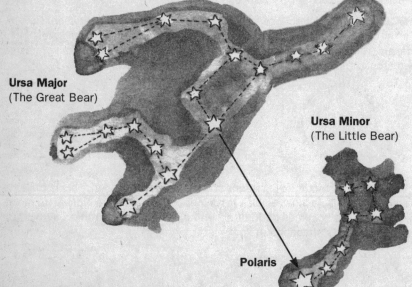

Ursa Major
(The Great Bear)

Ursa Minor
(The Little Bear)

Polaris

THE BIG AND LITTLE DIPPERS

The picture shows stars in the constellations
thought to resemble bears—Ursa Major (Great Bear)
and Ursa Minor (Little Bear). The tail and hips of the Great Bear are also
known as the Big Dipper. Ursa Minor is also known as the Little Dipper.

THE NORTH STAR

The last star in the handle of the Little Dipper is called Polaris, or the North Star.
Polaris always shines to the north. Throughout history, people have been using
Polaris to guide them in their travels. The two stars at the end of the bowl of the
Big Dipper always point in the direction of Polaris, making it easy to find.

The ZODIAC

The **zodiac** is an imaginary belt (or path) that goes around the sky. The orbits of the sun, the moon, and most of the planets are within the zodiac. Twelve of the constellations can also be found within the belt of the zodiac. The zodiac is divided into 12 equal sections. Each section is named for the constellation that occupies most of its space. Below are the symbols and signs of the zodiac.

Aries (Ram)	Taurus (Bull)	Gemini (Twins)	Cancer (Crab)
Leo (Lion)	Virgo (Maiden)	Libra (Balance)	Scorpio (Scorpion)
Sagittarius (Archer)	Capricorn (Goat)	Aquarius (Water Bearer)	Pisces (Fishes)

WHO IS INTERESTED IN THE SIGNS OF THE ZODIAC?

The stars in the constellations interest both astronomers and astrologers.
Astronomers are scientists who study the sky, including the stars, planets, moons, comets, asteroids, and meteors. Astronomers study what these are made of, how they behave, what they measure, how fast they move, and what gases they are made up of.
Astrologers are not scientists. Astrologers believe that the positions and movements of the sun, the moon, and the planets have an influence on the lives of people on Earth and can be used to predict the future.

Heavenly QUESTIONS and ANSWERS

WHAT IS A GALAXY?

A **galaxy** is a group of billions of stars that are held together by gravity. There may be about 50 billion galaxies in the universe. The galaxy we live in is called the **Milky Way**. The sun and every star we see at night are just a few of the 200 billion stars in the Milky Way. The Milky Way is so large that the light from a star along the edge of the galaxy would take about 100,000 years to reach the other side. Astronomers measure the distance between stars and between galaxies in light years. One **light year** is the distance that light travels in one year. Light travels about 186,282 miles in one second. In one year, light travels about 5.9 trillion miles.

? **DID YOU KNOW?** Light can travel around Earth seven times in one second. It takes light about eight minutes to travel from the sun to Earth.

WHAT ARE METEORS, METEORITES, AND METEOR SHOWERS?

On a clear night, you may see a sudden streak of light in the sky. It may be caused by chunks of rock or metal called **meteoroids** speeding through space. When a meteoroid enters Earth's atmosphere, friction with air molecules causes it to burn brightly. The streak we see is called a **meteor**, or **shooting star**.

Many meteoroids follow in the path of a comet as it orbits the sun. As these meteoroids enter Earth's atmosphere, large numbers of meteors can be seen coming from about the same point in the sky. These streaks are called **meteor showers**. If a meteoroid is large enough to reach the ground without burning up completely, it is called a **meteorite**.

? **DID YOU KNOW?** The largest known meteorite was found in Namibia in 1920. It is 9 feet long, 8 feet wide, and is estimated to weigh around 65 tons. The largest meteorite that can be seen in a museum is at the American Museum of Natural History in New York City. This meteorite weighs over 68,000 pounds. It was found in Greenland in 1897.

WHAT IS A BLACK HOLE?

Black holes cannot be seen, but astronomers know they are what remain at the end of the life of a star. Stars have limited life spans. Our sun, which is a star, is about 5 billion years old. It is expected to last another 5 billion years.

Eventually some stars merely stop shining, while others explode. Many astronomers believe that when a star explodes it may leave behind a chunk of matter as heavy as our sun yet only a few miles across. The force of gravity of this tiny star is so strong that nothing that comes close to it can escape its pull, not even light. These tiny stars are called black holes.

HOW DID THE UNIVERSE BEGIN?

Most astronomers believe that the universe began in a massive explosion 10 to 20 billion years ago and that it has been expanding ever since. This is called the **big bang theory**. Some believe that the universe will keep expanding forever. Others believe that the expansion will slow down over billions of years and that gravity will begin to cause the universe to collapse.

TRAVELING INTO OUTER SPACE

American exploration into space began in January 1958, when the United States launched the *Explorer 1* satellite into orbit. Several months later, on October 1, 1958, NASA (National Aeronautics and Space Administration) was formed to explore space for peaceful and scientific purposes. The rapid entry of the United States into space was in response to the Soviet Union's launching of its satellite *Sputnik 1* into orbit on October 4, 1957. In 1961, President John F. Kennedy promised Americans that the United States would land a person on the moon by the end of the 1960s. The "space race" between the United States and the Soviet Union continued throughout the 1960s and 1970s.

The following time line gives some of the major flights of astronauts into space, including the U.S. Apollo flights to the moon.

1961 — On April 12, Soviet cosmonaut Yuri Gagarin, in Vostok 1, became the **first human to orbit Earth**. On May 5, U.S. astronaut Alan B. Shepard Jr. of the Mercury 3 mission became the **first American in space**.

1962 — On February 20, U.S. astronaut John H. Glenn Jr. of Mercury 6 became the **first American to orbit Earth**.

1963 — From June 16 to 19, the Soviet spacecraft Vostok 6 carried the **first woman in space,** Valentina V. Tereshkova.

1965 — On March 18, Soviet cosmonaut Aleksei A. Leonov became the **first person to walk in space.** He spent 10 minutes outside the spaceship. On December 15, U.S. Gemini 6A and 7 (with astronauts) became the **first vehicles to rendezvous** (approach and see each other) **in space**.

1966 — On March 1, the Soviet probe Venera 3 crashed into Venus and became the **first humanmade object to land on another planet**. On March 16, U.S. Gemini 8 became the **first craft to dock with** (become attached to) **another vehicle** (an unmanned Agena rocket).

1967 — On January 27, a fire in a U.S. Apollo spacecraft killed astronauts Virgil I. Grissom, Edward H. White, and Roger B. Chaffee. On April 23, Soyuz 1 crashed to the ground, killing Soviet cosmonaut Vladimir Komarov.

1969 — On July 20, after successful flights of Apollo 8, 9, and 10, **U.S. Apollo 11's lunar module Eagle landed on the moon's surface** in the area known as the Sea of Tranquillity. Neil Armstrong became the **first person to walk on the moon**.

1970 — In April, Apollo 13 astronauts returned safely to Earth after an explosion damaged their spacecraft and prevented them from landing on the moon.

1971 — In July and August, U.S. Apollo 15 astronauts tested the **Lunar Rover** on the moon.

1972 — In December, Apollo 17 was the sixth and **final U.S. mission to land successfully on the moon**.

1973 — On May 14, the U.S. put the **first space station**, **Skylab**, **into orbit**. Crews worked in Skylab until January 1974, when the last crew left.

▲ *Lunar Rover on the Moon*

1975 — On July 15, the U.S. launched Apollo 18 and the U.S.S.R. launched Soyuz 19. Two days later, the **American and Soviet spacecraft docked**, and for several days their crews worked and spent time together in space. This was NASA's last space mission with astronauts until the Space Shuttle.

COOPERATION IN SPACE: The Space Shuttle and the Space Station

In an effort to reduce costs, NASA developed the space shuttle program during the 1970s. The U.S. space shuttle became the first reusable spacecraft. Earlier space capsules could not be used again after returning to Earth, but the space shuttle lands on a runway like an airplane and can be launched again at a later date. On space shuttle missions, astronauts perform many experiments, test equipment, and sometimes place satellites into orbit.

The European Space Agency, which was formed by some European countries in 1975, constructed the Spacelab scientific laboratory. Spacelab first rode a space shuttle in 1983. In 1986, the Soviet Union launched its successful Mir space station. By the mid-1990s, the United States and Russia were sharing projects in space.

1977 — On August 12, the first shuttle, **Enterprise**, tool off from the back of a 747 jet airliner.

1981 — On April 12, **Columbia** was launched and became the first shuttle to reach Earth orbit.

▲ U.S. Space Shuttle

1983 — In April, NASA began using a third shuttle, **Challenger**. Two more **Challenger** flights in 1983 included astronauts Sally K. Ride and Guion S. Bluford, Jr., the first American woman and African-American man in space. On November 28, **Columbia** was launched carrying the scientific laboratory Spacelab.

1984 — In August, the shuttle **Discovery** was launched for the first time.

1985 — In October, the shuttle **Atlantis** was launched for the first time.

1986 — On January 28, after 24 successful shuttle missions, **Challenger** exploded 73 seconds after takeoff. Astronauts Dick Scobee, Michael Smith, Ellison Onizuka, Judith Resnick, Greg Jarvis, and Ron McNair, and teacher Christa McAuliffe all died. In March, the Soviet space station **Mir** was launched into orbit.

1987 — On December 21, Soyuz TM-4 cosmonauts Vladimir Titov, Muso Manarov, and Anatoly Levchenko arrived at **Mir**. They stayed for one year, until December 21, 1988.

▲ Mir Space Station

1988 — On September 29, nearly two years after the Challenger disaster, new safety procedures led to the successful launch of **Discovery**.

1990 — On April 24, the **Hubble Space Telescope** was launched from **Discovery**, but the images sent back to Earth were fuzzy.

1992 — In May, NASA launched a new shuttle, **Endeavour**.

1993 — In December, a crew aboard **Endeavour** repaired the Hubble telescope.

1995 — On February 6, the U.S. shuttle **Discovery** approached within 40 feet of the orbiting Russian **Mir** station. In March, an American astronaut traveled in a Russian spacecraft and joined cosmonauts on **Mir**. In June and November, **Atlantis** docked with **Mir**, and they orbited Earth while joined together.

1996 — **Atlantis** docked with the **Mir** space station in March, and Dr. Shannon Lucid became the first American woman to join the **Mir** crew.

SENDING ROBOTS TO WORK

Another way to learn about our solar system is to send unmanned space probes into space to collect information to send back to Earth. These are less expensive and much less dangerous than space missions with astronauts. Below are the names, launch dates, and missions of some successful U.S. unmanned probe missions.

Mariner 2 (August 27, 1962):
First successful flyby of Venus. Reached Venus in December 1962.

Mariner 4 (November 28, 1964):
First probe to reach Mars. Reached Mars July 1965.

Ranger 7 (July 28, 1964):
Sent back over 4,000 close-up pictures of the moon.

Pioneer 10 (March 2, 1972):
First probe to reach Jupiter. Reached Jupiter in December 1973.

Mariner 10 (November 3, 1973):
Only U.S. probe to reach Mercury. Reached Mercury in March 1974.

Viking 1 (August 20, 1975):
Landed on Mars July 20, 1976. Followed soon after by Viking 2.

Voyager 1 (September 5, 1977):
Reached Jupiter in March 1979. Reached Saturn in November 1980.

Voyager 2 (August 20 1977):
Reached Jupiter in July 1979, Saturn in August 1981, Uranus in January 1986, and Neptune in August 1989.

Pioneer Venus 1 (May 20, 1978):
Operated in Venus orbit for 14 years, until October 1992.

Magellan (May 4, 1989):
After extensive mapping of Venus, *Magellan* burned up in its atmosphere on October 11, 1994.

Galileo (October 18, 1989):
Reached Jupiter in December 1995. Sent back data about Jupiter's atmosphere.

? **DID YOU KNOW?** The **NEAR** satellite was launched on February 17, 1995, and is scheduled to reach the asteroid Eros in 1997. The **Cassini** probe is scheduled to be launched in 1997 and to reach Saturn in 2004.

EXPLORING THE PLANETS PUZZLE

Look at the clues below and see if you know the names of the planets they describe. If not, look at pages 154-156 to help find out. The letters in the box going down spell out the planet with the most moons. (Answers are on page 305.)

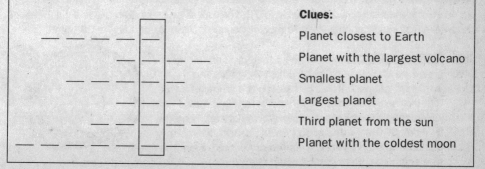

Clues:

Planet closest to Earth

Planet with the largest volcano

Smallest planet

Largest planet

Third planet from the sun

Planet with the coldest moon

What Makes a PLANT a PLANT?

Plants were the first living things on Earth. They appeared around three billion years ago, long before animals appeared. The first plants, called algae, grew in or near water. Years later—about 300 or 400 million years ago—the first land plants appeared. These were ferns, club mosses, and horsetails. After these came plants that bear cones (called "conifers") and trees that were ancestors of the palm trees we see today.

Flowers, grass, weeds, oak trees, palm trees, and poison ivy have certain things in common with each other and with every other plant. All plants have the following three important characteristics:

- ☑ Plants create their own food from air, sunlight, and water.
- ☑ Plants are rooted in one place—they don't move around.
- ☑ Plant cells contain cellulose, a substance that keeps plants rigid and upright.

In order to grow, plants need air, water, light, and warmth. Not all plants need soil or the same climate, or the same amount of light, warmth, and water to grow. A cactus plant needs a lot of heat and light but not much water, while a fir tree will grow in a northern forest where it is cold much of the year and light is limited. Water lilies are really rooted in the soil underwater, while water hyacinths just float on the water's surface and grow to about two feet above it.

 DID YOU KNOW? You can grow plants from some common foods, such as a sweet potato, an avocado pit, grapefruit seeds, or the tops of carrots.

RECORD-BREAKING PLANTS
World's Oldest Living Plants: Bristlecone pine trees in California (4,700 years old)
World's Tallest Plants: The tallest tree ever measured was a eucalyptus tree in Victoria, Australia, measuring 435 feet tall in 1872. The tallest tree now standing is a giant sequoia tree in Redwood National Park, Humboldt County, California, standing at 365 feet.

DID YOU KNOW? Do you know that you can tell how old a tree is by looking at its rings? Rings are the irregularly shaped circles you see on the stump of a tree that has been cut down. As a tree gets taller, it also gets wider, and each year that a tree grows outward is marked by a ring. A year with a good growing season leaves a thicker ring than a year that is too dry or cold. From the size of tree rings, scientists can tell what the climate was like years and years ago.

PLANT TALK

agronomy
The growing of plants for food.

fertilizer
A natural or chemical substance applied to the soil to help plants grow bigger and faster.

herb
A plant used for flavoring or seasoning, for its scent, or as medicine. Mint, lavender, and rosemary are all herbs.

horticulture
The growing of plants for beauty.

house plant
A plant that is grown indoors. Many plants that are grown outdoors in tropical and desert regions have become popular as house plants.

hybrid
A plant that has been scientifically combined with another plant or has been changed to make it more beautiful, larger, stronger, or better in some other way. Many roses are hybrids.

hydroponics
A way of growing plants in a nutritional liquid rather than in soil.

mulch
A covering of bark, compost (decomposed garbage), hay, or other substance used to conserve water and control weeds. Mulch can also provide nutrients for plants and keep plants warm in winter.

native
A plant that has always grown in a certain place, rather than being brought there from somewhere else. Corn is native to North America.

photosynthesis
The process that allows plants to make their own food from air, sunlight, and water.

phototropism
The turning of plants toward the light.

propagation
The reproduction of plants. Plants can be reproduced from seeds, or by dividing the roots of a plant, or sometimes by simply placing a piece of the leaf on soil.

terrarium
A glass box containing small plants and animals, such as moss, ferns, lizards, and turtles.

transplant
A plant that is dug up and moved from one place to another.

wildflower
A flowering plant that grows on its own in the wild, rather than being planted by a person.

evergreen
A tree that keeps its leaves or needles all year long.

deciduous
A tree that loses its leaves in autumn and gets new ones in the spring.

annual
A plant that grows, flowers, and dies in one year. Most annuals produce seeds that can be planted the following spring.

biennial
A plant that takes two years to mature. The first year the plant produces a stem and leaves, and the second year it produces flowers and seeds.

perennial
A plant that stops growing and may look dead in the fall, but comes back year after year.

WHERE DO PLANTS GROW?

Plants grow almost everywhere on Earth. Even the highest mountaintops and the driest deserts have plant life. In fact, the only places on Earth where plants don't grow are in most of Antarctica and near the North Pole. Plants can't grow there because the ground stays frozen all year round. The Earth is sometimes divided into plant-growing regions.

TUNDRA and ALPINE REGION

The northernmost regions of North America, Europe, and Asia surrounding the Arctic Ocean are called the **tundra**. The temperature rarely rises above 45 degrees Fahrenheit, and it is too cold for trees to grow there. Most tundra plants are mosses and lichens that hug the ground for warmth. A few wildflowers and small shrubs also grow where the soil thaws for about two months of the year. This kind of climate and plant life also exist on top of the highest mountains (the Himalayas, Alps, Andes, Rockies), where small Alpine flowers also grow.

What Is the Tree Line? On mountains in the north (such as the Rockies) and in the far south (such as the Andes), there is an altitude above which trees will not grow. This is called the **tree line** or **timberline.** Above the tree line, low shrubs and small plants, like Alpine flowers, can be seen. As you move farther from the poles to the edge of the tundra, small dwarfed and twisted trees begin to appear just below the tree line. This is the beginning of the forest region.

FORESTS

Where Evergreens Grow. Forests cover much of Earth's land surface. Evergreen trees, such as pines, hemlocks, firs, and spruces, grow in the forest regions farthest from the equator. These trees are called **conifers** because they produce cones. Here the summers are longer than in the tundra, and temperatures reach 50 degrees Fahrenheit or a little warmer.

Temperate Forests. Between the cool evergreen forests and the hotter tropical rain forests, there are temperate forests with warm, rainy summers and cold, snowy winters. Here **deciduous trees** (trees that lose their leaves in the fall and grow new ones in the spring) join the evergreens in the forest. Temperate forests are home to such trees as maples, oaks, beeches, and poplars, and to many kinds of wildflowers and shrubs. Temperate forests are found in the eastern United States, southeastern Canada, northern Europe and Asia, and southern Australia.

Tropical Rain Forests. Moving still closer to the equator, we come to the tropical rain forests, where the greatest variety of plants on Earth can be found. The temperature never falls below freezing except on the mountain slopes, and there is plenty of rain all year long. Trees there stay green throughout the year. There are also many climbing vines, orchids, and tree ferns. Other typical plants of the moist tropics are cacao, coffee, sugarcane, bananas, pineapples, and cashews. Woods such as mahogany and teak also come from the tropics. Tropical rain forests are found in Central America, South America, Asia, and Africa.

GRASSLAND

The areas of the world that are too dry to have green forests, but not dry enough to be deserts, are called **grasslands.** The most common plants found there are grasses. Cooler grasslands are found in the Great Plains of the United States and Canada, in the steppes of Europe and Asia, and in the pampas of Argentina. The drier grasslands are used for grazing cattle and sheep. In the **prairies**, where there is a little more rain, important grains, such as wheat, rye, oats, and barley are grown. The warmer grasslands, called **savannas,** are found in central and southern Africa, Venezuela, southern Brazil, and Australia. Most savannas have moist summers and cool, dry winters.

DESERTS

The driest areas of the world are the **deserts.** They can be hot or cold, but they also contain an amazing number of plants. Cactuses and sagebrush are native to dry regions of North and South America, while the deserts of Africa and Asia contain plants called euphorbias. Dates have grown in the deserts of the Middle East and North Africa for thousands of years. In the southwestern United States and northern Mexico, there are many types of cactuses, including prickly pear, barrel, and saguaro.

FASCINATING PLANTS
Plants That "Eat" Bugs

You probably know that bugs sometimes eat plants. But did you know that some plants trap insects and use them as food? These are known as "carnivorous plants." The **pitcher-plant**, *Venus's-flytrap*, and **sundew** are three examples. Most carnivorous plants live in poor soils where they don't get enough nourishment. They digest their prey very slowly over a long period of time.

Flowering Stones

Did you know that plants have ways of protecting themselves, just as animals do? **Lithops** (or flowering stones) are plants in the South African desert that look like small, gray stones. They are much less likely to be eaten by animals than something that looks green and delicious.

Plants That Give Us Colors

Many natural dyes that are used to color fabrics come from plants. **Indigo** was grown by the American colonists in the South for the beautiful blue dye produced from its leaves. Weavers in Mexico still use indigo dyes. And people living in the Himalayan mountains in Asia use **rhubarb** to produce yellow dye. In Japan, some of the finest silks are dyed with barks and roots from several plants. In Australia, the leaves of the **eucalyptus tree** are used to make a dye for wool. Common garden flowers that can be boiled to produce dyes are **black-eyed Susans**, **coreopsis**, **dahlias**, **goldenrod**, and **marigolds**.

The LARGEST and SMALLEST PLACES in the World

If someone asks you what the largest country is, you would have to ask that person another question before you can answer: The largest country in area, or the largest in population (the one with the most people)? The world's largest country in area is Russia. The world's largest country in population is China. Vatican City is the smallest country in area and population. Below are lists of the world's largest and smallest countries and the largest cities, with their populations.

Total Population of the World in 1995: 5,734,000,000

LARGEST COUNTRIES (Most People)	
Population	Country
1,203,097,000	China
936,546,000	India
262,755,000	United States
203,584,000	Indonesia
160,737,000	Brazil
149,909,000	Russia
131,542,000	Pakistan
128,095,000	Bangladesh
125,506,000	Japan
101,232,000	Nigeria
93,986,000	Mexico
81,337,000	Germany
74,393,000	Vietnam
73,265,000	Philippines
64,625,000	Iran
63,405,000	Turkey
60,271,000	Thailand
58,295,000	Great Britain
58,262,000	Italy
58,109,000	France
55,979,000	Ethiopia
51,868,000	Ukraine
45,554,000	South Korea
45,104,000	Myanmar (Burma)
45,095,000	South Africa

SMALLEST COUNTRIES (Fewest People)	
Population	Country
811	Vatican City
10,000	Nauru
10,000	Tuvalu
17,000	Palau
24,000	San Marino
31,000	Liechtenstein

LARGEST CITIES (Most People)

Below are the 10 cities in the world that have the most people. The numbers include people from the cities themselves and the built-up areas around them (called the metropolitan area).

City, Country	Population
Tokyo, Japan	26,518,000
New York City, U.S.	16,271,000
Sao Paulo, Brazil	16,110,000
Mexico City, Mexico	15,525,000
Shanghai, China	14,709,000
Bombay, India	14,496,000
Los Angeles, U.S.	12,232,000
Beijing, China	12,030,000
Calcutta, India	11,485,000
Seoul, South Korea	11,451,000

POPULATION of the UNITED STATES

Total Population of the United States in 1995: 262,755,270

Population of the STATES and DISTRICT OF COLUMBIA in 1995			
Rank & State Name	**Population**	**Rank & State Name**	**Population**
1. California	31,589,153	27. Oklahoma	3,277,687
2. Texas	18,723,991	28. Connecticut	3,274,662
3. New York	18,136,081	29. Oregon	3,140,585
4. Florida	14,165,570	30. Iowa	2,841,764
5. Pennsylvania	12,071,842	31. Mississippi	2,697,243
6. Illinois	11,829,940	32. Kansas	2,565,328
7. Ohio	11,150,506	33. Arkansas	2,483,769
8. Michigan	9,549,353	34. Utah	1,951,408
9. New Jersey	7,945,298	35. West Virginia	1,828,140
10. Georgia	7,200,882	36. New Mexico	1,685,401
11. North Carolina	7,195,138	37. Nebraska	1,637,112
12. Virginia	6,618,358	38. Nevada	1,530,108
13. Massachusetts	6,073,550	39. Maine	1,241,382
14. Indiana	5,803,471	40. Hawaii	1,186,815
15. Washington	5,430,940	41. Idaho	1,163,261
16. Missouri	5,323,523	42. New Hampshire	1,148,253
17. Tennessee	5,256,051	43. Rhode Island	989,794
18. Wisconsin	5,122,871	44. Montana	870,281
19. Maryland	5,042,438	45. South Dakota	729,034
20. Minnesota	4,609,548	46. Delaware	717,197
21. Louisiana	4,342,334	47. North Dakota	641,367
22. Alabama	4,252,982	48. Alaska	603,617
23. Arizona	4,217,940	49. Vermont	584,771
24. Kentucky	3,860,219	50. District of Columbia	554,256
25. Colorado	3,746,585	51. Wyoming	480,184
26. South Carolina	3,673,287		

THE LARGEST CITIES IN THE UNITED STATES IN 1995

Cities grow and shrink in population. Below is a list of the largest cities in the United States in 1995 compared with their populations in 1950. Can you find the 6 cities that increased in population? And the 4 that decreased?

Rank & City	1995	1950
1. New York, NY	7,333,253	7,891,957
2. Los Angeles, CA	3,448,613	1,970,358
3. Chicago, IL	2,731,743	3,620,962
4. Houston, TX	1,702,086	596,163
5. Philadelphia, PA	1,524,249	2,071,605
6. San Diego, CA	1,151,977	334,387
7. Phoenix, AZ	1,048,949	106,818
8. Dallas, TX	1,022,830	434,462
9. San Antonio, TX	998,905	408,442
10. Detroit, MI	992,038	1,849,568

Taking the Census: EVERYONE COUNTS

WHAT IS A CENSUS?

Every ten years the United States government counts the people who live in the United States. This is called taking the census. The census is taken to find out how many people live in the United States, where they live, how old they are, what they do, how much money they earn, the number of children in families, and other things about them.

WHEN WAS THE FIRST U.S. CENSUS TAKEN?

The first census was taken in 1790, after the American Revolution. That year there were 3,929,200 people in the United States. Most of the people then lived in the eastern part of the country, on farms or in small towns.

WHY DO WE NEED TO BE COUNTED?

Census information is important for many reasons.

☑ **Congress.** The number of representatives from each state in the U.S. House of Representatives is determined by the population of each state.

☑ **National government.** Census information helps the national government make plans to provide public services such as health care, highways, and parks.

☑ **State and local governments.** Census information helps state and local governments decide local questions, such as whether to build more schools for children or homes for elderly people.

☑ **Private companies.** It gives private companies information that helps them—such as how many people use cars, refrigerators, baby food, and other products; how many people read newspapers; and where these people live.

WHAT DOES THE LATEST CENSUS TELL US ABOUT THE UNITED STATES?

☑ By 1990, the population had increased to 248,709,873.

☑ More than half of the people in the United States live in the southern and western sections of the country.

☑ About 80% of Americans live in cities or suburbs.

☑ The United States is known for its large population that includes people of different races and nationalities.

The chart below shows how many Americans called themselves white, black, Asian, American Indian, and Hispanic in the 1990 census. The percentages add up to more than 100% because Hispanics may be of Mexican, Puerto Rican, Cuban or Spanish decent, or they may have roots in other Spanish-speaking countries of the Caribbean, or in Central or South America. Hispanics may be of any race.

White, 199,686,070 ....80%

Black, 29,986,060 ....12%

Hispanic, 22,354,059 ....9%

Asian, 7,276,662...................................3%
 (including the Pacific Islands)

American Indian, 1,959,234....................1%
 (including Eskimo, or Aleut)

Other race, 9,804,847 ....4%
 (people who said "other race")

COUNTING THE FIRST AMERICANS

WHERE DID THEY COME FROM?
American Indians, also called Native Americans, lived in North and South America long before the first European explorers arrived. Their ancestors are thought to have come from northeast Asia more than 20,000 years ago. American Indians are not one people, but many different peoples, each with their own traditions and way of life.

HOW MANY WERE THERE IN THE BEGINNING?
It is believed that many millions of Indians lived in the Americas before Columbus came. About 850,000 lived in what is now the United States.

HOW MANY ARE THERE NOW?
During the 17th, 18th, and 19th centuries, disease and wars with white settlers and soldiers caused the death of thousands of American Indians. By 1910 there were only about 220,000 left in the United States. Since then, the American Indian population has increased dramatically. In 1990, the last year a census was taken, the total number of Native Americans was close to 2 million.

WHERE DO NATIVE AMERICANS LIVE?
Below are the states with the largest Native American populations.

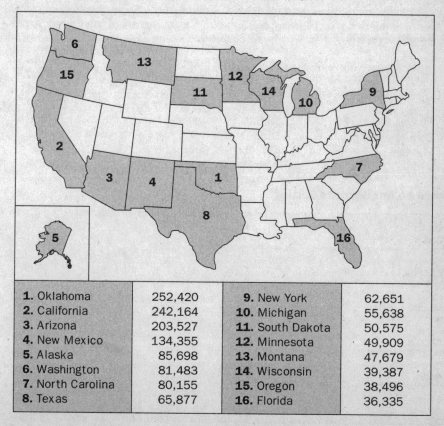

1. Oklahoma	252,420		9. New York	62,651
2. California	242,164		10. Michigan	55,638
3. Arizona	203,527		11. South Dakota	50,575
4. New Mexico	134,355		12. Minnesota	49,909
5. Alaska	85,698		13. Montana	47,679
6. Washington	81,483		14. Wisconsin	39,387
7. North Carolina	80,155		15. Oregon	38,496
8. Texas	65,877		16. Florida	36,335

The MANY FACES of America: IMMIGRATION

You have probably heard it said that America is a nation of immigrants. Many Americans are descended from Europeans or from Africans or from Asians. Do you know someone who was born in another country?

Why Do People Come to the United States?

Have you ever wondered why so many people want to leave their native country and come and live in the United States? It isn't usually because they don't love their own country. Most people are very attached to the place where they were born. Immigrants come to America for many reasons: to live in freedom, to worship as they choose, to escape poverty, to make a better life for themselves and their children.

Millions of people have immigrated to the United States from all over the world—more than 40 million since 1820. Much of the art we see or the music we hear, and many of the scientific discoveries and inventions we use, foods we eat, and languages we speak were introduced to us by people who came from other countries.

What Countries Do Immigrants Come From?

Immigrants come to the United States from many countries. Below are some of the countries immigrants came from in 1994. The name of the country is followed by the number of immigrants. In 1994, immigration from all countries to the United States totaled 804,416.

Mexico	111,398	Poland	28,048
Russia and other former Soviet republics	63,420	El Salvador	17,644
		Ireland	17,256
China	53,985	Great Britain	16,326
Philippines	53,535	Canada	16,068
Dominican Republic	51,189	North and South Korea	16,011
Vietnam	41,345	Cuba	14,727
India	34,921	Jamaica	14,349

Where Do Immigrants Settle?

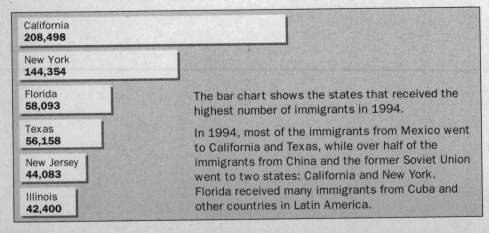

California
208,498

New York
144,354

Florida
58,093

Texas
56,158

New Jersey
44,083

Illinois
42,400

The bar chart shows the states that received the highest number of immigrants in 1994.

In 1994, most of the immigrants from Mexico went to California and Texas, while over half of the immigrants from China and the former Soviet Union went to two states: California and New York. Florida received many immigrants from Cuba and other countries in Latin America.

Becoming an AMERICAN CITIZEN: NATURALIZATION

When a foreign-born person becomes a citizen of the United States, we say the person has become **naturalized.** To apply for American citizenship, a person

- ☑ Must be at least 18 years old.
- ☑ Must have lived legally in the United States for at least 5 years.
- ☑ Must have an understanding of English if under the age of 55.
- ☑ Must be of good moral character.
- ☑ Must demonstrate a knowledge of the history and form of government of the United States.

ELLIS ISLAND and THE STATUE OF LIBERTY

ELLIS ISLAND: THE GATEWAY TO AMERICA

Until this century, people could immigrate freely to the United States. They piled on to ships and came, hoping to find a better life. Between 1892 and 1924, more than 12 million people came into the country by passing through Ellis Island, a huge immigration center in New York harbor. There they were screened for certain contagious diseases and some sick people were sent back, but most immigrants were allowed to stay.

Immigrants who passed through Ellis Island came from many places—Italy, Russia, Hungary, Austria, Germany, England, Ireland, Sweden, Greece, Norway, Turkey, Scotland, the West Indies, Poland, Portugal, France, and others.

Ellis Island as a Museum. As an immigration center, Ellis Island was closed in 1954. But in 1990, it reopened as a museum to tell the story of the immigrants who helped make the United States a great country. The names of many of the immigrants who came through Ellis Island are inscribed on a wall in their memory.

THE STATUE OF LIBERTY. Many of the immigrants who steamed into New York harbor passed by the Statue of Liberty. Set on her own island, the "Lady With the Lamp" was given to the United States by France and has served
as a symbol of freedom and a welcome to Americans-to-be since she was erected in 1886. In 1903, a sonnet by the U.S. poet Emma Lazarus was inscribed at the base of the statue. Two of its lines read: "Give me your tired, your poor, your huddled masses yearning to breathe free...."

ENTERTAINMENT AWARDS

Who is your favorite movie actor or actress? What is your all-time favorite film? If you are interested in the movies, you probably know that an Oscar is a golden statuette that is awarded for the best movie, best actor, best actress, and so on. The Oscar presentations are watched on television by millions of people all over the world. Among other awards given for the best in entertainment are Grammys, Emmys, and Tonys.

ACADEMY AWARDS: THE OSCARS

The Oscars are given every year by the Academy of Motion Picture Arts and Sciences for the best movie, best actor and actress, best supporting actor and actress, best director, best original song, and so on. Here are some of the films and people who won an Oscar in 1996.

▲ *Actor James Cromwell, with "Babe"*

Best Picture: *Braveheart*

Best Actor: Nicolas Cage in *Leaving Las Vegas*

Best Actress: Susan Sarandon in *Dead Man Walking*

Best Supporting Actor: Kevin Spacey in *The Usual Suspects*

Best Supporting Actress: Mira Sorvino in *Mighty Aphrodite*

Best Director: Mel Gibson for *Braveheart*

Best Original Song: "Colors of the Wind" from *Pocahontas*

Best Original Musical Score: Alan Menken and Stephen Schwartz for *Pocahontas*

Best Visual Effects: *Babe*

Best Makeup: *Braveheart*

? **DID YOU KNOW?** Walt Disney won 20 Oscars—more than anyone else. The youngest person ever to receive an Oscar was Shirley Temple. She won an honorary Oscar in 1934 at the age of 5. The oldest was Jessica Tandy. In 1990, at the age of 80, she won an Oscar for Best Actress in the film *Driving Miss Daisy*.

THE GRAMMYS

Grammys are awards given out each year by the National Academy of Recording Arts & Sciences for the best in popular music. Some of the winners in 1996 were:

Best Record: Seal, "Kiss From a Rose"
Best Album: Alanis Morissette, *Jagged Little Pill*
Best New Artist: Hootie and the Blowfish
Best Pop Album: *Turbulent Indigo*, Joni Mitchell
Best Rock Group: Blues Traveler
Best Hard Rock Group: Pearl Jam
Best Rhythm-and-Blues Group: T. L. C.
Best Rap Soloist: Coolio
Best Country Group: The Mavericks
Best Country Album: Shania Twain, *The Woman in Me*
Best Contemporary Jazz Album: Pat Metheny Group, *We Live Here*
Best Film or Television Song: "Colors of the Wind" (from *Pocahontas*), by Alan Menken and Stephen Schwartz

THE EMMYS

The Emmy Awards are given each year by the Academy of Television Arts and Sciences for the best of television. These include the best series, best actors and actresses, and best writers and directors. Here are some of the major winners for the 1994-1995 season for prime-time television. (Prime time is the evening hours when the TV audience is the largest.)

Best Drama Series: *NYPD Blue* (ABC)
Best Actor in a Drama Series: Mandy Patinkin, in *Chicago Hope* (CBS)
Best Actress in a Drama Series: Kathy Baker, in *Picket Fences* (CBS)
Best Comedy Series: *Frasier* (NBC)
Best Actor in a Comedy Series: Kelsey Grammer, in *Frasier*
Best Actress in a Comedy Series: Candice Bergen, in *Murphy Brown* (CBS)
Best Miniseries: *Joseph* (TNT)
Best Talk Show: *The Oprah Winfrey Show* (ABC)
Best Game Show: *Jeopardy!* (ABC)

THE TONYS

The Antoinette Perry Awards, known as the "Tonys," are annual awards given to the best Broadway plays and to those who write them, act in them, and direct them. The 50th Tony Awards were given out in 1996. Winners for the 1995-1996 season were:

Best Play: *Master Class*, by Terrence McNally
Best Musical: *Rent*, by Jonathan Larson
Best Musical Revival: *The King and I*, a 1952 musical by Richard Rodgers and Oscar Hammerstein II
Leading Actor in a Play: George Grizzard in *A Delicate Balance*
Leading Actress in a Play: Zoe Caldwell in *Master Class*
Leading Actor in a Musical: Nathan Lane in *A Funny Thing Happened on the Way to the Forum*
Leading Actress in a Musical: Donna Murphy in *The King and I*

Other PRIZES and AWARDS

NOBEL PRIZES

The Nobel Prizes are named after Alfred B. Nobel (1833-1896), a Swedish scientist who left money to be awarded every year to people who have done something important to help humankind. The world-famous German-born physicist Albert Einstein won the physics prize in 1921, and the Polish-French scientist Marie Curie won two Nobel Prizes—one in physics in 1903 (with Pierre Curie, her husband, and Henry Becquerel) and one in chemistry in 1911. There are also prizes for medicine-physiology, literature, economics, and peace. The Nobel Peace Prize goes to a person or group that the judges think has done the most the previous year to help achieve peace between nations.

 DID YOU KNOW? Two American presidents have won the Nobel Peace Prize: Theodore Roosevelt in 1906 and Woodrow Wilson in 1919.

PULITZER PRIZES

The Pulitzer Prizes are named after Joseph Pulitzer (1847-1911), a journalist and publisher, who gave the money to set them up. The prizes are given yearly in the United States for journalism, literature, and music.

SPINGARN MEDAL

The Spingarn Medal was established in 1914 by Joel Elias Spingarn, then the chairperson of the National Association for the Advancement of Colored People (NAACP). It is awarded every year by the NAACP for the highest achievement by a black American. Here are some well-known winners and the year they won.

1995: Historian John Hope Franklin
1994: Writer and poet Maya Angelou
1991: General Colin L. Powell,
    then the Chairman of the
    Joint Chiefs of Staff

1985: Actor Bill Cosby
1979: Civil rights activist Rosa L. Parks
1975: Baseball player Hank Aaron
1957: Civil rights leader
    Martin Luther King, Jr.

THE MEDAL OF HONOR

The Congressional Medal of Honor is the highest award that is given by the government of the United States. It is a military award for extraordinary personal bravery in war against an enemy. The first Medals of Honor were awarded in 1863. By the beginning of 1996, 3,420 Medals of Honor had been awarded.

Army   *Navy*   *Air Force*

HALLS of FAME

Halls of fame are special museums created to honor people who are best in their field. The first hall of fame, which was opened in 1900 in New York, honors great Americans from President George Washington to agricultural scientist George Washington Carver (who developed peanut butter), from early feminist Susan B. Anthony to composer and marching band leader John Philip Sousa. Below are some halls of fame. For others, look at the pages on SPORTS and INVENTIONS.

ROCK AND ROLL HALL OF FAME AND MUSEUM
1 Key Plaza, Cleveland, Ohio 44114   Phone: (216) 781-7625.

The Rock and Roll Hall of Fame and Museum opened September 1, 1995, in Cleveland, Ohio, with a huge celebration, parade, and rock concert. Some people say that from the shoreline of Lake Erie, the building looks like a gigantic turntable. Inside, the Hall of Fame honors famous rock-and-roll artists and people who influenced their music. Musicians honored in 1996 include: The Velvet Underground, David Bowie, Gladys Knight and the Pips, Jefferson Airplane, Little Willie John, Pink Floyd, the Shirelles, and Pete Seeger. To be in the Hall of Fame, musicians must have recorded their first song at least 25 years ago. The museum honors current rockers through films, photographs, videos, and displays of costumes and possessions, including the first glove Michael Jackson wore on stage and Queen Latifah's high school yearbook.

Conservation Hall of Fame
National Wildlife Federation
1400 16th Street NW
Washington, DC 20036-2266
Contains a wildlife gallery of art.

Hall of Fame for Great Americans
University Avenue and
W. 181st Street
Bronx, NY 10453

National Band and Choral Directors Hall of Fame
519 N. Halifax Avenue
Daytona Beach, FL 32118
Honors school band and choral directors. Holds marching band and choral music contests.

National Cowboy Hall of Fame and Western Heritage Center
1700 NE 63rd Street
Oklahoma City, OK 73111
Honors the pioneers who developed the American West. Offers exhibitions, lectures, and tours.

National Women's Hall of Fame
76 Fall Street
Seneca Falls, NY 13148
Honors American women who have made great contributions to their country. Holds essay and poster contests and sponsors special activities for school groups.

CONTESTS

Some kids like to compete in soccer or gymnastics. Others like to enter contests for making posters, writing stories, or creating science projects. And others prefer not to compete at all. If you like contests, there are many kinds to choose from. Some contests appear in magazines or newspapers, and you can enter them on your own. Others are run only through schools.

MAGAZINE CONTESTS

If you like history, *The American History Magazine for Young People* runs a contest each year asking readers (ages 8-14) to create a short video, poster, or essay telling why they think a particular person played an important role in history. If you like science projects, the magazine *Odyssey, Science That Is Out of This World* holds contests in which kids do artwork, write science fiction stories, or design science projects. For more information on either contest, you may contact: Cobblestone Publishing, 7 School Street, Peterborough, NH 03458. Phone: (800) 821-0115

Other magazines also hold contests for kids or print kids' original stories, poems, opinions, artwork, photographs, and even jokes and riddles. Some of them are: *Contact, Highlights for Children, Sports Illustrated for Kids, Stone Soup: The Magazine by Young Writers and Artists,* and *Zillions.* You can look for these and others in your library.

CONTESTS THROUGH SCHOOLS

National Spelling Bee. Are you a good speller? A company named Scripps Howard runs spelling bees for kids 15 years old and under. Winners go on to county contests, and then possibly to the National Spelling Bee in Washington, D.C. For information, a school principal may contact: The Scripps Howard National Spelling Bee, P.O. Box 5380, Cincinnati, OH 45201. Phone: (513) 977-3040

Contests in Photography, Writing, Music, and Art. Do you like to take photographs, write stories or poems, compose music, or create art? If so, contests through the P.T.A. (Parent Teacher Association) Reflections Program may interest you. The contests are based on a different theme each year, and entries may be in photography, writing, music, or art. Students compete from local to national levels. For information, a school P.T.A. may contact: National P.T.A. Reflections Program, 330 North Wabash Avenue, Suite 2100, Chicago, IL 60611. Phone: (312) 670-6782

National Geography Bee. How would you like to test your knowledge of geography? The National Geographic Society sponsors The National Geography Bee. In this contest, fourth through eighth graders compete on local, state, and national levels by answering oral and written questions about geography. For information, a school principal may write to: National Geography Bee, National Geographic Society, 1145 15th Street N.W., Washington, D.C., 20036-4688.

RELIGION
Around the WORLD

Have you ever asked yourself questions like these: How did the universe begin? Why are we here on earth? What happens to us after we die? For many people, religion is a way of answering such questions. Believing in a God or gods, or in a Divine Being, is one way of making sense of the world around us. Religions can also help guide people's lives. More than 5 billion people all over the world belong to some religious group. Different religions have different beliefs. For example, Christians, Jews, and Muslims believe in one God, while Hindus believe in many gods. On this page and the next page are some facts about the world's major religions.

CHRISTIANITY

Who Started Christianity? Jesus Christ, in the first century. He was born in Bethlehem between 8 B.C. and 4 B.C. and died about A.D. 29.

What Do Christians Believe? That there is one God. That Jesus Christ is the Son of God, who came on earth to save humankind.

How Many Christians Are There? Christianity is the world's biggest religion. In 1995 there were almost 2 billion Christians, in nearly all parts of the world. Nearly one billion of the Christians were Roman Catholics. Among the Christians are:

Roman Catholics, for whom the pope in Rome is the leader of their church.

Orthodox Christians, who accept most Catholic teachings, but follow their bishop as their spiritual leader.

Protestants, who accept the Bible, as well as insights of the laity (members of the church who are not ordained as clergy). They are divided into many different groups.

JUDAISM

Who Started Judaism? Abraham is considered the founder of Judaism. He lived around 1300 B.C.

What Do Jews Believe? That there is one God who created the universe and rules over it. That they should be faithful to God and carry out God's commandments.

How Many Are There? In 1995, there were more than 14 million Jews, spread around the world. Many live in Israel or the United States.

What Kinds Are There? In the United States there are three main kinds: **Orthodox**, **Conservative**, and **Reform**. Orthodox Jews are the most traditional. Traditional means that they follow strict laws about how they dress, what they can eat, and how they conduct their lives. Conservative Jews follow many of the traditions. Reform Jews are the least traditional.

ISLAM

Who Started Islam? Muhammad, the Prophet, in A.D. 622.

What Do Muslims Believe? People who believe in Islam are called Muslims. They believe: That there is one God. That Muslims should follow the laws of God, as told to Muhammad. That they should pray five times a day. That they should try, during their lives, to make at least one trip to the holy city of Mecca in Saudi Arabia.

How Many Muslims Are There? In 1995, there were about 1 billion Muslims, mostly in parts of Africa and Asia. The two main kinds of Muslims are: **Sunni Muslims**, who make up about 85 percent of Muslims today, and **Shiite Muslims**, who broke away in a dispute over who should lead them.

HINDUISM

Who Started Hinduism? No single person. Aryan invaders of India, around 1500 B.C., brought their own beliefs with them, which were mixed with the beliefs of the people who already lived in India.

What Do Hindus Believe? That there are many gods and many ways of worshipping. That people die and are reborn many times as another living thing. That there is a universal soul or principle known as *Brahman*. That the goal of life is to escape the cycle of birth and death and become part of the *Brahman*. This is achieved by leading a pure and good life.

How Many Are There? In 1995, there were about 780 million Hindus, mainly in India and places where people from India have gone to live.

What Kinds Are There? There are many kinds of Hindus, who worship different gods or goddesses.

BUDDHISM

Who Started Buddhism? Gautama Siddhartha (the Buddha), around 525 B.C.

What Do Buddhists Believe? Buddha taught that life is filled with suffering. In order to be free of that suffering, believers have to give up worldly possessions and worldly goals and strive to achieve a state of perfect peace known as *nirvana*.

How Many Are There? In 1995, there were about 320 million Buddhists, mostly in Asia.

What Kinds Are There? There are two main kinds. **Theravada** ("Path of the Elders") **Buddhism,** the older kind, is more common in southern Asia. **Mahayana** ("Great Vessel") **Buddhism** is more common in northern Asia.

RELIGIOUS MEMBERSHIP
in the United States

Did you know that Protestants are the largest religious group in the United States, and that Catholics are the second largest? In the box below you can see how many people belong to the major religious groups. These numbers are estimates, because no one knows exactly how many people belong to each group.

Protestants				over 100 million
Including:	Baptists	37 million	Mormons	5 million
	Methodists	14 million	Presbyterians	4 million
	Pentecostals	11 million	Episcopalians	3 million
	Lutherans	8 million	Reformed Churches	2 million

Roman Catholics	60 million
Jews	6 million
Orthodox Christians	6 million
Muslims	5 million

RELIGIOUS TEXTS

Every religion has its writings or sacred texts that set out its laws and beliefs. Among them are:

THE BIBLE
The Old Testament. Also known as the Hebrew Bible, this is a collection of laws, history, and other writings that are holy books for Jews and also for Christians. The first five books of the Old Testament are known by Jews as the Torah. These contain the stories of creation and the beginnings of human life, as well as the laws handed down by the prophet Moses.

The New Testament. A collection of Gospels (stories about Jesus), epistles (letters written to guide the early Christians), and other writings. The Old Testament and New Testament together make up the Bible that is read by Christians.

THE KORAN
The Koran sets out the central beliefs of Islam, the religion of Muslims. Muslims believe that the Koran was revealed by God to the prophet Muhammad through the angel Gabriel. The Koran is also spelled "Qur'an."

THE BHAGAVAD GHITA
The Bhagavad Ghita is one of several Hindu religious writings. Part of a long poem about war, it is familiar to almost every Hindu. In it the god Krishna, in the form of a man, drives the chariot of Prince Arjuna into battle and teaches him about how to live.

Major HOLY DAYS
for Christians, Jews, and Muslims

CHRISTIAN HOLY DAYS

	1996	1997	1998
Ash Wednesday	February 21	February 12	February 25
Good Friday	April 5	March 28	April 10
Easter Sunday	April 7	March 30	April 12
Easter for Orthodox Churches	April 14	April 27	April 19
Christmas	December 25	December 25	December 25

JEWISH HOLY DAYS
The Jewish holy days begin at sundown and end at sundown. The days listed below are the first full day of the holy day.

	1996 (5756-57)	1997 (5757-58)	1998 (5758-59)
Passover	April 4	April 22	April 11
Rosh Hashanah (New Year)	September 14	October 2	September 21
Yom Kippur	September 23	October 11	September 30
Chanukah	December 6	December 24	December 14

ISLAMIC (MUSLIM) HOLY DAYS

	1996-97 (1417)	1997-98 (1418)	1998-99 (1419)
Muharram 1 (New Year)	May 18	May 8	April 27
Mawlid (Birthday of Muhammad)	July 28	July 17	July 6
Ramadan 1	January 10	December 31	December 20
al-Adha Dhu al-Hijjah 10	April 17	April 7	March 28

CHEMICAL ELEMENTS

People, dogs, butterflies, flowers, rocks, air, water, CDs, baseball cards, telephones—everything we see and use is made up of "basic ingredients" called **elements**. There are 111 elements. Most of them have been found in nature. Some have been created in laboratories. The charts below show the elements found in Earth's crust and those found in the atmosphere:

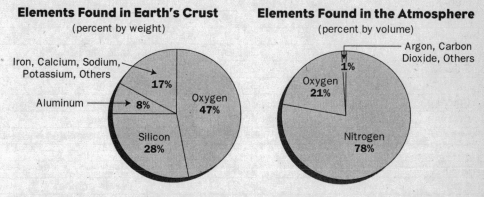

Elements Found in Earth's Crust
(percent by weight)

Iron, Calcium, Sodium, Potassium, Others
17%
Aluminum — 8%
Oxygen 47%
Silicon 28%

Elements Found in the Atmosphere
(percent by volume)

Argon, Carbon Dioxide, Others
1%
Oxygen 21%
Nitrogen 78%

How Can Scientists Tell One Element From Another? The smallest possible piece of an element that has all the properties of the original element is called an **atom**. Each tiny atom is made up of even smaller particles called **protons**, **neutrons**, and **electrons**.

To tell one element from another, scientists count the number of protons in an atom. The total number of protons is called the element's **atomic number**. All of the atoms of an element have the same number of protons and electrons, but some atoms have a different number of neutrons. For example, carbon–12 has 6 protons and 6 neutrons, and carbon–13 has 6 protons and 7 neutrons.

We call the amount of matter in an atom its **atomic mass**. Carbon–13 has a greater atomic mass than carbon–12. The average atomic mass of all of the different atoms of the same element is called the element's **atomic weight**. Every element has a different atomic number and a different atomic weight.

Chemical Symbols Are Scientific Shorthand. When scientists write the names of elements, they often use a symbol instead of spelling out the full name. Just as we sometimes use $ instead of writing "dollars," scientists write O for oxygen and He for helium. The symbol for each element is one or two letters. The symbols usually come from the English name for the element (C for carbon). The symbols for some of the elements come from the element's Latin name. For example, the symbol for gold is Au, which is short for *Aurum,* the Latin word for gold.

A LOOK at Some COMMON ELEMENTS

The table below shows some common elements with their symbol, atomic number, atomic weight, the year they were discovered, and some of their common uses.

NAME OF ELEMENT	SYMBOL	ATOMIC NUMBER	ATOMIC WEIGHT	YEAR FOUND	COMMON USE
Hydrogen	H	1	1.01	1766	in welding
Helium	He	2	4.00	1868	inflate balloons
Carbon	C	6	12.01	B.C.	pencils, diamonds
Nitrogen	N	7	14.01	1772	fertilizers
Oxygen	O	8	16.00	1774	breathing
Fluorine	F	9	19.00	1771	toothpastes
Neon	Ne	10	20.18	1898	electric signs
Sodium	Na	11	22.99	1807	in salt
Aluminum	Al	13	26.98	1825	soda cans
Silicon	Si	14	28.09	1823	in sand
Sulfur	S	16	32.06	B.C.	matches
Chlorine	Cl	17	35.45	1774	purifies water, in salt
Calcium	Ca	20	40.08	1808	in bones
Iron	Fe	26	55.85	B.C.	steel, magnets
Copper	Cu	29	63.55	B.C.	water pipes, wire
Silver	Ag	47	107.87	B.C.	jewelry, dental fillings
Gold	Au	79	196.97	B.C.	jewelry, coins
Mercury	Hg	80	200.59	B.C.	in thermometers
Lead	Pb	82	207.19	B.C.	in car batteries

ELEMENTS ARE ALL AROUND US. Neon signs light up store windows. Car batteries contain lead. Soda cans are made from aluminum. Chips using silicon are found in computers. Jewelry is made from gold and silver.

When elements join together, they form **compounds**. Water is a compound made up of hydrogen and oxygen. Salt is a compound made up of sodium and chlorine. Many things we use at home or in school are compounds.

Common Name	Contains the Compound	Contains the Elements
Vinegar	Acetic acid	carbon, hydrogen, oxygen
Chalk	Calcium carbonate	calcium, carbon, oxygen
Soda bubbles	Carbon dioxide	carbon, oxygen
Rust	Iron oxide	iron, oxygen
Baking soda	Sodium bicarbonate	sodium, hydrogen, carbon, oxygen
Toothpaste	Sodium fluoride	sodium, fluorine

Some ANSWERS to SCIENCE QUESTIONS

WHAT IS A MAGNET?

Have you ever seen paper clips or pins sliding toward a magnet and then sticking to it? Magnets have two areas, called **poles**, where magnetic effects are strongest. A bar magnet has a pole at each end. Around each pole is a region called a **magnetic field**. A magnetic field cannot be seen, but it can be felt when a another magnet enters the field or when an object that has iron in it, such as a paper clip or a pin, enters the magnetic field. Such an object will be attracted to one of the poles of the magnet.

HOW DO MAGNETS REACT TO OTHER MAGNETS?

Magnets have two poles. One is called the north pole and the other is called the south pole. The north pole of one magnet will attract the south pole of another magnet—in other words, opposites attract. But when the north poles of two magnets are brought near each other, they will push away (repel) each other. Magnets can have different shapes and can be made of different materials.

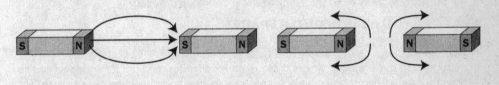

? **DID YOU KNOW?** Do you know that Earth is a giant magnet whose magnetic field exists at all locations? Like a bar magnet, Earth has two magnetic poles—one of them is near the geographical north pole and the other is near the geographical south pole. If you have ever used a compass, you have seen that the compass needle always points in the same direction—toward the north—no matter which way you turn. The needle is a small bar magnet that can rotate easily. The needle points north because the north pole of the magnet is attracted to the magnetic pole of Earth near the geographical north pole.

WHEN DOES WATER MELT AND FREEZE?

We usually think of water as a liquid. But it can also be a solid or a gas, depending on its temperature. At low temperatures, below freezing (32 degrees Fahrenheit or 0 degrees Celsius), water is a solid called **ice**. At warmer temperatures, it is a **liquid**. At very high temperatures (212 degrees Fahrenheit or 100 degrees Celsius or higher), water boils and becomes a **gas** called steam. It also becomes a gas, often called water vapor, when it evaporates, as it does when wet clothes are hung out to dry. Water vapor condenses into a liquid when it is chilled. That is why liquid water coats the outside of a cold glass on a humid day.

WHAT CAUSES FROST PATTERNS ON WINDOWS IN WINTER?

Have you ever seen feathery patterns of frost on windows in very cold weather? When water vapor in the air comes in contact with the extremely cold glass of a window, the water vapor immediately turns to ice. The ice forms on the windows in patterns of ice crystals.

Some LIGHT and SOUND Subjects

WHAT IS LIGHT?

Light is a form of energy that travels in **rays**. Light rays generally move in straight lines, at a speed of 186,000 miles per second through empty space. It takes over 8 minutes for the light from the sun to reach Earth. Light also moves through materials like water and glass, but more slowly.

WHAT IS A RAINBOW?

The light we usually see (visible light) is made up of colors called the **spectrum**. The colors of the spectrum are red, orange, yellow, green, blue, indigo, and violet. White light is formed from a mixture of all the colors of the spectrum. A prism can separate the colors in a beam of white light. When you see a rainbow, the tiny water droplets in the air are separating the white light into the spectrum.

WHERE DOES SOUND COME FROM?

When objects vibrate quickly back and forth in the air, they create **sound**. The vibrating objects cause the molecules in the air around the objects to move. As the molecules move, the vibrations travel through the air in **waves**. These sound waves move outward in every direction from the place where they started—like ripples in a pond moving away from the point where a pebble is dropped.

WHAT CAN YOU HEAR IN OUTER SPACE?

Sound waves have to have a medium to move through. Usually air serves as the medium. But sounds can also travel through water, wood, glass, and other materials. In outer space, where there is no air or other medium for sound waves to travel through, there is no sound. Astronauts in space communicate with Earth over radio waves, not sound waves.

HOW LOUD ARE THOSE SOUNDS?

The loudness of a sound (called **volume**) is measured in **decibels**. The volume depends on how many air molecules are vibrating and how strongly they are vibrating. The quietest sound that can be heard has a value of zero decibels. The louder the sound, the higher the decibel level.

0 decibels
faintest sound heard

10-20 decibels
rustling leaves

20-30 decibels
whispering

50-70 decibels
conversation

80-100 decibels
heavy traffic and trains

100-120 decibels
loud music

140-150 decibels
nearby jet engine

MINERALS, ROCKS, and GEMS

WHAT ARE MINERALS?

Minerals are natural solid materials in the soil that were never alive. All of the land on our planet and even the ocean floor rest on a layer of rock made up of minerals. Minerals have also been found on other planets, on our moon, and in meteorites that landed on Earth. Some minerals, such as gold and silver, are made up entirely of one element. But most minerals are formed from two or more elements joined together. The most common mineral is quartz, which is made of silicon and oxygen and is found all over the world. Sand is made up mostly of quartz. Graphite, which is used in pencils, is another common mineral. Other minerals, like diamonds, are very rare and valuable. Oddly enough, diamonds and graphite are different forms of the same element—carbon.

WHAT ARE ROCKS?

Rocks are combinations of minerals. There are three kinds of rocks:

1. **Igneous rocks** are rocks that form from melted minerals in the Earth that cool and become solid. Granite is an igneous rock made from quartz, feldspar, and mica.
2. **Sedimentary rocks** are rocks that usually form in sea and river beds from tiny pieces of other rocks, sand, and shells that get packed together. It takes millions of years for these pieces to form sedimentary rocks. Limestone is a kind of sedimentary rock.
3. **Metamorphic rock.** Over millions of years, the heat and pressure inside Earth can change the minerals in igneous and sedimentary rocks. When the minerals in a rock change, the new rock is called a **metamorphic rock.** Marble is a metamorphic rock formed from limestone.

WHAT ARE GEMS?

Most **gems** are minerals that have been cut and polished to be used as jewelry or other kinds of decoration. Some gems are not minerals. A pearl is a gem that is not a mineral, because it comes from an oyster, which is a living thing. The most valued gems—diamonds, emeralds, rubies, and sapphires—are minerals called **precious stones.** Below are some popular gems, the kind of mineral each one is, the elements each is made up of, and the usual colors for the gem.

Gem Name	Mineral	Element It Is Made Of	Usual Colors
Amethyst	quartz	silicon, oxygen	purple
Diamond	carbon	carbon	bluish white
Emerald	beryl	beryllium, silicon, aluminum, oxygen	green
Opal	opal	silicon, oxygen	red, green, blue
Ruby	corundum	aluminum, oxygen	red
Sapphire	corundum	aluminum, oxygen	blue

? **DID YOU KNOW?** Some minerals glow in the dark. Those that change color under ultraviolet light—like diamonds, opals, and rubies—are called **fluorescent minerals.** Fluorescent minerals that glow in the dark even after ultraviolet light is taken away are called **phosphorescent minerals.**

Some FAMOUS SCIENTISTS

Archimedes (about 287 B.C.-212 B.C.), a Greek mathematician who discovered that heavy objects could be moved with little force. He was one of the first people to test his ideas with experiments.

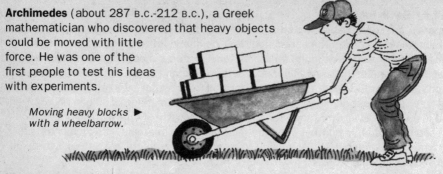

Moving heavy blocks ▶ with a wheelbarrow.

Nicolaus Copernicus (1473-1543), a Polish scientist known as the founder of modern astronomy. He believed that Earth and other planets revolved around the sun. His ideas were not accepted during his lifetime.

Galileo Galilei (1564-1642), an Italian astronomer who, like Copernicus, believed that the sun was at the center of the solar system, and that the planets revolved around it. He also proved that all objects, whether heavy or light, fall at the same rate.

Sir Isaac Newton (1642-1727), a British scientist famous for discovering the laws of gravity. He also discovered that sunlight is made up of all the colors of the rainbow.

Edward Jenner (1749-1823), a British doctor who discovered a way to prevent smallpox by injecting healthy people with cowpox vaccine. Today's vaccines work in a similar way.

Michael Faraday (1791-1867), a British scientist who discovered that magnets can be used to create electricity in copper wires. His discoveries enable us to produce massive amounts of electricity.

Charles Darwin (1809-1882) was a British scientist best known for his theory of evolution. According to Darwin's theory of evolution, living creatures slowly develop and change over millions of years.

Gregor Johann Mendel (1822-1884), an Austrian monk who discovered the laws of heredity by showing how characteristics are passed from one generation of plants to the next.

Louis Pasteur (1822-1895), a French chemist who discovered a process called pasteurization, in which heat is used to kill germs. This process is still used to purify milk and many other food products.

Marie Curie (1867-1934), a Polish-French physical chemist known for discovering radium, which is used to treat some diseases. She won the Nobel Prize for chemistry in 1911. She and her husband, **Pierre Curie**, also won the Nobel Prize for physics in 1903 for their work in radiation.

▲ *Pasteurized milk*

Albert Einstein (1879-1955), a German-American physicist who developed a revolutionary theory about the relationships between time, space, matter, and energy. He won a Nobel Prize in 1921.

Francis Crick (born 1916) and **Maurice Wilkins** (born 1916) of England and **James D. Watson** (born 1928) of the United States won a Nobel Prize in 1962 for their discoveries about DNA, the basic chemical that controls inheritance in all living cells.

SCIENCE MUSEUMS

Seeing is believing—and you made it happen! If you like hands-on exhibits and like to learn about robots, computers, the Ice Age, dinosaurs, the brain, how the body works, and many other areas of science, a visit to a science museum is in order. There are many science museums in the United States. Below are a few of them. Look in the INDEX for museums about natural history and computers.

National Air and Space Museum, Washington, D.C. Houses the Wright brothers' plane, Charles Lindbergh's *Spirit of St. Louis*, and *Skylab*, as well as many other planes and rockets. Visitors (1995), 8,700,000.

California Museum of Science and Industry, Los Angeles, California. Includes a giant electromagnet activated by visitors; exhibits on electricity, earthquakes, computer-assisted design, aerospace, and health sciences. Visitors (1995), 2,500,000.

Museum of Science and Industry, Chicago, Illinois. Includes a reproduction of a coal mine, as well as displays on health, human intelligence, and how people live. Visitors (1995), 1,900,000.

The Franklin Institute Science Museum, Philadelphia, Pennsylvania. Includes an exhibit on the environment called Earth Quest; a giant heart people can walk through; exhibits on astronomy (including an observatory), communications, mathematics, shipbuilding, and railroads. Features many hands-on exhibits. Visitors (1995), 1,000,000.

Liberty Science Center, Liberty State Park, Jersey City, New Jersey. Features more than 250 interactive exhibits and an OMNIMAX theater. The ferry to the Statue of Liberty and Ellis Island Museum is also in Liberty State Park. Visitors (1995), 900,000.

Southwest Museum of Science and Technology, The Science Place, Dallas, Texas. Includes hands-on science exhibits; water and sound experiments; an exhibit on special effects in movies; mathematical puzzles, and a planetarium. Visitors (1995), 600,000.

Signs and symbols give us information at a glance. Some signs indicate where something is located, such as Hospitals or Rest Rooms. Others give commands, such as Stop or Yield. Still others warn us of danger. Long ago, when most people did not know how to read, simple pictures and symbols were used on signs to help strangers find the shops in a town. Each sign shown here uses a symbol to describe something in a simple way, so you do not have to read the language to understand the sign.

Telephone	Gasoline	Hospital	First Aid	Drug Store
Handicapped Access	Men's Restroom	Women's Restroom	Food	Lodging
Airport	Information	Lost and Found	School Zone	No Bicycles
Picnic Area	Camping	Swimming	Fishing	Hiking Trail
No Smoking	Flammable	Poison	Radioactive	Explosives

ROAD SIGNS

Stop

One Way

No Entry

No Parking

Right Turn

No Left Turn

Hill

Signal Ahead

No U Turn

Pedestrian Crossing

Deer Crossing

Railroad Crossing

Road Work Ahead

Cross Road

Winding Road

Slippery Road

Divided Highway

Yield

Merging Traffic

SOME USEFUL SYMBOLS

$ Dollar

¢ Cent

% Percent

& Ampersand (and)

℞ Prescription

© Copyright

® Registered Trademark

♂ Male

♀ Female

± Plus or Minus

= Is Equal To

≠ Is Not Equal To

< Is Less Than

> Is Greater Than

( ) Parentheses

BRAILLE

Blind people read with their fingers using a system of raised dots called Braille. Braille was developed by Louis Braille (1809-1852) in France in 1826, when he was in his teens. The Braille alphabet, numbers, punctuation, and speech sounds are represented by 63 different combinations of 6 raised dots arranged in a grid like this:

1	4
2	5
3	6

The letters in the basic alphabet are lowercase. Special symbols are placed before the lowercase letters to form capital letters and numbers. The dark dots show the grid. The light dots show the raised dots.

BRAILLE ALPHABET AND NUMBERS

a b c d e f g h i j k l m

n o p q r s t u v w x y z

1 2 3 4 5 6 7 8 9 0

SIGN LANGUAGE

Many people who are deaf or hearing-impaired, and cannot hear spoken words, talk with their fingers instead of their voices. To do this, they use a system of manual signs (the manual alphabet), or finger spelling, in which the fingers are used to form letters and words. Originally developed in France by Abbe Charles Michel De l'Epee in the late 1700s, the manual alphabet was later brought to the United States by Laurent Clerc (1785-1869), a Frenchman who taught people who were deaf.

AMERICAN MANUAL ALPHABET

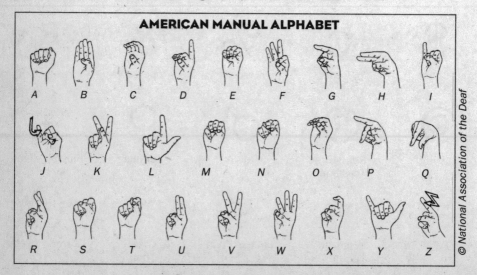

A B C D E F G H I

J K L M N O P Q

R S T U V W X Y Z

© National Association of the Deaf

SEC RETMES SAG ESAN DOT HERCO DES

Can you guess what the title of this page says? If you look closely, you will see that it is "secret messages and other codes" with the spaces between words changed. Changing the spaces between words is one of many ways to create secret codes. Different kinds of codes have been used since ancient times to keep military plans secret. Secret codes are still used today by the military, by banks for ATM machines, and in many other places. The science of writing and reading secret messages is called **cryptography.**

CIPHERS

One system of cryptography is called **ciphers.** In this system, letters are rearranged in different ways or letters may be substituted for other letters. In the examples below, you can see four ways that ciphers are used to hide the sentence "I WANT TO GO TO THE MOVIES."

1. Changing the spaces: IWA NTT OGO TOT HEMO VIES.

2. Writing the sentence backwards: SEIVOM EHT OT OG OT TNAW I.

3. Writing the sentence using the alphabet from Z to A instead of A to Z, so that A=Z, B=Y, C=X, D=W, and so on: R DZMG GL TL GL GSV NLERVH.

4. Writing the sentence using an alphabet with the letters rearranged, for example, O R A N G E B C D F H I J K L M P Q S T U V W X Y Z (O=A, R=B, A=C, N=D, and so on): D WOKT TL BL TL TCG JLVDGS.

NUMBERS FOR LETTERS

Numbers can also be used in place of some or all of the letters of the alphabet. If you know that 1=W, 2=T, 3=R, 4=O, 5=M, 6=K, 7=G, 8=E, and 9=A, you can read the message below.

73882IN7S F345 2H8 143LD 9L59N9C F43 6IDS

SECRET MESSAGE PUZZLE

To decipher (figure out) this secret message, look at the telephone buttons. Notice that most buttons contain one number and three letters. Let A=2, B=2, and C=(2). Do the same thing with the other buttons, so that D=3, E=3, and F=(3), and so on. If you need Q and Z, let Q=*, and Z=#. Now can you crack the code for this sentence? (Answers are on page 305.)

(9)(6)8 273 2 4(6)(6)3 3383(2)8(4)(8)3

193

The OLYMPIC GAMES

The first Olympic Games were played in Greece more than 2,500 years ago. They began in 776 B.C. and featured just one event—a footrace. The ancient Greeks later added boxing, wrestling, chariot racing, and the pentathlon (which consists of five different events). The ancient Olympic Games were held every four years for more than 1,000 years, until A.D. 393, when a Roman Emperor stopped them. The modern Olympic Games were organized by a French educator named Baron Pierre de Coubertin. In 1894, he helped set up the International Olympic Committee, which organized the Games.

1996: THE 100TH ANNIVERSARY OF THE OLYMPIC GAMES

The 100th anniversary of the modern Olympic Games was celebrated in Atlanta, Georgia, during the summer of 1996, from July 19 to August 4. Thousands of Olympic athletes from around the world competed in a total of 271 medal events. The 1996 Games marked the fourth time the summer Olympics took place in the United States. Previous Games were in St. Louis in 1904 and Los Angeles in 1932 and 1984.

TM © 1993 ACOG

▲ *Izzy, the 1996 Olympic mascot*

SOME OLYMPIC FIRSTS

1896 — **The first modern Olympic Games were held in Athens, Greece.** Thirteen countries and 311 athletes took part.

1900 — **Women competed in the Olympic Games for the first time.**

1908 — **For the first time, medals were awarded to the first three people to finish each event**—a gold medal for first place, a silver medal for second, and a bronze medal for third.

1920 — **The Olympic flag was raised for the first time, and the Olympic oath was introduced**. The five interlaced rings of the flag represent: North America, South America, Europe, Asia, and Africa.

1924 — **The Winter Olympics, featuring skiing and skating events, were held for the first time.**

1928 — **The Olympic flame was introduced at the Olympic Games.** The flame is carried by runners in a relay, from Olympia in Greece to the site of the Games. It traveled by air for the first time in 1956, when the Games were held in Australia.

1994 — **Starting with the 1994 Winter Olympics, the winter and summer Games have been held two years apart,** instead of in the same year.

SITES OF OLYMPIC GAMES

Winter Games:
1998 Nagano, Japan
2002 Salt Lake City, Utah, U.S.

Summer Games:
1996 Atlanta, Georgia, U.S.
2000 Sydney, Australia

OLYMPIC SPORTS

1996 Summer Olympic Sports

Archery	Football (Soccer)	Softball
Badminton	Gymnastics	Swimming
Baseball	Rhythmic Gymnastics	Synchronized Swimming
Basketball		
Boxing	Judo	Table Tennis
Canoe/Kayak	Modern Pentathlon (cross-country riding, fencing, pistol shooting, swimming, cross-country running—one event per day for 5 days)	Team Handball
Cycling		Tennis
Diving		Track and Field
Equestrian (dressage, show jumping, 3-day event)		Volleyball
		Water Polo
		Weight Lifting
Fencing	Rowing	Wrestling
Field Hockey	Shooting	Yachting

1998 Winter Olympic Sports

Biathlon (cross-country skiing, rifle marksmanship)
Bobsled
Curling
Ice Hockey
Luge (Toboggan)
Figure Skating
Speed Skating
Alpine Skiing
Freestyle Skiing
Nordic Skiing
Cross-Country
Ski Jumping
Nordic Combined
Snowboarding

? DID YOU KNOW?

☑ Snowboarding, one of the most popular and fastest-growing sports in the world, will officially become an Olympic event at the 1998 Winter Games.

☑ The Paralympic Games are for international athletes who are wheelchair bound, are blind or visually impaired, or have other physical disabilities. These Games, which are held after the Summer and the Winter Olympic Games, were first held in 1960. The 1996 Paralympic Games were held in August in Atlanta, where 3,500 athletes from more than 100 nations competed for medals in 19 sports.

BASEBALL

For Major League Baseball, 1995 was a comeback year. The longest players' strike in history began on August 12, 1994, and caused the 1994 World Series to be canceled. The strike finally ended on April 2, 1995, but the 1995 season was shortened from the normal 162 games to 144. The fans didn't return immediately. Attendance at ballparks generally was down all season long. But for the first time ever, baseball used its new playoff setup, with three divisions in each league leading to an extra playoff series. Those playoffs and the World Series between the Atlanta Braves and Cleveland Indians brought some of the excitement back to baseball.

FINAL 1995 STANDINGS

AMERICAN LEAGUE

Eastern Division	Won	Lost
Boston Red Sox	86	58
New York Yankees*	79	65
Baltimore Orioles	71	73
Detroit Tigers	60	84
Toronto Blue Jays	56	88

Central Division	Won	Lost
Cleveland Indians	100	44
Kansas City Royals	70	74
Chicago White Sox	68	76
Milwaukee Brewers	65	79
Minnesota Twins	56	88

Western Division	Won	Lost
Seattle Mariners	79	66
California Angels	78	67
Texas Rangers	74	70
Oakland Athletics	67	77

*Wild card team

NATIONAL LEAGUE

Eastern Division	Won	Lost
Atlanta Braves	90	54
New York Mets	69	75
Philadelphia Phillies	69	75
Florida Marlins	67	76
Montreal Expos	66	78

Central Division	Won	Lost
Cincinnati Reds	85	59
Houston Astros	76	68
Chicago Cubs	73	71
St. Louis Cardinals	62	81
Pittsburgh Pirates	58	86

Western Division	Won	Lost
Los Angeles Dodgers	78	66
Colorado Rockies*	77	67
San Diego Padres	70	74
San Francisco Giants	67	77

*Wild card team

PLAYOFF RESULTS

Division Series
 Cleveland defeated Boston 3-0
 Seattle defeated New York 3-2
Championship Series
 Cleveland defeated Seattle 4-2

Division Series
 Atlanta defeated Colorado 3-1
 Cincinnati defeated Los Angeles 3-0
Championship Series
 Atlanta defeated Cincinnati 4-0

WORLD SERIES
Atlanta defeated Cleveland 4 games to 2

? **DID YOU KNOW?** In Major League Baseball, the distance between bases is 90 feet. The distance from the pitcher's mound to home plate is 60 feet, 6 inches.

1995 MAJOR LEAGUE LEADERS

Most Valuable Players
  American League: Mo Vaughn, Boston Red Sox
  National League: Barry Larkin, Cincinnati Reds
Cy Young Award Winners (Top Pitcher)
  American League: Randy Johnson, Seattle Mariners
  National League: Greg Maddux, Atlanta Braves
Rookies of the Year
  American League: Marty Cordova, Minnesota Twins
  National League: Hideo Nomo, Los Angeles Dodgers
Batting Champs
  American League: Edgar Martinez, Seattle Mariners, .356
  National League: Tony Gwynn, San Diego Padres, .368
Home Run Leaders
  American League: Albert Belle, Cleveland Indians, 50
  National League: Dante Bichette, Colorado Rockies, 40
Runs Batted In (RBI) Leaders
  American League: Albert Belle, Cleveland Indians, 126
                Mo Vaughn, Boston Red Sox, 126
  National League: Dante Bichette, Colorado Rockies, 128
Most Pitching Victories
  American League: Mike Mussina, Baltimore Orioles, 19
  National League: Greg Maddux, Atlanta Braves, 19

▲ *Greg Maddux*

 DID YOU KNOW?

☑ On September 6, 1995, Cal Ripkin, Jr., of the Baltimore Orioles broke one of baseball's most amazing records. On that day, Ripkin played his 2,131st straight game, breaking the record of 2,130 set by the Yankees' Lou Gehrig in 1939. Ripkin didn't miss a single game for more than 13 years.

☑ By winning the National League's Cy Young Award in 1995, Greg Maddux of the Atlanta Braves became the first pitcher in baseball history to win the coveted prize four straight years.

BASEBALL HALL OF FAME

The National Baseball Hall of Fame and Museum opened on June 12, 1939, in Cooperstown, New York. To be nominated for membership, players must be retired from baseball for five years. **Address:** Post Office Box 590, Cooperstown, NY 13326. **Phone:** (607) 547-7200.

LITTLE LEAGUE

The Little League is the largest youth sports program in the world. Little League baseball began in 1939 in Williamsport, Pennsylvania, with 30 boys playing on 3 teams. By 1996, 3 million boys and girls ages 5 to 18 were playing on 198,000 Little League teams in 84 countries. The Little League celebrated the 50th anniversary of its World Series in 1996.

DID YOU KNOW? A Little League baseball field is smaller than a Major League field. The distance between the bases is 60 feet (instead of 90 feet), and the distance from home plate to the outfield wall is 200 feet (much shorter than in the majors).

BASKETBALL

Basketball began in 1891 in Springfield, Massachusetts, when Dr. James Naismith invented it using peach baskets as hoops. Big-time professional basketball was born in 1949, when the National Basketball Association (NBA) was formed. In the 1995-1996 season, there were 29 NBA teams.

PROFESSIONAL BASKETBALL

FINAL 1995-1996 NBA STANDINGS

EASTERN CONFERENCE

Atlantic Division	Won	Lost
Orlando Magic	60	22
New York Knicks	47	35
Miami Heat	42	40
Washington Bullets	39	43
Boston Celtics	33	49
New Jersey Nets	30	52
Philadelphia 76ers	18	64

Central Division	Won	Lost
Chicago Bulls	72	10
Indiana Pacers	52	30
Cleveland Cavaliers	47	35
Atlanta Hawks	46	36
Detroit Pistons	46	36
Charlotte Hornets	41	41
Milwaukee Bucks	25	57
Toronto Raptors	21	61

WESTERN CONFERENCE

Midwest Division	Won	Lost
San Antonio Spurs	59	23
Utah Jazz	55	27
Houston Rockets	48	34
Denver Nuggets	35	47
Minnesota Timberwolves	26	56
Dallas Mavericks	26	56
Vancouver Grizzlies	15	67

Pacific Division	Won	Lost
Seattle SuperSonics	64	18
Los Angeles Lakers	53	29
Portland Trail Blazers	44	38
Phoenix Suns	41	41
Sacramento Kings	39	43
Golden State Warriors	36	46
Los Angeles Clippers	29	53

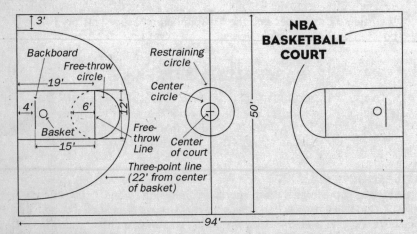

NBA BASKETBALL COURT

CONFERENCE FINALS

Eastern Conference: Chicago Bulls defeated Orlando Magic, 4 games to 0.
Western Conference: Seattle SuperSonics defeated Utah Jazz, 4 games to 3.

CHAMPIONSHIP SERIES

Chicago Bulls defeated Seattle SuperSonics, 4 games to 2.

HIGHLIGHTS OF THE 1995-1996 BASKETBALL SEASON

Most Valuable Player: Michael Jordan, Chicago Bulls
Defensive Player of the Year: Gary Payton, Seattle SuperSonics
Rookie of the Year: Damon Stoudamire, Toronto Raptors
Coach of the Year: Phil Jackson, Chicago Bulls
Most Valuable Player in the Finals: Michael Jordan, Chicago Bulls
Scoring Leader: Michael Jordan, Chicago Bulls

| Games: 82 | Points: 2,491 | Average: 30.4 |

Rebounding Leader: Dennis Rodman, Chicago Bulls

| Games: 64 | Rebounds: 952 | Average: 14.9 |

Assists Leader: John Stockton, Utah Jazz

| Games: 82 | Assists: 916 | Average: 11.2 |

Steals Leader: Gary Payton, Seattle SuperSonics

| Games: 81 | Steals: 231 | Average: 2.85 |

Blocked Shots Leader: Dikembe Mutombo, Denver Nuggets

| Games: 74 | Blocks: 332 | Average: 4.49 |

BASKETBALL HALL OF FAME

The Naismith Memorial Basketball Hall of Fame was founded in 1959 to honor great basketball players, coaches, referees, and other people who have made important contributions to the game. Named after the inventor of basketball, the museum features exhibits on the history of the game. **Address:** 1150 West Columbus Avenue, Springfield, MA 01101-0179. **Phone:** (413) 781-5759.

DID YOU KNOW?

☑ By winning 72 games in the 1995-1996 season, the Chicago Bulls set a new NBA record.

☑ The Boston Celtics have won 16 NBA championships, more than any other team.

☑ In the 1961-1962 season, Wilt Chamberlain averaged an incredible 50.4 points per game, and he had a game against the New York Knicks in which he scored a record 100 points.

☑ When he retired in 1989 after 20 NBA seasons, Kareem Abdul-Jabbar had scored a record 38,387 points.

☑ A basketball is made from an inflated bladder with a cemented leather or rubber cover. It weighs 20-22 ounces and has a circumference of 30 inches.

MAGIC'S 1996 COMEBACK

On January 30, 1996, midway through the 1995-1996 season, Earvin "Magic" Johnson rejoined the Los Angeles Lakers. In November 1991, he had shocked the sports world by retiring from the NBA because he had HIV, the virus that causes AIDS. One of the all-time greats, Magic quickly showed he hadn't lost his touch. In his first game back, he scored 19 points, had 10 assists, and grabbed 8 rebounds. Magic helped lead the Lakers into the playoffs, but at the end of the season he decided to retire again.

▲ Magic Johnson

COLLEGE BASKETBALL

College basketball has become a huge sport. The National Collegiate Athletic Association (NCAA) Tournament began in 1939. Today, it is a spectacular 64-team extravaganza that is considered the national championship tournament. The Final Four weekend, when the semi-finals and finals are played, is one of the most watched sports events in America. The NCAA Tournament for women's basketball began in 1982. Since then, the popularity of the women's game has grown by leaps and bounds.

THE 1995-1996 NCAA TOURNAMENT RESULTS

MEN'S FINAL FOUR RESULTS

Semi-Finals:
Kentucky 81 Massachusetts 74
Syracuse 77 Mississippi State 69
Championship Game:
Kentucky 76 Syracuse 67

DID YOU KNOW? When the University of Kentucky defeated Syracuse University to win the 1995-1996 national championship, it was the sixth time the Wildcats reached the top of the college basketball world. Their six national crowns are second only to UCLA, which has won 11 times.

WOMEN'S FINAL FOUR RESULTS

Semi-Finals:
Tennessee 88 Connecticut 83 (OT)
Georgia 86 Stanford 76
Championship Game:
Tennessee 83 Georgia 65

DID YOU KNOW? With their national championship in 1995-1996, the Lady Vols of the University of Tennessee won for the fourth time in 15 years of women's NCAA championship play. That's twice as many titles as any other school. The University of Connecticut in 1995 and the University of Texas in 1986 remain the only schools to have won women's titles with undefeated teams.

▲ Marcus Camby

BOOST/NAISMITH AWARD WINNERS 1995-1996

MEN
Player of the Year: Marcus Camby, Massachusetts
Coach of the Year: John Calipari, Massachusetts

WOMEN
Player of the Year: Saudia Roundtree, Georgia
Coach of the Year: Andy Landers, Georgia

FOOTBALL

American football began as a college sport. The first game that was like today's football took place between Yale and Harvard in New Haven, Connecticut, on November 13, 1875. The sport was largely shaped by Walter Camp in the 1880s. He reduced the number of players to 11 on each side and introduced the idea of each play beginning from the line of scrimmage. He also introduced the concept of "downs" and was the first to have the field lined with chalk every five yards.

PROFESSIONAL FOOTBALL

The 1995 National Football League season ended on January 28, 1996, with the Dallas Cowboys winning the Super Bowl for the third time in four years. This time, the NFC Cowboys defeated the AFC Pittsburgh Steelers, 27-17, in Super Bowl XXX. It was also a year of great individual performances. Dallas's Emmitt Smith won another rushing title and set a record with 25 touchdowns. Herman Moore of the Detroit Lions set a receiving record with 123 catches, while Green Bay quarterback Brett Favre became the league's Most Valuable Player.

FINAL NFL STANDINGS FOR THE 1995 SEASON

National Football Conference

Eastern Division	Won	Lost
Dallas Cowboys	12	4
Philadelphia Eagles	10	6
Washington Redskins	6	10
New York Giants	5	11
Arizona Cardinals	4	12

Central Division	Won	Lost
Green Bay Packers	11	5
Detroit Lions	10	6
Chicago Bears	9	7
Minnesota Vikings	8	8
Tampa Bay Buccaneers	7	9

Western Division	Won	Lost
San Francisco 49ers	11	5
Atlanta Falcons	9	7
New Orleans Saints	7	9
St. Louis Rams	7	9
Carolina Panthers	7	9

American Football Conference

Eastern Divison	Won	Lost
Buffalo Bills	10	6
Indianapolis Colts	9	7
Miami Dolphins	9	7
New England Patriots	6	10
New York Jets	3	13

Central Division	Won	Lost
Pittsburgh Steelers	11	5
Cincinnati Bengals	7	9
Houston Oilers	7	9
Cleveland Browns	5	11
Jacksonville Jaguars	4	12

Western Division	Won	Lost
Kansas City Chiefs	13	3
San Diego Chargers	9	7
Oakland Raiders	8	8
Denver Broncos	8	8
Seattle Seahawks	8	8

1995 Conference Championship Games
National Football Conference: Dallas Cowboys 38, Green Bay Packers 27
American Football Conference: Pittsburgh Steelers 20, Indianapolis Colts 16

Super Bowl XXX, January 28, 1996, Sun Devil Stadium, Tempe, Arizona
Dallas Cowboys 27, Pittsburgh Steelers 17

NFL FOOTBALL FIELD

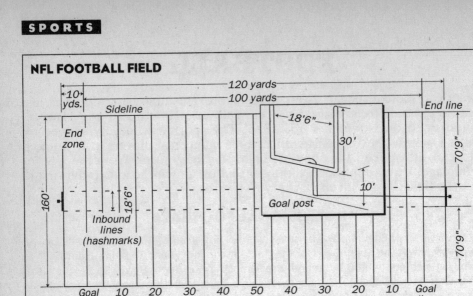

TOP NFL PERFORMERS OF 1995

Rushing Leader: Emmitt Smith, Dallas Cowboys
   Carries: 377; **Yards:** 1,773; **Average:** 4.7
Passing Leader: Jim Harbaugh, Indianapolis Colts
   Passing Attempts: 314; **Passing Completions:** 200;
   Passing Yards: 2,575;
   Passing Completion Percentage: 63.7;
   Touchdown Passes: 17; **Passes Intercepted:** 5;
   Quarterback rating: 100.7
Pass Receiving Leader: Herman Moore, Detroit Lions
   Catches: 123 (new record); **Yards:** 1,686; **Average:** 13.7

The following awards were all chosen by the Associated Press
   Most Valuable Player: Brett Favre, Green Bay Packers
   Offensive Player of the Year: Brett Favre, Green Bay Packers
   Defensive Player of the Year: Bryce Paup, Buffalo Bills
   Coach of the Year: Ray Rhodes, Philadelphia Eagles
   Offensive Rookie of the Year: Curtis Martin, New England Patriots
   Defensive Rookie of the Year: Hugh Douglas, New York Jets

▲ *Emmitt Smith*

? DID YOU KNOW? A football is 11 to 11¼ inches long and weighs 14-15 ounces. It is oval in shape and somewhat pointed at the ends. It is made up of an inflated bladder covered with pebbled grain leather.

PRO FOOTBALL HALL OF FAME

Football's Hall of Fame was founded in 1963 by the National Football League to honor the game's outstanding players, coaches, and contributors. To be nominated, players must be retired from football for five years. **Address:** Football Hall of Fame, 2121 George Halas Drive, Canton, OH 44708. **Phone:** (216) 456-8207.

COLLEGE FOOTBALL

College football is one of America's most colorful and exciting sports. The National Collegiate Athletic Association (NCAA), which was founded in 1906, oversees college football today. There is no one tournament to determine the best team in college football. The national champion is chosen by several football polls, which sometimes disagree.

1995 TOP 10 COLLEGE TEAMS					
Chosen by the Associated Press Poll and the USA Today/CNN Poll.					
Rank	AP	USA Today/CNN	Rank	AP	USA Today/CNN
1.	Nebraska	Nebraska	6.	Ohio State	Kansas State
2.	Florida	Tennessee	7.	Kansas State	Northwestern
3.	Tennessee	Florida	8.	Northwestern	Ohio State
4.	Florida State	Colorado	9.	Kansas	Virginia Tech
5.	Colorado	Florida State	10.	Virginia Tech	Kansas

THE BOWL GAMES

Post-season "bowl" games held on or near New Year's Day have become a great part of college football tradition. The Bowl Alliance, which includes the Sugar, Fiesta, and Orange Bowls, has been formed to try to get the best matchups in these Bowls, with the hope that one will determine the national champion. The Rose Bowl is the oldest bowl game, having been played first in 1902. There are now some 18 bowl games.

SOME 1995 SEASON MAJOR BOWL RESULTS

Rose Bowl (Pasadena, California): Southern Cal 41, Northwestern 32
Orange Bowl (Miami, Florida): Florida State 31, Notre Dame 26
Cotton Bowl (Dallas, Texas): Colorado 38, Oregon 6
Sugar Bowl (New Orleans, Louisiana): Virginia Tech 28, Texas 10
Fiesta Bowl* (Tempe, Arizona): Nebraska 62, Florida 24
*The Fiesta Bowl matchup determined the
 national champion.

▲ Eddie George

HEISMAN TROPHY. The Heisman Trophy is given to the most outstanding college football player in the United States. It was first presented in 1935. The **1995 Heisman Trophy Winner** was running back Eddie George of Ohio State, who led all Division I-A players in touchdowns, with 24, and was fifth in the nation in rushing, with an average of 152 yards per game.

COLLEGE FOOTBALL HALL OF FAME

The College Football Hall of Fame was established in 1955 by the National Football Foundation. To be nominated, a player must be out of college 10 years and must have been a first team All-American pick by a major selector during his career. Coaches must be retired three years.
Address: 111 South St. Joseph Street, P.O. Box 11146, South Bend, Indiana 46601. **Phone:** (219) 235-9999.

GYMNASTICS

It takes a combination of strength, coordination, and grace to become a top gymnast. Although the sport goes back to ancient Greece, present-day gymnastics began in Sweden in the early 1800s. The sport has been part of the Olympic Games since 1896. An Olympic gold medal is the highest honor that a gymnast can receive. There is also an annual World Gymnastics Championship meet.

GYMNASTIC EVENTS

FOR WOMEN
1. All-Around
2. Side Horse Vault
3. Asymmetrical (Uneven) Bars
4. Balance Beam
5. Floor Exercises
6. Team Combined Exercises
7. Rhythmic All-Around

FOR MEN
1. All-Around
2. Horizontal Bar
3. Parallel Bars
4. Rings
5. Long Horse Vault
6. Side Horse (Pommel Horse)
7. Floor Exercises
8. Team Combined Exercises

HOW ARE GYMNASTS JUDGED?

Gymnasts must do both compulsory and optional exercises during a routine. **Compulsory exercises** are rated for mechanical correctness, grace, rhythm, ease, form, continuity, posture, and timing. **Optional exercises** are judged for their difficulty, combination of movements, risk, originality, and execution. Scores range from 1 to a perfect 10. There are four or six judges at a competition. The highest and lowest scores are dropped, and the remaining scores are averaged for the contestant's mark.

ALL-AROUND CHAMPIONSHIP AT THE OLYMPICS

In women's Olympics competition, the All-Around championship is decided by adding the scores of four individual events (balance beam, floor exercise, uneven bars, vault). In men's competition, the All-Around is decided by adding the scores of six individual events (floor exercise, horizontal bar, parallel bars, pommel horse, rings, vault).

? **DID YOU KNOW?** Gymnastics is a sport in which teenage girls often excel.

☑ At the 1976 Olympics, 14-year-old Nadia Comanici of Romania became the first gymnast ever to receive a perfect score of 10 on both the uneven bars and the balance beam. Before the Olympics ended, she had been awarded seven perfect 10s. She also won three gold medals. Today, women must be at least 15 years of age to compete, and men must be at least 16.

☑ At the 1984 Olympics, 16-year-old Mary Lou Retton from Fairmont, West Virginia, became the first American woman to win the All-Around gold medal.

☑ When Shannon Miller became World Champion by winning the All-Around competition in 1994, she became the first U.S. women's gymnast to win this prestigious title two years in a row.

▲ *Shannon Miller*

ICE HOCKEY

Ice hockey began in Canada in the mid-1800s. By the beginning of the 1900s, hockey was becoming a major Canadian sport. The National Hockey League was formed in 1916 and has been in operation ever since. In the 1995-1996 season, there were 26 teams in the NHL, 19 in the United States and 7 in Canada.

FINAL 1995-1996 STANDINGS

EASTERN CONFERENCE

Northeast Division

	W	L	T	Pts
Pittsburgh Penguins	49	29	4	102
Boston Bruins	40	31	11	91
Montreal Canadiens	40	32	10	90
Hartford Whalers	34	39	9	77
Buffalo Sabres	33	42	7	73
Ottawa Senators	18	59	5	41

Atlantic Division

	W	L	T	Pts
Philadelphia Flyers	45	24	13	103
New York Rangers	41	27	14	96
Florida Panthers	41	31	10	92
Washington Capitals	39	32	11	89
Tampa Bay Lightning	38	32	12	88
New Jersey Devils	37	33	12	86
New York Islanders	22	50	10	54

WESTERN CONFERENCE

Central Division

	W	L	T	Pts
Detroit Red Wings	62	13	7	131
Chicago Blackhawks	40	28	14	94
Toronto Maple Leafs	34	36	12	80
St. Louis Blues	32	34	16	80
Winnipeg Jets	36	40	6	78
Dallas Stars	26	42	14	66

Pacific Division

	W	L	T	Pts
Colorado Avalanche	47	25	10	104
Calgary Flames	34	37	11	79
Vancouver Canucks	32	35	15	79
Anaheim Mighty Ducks	35	39	8	78
Edmonton Oilers	30	44	8	68
Los Angeles Kings	24	40	18	66
San Jose Sharks	20	55	7	47

? DID YOU KNOW? In 1995-1996 the Detroit Red Wings set a new league record for most victories in a season, with 62.

CONFERENCE FINALS

Eastern Conference: Florida Panthers defeated Pittsburgh Penguins, 4 games to 3.
Western Conference: Colorado Avalanche defeated Detroit Red Wings, 4 games to 2.
NHL CHAMPIONSHIP: Colorado Avalanche defeated Florida Panthers, 4 games to 0, to win the Stanley Cup.

? DID YOU KNOW? Mario Lemieux, of the Pittsburgh Penguins, made a great comeback in the 1995-1996 NHL season. After sitting out 1994-1995 because of illness, "Super Mario" returned to win his fifth scoring title with 161 points (69 goals, 92 assists) and his third Most Valuable Player award.

▲ *Mario Lemieux*

HOCKEY HALL OF FAME

The Hockey Hall of Fame was opened in 1961 to honor important hockey figures.
Address: BCE Place, 30 Yonge Street, Toronto, Ontario, Canada M5E 1X8.
Phone: (416) 360-7735.

ICE SKATING

People have enjoyed ice skating for hundreds of years. The first skates were made from animal bones ground to a smooth, flat surface. Wooden skates with iron blades appeared in the Netherlands around the 13th or 14th century. Steel skating blades appeared around 1860 and allowed skaters to move quickly and with more control.

FIGURE SKATING

There are two types of competitive ice skating—figure skating and speed skating. Figure skating, which is almost like ballet, is judged by the way the skaters perform certain turns and jumps and by the creative difficulty of their programs. There are singles competitions for both men and women, pairs skating, and ice dancing.

1996 World Championships

The figure skating World Championships took place in Edmonton, Alberta, Canada in March of 1996. Below are the winners for the singles competition.

	Women's Singles	Men's Singles
Gold Medal:	Michelle Kwan (U.S.)	Todd Eldredge (U.S.)
Silver Medal:	Chen Lu (China)	Ilia Kulik (Russia)
Bronze Medal:	Irina Slutskaya (Russia)	Rudy Galindo (U.S.)

? **DID YOU KNOW?** When Michelle Kwan and Todd Eldredge won gold medals at the 1996 figure skating World Championships, it marked the first time that both the women's and men's champions were from the United States since 1986. That year, Debi Thomas and Brian Boitano brought home the gold. At age 15, Michelle Kwan was the youngest American and the third youngest woman to win a world title. Sonia Henie was just 14 when she won in 1927, and Oksana Baiul was 15, but a few months younger than Kwan, when she was victorious in 1993.

Michelle Kwan ▶

America's Olympic Champions

Below are America's Olympic gold medalists in singles competition:

Men: Dick Button (1948, 1952), Hayes Alan Jenkins (1956), David Jenkins (1960), Scott Hamilton (1984), Brian Boitano (1988).

Women: Tenley Albright (1956), Carol Heiss (1960), Peggy Fleming (1968), Dorothy Hamill (1976), Kristi Yamaguchi (1992).

SPEED SKATING

Speed skating is a race around an oval track. The traditional track is 400 meters around with two lanes. The skaters, who skate two at a time, are racing the clock. The winner is the skater with the fastest time of any competitor. Speed skating for men became part of the Winter Olympics in 1924, for women in 1960. Men compete in five events: the 500 meters, 1,000 meters, 1,500 meters, 5,000 meters, and 10,000 meters. Women also compete in five events: the 500 meters, 1,000 meters, 1,500 meters, 3,000 meters, and 5,000 meters.

SOCCER

Soccer, which is called football in many countries, is the number one sport worldwide. It is estimated that soccer is played by more than 100,000,000 people in over 150 countries. The first rules for the game were published in 1863 by the London Football Association. Since then, the sport has spread rapidly from Europe to almost every part of the world. The United States Youth Soccer Association runs age-group programs for more than one million kids all around the country.

THE WORLD CUP. The biggest soccer tournament is the World Cup. It is held every four years. Teams from more than 100 nations compete, and the top 24 teams represent their countries in a three-week long tournament. In 1994, the World Cup tournament was held in the United States for the first time.

1994 World Cup Results

Semifinals:	Brazil 1	Sweden 0
	Italy 2	Bulgaria 1
Championship:	Brazil 3	Italy 2
	(Game decided by penalty kicks)	

▲ *Tony Meola*

? **DID YOU KNOW?** In April 1996, Major League Soccer, a new professional league, started play with ten teams in major United States cities. Three quarters of the players were born in the United States. League officials hope exciting players such as goalkeeper Tony Meola and others from the 1994 U.S. World Cup team will help make professional soccer popular in America.

SWIMMING

Competitive swimming as an organized sport began in the second half of the 19th century. When the modern Olympic Games began in Athens, Greece, in 1896, the only racing stroke was the breaststroke. Today, men and women at the Olympics swim the backstroke, breaststroke, butterfly, and freestyle, in events ranging from 50 meters to 1,500 meters.

SWIMMERS SWIM FASTER AND FASTER. When Johnny Weissmuller won the 100-meter freestyle at the 1924 Olympics, his winning time was 59.0 seconds. When Matt Biondi won it in 1988, his winning time was 48.63 seconds, more than 10 seconds faster than Weissmuller's. Swimming records continue to be broken nearly every year.

Some Great U.S. Olympic Swimmers

☑ **Johnny Weissmuller** won three gold medals at the 1924 and 1928 Games and later became even more famous playing Tarzan in movies.

☑ **Mark Spitz** won two gold medals in relays at the 1968 Games and returned in 1972 to make Olympic swimming history by winning seven gold medals.

☑ **Janet Evans**, at age 17, won three gold medals at the 1988 Olympics in Seoul, South Korea. In 1992, she won another gold and a silver in Barcelona, Spain.

☑ **Matt Biondi** won seven medals at the 1988 Olympics, including five golds.

TENNIS

The modern game of tennis began in 1873 when a British officer, Major Walter Wingfield, developed it from the earlier game of court tennis. In 1877, the first championship matches were held at the old Wimbledon Grounds near London. The United States Lawn Tennis Association was founded in 1881, and that same year the first United States men's championships were held at Newport, Rhode Island. Six years later the first women's championships took place in Philadelphia.

GRAND SLAM TOURNAMENTS

Today, professional tennis players from all over the world compete in dozens of tournaments. The four most important, called the **grand slam** tournaments, are the Australian Open, the French Open, the All-England (Wimbledon) Championships, and the United States Open. There are separate competitions for men and women in singles and doubles. There are also mixed doubles, where men and women team together.

Men's and Women's Singles Champions

1996 Australian Open Finals
Men: Boris Becker (Germany) defeated Michael Chang (U.S.) 6-2, 6-4, 2-6, 6-2
Women: Monica Seles (U.S.) defeated Anka Huber (Germany) 6-4, 6-1

1995 Wimbledon Finals
Men: Pete Sampras (U.S.) defeated Boris Becker (Germany) 6-7, 6-2, 6-4, 6-2
Women: Steffi Graf (Germany) defeated Arantxa Sanchez Vicario (Spain) 4-6, 6-1, 7-5

1996 French Open Finals
Men: Yevgeny Kafelnikov (Russia) defeated Michael Stich (Germany) 7-6, 7-5, 7-6
Women: Steffi Graf (Germany) defeated Arantxa Sanchez Vicario (Spain) 6-3, 6-7, 10-8

1995 United States Open Finals
Men: Pete Sampras (U.S.) defeated Andre Agassi (U.S.) 6-4, 6-3, 4-6, 7-5
Women: Steffi Graf (Germany) defeated Monica Seles (U.S.) 7-6, 0-6, 6-4

RANKINGS FOR 1995.
The Association of Tennis Professionals (ATP) and the Women's Tennis Association (WTA) now keep computer rankings of all the players on the tour. The final top five rankings for men and women in 1995 were as follows.

Women
1. Steffi Graf, Germany; Monica Seles, United States (co-number one)
2. Conchita Martinez, Spain
3. Arantxa Sanchez Vicario, Spain
4. Kimiko Date, Japan
5. Mary Pierce, France

Men
1. Pete Sampras, United States
2. Andre Agassi, United States
3. Thomas Muster, Austria
4. Boris Becker, Germany
5. Michael Chang, United States

? DID YOU KNOW? After winning seven grand slam championships by the time she was 19, Monica Seles saw her career almost end when she was stabbed during a match in April 1993. Seles stayed out of tennis for more than two years. When she returned in 1995, she made it to the finals of the U.S. Open. A few months later, she won the 1996 Australian Open.

▲ *Monica Seles*

SPECIAL OLYMPICS

The Special Olympics is the world's largest program of sports training and athletic competition for children and adults with mental retardation. Founded in 1968, Special Olympics International has offices in all 50 U.S. states and Washington, D.C., and in many countries throughout the world. The organization offers year-round training and competition in 17 summer sports and 6 winter sports to nearly 1.5 million athletes in more than 140 countries.

The first Special Olympics competition was held in Chicago in 1968. After holding national events in individual countries, Special Olympics International holds World Games. The World Games alternate between summer and winter sports every two years. The 1995 Special Olympics World Summer Games were held in New Haven, Connecticut, in July. The 1997 Special Olympics World Winter Games are to be held in Toronto and Collingwood, Canada, in February.

SPECIAL OLYMPICS OFFICIAL SPORTS

Summer: aquatics, athletics (track and field), basketball, bowling, cycling, equestrian, gymnastics, roller skating, soccer, softball, tennis, volleyball
Demonstration sports: badminton, golf, poly hockey (similar to floor hockey), powerlifting, table tennis, team handball
Winter: alpine and cross-country skiing, figure and speed skating, floor hockey

WHERE TO GET MORE INFORMATION ON THE SPECIAL OLYMPICS

Anyone wanting more information on the Special Olympics can write to:
Special Olympics International Headquarters,
1325 G Street Washington, D.C. 20005.

SPORTS MATCHING PUZZLE

How many of the athletes in the first column can you match with the sports in the second column? All of the names can be found in the SPORTS section. (Answers are on page 305.)

ATHLETES	SPORTS
Monica Seles	BASEBALL
Mario Lemieux	FOOTBALL
Mary Lou Retton	BASKETBALL
Jim Harbaugh	HOCKEY
Kristi Yamaguchi	TENNIS
Dennis Rodman	SWIMMING
Greg Maddux	GYMNASTICS
Janet Evans	FIGURE SKATING

What Are TIME ZONES?

The length of a day is 24 hours—the time it takes Earth to complete one rotation on its axis. The system we use to tell time is called **standard time**. In standard time, Earth is divided into 24 time zones. The time zones run north to south, from the North Pole to the South Pole. To figure out the time in a particular zone, you must count the number of zones east or west of the **prime meridian**, or 0 degrees, which runs through Greenwich, England. When it is midnight, or 0 hour, in Greenwich, it is 5 hours earlier in New York, because New York is 5 zones away. Forty-eight states of the United States are in 4 of the 24 time zones (Alaska and Hawaii are in different time zones).

WHEN IT IS 12 NOON IN NEW YORK, IT IS

12 noon in Atlanta, Georgia
11 A.M. in St. Louis, Missouri
11 A.M. in Dallas, Texas
10 A.M. in Denver, Colorado
 9 A.M. in Los Angeles, California
 8 A.M. in Juneau, Alaska
 7 A.M. in Honolulu, Hawaii

TRAVEL TIME

1492 — Christopher Columbus's first trip across the Atlantic Ocean from Spain to San Salvador took 70 days.

1650s — It took 50 days to sail from London, England, to Boston, Massachusetts.

1829 — The first Atlantic Ocean crossing by a ship powered in part by steam (*Savannah*, sailing from Savannah, Georgia, to Liverpool, England) took 29 days.

1903 — The first flight in a heavier-than-air craft was performed by Wilbur Wright at Kitty Hawk, North Carolina, and lasted for 59 seconds.

1927 — Charles Lindbergh flew from New York to Paris in 33 hours, 29 minutes, 30 seconds in the first nonstop flight across the Atlantic Ocean by one person.

1961 — The flight of the first U.S. satellite carrying an astronaut (Alan Shepard, Jr.) lasted 15 minutes.

1990s — Travel by supersonic plane, the Concorde, between London and New York now takes 3 ½ hours.

CALENDARS

WHAT IS A CALENDAR?

Calendars divide time into units, such as days, weeks, months, and years. Calendar divisions are based on movements of Earth and on the sun and the moon. A day is the average time it takes for one rotation of Earth on its axis (24 hours). A year is the average time it takes for one revolution of Earth around the sun (365.3 days).

EARLIEST CALENDAR: The Egyptian Calendar

In ancient times, calendars were based upon the movements of the moon across the sky. The ancient Egyptians were the first to develop a solar calendar, a calendar based on the movements of the sun.

ROMAN CALENDARS: The Julian and Gregorian Calendars

At first the ancient Romans had a calendar with a year of 304 days, but it was not a solar calendar and became confusing. Later, in 45 B.C., the emperor Julius Caesar decided to use a calendar based on the movements of the sun. This calendar, called the **Julian calendar,** fixed the normal year at 365 days and added one day every fourth year (leap year). The Julian calendar also established the months of the year and the days of the week.

The Julian calendar was used until A.D. 1582, when it was revised by Pope Gregory XIII, because the Julian calendar year was 11 minutes and 14 seconds longer than the solar year. Pope Gregory shortened the calendar year slightly to match the solar year. This new calendar, called the **Gregorian calendar,** is the one we use today in the United States.

OTHER CALENDARS: Jewish and Islamic Calendars

Other calendars are also used. The Jewish calendar, which starts in the year 3761 B.C., is the official calendar of the State of Israel. The year 1997 is equivalent to the year 5757-5758 on the Jewish calendar, beginning at Rosh Hashanah (New Year). The Islamic calendar starts counting years in A.D. 622. The year 1997 is equivalent to the year 1417-1418 on the Islamic calendar, beginning at Muharram (New Year).

? DID YOU KNOW? Stonehenge, the ancient stone monument in Salisbury, England, is between 3,000 and 5,000 years old. Most scientists think it was used to predict the positions of the sun and moon—a kind of huge calendar.

BIRTHSTONES					
January	Garnet	May	Emerald	September	Sapphire
February	Amethyst	June	Pearl	October	Opal
March	Aquamarine	July	Ruby	November	Topaz
April	Diamond	August	Peridot	December	Turquoise

UNITED NATIONS

The United Nations—or UN for short—was established in 1945 after World War II to promote peace and cooperation throughout the world. The UN conducts its business in six official languages: Arabic, Chinese, English, French, Russian, and Spanish. The first members of the UN were the 50 countries that met and signed the Charter in 1945. By the middle of 1996, 185 countries (most of the world) were members. For the names of the countries that belong to the UN, see the COUNTRIES section, pages 44-63.

What Are the UN's Goals?

☑ To keep worldwide peace and security.
☑ To develop friendly relations among countries.
☑ To help countries cooperate in solving economic, social, cultural, and humanitarian problems.

☑ To promote respect for human rights and basic freedoms.
☑ To be a center that helps countries to achieve these goals.

How the UN Is ORGANIZED

The work of the UN is carried out almost all over the world. It is done through six main organs, each with a different purpose. The Secretary-General is the Chief Officer of the UN.

GENERAL ASSEMBLY

The General Assembly can discuss any problem important to the world. The Assembly admits new members to the UN, appoints the Secretary-General, and decides the UN's budget. It meets once a year for three months, but emergency meetings can be called at any time.

Who Are Its Members? All members of the UN are represented in the General Assembly.

How Do Members Vote? When the General Assembly votes, each country—whether large or small, rich or poor—has one vote. Two thirds of the members must agree for a resolution to be decided.

SECURITY COUNCIL

The Security Council discusses questions of peace and security.

Who Are Its Members? The Security Council is made up of 5 permanent members (China, France, Great Britain, Russia, and the United States) and 10 members that are elected by the General Assembly for two-year terms.

How Do Members Vote? To pass a resolution, at least 9 of the 15 members, including all the permanent members, must vote "yes." If any permanent member vetoes (votes "no" on) the resolution, it is not passed.

UN SECRETARIES-GENERAL

The Secretary-General is the Chief Officer of the United Nations, appointed by the General Assembly for a five-year term. The Secretary-General can bring any problem that threatens world peace to the Security Council or the General Assembly.

1992-present	Boutros Boutros-Ghali, Egypt
1982-1991	Javier Perez de Cuellar, Peru
1972-1981	Kurt Waldheim, Austria
1961-1971	U Thant, Burma (Myanmar)
1953-1961	Dag Hammarskjold, Sweden
1945-1952	Trygve Lie, Norway

DID YOU KNOW? The headquarters for the UN is located in New York City, but the land and the buildings are not part of the United States. The United Nations is an international zone, with its own flag, post office, stamps, and security.

United Nations Day is celebrated every October 24th, because the UN Charter was officially approved on October 24, 1945.

To get more information about the United Nations, you can write to the Public Inquiries Unit, Room GA-57, United Nations, NY 10017 or call the UN at (212) 963-4475.

INTERNATIONAL COURT OF JUSTICE

The International Court of Justice, or World Court, is the highest court of law for legal disputes between countries. When countries have a dispute, they can take their case before the International Court of Justice, which is located at The Hague, Netherlands. Countries that come before the Court must promise to obey the decision of the judges.

Who Are Its Members? There are 15 judges on the Court, each from a different country, elected by the General Assembly and the Security Council.

SECRETARIAT

The Secretariat is the UN staff that carries out the day-to-day operations of the United Nations. Its head is the Secretary-General, currently Boutros Boutros-Ghali. Members of the Secretariat collect background information for the delegates to study and help carry out UN decisions.

ECONOMIC AND SOCIAL COUNCIL

The Economic and Social Council deals with world problems such as trade, economic development, industry, population, children, food, education, health, and human rights. The Council works closely with many commissions and special agencies, such as FAO (Food and Agriculture Organization), UNICEF (United Nations International Children's Fund), and WHO (World Health Organization).

Who Are Its Members? It has 54 member countries elected by the General Assembly for three-year terms.

TRUSTEESHIP COUNCIL

The Trusteeship Council was formed to watch over the people living in territories that were placed under UN trust until they could become independent.

Who Are Its Members? Its members are the permanent members of the Security Council.

United States: FACTS & FIGURES

AREA	Land: 3,536,278 square miles	Water: 251,041 square miles	Total: 3,787,319 square miles

POPULATION (1995): 262,755,270 **CAPITAL:** Washington, D.C.

LARGEST, HIGHEST, AND OTHER STATISTICS

Largest state: Alaska (656,424 square miles)
Smallest state: Rhode Island (1,545 square miles)
Northernmost city: Barrow, Alaska (71°17' north latitude)
Southernmost city: Hilo, Hawaii (19°43' north latitude)
Easternmost city: Eastport, Maine (66°59'02" west longitude)
Westernmost city: Atka, Alaska (174°20' west longitude)
Highest town: Climax, Colorado (11,560 feet)
Lowest town: Calipatria, California (185 feet below sea level)
Oldest national park: Yellowstone National Park (Idaho, Montana, Wyoming), 2,219,791 acres, established 1872
Largest national park: Wrangell-St. Elias, Alaska (8,323,618 acres)
Longest river: Mississippi-Missouri (3,710 miles)
Deepest lake: Crater Lake, Oregon (1,932 feet)
Highest mountain: Mount McKinley, Alaska (20,320 feet)
Lowest point: Death Valley, California (282 feet below sea level)
Rainiest spot: Mt. Waialeale, Hawaii (average annual rainfall 460 inches)
Tallest building: Sears Tower, Chicago, Illinois (1,454 feet)
Tallest structure: TV tower, Blanchard, North Dakota (2,063 feet)
Longest bridge span: Verrazano-Narrows Bridge, New York (4,260 feet)
Highest bridge: Royal Gorge, Colorado (1,053 feet)

INTERNATIONAL BOUNDARY LINES OF THE U.S.

U.S.-Canadian border ....3,987 miles (excluding Alaska)
Alaska-Canadian border ....1,538 miles
U.S.-Mexican border (Rio Grande) ....1,933 miles
Atlantic coast ....2,069 miles
Gulf of Mexico coast....................................1,631 miles
Pacific coast ....7,623 miles
Arctic coast, Alaska ....1,060 miles

TERRITORIAL SEA OF THE U.S. The territorial sea of the United States is the surrounding waters that the country claims as its own. A proclamation issued by President Ronald Reagan on December 27, 1988, stated that the territorial sea of the United States extends 12 nautical miles from the shores of the country.

SYMBOLS of the United States

THE MOTTO

The U.S. motto, "In God We Trust," was originally put on coins during the Civil War (1861-1865). Its use disappeared and reappeared on various coins until 1955, when Congress ordered it placed on all paper money and coins.

THE GREAT SEAL OF THE U.S.

The Great Seal of the U.S. shows an American bald eagle with a ribbon in its mouth bearing the Latin words "e pluribus unum" (one out of many). In its talons are the arrows of war and an olive branch of peace. On the back of the Great Seal is an unfinished pyramid with an eye (the eye of Providence) above it. The seal was approved by Congress on June 20, 1782.

THE FLAG

The flag of the United States has 50 stars (one for each state) and 13 stripes (one for each of the original 13 states). It is called unofficially the "Stars and Stripes." The first U.S. flag was commissioned by the Second Continental Congress in 1777 but did not exist until 1783, after the American Revolution. Historians are not certain who designed the Stars and Stripes. Many different flags are believed to have been used during the American Revolution.

The flag of 1777 was used until 1795. In that year President George Washington ordered that a new flag have 15 stripes, alternate red and white, and 15 stars on a blue field. In 1818, Congress directed that the flag have 13 stripes and that a new star be added for each new state of the Union. The last star was added in 1960 for the state of Hawaii.

| 1777 | 1795 | 1818 |

PLEDGE OF ALLEGIANCE TO THE FLAG

"I pledge allegiance to the flag of the United States of America and to the republic for which it stands, one nation under God, indivisible, with liberty and justice for all."

NATIONAL ANTHEM: "THE STAR-SPANGLED BANNER"

"The Star-Spangled Banner" was a poem written in 1814 by Francis Scott Key as he watched British ships bombard Fort McHenry, Maryland, during the War of 1812. It became the National Anthem by an act of Congress in 1931. Although it has four stanzas, the one most commonly sung is the first stanza. The music to "The Star-Spangled Banner" was originally a tune called "Anacreon in Heaven."

The U.S. GOVERNMENT
and How It Works

THE U.S. CONSTITUTION: The Foundation of American Government

The Constitution is the document that created the present government of the United States. It was written in 1787 and went into effect in 1789. The Constitution establishes the three branches of the U.S. government, which are the executive (headed by the president), the legislative (the Congress), and the judicial (the Supreme Court and other federal courts). The first 10 amendments to the Constitution (the Bill of Rights) explain the basic rights of all American citizens.

The Preamble to the Constitution

The Constitution begins with a short statement called the **Preamble.** The Preamble states that the government of the United States was established by the people.

"We, the people of the United States, in order to form a more perfect Union, establish justice, insure domestic tranquility, provide for the common defense, promote the general welfare, and secure the blessings of liberty to ourselves and our posterity do ordain and establish this Constitution for the United States of America."

The Articles

The original Constitution contained seven articles. The first three articles of the Constitution establish the three branches of the U.S. government.

Legislative Branch
ARTICLE 1 creates the Senate and House of Representatives and describes their functions and powers.

Executive Branch
ARTICLE 2 creates the Office of the President and the Electoral College and lists their powers and responsibilities.

Judicial Branch
ARTICLE 3 creates the Supreme Court and gives Congress power to create lower courts. The powers of the courts and certain crimes are defined.

The States
ARTICLE 4 discusses relationship of states to each other and to citizens. Defines powers.

Amending the Constitution
ARTICLE 5 describes how the Constitution may be amended (changed).

Federal Law
ARTICLE 6 makes the Constitution the supreme law of the land over state laws and constitutions.

Ratifying the Constitution
ARTICLE 7 establishes how to ratify (approve) the Constitution.

AMENDMENTS TO THE CONSTITUTION

The creators of the Constitution understood that the Constitution might need to be amended, or changed, in the future. Article 5 describes how the Constitution may be amended. In order to pass, an amendment must be approved by a two-thirds majority in the House of Representatives and a two-thirds majority in the Senate. An amendment must then be approved by three fourths of the states (38 states). Between 1791 and 1995 the Constitution was amended 27 times.

The Bill of Rights: The First 10 Amendments

The first ten amendments were adopted in 1791 and contain the basic freedoms Americans enjoy as a people. These amendments are known as the Bill of Rights. They are summarized below.

1. Guarantees freedom of religion, speech, and the press
2. Guarantees the right of the people to have firearms
3. Guarantees that soldiers cannot be lodged in private homes except with consent of the owner
4. Protects citizens against being searched or having their property searched or taken away by the government without a good reason
5. Protects rights of people on trial for crimes
6. Guarantees people accused of crimes the right to a speedy public trial by jury
7. Guarantees people the right to a trial by jury for other kinds of cases
8. Prohibits cruel and unusual punishments
9. States that specific rights listed in Constitution do not take away rights that may not be listed
10. Establishes that powers not granted specifically to the federal government are reserved for state governments or the people

Other Important Amendments

13 **(1865):** Abolishes slavery in the United States

14 **(1868):** Establishes the Bill of Rights as protection against actions by a state government; guarantees equal protection under the law for all citizens

15 **(1870):** Guarantees that a person of any race or color cannot be denied the right to vote

19 **(1920):** Grants women the right to vote

22 **(1951):** Limits the president to two four-year terms of office

24 **(1964):** Outlaws the poll tax (a tax people had to pay before they could vote) in federal elections. (The poll tax had been used to keep African-Americans in the South from voting.)

25 **(1967):** Grants the president the power to appoint a new vice president, with the approval of Congress, if a vice president dies or leaves office in the middle of a term

26 **(1971):** Lowers the voting age to eighteen

The Executive Branch:
The PRESIDENT and the CABINET

The executive branch of the federal government is headed by the president of the United States. It also consists of the vice president, people who work for the president or vice president, the major departments of the government, and many special agencies. The cabinet is made up of the vice president, the heads of the major departments, and a few other important people. It meets when the president asks for its advice. As head of the executive branch, the president is responsible for enforcing the laws passed by Congress. The president is also commander in chief of all U.S. armed forces.

Organization of the Executive Branch.

The chart below shows how the executive branch is organized.

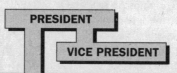

| PRESIDENT |
| VICE PRESIDENT |

CABINET DEPARTMENTS			
State	Interior	Health and	Transportation
Treasury	Agriculture	Human Services	Energy
Defense	Commerce	Housing and Urban	Education
Justice	Labor	Development	Veterans Affairs

How Long Does the President Serve?

The president serves a four-year term, starting on January 20.

What Happens If the President Dies?

If the president dies in office or cannot complete the term, the vice president becomes president. If the president is disabled, the vice president can become acting president until the president is able to work again. The next person to become president after the vice president would be the Speaker of the House of Representatives.

? DID YOU KNOW?

The White House has an address on the World Wide Web. It is:

http://www.whitehouse.gov

You can use that Web site to "tour" the White House and learn more about the First Family.

▲ The White House, the home of the President

The Judicial Branch:
The SUPREME COURT

The highest court in the United States is the **Supreme Court.** It consists of nine justices who are appointed for life by the president with the approval of the Senate. Eight of the nine members are called associate justices. The ninth is the chief justice, who presides over the Court's meetings.

What Does the Supreme Court Do?   The Supreme Court's major responsibilities are to review federal laws, actions of the president, treaties of the United States, and laws passed by state governments to be sure that they do not conflict in any way with the U.S. Constitution. The Supreme Court carries out these responsibilities by deciding cases that come before it. This process is known as **judicial review.** If the Supreme Court finds that a law or action violates the Constitution, the justices declare it **unconstitutional.**

The Supreme Court's Decision Is Final.   Most cases must go through other federal courts or state courts before they go to the Supreme Court. The Supreme Court is the final court for a case, and the justices usually decide which cases they will review. After the Supreme Court hears a case, it may agree or disagree with the decision by an earlier court. When the Supreme Court makes a ruling, its decision is final, and all people involved in the case must abide by it.

Who Is on the Supreme Court?   Below are the nine justices sitting on the Supreme Court for its 1995–1996 session.

Back row (from left to right): Ruth Bader Ginsburg, David H. Souter, Clarence Thomas, Stephen Breyer.
Front row (from left to right): Antonin Scalia, John Paul Stevens, Chief Justice William H. Rehnquist, Sandra Day O'Connor, Anthony M. Kennedy.

? DID YOU KNOW? In 1967, Thurgood Marshall became the first African-American to serve on the Supreme Court. In 1981, Sandra Day O'Connor became the first woman to serve on the Court.

The Legislative Branch: CONGRESS

The Congress of the United States is the legislative branch of the federal government. Congress's major responsibility is to pass the laws that govern the country. It is the president's responsibility to enforce them. Congress consists of two parts—the Senate and the House of Representatives. They are known as the houses of Congress.

THE SENATE

The Senate has 100 members, two from each state. Senators are elected for six-year terms. The framers (writers) of the Constitution created the Senate so that one house of Congress could provide equal representation for each state, whether the state is large or small. Thus, the state with the greatest population (California) has two senators, the same number as the state with the smallest population (Wyoming).

In addition to passing laws, the Senate has the responsibility of approving people the president appoints for certain jobs, for example, cabinet members and Supreme Court justices. It also has the responsibility under the Constitution of trying federal officials who have been impeached (see box below) by the House of Representatives.

THE HOUSE OF REPRESENTATIVES

The House of Representatives has 435 members. The number of representatives a state has is determined by the state's population, so California has many more representatives than Wyoming. Each state is entitled to at least one representative—no matter how small its population. The first House of Representatives in 1789 had 65 members. As the country's population grew, the number of representatives increased. The total membership has been fixed at 435 since the 1910 census.

What Impeachment Means

A president, vice president, and other high-ranking officials of the United States (for example, federal judges) can be formally charged by the House of Representatives and removed from office for committing treason, bribery, or other serious crimes. Under the Constitution, the House of Representatives has the sole authority to impeach federal officials accused of crimes. "Impeachment" means that the House of Representatives formally charges a federal official with committing a crime. Once an official has been impeached (charged with a crime), he or she must be tried by the Senate. If the Senate finds the official guilty of the charges, he or she is then removed from office.

In 1868, the House impeached President Andrew Johnson, but he was acquitted (found not guilty) after a trial in the Senate. In 1974, a House committee recommended that the House of Representatives impeach President Richard Nixon, but before a vote was taken, President Nixon resigned.

The House of Representatives— STATE BY STATE

Each state has the following number of representatives in the House:

Alabama...............7	Minnesota..............8	Texas...................30
Alaska..................1	Mississippi.............5	Utah......................3
Arizona.................6	Missouri.................9	Vermont................1
Arkansas...............4	Montana................1	Virginia................11
California............52	Nebraska...............3	Washington............9
Colorado...............6	Nevada..................2	West Virginia..........3
Connecticut...........6	New Hampshire.......2	Wisconsin..............9
Delaware...............1	New Jersey...........13	Wyoming...............1
Florida.................23	New Mexico...........3	
Georgia...............11	New York..............31	
Hawaii..................2	North Carolina.......12	
Idaho...................2	North Dakota..........1	
Illinois.................20	Ohio......................19	
Indiana................10	Oklahoma...............6	
Iowa.....................5	Oregon..................5	
Kansas..................4	Pennsylvania.........21	
Kentucky...............6	Rhode Island...........2	
Louisiana..............7	South Carolina........6	
Maine....................2	South Dakota.........1	
Maryland...............8	Tennessee..............9	
Massachusetts......10		
Michigan..............16		

The District of Columbia (Washington, D.C.) has one nonvoting member of the House of Representatives.

221

How CONGRESS Makes LAWS

1. Senators and Representatives Propose a Bill.

A proposed law is called a bill. Any member of Congress may propose (introduce) a bill. A bill is introduced in each house of Congress. The House of Representatives and the Senate consider a bill separately. A member of Congress who introduces a bill is known as the bill's *sponsor*.

2. House and Senate Committees Consider the Bill.

The bill is then sent to appropriate committees for consideration. A committee is made up of a small number of members of the House or Senate. A bill relating to agriculture, for example, would be sent to the agriculture committees in the House and in the Senate. When committees are considering a bill, they hold hearings at which people can speak for or against the bill.

3. Committees Change the Bill.

The committees then consider the bill and change it as they see fit. They vote on the bill.

4. The Bill Is Debated in the House and Senate.

If the committees vote in favor of the bill, it goes to the full House and Senate, where it is debated and changed further. The House and Senate then vote on the bill.

5. From the House and Senate to Conference Committee.

If the House and the Senate pass different versions of the same bill, the bill must then go to a "conference committee," where differences between the two versions must be worked out. A conference committee is a special committee made up of Senate and House members who meet to resolve the differences in versions of the same bill.

8. What If the President Doesn't Sign the Bill?

Sometimes the president does not approve of a bill and refuses to sign it. This is called vetoing the bill. A bill that has been vetoed goes back to Congress, where the members can vote on it again. If the House and the Senate pass the bill again with a two-thirds majority vote, the bill becomes law. This is called overriding the president's veto. A law passed in 1996 also allows the president, as of 1997, to veto parts of a bill about how the government spends money, rather than vetoing the entire bill.

6. Final Vote in the House and Senate.

The conference committee version is then voted on by the House and the Senate. In order for a bill to become a law, it must be approved in exactly the same form by a majority of members of both houses of Congress and signed by the president.

7. The President Signs the Bill Into Law.

If the bill passes both houses of Congress, it then goes to the president for his signature. Once the president signs a bill, it becomes law.

Major GOVERNMENT AGENCIES

Government agencies have a variety of functions. Some set rules and regulations or enforce laws. Others investigate or gather information. Some major agencies are listed below:

Central Intelligence Agency (CIA)
Gathers secret information on other countries and their leaders.

Commission on Civil Rights
Makes sure that the laws that protect people against discrimination are obeyed.

Consumer Product Safety Commission
Examines the products that people buy to be sure they are safe.

Environmental Protection Agency (EPA)
Enforces laws on clean air and water and is responsible for cleaning up hazardous waste sites.

Equal Employment Opportunity Commission (EEOC)
Makes sure that people are not discriminated against when they apply for a job and when they are at work.

Federal Communications Commission (FCC)
Issues licenses to radio and TV stations and makes broadcasting rules.

Federal Emergency Management Agency (FEMA)
Helps local communities recover from disasters such as hurricanes, earthquakes, and floods.

Federal Trade Commission (FTC)
Makes sure that businesses operate fairly and that they obey the law.

Library of Congress
The main library of the United States, collects most of the books published in the United States. It also has many historic documents and photographs.

National Archives and Records Administration
Stores major historic records of U.S. government.

National Foundation on the Arts and the Humanities
Gives government money to museums and artists.

Occupational Safety and Health Administration (OSHA)
Makes sure that places where people work are safe and will not harm their health.

Peace Corps
Sends American volunteers to foreign countries for two years to help with special projects such as teaching and farming.

Securities and Exchange Commission (SEC)
Makes sure that the stock market operates fairly and obeys the laws.

ELECTIONS: Electing the PRESIDENT and VICE PRESIDENT

You may be amazed to learn that the president and vice president of the United States are not really elected in November on Election Day. They are actually elected one month later, in December, by 538 people called the Electoral College.

WHAT IS THE ELECTORAL COLLEGE?

The system for electing presidents was established by the U.S. Constitution in 1789. Each state must choose a group of "electors," equal to the total number of Senators and Representatives the state sends to Congress. For example, the state of Missouri has 9 Representatives and 2 Senators and thus has 11 electors. The District of Columbia has 3 electors. Electors from the 50 states and the District of Columbia are called the Electoral College. Actually, they are not a college at all, but are a group of people (usually members of political parties) who officially elect the president and vice president.

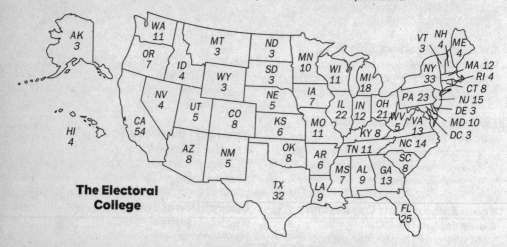

The Electoral College

HOW ARE THE PRESIDENT AND VICE PRESIDENT ELECTED?

Every four years on Election Day, in November, the names of the candidates for president and vice president appear on the voting machine or ballot, and voters select the people they prefer. Although the voter usually cannot see the names of the electors on the voting machine, when he or she pulls the lever for the president, the voter is really voting for a group of electors who have promised to support (are "pledged to") the voter's presidential candidate.

When the election polls close, each state then counts the votes cast for each presidential and vice presidential candidate. The electors in the Electoral College who are pledged to the candidate with the most votes in each state meet in their home state in December and officially cast their ballots for president and vice president. To be elected, a candidate must receive a majority of the Electoral College votes, or 270 votes. The results are announced in Congress the following January. If no candidate receives 270 electoral votes, the election goes to the House of Representatives, where the president is selected from the top three candidates.

Using a VOTING MACHINE

Although some people in the United States still vote on paper ballots, most people now vote on voting machines. There are different kinds of voting machines, but they all work in the same basic way. When the voter goes into the voting booth, he or she pulls a master lever that locks the machine. The voter sees the names of the candidates from different political parties and pulls a small lever next to the candidate the voter chooses for each office. The votes are then recorded in the machine when the voter pulls the master lever back into its original position.

Space for a question to be explained

Name of political party

Name of candidate

Lever for candidate

Voter

Master lever

? DID YOU KNOW?
In the past twenty years, only around half the people who could vote for the president actually did vote.

WHO CAN VOTE IN THE UNITED STATES: A TIMELINE

1789 — The U.S. Constitution is adopted in 1789, and all states allow white men who own land to vote. In New Jersey, women who own land are also allowed to vote.

1807 — New Jersey ends women's right to vote.

1830s — All states allow all white men to vote, even those who don't own land.

1848 — At a convention in Seneca Falls, New York, women call for the right to vote.

1870 — The Fifteenth Amendment to the Constitution is adopted, guaranteeing the right to vote to men regardless of race or color.

1890s — Some states allow women to vote in state and local elections (but not elections for president or members of Congress).

1920 — The Nineteenth Amendment to the Constitution is adopted, guaranteeing women the right to vote in all elections.

1964 — The Civil Rights Act of 1964 bans the use of literacy tests and poll taxes, which were used to prevent African-Americans from voting.

1971 — The Twenty-sixth Amendment to Constitution is adopted, lowering the voting age from 21 to 18.

PRESIDENTS and VICE PRESIDENTS
of the UNITED STATES

PRESIDENT VICE PRESIDENT	TERM	PRESIDENT VICE PRESIDENT	TERM
1 George Washington	**1789-1797**	**22 Grover Cleveland**	**1885-1889**
John Adams	1789-1797	Thomas A. Hendricks	1885
2 John Adams	**1797-1801**	**23 Benjamin Harrison**	**1889-1893**
Thomas Jefferson	1797-1801	Levi P. Morton	1889-1893
3 Thomas Jefferson	**1801-1809**	**24 Grover Cleveland**	**1893-1897**
Aaron Burr	1801-1805	Adlai E. Stevenson	1893-1897
George Clinton	1805-1809	**25 William McKinley**	**1897-1901**
4 James Madison	**1809-1817**	Garret A. Hobart	1897-1899
George Clinton	1809-1812	Theodore Roosevelt	1901
Elbridge Gerry	1813-1814	**26 Theodore Roosevelt**	**1901-1909**
5 James Monroe	**1817-1825**	Charles W. Fairbanks	1905-1909
Daniel D. Tompkins	1817-1825	**27 William Howard Taft**	**1909-1913**
6 John Quincy Adams	**1825-1829**	James S. Sherman	1909-1912
John C. Calhoun	1825-1829	**28 Woodrow Wilson**	**1913-1921**
7 Andrew Jackson	**1829-1837**	Thomas R. Marshall	1913-1921
John C. Calhoun	1829-1832	**29 Warren G. Harding**	**1921-1923**
Martin Van Buren	1833-1837	Calvin Coolidge	1921-1923
8 Martin Van Buren	**1837-1841**	**30 Calvin Coolidge**	**1923-1929**
Richard M. Johnson	1837-1841	Charles G. Dawes	1925-1929
9 William H. Harrison	**1841**	**31 Herbert Hoover**	**1929-1933**
John Tyler	1841	Charles Curtis	1929-1933
10 John Tyler	**1841-1845**	**32 Franklin D. Roosevelt**	**1933-1945**
No Vice President		John Nance Garner	1933-1941
11 James Knox Polk	**1845-1849**	Henry A. Wallace	1941-1945
George M. Dallas	1845-1849	Harry S. Truman	1945
12 Zachary Taylor	**1849-1850**	**33 Harry S. Truman**	**1945-1953**
Millard Fillmore	1849-1850	Alben W. Barkley	1949-1953
13 Millard Fillmore	**1850-1853**	**34 Dwight D. Eisenhower**	**1953-1961**
No Vice President		Richard M. Nixon	1953-1961
14 Franklin Pierce	**1853-1857**	**35 John F. Kennedy**	**1961-1963**
William R. King	1853	Lyndon B. Johnson	1961-1963
15 James Buchanan	**1857-1861**	**36 Lyndon B. Johnson**	**1963-1969**
John C. Breckinridge	1857-1861	Hubert H. Humphrey	1965-1969
16 Abraham Lincoln	**1861-1865**	**37 Richard M. Nixon**	**1969-1974**
Hannibal Hamlin	1861-1865	Spiro T. Agnew	1969-1973
Andrew Johnson	1865	Gerald R. Ford	1973-1974
17 Andrew Johnson	**1865-1869**	**38 Gerald R. Ford**	**1974-1977**
No Vice President		Nelson A. Rockefeller	1974-1977
18 Ulysses S. Grant	**1869-1877**	**39 Jimmy Carter**	**1977-1981**
Schuyler Colfax	1869-1873	Walter F. Mondale	1977-1981
Henry Wilson	1873-1875	**40 Ronald Reagan**	**1981-1989**
19 Rutherford B. Hayes	**1877-1881**	George Bush	1981-1989
William A. Wheeler	1877-1881	**41 George Bush**	**1989-1993**
20 James A. Garfield	**1881**	Dan Quayle	1989-1993
Chester A. Arthur	1881	**42 Bill Clinton**	**1993-**
21 Chester A. Arthur	**1881-1885**	Al Gore	1993-
No Vice President			

PRESIDENTS of the United States and their FAMILIES

1. GEORGE WASHINGTON (1789-1797)
Political Party: Federalist
Born: Feb. 22, 1732, at Wakefield, Westmoreland County, Virginia
Married: Martha Dandridge Custis (1731-1802); no children
Died: Dec. 14, 1799; buried at Mount Vernon, Fairfax County, Virginia
Early Career: Soldier; head of the Virginia militia; commander in chief of the Continental Army; chairman of Constitutional Convention (1787)

2. JOHN ADAMS (1797-1801)
Political Party: Federalist
Born: Oct. 30, 1735, in Quincy, Massachusetts
Married: Abigail Smith (1744-1818); 3 sons, 2 daughters
Died: July 4, 1826; buried in Quincy, Massachusetts
Early Career: Lawyer; delegate to Continental Congress; signer of the Declaration of Independence; first vice president

3. THOMAS JEFFERSON (1801-1809)
Political Party: Democratic-Republican
Born: Apr. 13, 1743, at Shadwell, Albemarle County, Virginia
Married: Martha Wayles Skelton (1748-1782); 1 son, 5 daughters
Died: July 4, 1826; buried at Monticello, Albemarle County, Virginia
Early Career: Lawyer; member of the Continental Congress; author of the Declaration of Independence; governor of Virginia; first secretary of state; author of the Virginia Statute on Religious Freedom

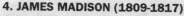

4. JAMES MADISON (1809-1817)
Political Party: Democratic-Republican
Born: Mar. 16, 1751, at Port Conway, King George County, Virginia
Married: Dolley Payne Todd (1768-1849); no children
Died: June 28, 1836; buried at Montpelier, Orange County, Virginia
Early Career: Member of the Virginia Constitutional Convention (1776); member of the Continental Congress; major contributor to the U.S. Constitution; writer of the Federalist Papers; secretary of state

5. JAMES MONROE (1817-1825)
Political Party: Democratic-Republican
Born: Apr. 28, 1758, in Westmoreland County, Virginia
Married: Elizabeth Kortright (1768-1830); 2 daughters
Died: July 4, 1831; buried in Richmond, Virginia
Early Career: Soldier; lawyer; U.S. senator; governor of Virginia; secretary of state

6. JOHN QUINCY ADAMS (1825-1829)
Political Party: Democratic-Republican
Born: July 11, 1767, in Quincy, Massachusetts
Married: Louisa Catherine Johnson (1775-1852); 3 sons, 1 daughter
Died: Feb. 23, 1848; buried in Quincy, Massachusetts
Early Career: Diplomat; U.S. senator; secretary of state

7. ANDREW JACKSON (1829-1837)
Political Party: Democratic
Born: Mar. 15, 1767, in New Lancaster County, South Carolina
Married: Rachel Donelson Robards (1767-1828); no children
Died: June 8, 1845; buried in Nashville, Tennessee
Early Career: Lawyer; U.S. representative and senator; Indian fighter; general in the U.S. Army

8. MARTIN VAN BUREN (1837-1841)
Political Party: Democratic
Born: Dec. 5, 1782, at Kinderhook, New York
Married: Hannah Hoes (1783-1819); 4 sons
Died: July 24, 1862; buried at Kinderhook, New York
Early Career: Governor of New York; secretary of state; vice president

9. WILLIAM HENRY HARRISON (1841)
Political Party: Whig
Born: Feb. 9, 1773, at Berkeley, Charles City County, Virginia
Married: Anna Symmes (1775-1864); 6 sons, 4 daughters
Died: Apr. 4, 1841; buried in North Bend, Ohio
Early Career: First governor of Indiana Territory; superintendent of Indian affairs; U.S. representative and senator

10. JOHN TYLER (1841-1845)
Political Party: Whig
Born: Mar. 29, 1790, in Greenway, Charles City County, Virginia
Married: Letitia Christian (1790-1842); 3 sons, 5 daughters
　　　　　Julia Gardiner (1820-1889); 5 sons, 2 daughters
Died: Jan. 18, 1862; buried in Richmond, Virginia
Early Career: U.S. representative and senator; vice president

11. JAMES KNOX POLK (1845-1849)
Political Party: Democratic
Born: Nov. 2, 1795, in Mecklenburg County, North Carolina
Married: Sarah Childress (1803-1891); no children
Died: June 15, 1849; buried in Nashville, Tennessee
Early Career: U.S. representative; Speaker of the House; governor of Tennessee

12. ZACHARY TAYLOR (1849-1850)
Political Party: Whig
Born: Nov. 24, 1784, in Orange County, Virginia
Married: Margaret Smith (1788-1852); 1 son, 5 daughters
Died: July 9, 1850; buried in Louisville, Kentucky
Early Career: Indian fighter; general in the U.S. Army

13. MILLARD FILLMORE (1850-1853)
Political Party: Whig
Born: Jan 7, 1800, in Cayuga County, New York
Married: Abigail Powers (1798-1853); 1 son, 1 daughter
　　　　　Caroline Carmichael McIntosh (1813-1881); no children
Died: Mar. 8, 1874; buried in Buffalo, N.Y.
Early Career: Teacher; lawyer; U.S. representative; vice president

14. FRANKLIN PIERCE (1853-1857)
Political Party: Democratic
Born: Nov. 23, 1804, in Hillsboro, New Hampshire
Married: Jane Means Appleton (1806-1863); 3 sons
Died: Oct. 8, 1869, in Concord, New Hampshire
Early Career: U.S. representative, senator

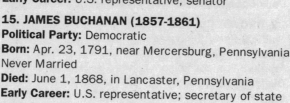

15. JAMES BUCHANAN (1857-1861)
Political Party: Democratic
Born: Apr. 23, 1791, near Mercersburg, Pennsylvania
Never Married
Died: June 1, 1868, in Lancaster, Pennsylvania
Early Career: U.S. representative; secretary of state

16. ABRAHAM LINCOLN (1861-1865)
Political Party: Republican
Born: Feb. 12, 1809, in Larue, Kentucky
Married: Mary Todd (1818-1882); 4 sons
Died: Apr. 15, 1865; buried in Springfield, Illinois
Early Career: Lawyer; U.S. representative

17. ANDREW JOHNSON (1865-1869)
Political Party: Republican
Born: Dec. 29, 1808, in Raleigh, North Carolina
Married: Eliza McCardle (1810-1876); 3 sons, 2 daughters
Died: July 31, 1875; buried in Greeneville, Tennessee
Early Career: State representative and senator;
   U.S. representative; governor of Tennessee; U.S. senator;
   vice president

18. ULYSSES S. GRANT (1869-1877)
Political Party: Republican
Born: Apr. 27, 1822, in Point Pleasant, Ohio
Married: Julia Dent (1826-1902); 3 sons, 1 daughter
Died: July 23, 1885; buried in New York City
Early Career: Army officer; commander of Union forces during
   Civil War

19. RUTHERFORD B. HAYES (1877-1881)
Political Party: Republican
Born: Oct. 4, 1822, in Delaware, Ohio
Married: Lucy Ware Webb (1831-1889); 7 sons, 1 daughter
Died: Jan. 17, 1893; buried in Fremont, Ohio
Early Career: Lawyer; general in Union Army; U.S. representative;
   governor of Ohio

20. JAMES A. GARFIELD (1881)
Political Party: Republican
Born: Nov. 19, 1831, in Orange, Cuyahoga County, Ohio
Married: Lucretia Rudolph (1832-1918); 4 sons, 1 daughter
Died: Sept. 19, 1881; buried in Cleveland, Ohio
Early Career: Teacher; Ohio state senator; general in Union Army;
   U.S. representative

21. CHESTER A. ARTHUR (1881-1885)
Political Party: Republican
Born: Oct. 5, 1829, in Fairfield, Vermont
Married: Ellen Lewis Herndon (1837-1880); 2 sons, 1 daughter
Died: Nov. 18, 1886; buried in Albany, New York
Early Career: Lawyer; vice president

22. GROVER CLEVELAND (1885-1889)
Political Party: Democratic
Born: Mar. 18, 1837, in Caldwell, New Jersey
Married: Frances Folsom (1864-1947); 2 sons, 3 daughters
Died: June 24, 1908; buried in Princeton, New Jersey
Early Career: Lawyer; mayor of Buffalo; governor of New York

23. BENJAMIN HARRISON (1889-1893)
Political Party: Republican
Born: Aug. 20, 1833, in North Bend, Ohio
Married: Caroline Lavinia Scott (1832-1892); 1 son, 1 daughter
　　　　　 Mary Scott Lord Dimmick (1858-1948); 1 daughter
Died: Mar. 13, 1901; buried in Indianapolis, Indiana
Early Career: Lawyer; general in Union Army; U.S. senator

24. GROVER CLEVELAND (1893-1897) See 22. above.

25. WILLIAM MCKINLEY (1897-1901)
Political Party: Republican
Born: Jan. 29, 1843, in Niles, Ohio
Married: Ida Saxton (1847-1907); 2 daughters
Died: Sept. 14, 1901; buried in Canton, Ohio
Early Career: Lawyer; U.S. representative; governor of Ohio

26. THEODORE ROOSEVELT (1901-1909)
Political Party: Republican
Born: Oct. 27, 1858, in New York City
Married: Alice Hathaway Lee (1861-1884); 1 daughter
　　　　　 Edith Kermit Carow (1861-1948); 4 sons, 1 daughter
Died: Jan. 6, 1919; buried in Oyster Bay, New York
Early Career: Assistant secretary of the navy; cavalry leader in
　Spanish-American War; governor of New York; vice president

27. WILLIAM HOWARD TAFT (1909-1913)
Political Party: Republican
Born: Sept. 15, 1857, in Cincinnati, Ohio
Married: Helen Herron (1861-1943); 2 sons, 1 daughter
Died: Mar. 8, 1930; buried in Arlington National Cemetery, Virginia
Early Career: Lawyer; judge; secretary of war

28. WOODROW WILSON (1913-1921)
Political Party: Democratic
Born: Dec. 28, 1856, in Staunton, Virginia
Married: Ellen Louise Axson (1860-1914); 3 daughters
　　　　　 Edith Bolling Galt (1872-1961); no children
Died: Feb. 3, 1924; buried in Washington, D.C.
Early Career: Lawyer; college professor; governor of New Jersey

29. WARREN G. HARDING (1921-1923)
Political Party: Republican
Born: Nov. 2, 1865, near Blooming Grove, Ohio
Married: Florence Kling De Wolfe (1860-1924); no children
Died: Aug. 2, 1923; buried in Marion, Ohio
Early Career: Ohio state senator; U.S. senator

30. CALVIN COOLIDGE (1923-1929)
Political Party: Republican
Born: July 4, 1872, in Plymouth, Vermont
Married: Grace Anna Goodhue (1879-1957); 2 sons
Died: Jan. 5, 1933; buried in Plymouth, Vermont
Early Career: Massachusetts state senator, lieutenant governor, and
governor; vice president

31. HERBERT HOOVER (1929-1933)
Political Party: Republican
Born: Aug. 10, 1874, in West Branch, Iowa
Married: Lou Henry (1875-1944); 2 sons
Died: Oct. 20, 1964; buried West Branch, Iowa
Early Career: Mining engineer; secretary of commerce

32. FRANKLIN DELANO ROOSEVELT (1933-1945)
Political Party: Democratic
Born: Jan. 30, 1882, in Hyde Park, New York
Married: Anna Eleanor Roosevelt (1884-1962); 4 sons, 1 daughter
Died: Apr. 12, 1945; buried in Hyde Park, New York
Early Career: Lawyer; New York state senator; assistant secretary of
the navy; governor of New York

33. HARRY S. TRUMAN (1945-1953)
Political Party: Democratic
Born: May 8, 1884, in Lamar, Missouri
Married: Elizabeth Virginia "Bess" Wallace (1885-1982); 1 daughter
Died: Dec. 26, 1972; buried in Independence, Missouri
Early Career: Haberdasher (ran men's clothing store); judge; U.S.
senator; vice president

34. DWIGHT D. EISENHOWER (1953-1961)
Political Party: Republican
Born: Oct. 14, 1890, in Denison, Texas
Married: Mamie Geneva Doud (1896-1979); 1 son
Died: Mar. 28, 1969; buried in Abilene, Kansas
Early Career: Commander, Allied landing in North Africa and later
Supreme Allied Commander in Europe during World War II;
president of Columbia University

35. JOHN FITZGERALD KENNEDY (1961-1963)
Political Party: Democratic
Born: May 29, 1917, in Brookline, Massachusetts
Married: Jacqueline Lee Bouvier (1929-1994); 1 son, 1 daughter
Died: Nov. 22, 1963; buried in Arlington National Cemetery, Virginia
Early Career: U.S. naval commander; U.S. representative and senator

36. LYNDON BAINES JOHNSON (1963-1969)
Political Party: Democratic
Born: Aug. 27, 1908, in Stonewall, Texas
Married: Claudia "Lady Bird" Alta Taylor (b. 1912); 2 daughters
Died: Jan. 22, 1973; buried in Stonewall, Texas
Early Career: U.S. representative and senator; vice president

37. RICHARD MILHOUS NIXON (1969-1974)
Political Party: Republican
Born: Jan. 9, 1913, in Yorba Linda, California
Married: Patricia Ryan (1912-1993); 2 daughters
Died: Apr. 22, 1994; buried in Yorba Linda, California
Early Career: Lawyer; U.S. representative and senator; vice president

38. GERALD R. FORD (1974-1977)
Political Party: Republican
Born: July 14, 1913, in Omaha, Nebraska
Married: Elizabeth Bloomer Warren (b. 1918);
        3 sons, 1 daughter
Early Career: Lawyer; U.S. representative; vice president

39. JIMMY (JAMES EARL) CARTER (1977-1981)
Political Party: Democratic
Born: Oct. 1, 1924, in Plains, Georgia
Married: Rosalynn Smith (b. 1927); 3 sons, 1 daughter
Early Career: Peanut farmer; Georgia state senator; governor
    of Georgia

40. RONALD REAGAN (1981-1989)
Political Party: Republican
Born: Feb. 6, 1911, in Tampico, Illinois
Married: Jane Wyman (b. 1914); 1 son, 1 daughter
        Nancy Davis (b. 1921); 1 son, 1 daughter
Early Career: Film and television actor; governor of California

41. GEORGE BUSH (1989-1993)
Political Party: Republican
Born: June 12, 1924, in Milton, Massachusetts
Married: Barbara Pierce (b. 1925); 4 sons, 2 daughters
Early Career: U.S. navy pilot; businessman; U.S. representative; U.S.
    ambassador to the United Nations; vice president

42. BILL (WILLIAM JEFFERSON) CLINTON (1993-   )
Political Party: Democratic
Born: Aug. 19, 1946, in Hope, Arkansas
Married: Hillary Rodham (b. 1947); 1 daughter
Early Career: Arkansas state attorney general; governor of Arkansas

Presidential FACTS, FAMILIES, and FIRST LADIES

PRESIDENTIAL FACTS

Youngest president: Theodore Roosevelt, who was 42 when he was sworn in.

Oldest president: Ronald Reagan, who was 78 when he left office.

Only president to serve more than two terms: Franklin Delano Roosevelt

Only president to serve two terms that were not back to back: Grover Cleveland

Only president who was unmarried: James Buchanan. His niece acted as White House hostess for her uncle.

Presidents who died in office: Eight U.S. presidents have died while they served as president. Four of them were assassinated: Abraham Lincoln, James Garfield, William McKinley, and John F. Kennedy. The other four presidents who died in office were William Henry Harrison, Zachary Taylor, Warren G. Harding, and Franklin Delano Roosevelt.

FAMOUS FIRST FAMILIES

Adams family: John Adams was the 2nd president, and his son, John Quincy Adams, became the 6th president.

Harrison family: Benjamin Harrison, the 23rd president, was the great-grandson of Benjamin Harrison, a signer of the Declaration of Independence, and the grandson of William Henry Harrison, the 9th president of the United States.

Roosevelt family: Theodore Roosevelt was the 26th president and his 5th cousin, Franklin Delano Roosevelt, the 32nd. Franklin's wife, Eleanor Roosevelt, was also Theodore Roosevelt's niece.

FAMOUS FIRST LADIES

Martha Washington was the first First Lady. A wealthy widow when she married George Washington, she helped his position as a Virginia planter.

Abigail Adams, the wife of John Adams, was a thoughtful, outspoken woman. She wrote hundreds of letters in which she clearly expressed her opinions on the issues of the day.

Dolley Madison, James Madison's wife, was famous as a hostess and for saving a portrait of George Washington during the War of 1812, when the British were about to burn the White House.

Eleanor Roosevelt, wife of Franklin D. Roosevelt, became a public figure herself after her husband became crippled by polio. She strongly urged her husband to support civil rights and the rights of workers.

Jacqueline Kennedy, wife of John F. Kennedy, known for her elegance and style, restored the White House and made it a symbol the country could be proud of.

Hillary Rodham Clinton, wife of Bill Clinton, a successful lawyer, and an outspoken defender of women's and children's rights. She wrote a book about children, *It Takes a Village,* which was published in 1995.

United States History Timeline

The First People in North America: Before 1492

40,000 B.C.-11,000 B.C.
First people (called Paleo-Indians) cross from Siberia to Alaska and begin to move into North America.

14,000 B.C.-11,000 B.C.
Paleo-Indians use stone points attached to spears to hunt big mammoths in northern parts of North America.

11,000 B.C.
Big mammoths disappear and Paleo-Indians begin to gather plants for food.

8000 B.C.-1000 B.C.
North American Indians begin using stone to grind food and to hunt bison and smaller animals.

1000 B.C.-A.D. 500
Woodland Indians, who lived east of the Mississippi River, bury people who have died under large burial mounds (which can still be seen today).

After A.D. 500
Anasazi peoples in the Southwestern United States live in homes on cliffs, called cliff dwellings. Anasazi pottery and dishes are well known for their beautiful patterns.

After A.D. 700
Mississippian Indian people in Southeastern United States develop farms and build burial mounds.

700-1492
Many different Indian cultures develop throughout North America.

Colonial America and the American Revolution: 1492-1783

1492
Christopher Columbus sails across the Atlantic Ocean and reaches an island in the Bahamas in the Caribbean Sea.

1513
Juan Ponce de León explores the Florida coast.

1524
Giovanni da Verrazano explores the coast from Carolina north to Nova Scotia, enters New York harbor.

1540
Francisco Vásquez de Coronado explores the southwestern United States north of the Rio Grande.

1565
St. Augustine, Florida, the first town established by Europeans in United States, is founded by the Spanish. Later burned by the English in 1586.

1607
Jamestown, Virginia, the first English settlement in North America, is founded by Captain John Smith.

1609
Henry Hudson sails into New York harbor and explores the Hudson River. Spaniards found Santa Fe, New Mexico.

1619
The first African slaves are brought to Jamestown. (Slavery is made legal in 1650.)

1620
Pilgrims from England arrive at Plymouth, Massachusetts, on the *Mayflower.*

1626
Peter Minuit buys Manhattan island for the Dutch from Man-a-hat-a Indians for $24. The island is renamed New Amsterdam.

1630
Boston is founded by Massachusetts colonists led by John Winthrop.

1634
Maryland is founded as a Catholic colony with religious freedom for all its settlers.

1664
The English seize New Amsterdam from the Dutch. The city is renamed New York.

1699
French settlers move into Mississippi and Louisiana.

1732
Benjamin Franklin begins publishing *Poor Richard's Almanack*.

1754-1763
French and Indian War between England and France. The French are defeated and lose their lands in Canada and the American Midwest.

1764-1767
England places taxes on sugar that comes from their North American colonies. England also requires colonists to purchase stamps to raise money to pay for the French and Indian War. Colonists protest and meet in the Stamp Act Congress.

1770
Boston Massacre: English troops fire on a group of people protesting English taxes.

1773
Boston Tea Party: English tea is thrown into the harbor to protest a tax on tea.

1775
Fighting at Lexington and Concord, Massachusetts, marks the beginning of the American Revolution.

1776
The Declaration of Independence is approved July 4 by the Continental Congress (made up of representatives from the American colonies).

1781
British General Cornwallis surrenders to the Americans at Yorktown, Virginia, ending the fighting in the Revolutionary War.

Benjamin Franklin (1706-1790) was a great American leader, printer, scientist, and writer. In 1732, he began publishing a magazine called *Poor Richard's Almanack*. Poor Richard was a make-believe person who gave advice about common sense and honesty. Many of Poor Richard's sayings are still known today. Among the most famous are "God helps them that help themselves" and "Early to bed, early to rise, makes a man healthy, wealthy, and wise."

Portion of The Declaration of Independence, July 4, 1776

"We hold these truths to be self-evident, that all men are created equal, that they are endowed by their Creator with certain unalienable rights, that among these are life, liberty, and the pursuit of happiness."

Who Attended the Convention?

The Constitutional Convention met in Philadelphia in the hot summer of 1787. Most of the great founders of America attended. Among those present were George Washington, James Madison, and John Adams. They met to form a new government that would be strong and, at the same time, protect the liberties that were fought for in the American Revolution. The Constitution they created is still the law of the United States.

The New Nation: 1783-1900

1783

The Treaty of Paris ending the American Revolutionary War is signed by the United States and England. The English recognize U.S. independence.

1784

The first successful daily newspaper, the *Pennsylvania Packet & General Advertiser,* is published.

1787

The Constitutional Convention meets in Philadelphia to write a new Constitution for the United States.

1789

The new Constitution is approved by the states. George Washington is chosen as the first president of the United States.

1800

The federal government moves to a new capital, Washington, D.C.

1803

President Thomas Jefferson makes the Louisiana Purchase from France. Millions of square miles of territory are added to the United States.

1804

Lewis and Clark explore far into the northwestern United States.

1812-1814

War of 1812 with Great Britain: British forces burn the Capitol and White House. Francis Scott Key writes "The Star-Spangled Banner."

1820

The Missouri Compromise in Congress bans slavery west of the Mississippi River and north of line 36°30' north latitude.

1823

The Monroe Doctrine (a statement by President Monroe) warns European countries not to interfere in North America.

1825

The Erie Canal opens in New York and links the east coast with the Midwest.

1831

The Liberator, a newspaper opposing slavery, is published in Boston.

Louisiana Purchase

"The Trail of Tears"

The Cherokee Indians living in Georgia were forced, by the state government of Georgia, to leave in 1838. They were sent to Oklahoma. On the long march, thousands died because of disease and the cold weather.

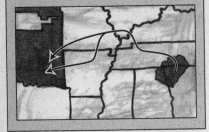

Uncle Tom's Cabin

Harriet Beecher Stowe's novel about the sufferings of slaves was an instant bestseller in the North and banned in most of the South. When President Abraham Lincoln met Stowe, he called her "the little lady who started this war" (the Civil War).

The Bloodiest War in U.S. History

The U.S. Civil War between the North and South lasted four years (1861-1865) and resulted in the deaths of more than 600,000 people—more than all other U.S. wars combined. Little was known at the time about the spread of diseases. As a result, many casualties were also the result of illnesses such as influenza, measles, and infections from battle wounds.

1836
Texans fighting for independence from Mexico are defeated by Mexican forces at the Alamo.

1838
Cherokee Indians are forced to move to Oklahoma, along "The Trail of Tears."

1844
The first telegraph line connects Washington and Baltimore.

1846-1848
U.S. war with Mexico: Mexico is defeated and the U.S. takes control of the Republic of Texas and of Mexican territories in the West.

1848
California "gold rush": The discovery of gold in California leads to a "rush" of more than 80,000 people to the West in search of gold.

1852
Uncle Tom's Cabin is published.

1858
Lincoln-Douglas debates during Senate campaign in Illinois: Abraham Lincoln and Stephen A. Douglas debate about slavery.

1860
Abraham Lincoln is elected president.

1861
The Civil War begins.

1863
President Lincoln issues the Emancipation Proclamation, freeing most slaves in the country.

1865
The Civil War ends as the South surrenders. Lincoln is assassinated.

1869
The first railroad connecting the east and west coasts is completed.

1878
The first telephone company begins operation.

1890
Battle of Wounded Knee is fought in South Dakota—the last major battle between Indians and U.S. troops.

1898
Spanish-American War: The U.S. defeats Spain and receives control of the Philippines and Puerto Rico.

World War I

In World War I the United States fought with Great Britain, France, and Russia (the Allies) against Germany and Austria-Hungary. The Allies won the war in 1918.

The Great Depression

The stock market crash of October 1929 led to a period of severe hardship for the American people—the Great Depression. As many as 25 percent of all workers could not find jobs. The Depression lasted until the early 1940s. The Depression also led to a great change in politics. In 1932, Democrat Franklin D. Roosevelt was elected president. He served as president for 12 years, longer than any other president.

The United States in the 20th Century

1903
The U.S. begins building the Panama Canal. The canal opens in 1914, connecting the Atlantic and Pacific oceans.

1908
Henry Ford introduces the Model T car, the first auto bought by thousands of people.

1916
The first woman—Jeanette Rankin of Montana—is elected to Congress.

1917-1918
The U.S. joins World War I on the side of the Allies against Germany.

1920
First licensed radio broadcast. Radio becomes extremely popular in 1920s.

1927
Charles A. Lindbergh becomes the first person to fly alone nonstop across the Atlantic Ocean.

1929
A stock market crash marks the beginning of the Great Depression.

1933
President Franklin D. Roosevelt's New Deal increases government help to people through programs such as Social Security.

1941
Japan attacks the U.S. navy base at Pearl Harbor, Hawaii. The U.S. enters World War II against Japan, Germany, and Italy.

1945
Germany and Japan surrender, ending World War II. Japan's surrender comes after the U.S. drops atomic bombs on Hiroshima and Nagasaki, Japan.

1950-1953
U.S. armed forces fight in the Korean War.

1954
The U.S. Supreme Court outlaws racial segregation in public schools.

1958
The first U.S. space satellite, *Explorer I*, goes into orbit.

1962
The U.S. forces the Soviet Union to pull its missiles out of Cuba (the Cuban missile crisis).

1963
President John F. Kennedy is assassinated in Dallas, Texas.

1964
Congress passes the Civil Rights Act, which outlaws discrimination in voting and jobs.

1965
The U.S. sends large numbers of soldiers to fight in the Vietnam War.

1968
Civil rights leader Martin Luther King, Jr., assassinated in Memphis. Senator Robert F. Kennedy assassinated in Los Angeles.

1969
U.S. astronaut Neil Armstrong becomes first person to walk on the moon.

1973
U.S. participation in the Vietnam War ends.

1974
President Nixon resigns because of the Watergate scandal. He is the only U.S. president to resign from office.

1979
U.S. hostages are taken in Iran, beginning a 444-day crisis until their release in 1981.

1981
Sandra Day O'Connor becomes the first woman appointed to U.S. Supreme Court.

1985
U.S. President Ronald Reagan and Soviet leader Mikhail Gorbachev begin working together to improve relations between their countries.

1989
General Colin Powell becomes the first African-American to head the U.S. military forces.

1991
The Persian Gulf War in the Middle East: The U.S. and its allies force Iraq to withdraw its invading forces from neighboring Kuwait.

1993
Bill Clinton, a Democrat, is inaugurated as president of the United States.

1994
The Republican Party wins majorities in both houses of Congress for the first time in 40 years.

1995-1996
President Clinton and Congress disagree over how to balance the federal budget in the next seven years.

Watergate
In June 1972, six men were arrested in the Watergate building in Washington, D.C., for trying to bug the telephones in the offices of the Democratic Party. Some of the men worked for the committee to reelect President Richard Nixon. In 1973, it was discovered that President Nixon had tape-recorded his conversations in the Oval Office of the White House. One of the tapes revealed that Nixon knew about a plan to hide information about "Watergate." Facing impeachment, Nixon resigned the presidency.

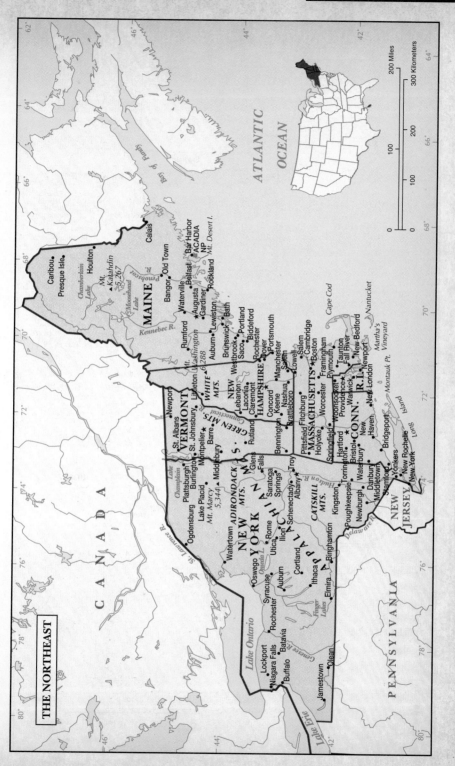

THE NORTHEAST

ATLANTIC OCEAN

CANADA

Bay of Fundy

MAINE

Calais
Caribou
Presque Isle
Houlton
Chamberlain Lake
Mt. Katahdin 5,267
Moosehead Lake
Old Town
Bangor
Bar Harbor
ACADIA NP
Mt. Desert I.
Waterville
Belfast
Rockland
Augusta
Gardiner
Lewiston
Auburn
Bath
Brunswick
Saco
Biddeford
Portland
Westbrook
Rumford
Kennebec R.
Penobscot R.

NEW HAMPSHIRE
WHITE MTS.
Mt. Washington 6,288
Littleton
Lebanon
Claremont
Concord
Keene
Manchester
Nashua
Rochester
Dover
Portsmouth

VERMONT
Newport
St. Albans
Burlington
Plattsburgh
Montpelier
Barre
Middlebury
Rutland
Bennington
Brattleboro
GREEN MTS.
Lake Champlain
Connecticut R.

MASSACHUSETTS
Pittsfield
Fitchburg
Lowell
Lawrence
Salem
Cambridge
Boston
Framingham
Worcester
Springfield
Holyoke
Plymouth
Taunton
Fall River
New Bedford
Cape Cod
Martha's Vineyard
Nantucket

R.I.
Woonsocket
Providence
Warwick
Newport

CONN.
Hartford
Bristol
New Britain
Waterbury
Danbury
New Haven
New London
Bridgeport
Stamford
Torrington
Middletown

NEW YORK
Ogdensburg
Watertown
Oneida L.
Oswego
Rome
Utica
Ilion
Syracuse
Rochester
Auburn
Cortland
Ithaca
Binghamton
Elmira
Jamestown
Olean
Batavia
Buffalo
Niagara Falls
Lockport
Finger Lakes
Genesee R.
Lake Ontario
Lake Erie
St. Lawrence R.
ADIRONDACK MTS.
Mt. Marcy 5,344
Lake Placid
Saratoga Springs
Glens Falls
Schenectady
Troy
Albany
Hudson
Kingston
Poughkeepsie
Newburgh
CATSKILL MTS.
APPALACHIAN MTS.
Yonkers
New Rochelle
New York
Long Island
Montauk Pt.
Delaware R.

NEW JERSEY

PENNSYLVANIA

200 Miles
300 Kilometers

EASTERN SEABOARD

MICHIGAN

CANADA

Lake Ontario

NEW YORK

Lake Erie

Erie • Bradford
• Oil City • Williamsport Wilkes-Barre • Scranton
• Sharon • Hazleton • Paterson
PENNSYLVANIA Easton • Newark
OHIO • New Castle • State College Pottsville Allentown • Bethlehem • Elizabeth New Brunswick
Altoona • Lebanon • Reading Jersey City
Weirton • Harrisburg Lancaster Pottstown • Trenton
McKeesport • Pittsburgh • Johnstown • Carlisle • Philadelphia Camden
Wheeling • York Chester • Glassboro
• Uniontown Wilmington **NEW**
Cumberland Newark Atlantic
Hagerstown • Middletown City
Parkersburg • Morgantown • Frederick **JERSEY** Vineland
Fairmont • Martinsburg Baltimore Dover
WEST Clarksburg • Winchester Silver Spring Milford Rehoboth
Elkins Spruce Knob Rockville Annapolis Lewes Beach
VIRGINIA 4861 Arlington ★ Washington Seaford **DEL.**
Huntington Harrisonburg D.C. Laurel Georgetown
• Charleston Staunton **SHENANDOAH** Alexandria Salisbury Ocean City
St. Albans NP Fredericksburg **MARYLAND**
Oak Hill Charlottesville Chesapeake
Beckley James R. Bay
KENTUCKY Princeton • Richmond
Bluefield Lynchburg • Petersburg
Roanoke **VIRGINIA** Hampton
Blacksburg Newport News • Norfolk
Martinsville Portsmouth • Virginia Beach
Danville Suffolk • Chesapeake
Bristol PLAIN Elizabeth City
TENNESSEE Winston- Greensboro
Salem Burlington Rocky Mount
High Point Durham • Wilson BANKS
Mt. Mitchell Chapel Raleigh Greenville
6684 Hickory Salisbury Hill
Asheville Kannapolis Concord **NORTH** Goldsboro Cape
GREAT SMOKY Gastonia Charlotte **CAROLINA** Kinston Hatteras
MTNS NP New Bern OUTER
Spartanburg Fayetteville Havelock Pamlico Sound
Easley • Greenville Rock Jacksonville
Clemson Hill
Anderson Florence
Greenwood **SOUTH** Lumberton
CAROLINA ★ Columbia Wilmington **ATLANTIC**
Aiken Sumter **OCEAN**
N. Augusta Orangeburg Myrtle Cape Fear
Beach
Summerville COASTAL
GEORGIA Charleston • Hanahan
Mount
Pleasant
Beaufort ATLANTIC
• Hilton Head Island

APPALACHIAN

0 100 200 Miles

0 100 200 300 Kilometers

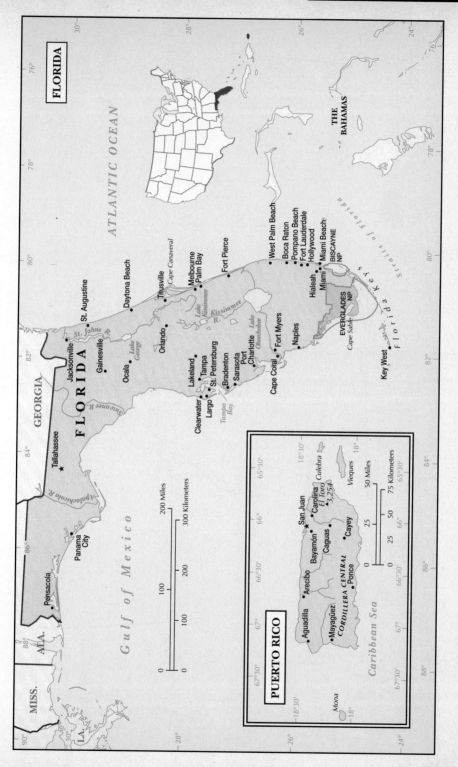

FLORIDA

ATLANTIC OCEAN

THE BAHAMAS

GEORGIA

ALA.

MISS.

LA.

FLORIDA

Tallahassee

Panama City

Pensacola

Gulf of Mexico

Apalachicola R.

Suwannee R.

Jacksonville

St. Augustine

Gainesville

St. Johns R.

Ocala

Lake George

Orlando

Daytona Beach

Titusville

Cape Canaveral

Melbourne
Palm Bay

Fort Pierce

West Palm Beach

Boca Raton
Pompano Beach
Fort Lauderdale
Hollywood
Miami Beach

Hialeah
Miami

BISCAYNE
NP

Lake Kissimmee

Lakeland
Tampa
St. Petersburg
Largo
Clearwater

Kissimmee R.

Lake Okeechobee

Bradenton
Sarasota
Port
Charlotte

Cape Coral

Fort Myers

Naples

EVERGLADES
NP

Cape Sable

Key West

Florida Keys

Straits of Florida

200 Miles
300 Kilometers

0   100   200

0   100   200

PUERTO RICO

San Juan

Arecibo

Aguadilla

Mayagüez

Bayamón

Caguas

Carolina
El Toro
3,254

Culebra

Vieques

Cayey

Ponce

CORDILLERA CENTRAL

Mona

Caribbean Sea

50 Miles
75 Kilometers

0   25   50

0   25   50

243

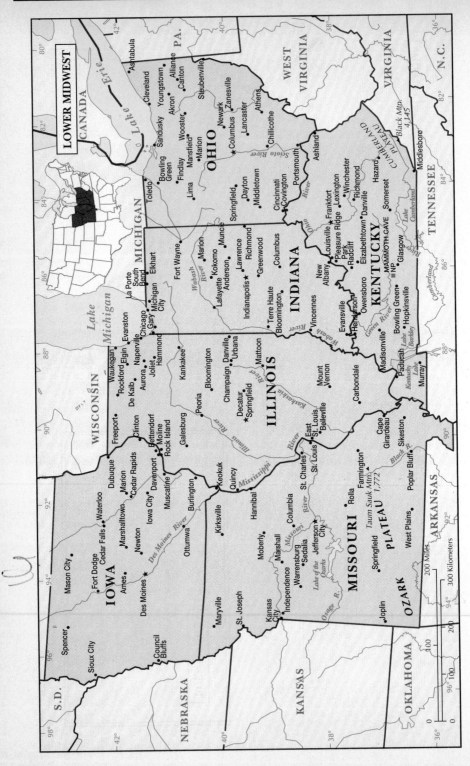

LOWER MIDWEST

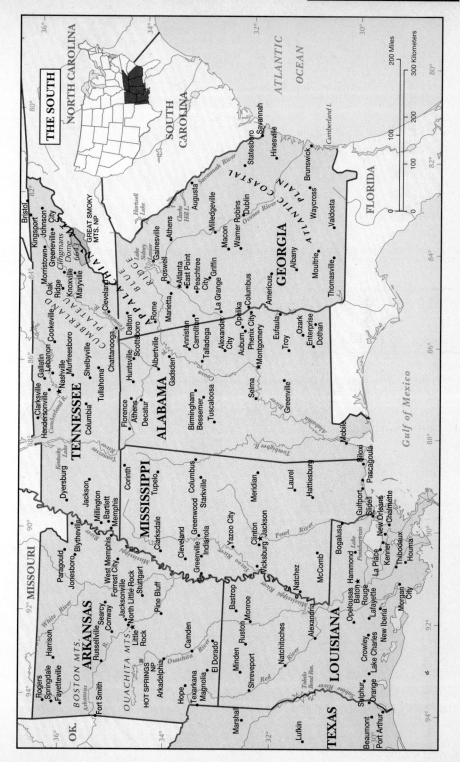

THE SOUTH

NORTH CAROLINA

SOUTH CAROLINA

FLORIDA

ATLANTIC OCEAN

200 Miles
300 Kilometers

GREAT SMOKY MTS. NP
Clingmans Dome 6643

BLUE RIDGE

APPALACHIAN

CUMBERLAND PLATEAU

Hartwell Lake
Clarks Hill L.
Savannah River
Oconee River

Savannah
Statesboro
Hinesville
Brunswick
Waycross
Valdosta
Moultrie
Thomasville
Albany
Americus
Dublin
Macon
Warner Robins
Milledgeville
Gainesville
Athens
Augusta

GEORGIA

ATLANTIC COASTAL PLAIN

Bristol
Kingsport
Johnson City
Greeneville
Morristown
Knoxville
Oak Ridge
Maryville
Cleveland
Chattanooga
Cookeville
Lebanon
Gallatin
Hendersonville
Clarksville
Nashville
Murfreesboro
Shelbyville
Columbia
Tullahoma

TENNESSEE

Roswell
Atlanta
East Point
Peachtree City
Griffin
La Grange
Columbus
Opelika
Auburn
Phenix City
Alexander City
Eufaula
Ozark
Troy
Enterprise
Dothan
Montgomery
Greenville

Rome
Marietta
Dalton
Scottsboro
Huntsville
Athens
Florence
Decatur
Albertville
Gadsden
Anniston
Talladega
Carrollton
Birmingham
Bessemer
Tuscaloosa
Selma

ALABAMA

Coosa River
Tombigbee R.
Alabama River

Mobile
Biloxi
Pascagoula
Gulfport
Slidell
New Orleans
Chalmette
Kenner
La Place
Thibodaux
Houma

Gulf of Mexico

Corinth
Tupelo
Columbus
Greenwood
Starkville
Indianola
Cleveland
Clarksdale
Greenville
Yazoo City
Jackson
Clinton
Vicksburg
Meridian
Laurel
Hattiesburg
Natchez
McComb

MISSISSIPPI

Pearl River
Yazoo River

MISSOURI

Paragould
Jonesboro
Blytheville
Dyersburg
Jackson
Millington
Bartlett
Memphis
West Memphis
Forrest City
Stuttgart
Jacksonville
North Little Rock
Little Rock
Pine Bluff

Rogers
Springdale
Fayetteville
Harrison
Russellville
Searcy
Conway

ARKANSAS

BOSTON MTS.
White River
Arkansas R.
OUACHITA MTS.
Ouachita River
Red River

Fort Smith
Camden
El Dorado
Magnolia
Hope
Texarkana
Arkadelphia
HOT SPRINGS NP

Marshall
Lufkin
Beaumont
Port Arthur
Orange
Sulphur

TEXAS

LOUISIANA

Toledo Bend Res.
Sabine River

Bastrop
Monroe
Ruston
Minden
Shreveport
Natchitoches
Alexandria
Bogalusa
Hammond
Opelousas
Baton Rouge
Lafayette
New Iberia
Crowley
Lake Charles
Morgan City

Lake Pontchartrain

OK.

Mississippi River
Tennessee River
Kentucky Lake
Cumberland R.

245

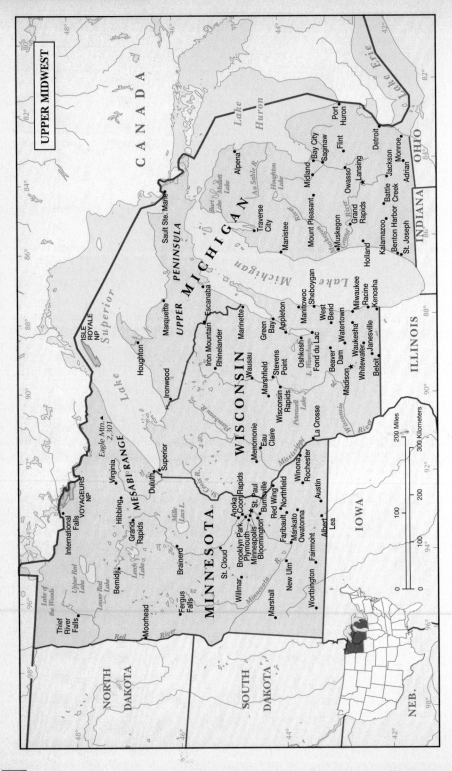

UPPER MIDWEST

CANADA

Lake Superior

Lake Huron

Lake Erie

Lake Michigan

ISLE ROYALE NP

MICHIGAN

UPPER PENINSULA

Sault Ste. Marie

Marquette

Houghton

Ironwood

Escanaba

Iron Mountain

Rhinelander

Marinette

Alpena

Burt Lake

Mullet Lake

Au Sable R.

Houghton Lake

Traverse City

Manistee

Mount Pleasant

Midland

Bay City

Saginaw

Flint

Port Huron

Detroit

Jackson

Lansing

Owosso

Grand Rapids

Muskegon

Holland

Kalamazoo

Battle Creek

Benton Harbor

St. Joseph

Monroe

Adrian

OHIO

INDIANA

ILLINOIS

Milwaukee

Racine

Kenosha

Sheboygan

Manitowoc

West Bend

Watertown

Waukesha

Whitewater

Janesville

Beloit

Madison

Beaver Dam

Fond du Lac

Oshkosh

Appleton

Green Bay

L. Winnebago

Stevens Point

Wisconsin Rapids

Marshfield

Wausau

Petenwell Lake

WISCONSIN

Eau Claire

Menomonie

La Crosse

Wisconsin River

Mississippi River

Chippewa R.

Wisconsin R.

St. Croix R.

Winona

Rochester

Red Wing

Northfield

Faribault

Owatonna

Austin

Albert Lea

Fairmont

Worthington

Mankato

New Ulm

Marshall

MINNESOTA

St. Paul

Minneapolis

Bloomington

Plymouth

Brooklyn Park

Coon Rapids

Anoka

Burnsville

St. Cloud

Willmar

Brainerd

Mille Lacs L.

Grand Rapids

Hibbing

Virginia

MESABI RANGE

Eagle Mtn. 2,301

VOYAGEURS NP

International Falls

Bemidji

Leech Lake

Upper Red Lake

Lower Red Lake

Lake of the Woods

Thief River Falls

Moorhead

Fergus Falls

Red River

Minnesota R.

Duluth

Superior

IOWA

NORTH DAKOTA

SOUTH DAKOTA

NEB.

200 Miles

300 Kilometers

0   100   200

0   100   200

80° 82° 84° 86° 88° 90° 92° 94° 96° 98°

48° 46° 44° 42°

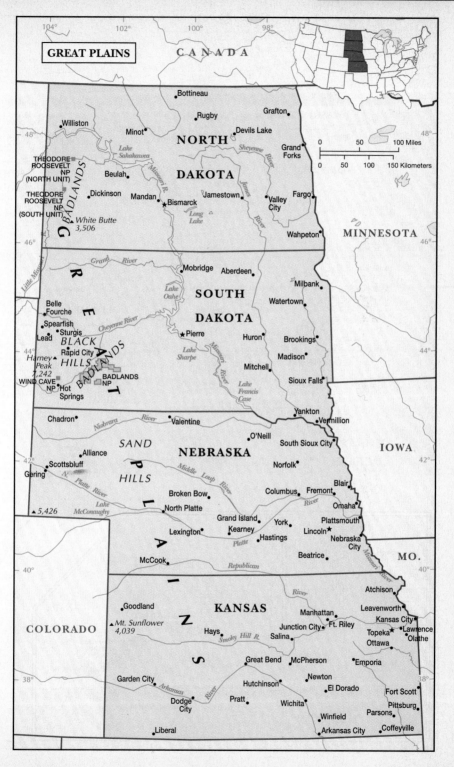

GREAT PLAINS

CANADA

104° 102° 100° 98°

Bottineau

Rugby · Grafton

Williston · Minot · Devils Lake

NORTH Grand Forks 48°

Lake Sakakawea · Sheyenne River

THEODORE ROOSEVELT NP (NORTH UNIT)

DAKOTA

Beulah · Mandan · Jamestown · Valley City · Fargo

THEODORE ROOSEVELT NP (SOUTH UNIT)

Dickinson · ★Bismarck

Missouri R. · James River

White Butte 3,506 · Long Lake

Wahpeton · **MINNESOTA** 46°

0 50 100 Miles
0 50 100 150 Kilometers

G R E A T

Grand River · Mobridge · Aberdeen

Little Missouri · Lake Oahe

SOUTH · Milbank

Belle Fourche · Watertown

Spearfish · Cheyenne River

Lead · Sturgis · **DAKOTA**

BLACK · ★Pierre · Huron · Brookings 44°

Harney Peak 7,242 · **HILLS** · Rapid City · Lake Sharpe · Madison

WIND CAVE NP · Hot Springs · **BADLANDS** · BADLANDS NP · Mitchell · Sioux Falls

Missouri River · Lake Francis Case

Yankton

Chadron · Niobrara River · Valentine · Vermillion

SAND · O'Neill · South Sioux City · **IOWA** 42°

Alliance · **NEBRASKA** · Norfolk

Scottsbluff · **HILLS** · Blair

Gering · Middle Loup River · Columbus · Fremont

N. Platte River · Broken Bow · Omaha

Lake McConaughy · ▲5,426 · North Platte · Grand Island · York · Plattsmouth

P · Lexington · Kearney · Hastings · Lincoln★ · Nebraska City

Platte ·

McCook · Beatrice · **MO.**

Republican · Missouri River 40°

L · Atchison

Goodland · **KANSAS** · Manhattan · Leavenworth · Kansas City

▲Mt. Sunflower 4,039 · Junction City · Ft. Riley · Topeka★ · Lawrence

COLORADO · **A** · Hays · Salina · Ottawa · Olathe

Smoky Hill R.

Great Bend · McPherson · Emporia

I · Garden City · Newton · Fort Scott 38°

Hutchinson · El Dorado · Pittsburg

N · Arkansas River · Dodge City · Pratt · Wichita · Parsons

S · Winfield · Coffeyville

Liberal · Arkansas City

247

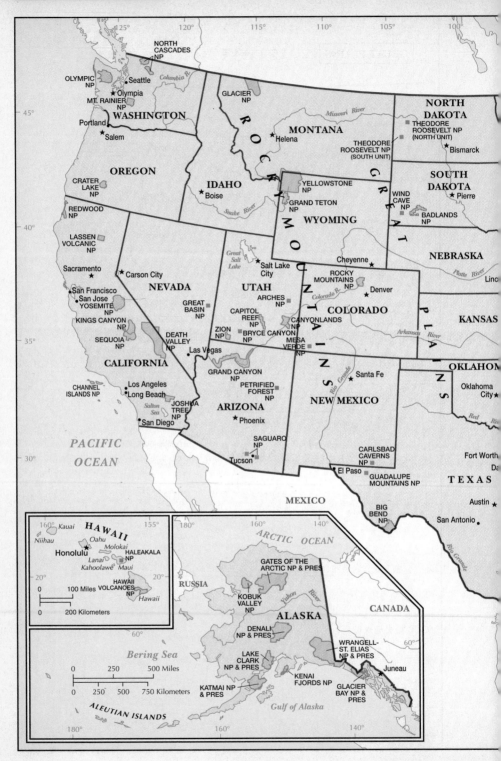

125°   120°   115°   110°   105°   100°

NORTH
CASCADES
NP

OLYMPIC
NP
• Seattle
Columbia R.
★ Olympia
MT. RAINIER
NP

GLACIER
NP

Missouri River

NORTH
DAKOTA

THEODORE
ROOSEVELT NP
(NORTH UNIT)

Portland ★

WASHINGTON

★ Salem

45°

MONTANA

• Helena

THEODORE
ROOSEVELT NP
(SOUTH UNIT)

• Bismarck

OREGON

CRATER
LAKE
NP

IDAHO

Boise ★

Snake River

ROCKY

YELLOWSTONE
NP

GRAND TETON
NP

WYOMING

SOUTH
DAKOTA

★ Pierre

WIND
CAVE
NP

BADLANDS
NP

REDWOOD
NP

40°

LASSEN
VOLCANIC
NP

Sacramento ★

★ Carson City

NEVADA

GREAT
BASIN
NP

Great
Salt
Lake

Salt Lake
City

UTAH

ARCHES
NP

Cheyenne ★

ROCKY
MOUNTAINS
NP

Colorado R.

Denver •

COLORADO

NEBRASKA

Platte River

Linc

KANSAS

GREAT

MOUNTAINS

PLAINS

San Francisco •
San Jose •
YOSEMITE
NP

KINGS CANYON
NP

35°

SEQUOIA
NP

CAPITOL
REEF
NP

ZION
NP

BRYCE CANYON
NP

CANYONLANDS
NP

MESA
VERDE
NP

Arkansas River

CALIFORNIA

DEATH
VALLEY
NP

Las Vegas •

Los Angeles •
Long Beach •

CHANNEL
ISLANDS NP

Salton
Sea

JOSHUA
TREE
NP

San Diego •

GRAND CANYON
NP

PETRIFIED
FOREST
NP

ARIZONA

★ Phoenix

Santa Fe ★

NEW MEXICO

Rio Grande

OKLAHOM

Oklahoma
City ★

Red
Riv

30°

SAGUARO
NP

Tucson •

CARLSBAD
CAVERNS
NP

El Paso •

GUADALUPE
MOUNTAINS NP

Fort Worth •

Da

TEXAS

PACIFIC
OCEAN

MEXICO

BIG
BEND
NP

Austin ★

San Antonio •

Rio Grande

160°   Kauai   HAWAII   155°

Niihau

Oahu
Molokai
Honolulu ★ Lanai HALEAKALA
Kahoolawe Maui NP

20°

HAWAII
VOLCANOES
NP

Hawaii

0   100 Miles

0   200 Kilometers

180°   160°   140°

ARCTIC OCEAN

GATES OF THE
ARCTIC NP & PRES

RUSSIA

KOBUK
VALLEY
NP

Yukon River

ALASKA

CANADA

DENALI
NP & PRES

WRANGELL-
ST. ELIAS
NP & PRES

60°

Bering Sea

LAKE
CLARK
NP & PRES

KENAI
FJORDS NP

Juneau ★

0   250   500 Miles

KATMAI NP
& PRES

GLACIER
BAY NP &
PRES

0   250   500   750 Kilometers

60°

ALEUTIAN ISLANDS

Gulf of Alaska

180°   160°   140°

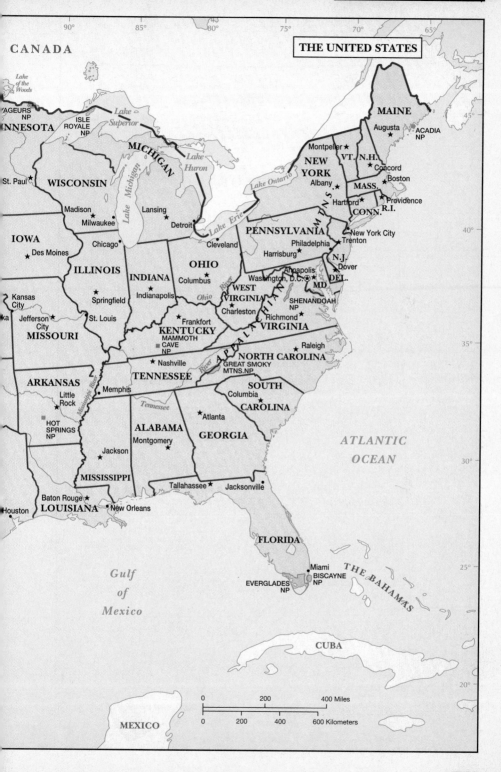

CANADA

THE UNITED STATES

Lake of the Woods

VOYAGEURS NP

ISLE ROYALE NP

MINNESOTA

MICHIGAN

Lake Superior

Lake Huron

Lake Michigan

St. Paul ★

WISCONSIN

Madison ★

Milwaukee ★

Lansing ★

Detroit ★

IOWA

Des Moines ★

Chicago ●

ILLINOIS

INDIANA

Springfield ★

Indianapolis ★

Columbus ★

OHIO

Cleveland ●

Lake Erie

Lake Ontario

MAINE

Augusta ★

ACADIA NP

Montpelier ★

VT. **N.H.**

Concord ★

NEW YORK

Albany ★

Boston ★

MASS.

Hartford ★

Providence ★

CONN. **R.I.**

PENNSYLVANIA

New York City ●

Trenton ★

Philadelphia ★

Harrisburg ★

N.J.

Dover ★

DEL.

Annapolis ★

Washington, D.C. ★

MD.

WEST VIRGINIA

Charleston ★

SHENANDOAH NP

Richmond ★

VIRGINIA

APPALACHIAN MTNS

Ohio River

Kansas City ★

Jefferson City ★

St. Louis ●

MISSOURI

Frankfort ★

KENTUCKY

MAMMOTH CAVE NP

Nashville ★

TENNESSEE

Tennessee River

Raleigh ★

NORTH CAROLINA

GREAT SMOKY MTNS.NP

ARKANSAS

Little Rock ★

Memphis ●

Mississippi River

HOT SPRINGS NP

Columbia ★

SOUTH CAROLINA

Atlanta ★

ALABAMA

Montgomery ★

Jackson ★

GEORGIA

MISSISSIPPI

Tallahassee ★

Jacksonville ●

Baton Rouge ★

LOUISIANA

New Orleans ●

Houston ●

FLORIDA

Miami ●

BISCAYNE NP

EVERGLADES NP

ATLANTIC OCEAN

THE BAHAMAS

Gulf of Mexico

CUBA

MEXICO

0	200	400 Miles	
0	200	400	600 Kilometers

90° 85° 80° 75° 70° 65°

45°

40°

35°

30°

25°

20°

249

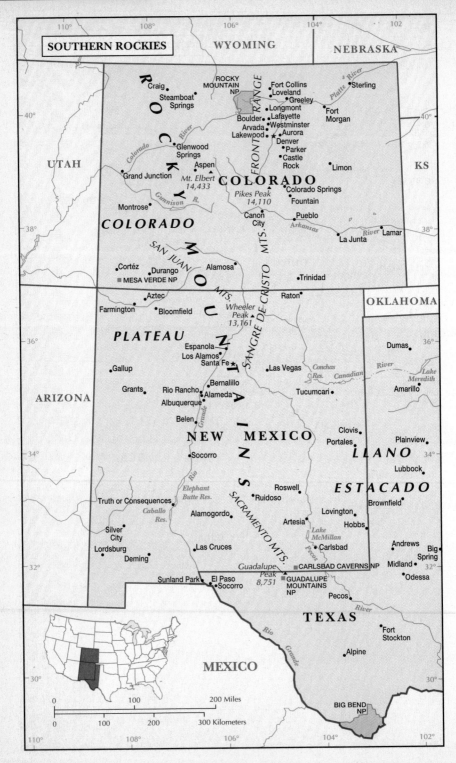

SOUTHERN ROCKIES

WYOMING

NEBRASKA

ROCKY MOUNTAIN NP

Craig

Steamboat Springs

Fort Collins
Loveland
Greeley
Longmont
Boulder
Lafayette
Arvada
Westminster
Lakewood
Aurora
Denver
Parker
Castle Rock

Sterling

Fort Morgan

FRONT RANGE

Glenwood Springs

Aspen

Grand Junction

Mt. Elbert 14,433

COLORADO

Pikes Peak 14,110

Colorado Springs

Fountain

Limon

Montrose

Canon City

Pueblo

Arkansas River

Lamar

La Junta

COLORADO

SAN JUAN MTS.

SANGRE DE CRISTO MTS.

Cortéz
Durango
MESA VERDE NP

Alamosa

Trinidad

Raton

OKLAHOMA

Aztec

Farmington
Bloomfield

Wheeler Peak 13,161

PLATEAU

Espanola
Los Alamos
Santa Fe

Dumas

Gallup

Grants

Rio Rancho
Bernalillo
Alameda
Albuquerque

Las Vegas

Conchas Res.

Canadian River

Lake Meredith

Amarillo

Belen

ROCKY MOUNTAIN

NEW MEXICO

Tucumcari

Socorro

Clovis
Portales

LLANO

Plainview

Lubbock

Truth or Consequences

Elephant Butte Res.

Caballo Res.

Roswell
Ruidoso

ESTACADO

Brownfield

Silver City

Lordsburg

Deming

Alamogordo

Las Cruces

Lovington

Artesia

Hobbs

SACRAMENTO MTS.

Lake McMillan

Pecos

Carlsbad

Andrews

Big Spring

Midland

Odessa

Sunland Park

El Paso
Socorro

Guadalupe Peak 8,751

CARLSBAD CAVERNS NP

GUADALUPE MOUNTAINS NP

Pecos

TEXAS

River

Fort Stockton

MEXICO

Rio Grande

Alpine

BIG BEND NP

0   100   200 Miles

0   100   200   300 Kilometers

UTAH

ARIZONA

KS

SOUTHERN PLAINS

KANSAS

100° 98° 96° 94°

Guymon

Woodward

Ponca City · Bartlesville · Miami

MO.

ARK.

Enid · Claremore

Dumas

Stillwater · Tulsa · Broken Arrow

Pampa

Clinton · El Reno · Edmond · Oklahoma City · Muskogee · Okmulgee

Amarillo

Lake Meredith

Shawnee

Chickasha · Norman

Altus · OKLAHOMA · Ada · McAlester

Lawton

Plainview

LLANO

Lubbock

ESTACADO

Brownfield

Wichita Falls · Sherman · Denison · Paris

Duncan · Ardmore · Lake Texoma · Durant

OUACHITA MTS

Texarkana

Denton · Greenville

Plano · Garland

Irving · Dallas · Mesquite

Fort Worth · Arlington

Marshall · Longview · Tyler

Andrews · Big Spring

Abilene

Midland

TEXAS

Corsicana

Odessa

Brownwood

Nacogdoches

San Angelo

Waco

Lufkin

Pecos

Fort Stockton

EDWARDS

Killeen · Temple

Bryan · College Station · Huntsville

PLATEAU

Round Rock

Austin

San Marcos

Houston · Baytown

New Braunfels · Seguin

Pasadena

Del Rio

San Antonio

Texas City · Galveston

BIG BEND NP

Freeport

Eagle Pass

MEXICO

Victoria

Matagorda Bay

Alice · Corpus Christi

Laredo · Kingsville

Gulf of Mexico

Padre Island

Edinburg · Mission · McAllen · Pharr · Weslaco · Harlingen · San Benito

Brownsville

0 100 200 Miles

0 100 200 300 Kilometers

102° 100° 98° 96°

KANSAS · 36°

Arkansas R. · Keystone Lake · 36°

Sapulpa

Robert S. Kerr Lake

Canadian River

Eufaula Lake

Red River · 34°

Sabine River

Colorado River

Brazos River

Sam Rayburn Res.

Lake Livingston

Amistad Res.

Rio Grande

Nueces River

Falcon Res.

Galveston Bay

30°

28°

26°

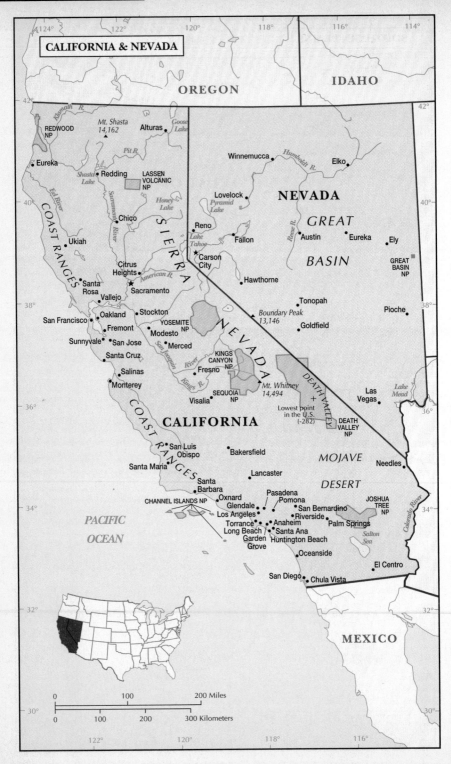

CALIFORNIA & NEVADA

OREGON

IDAHO

REDWOOD NP

Mt. Shasta 14,162

Alturas

Goose Lake

Klamath R.

Eureka

Pit R.

Shasta Lake Redding

LASSEN VOLCANIC NP

Chico

Honey Lake

Winnemucca

Humboldt R.

Elko

NEVADA

Lovelock

Pyramid Lake

GREAT

Ukiah

COAST RANGES

Sacramento River

Reno

Lake Tahoe

Fallon

Reese R.

Austin

Eureka

Ely

BASIN

SIERRA

Citrus Heights

★ Carson City

Hawthorne

GREAT BASIN NP

Santa Rosa

Vallejo

★ Sacramento

American R.

Tonopah

Pioche

San Francisco

Oakland

Stockton

YOSEMITE NP

Boundary Peak 13,146

Goldfield

Fremont

Modesto

NEVADA

Sunnyvale

San Jose

Merced

San Joaquin River

San Jose

Santa Cruz

KINGS CANYON NP

Fresno

Kings R.

DEATH VALLEY

Las Vegas

Lake Mead

Salinas

Monterey

Visalia

SEQUOIA NP

Mt. Whitney 14,494

Lowest point in the U.S. (-282)

DEATH VALLEY NP

CALIFORNIA

San Luis Obispo

Bakersfield

MOJAVE

Needles

Santa Maria

COAST RANGES

Lancaster

DESERT

Santa Barbara

CHANNEL ISLANDS NP

Oxnard

Pasadena

Pomona

JOSHUA TREE NP

Glendale

San Bernardino

PACIFIC

Los Angeles

Riverside

Palm Springs

Colorado River

Torrance

Anaheim

Santa Ana

Long Beach

Garden Grove

Huntington Beach

Salton Sea

OCEAN

Oceanside

El Centro

San Diego

Chula Vista

MEXICO

0   100   200 Miles

0   100   200   300 Kilometers

ARIZONA & UTAH

WYOMING

NEVADA

Bear Lake
• Logan
• Brigham City
Roy • Ogden
• Clearfield
• Layton
• Bountiful
Salt Lake City ★
West Jordan • Murray
Tooele • • Sandy
• Orem
• Provo
• Payson

GREAT SALT LAKE DESERT

Great Salt Lake

Utah Lake

WASATCH

UINTA

RANGE

▲ Kings Peak
13,528
MTS
• Vernal

Green River

• Price

Sevier Lake

• Richfield

UTAH

Green River •

ARCHES NP ■

CAPITOL REEF NP

CANYONLANDS NP

• Moab

COLORADO

Cedar City •

Sevier River

BRYCE CANYON NP ■

ZION NP

Saint George •

Lake Powell

• Blanding

San Juan River

• Page

• Kayenta

Colorado River

Lake Mead

GRAND CANYON

GRAND CANYON NP

PAINTED DESERT

NEW MEXICO

• Kingman
• Bullhead City

Humphreys Peak
12,633 ▲
• Flagstaff

• Winslow
Cottonwood •   • Holbrook

PETRIFIED FOREST NP ■

CALIFORNIA

Lake Havasu City •

Lake Havasu

• Prescott

Verde R.

ARIZONA

Colorado River

Peoria •
Glendale •   • Scottsdale
Phoenix ★ • Mesa
Tempe •
Chandler •

Salt River

• Globe

• Apache Junction

Gila R.

Gila River

Casa Grande •

• Coolidge

• Eloy

• Safford

Yuma •

SONORAN

DESERT

■ Tucson
SAGUARO NP ■

• Sierra Vista

• Nogales   • Bisbee   • Douglas

MEXICO

0   100   200 Miles

0   100   200   300 Kilometers

NORTHERN ROCKIES

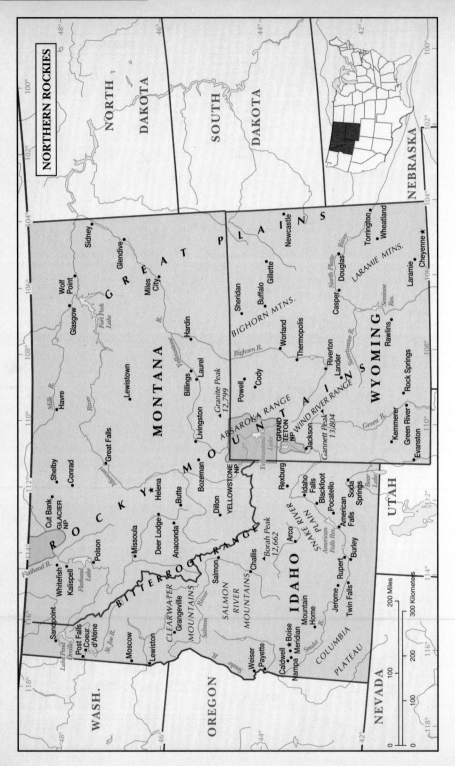

NORTH DAKOTA

SOUTH DAKOTA

NEBRASKA

GREAT PLAINS

WASH.

OREGON

NEVADA

UTAH

WYOMING

MONTANA

IDAHO

ROCKY MOUNTAINS

BITTERROOT RANGE

CLEARWATER MOUNTAINS

SALMON RIVER MOUNTAINS

COLUMBIA PLATEAU

SNAKE RIVER PLAIN

ABSAROKA RANGE

WIND RIVER RANGE

BIGHORN MTNS.

LARAMIE MTNS.

Sidney
Glendive
Wolf Point
Glasgow
Havre
Shelby
Conrad
Cut Bank
Whitefish
Kalispell
Sandpoint
Post Falls
Coeur d'Alene
Polson
Missoula
Deer Lodge
Anaconda
Butte
Helena ★
Great Falls
Lewistown
Miles City
Hardin
Billings
Laurel
Livingston
Bozeman
Dillon
Granite Peak 12,799 ▲

Moscow
Lewiston
Grangeville
Salmon
Challis
Borah Peak 12,662 ▲
Arco
Weiser
Payette
Caldwell
Nampa
Boise ★
Meridian
Mountain Home
Jerome
Rupert
Twin Falls
Burley
American Falls
Pocatello
Blackfoot
Idaho Falls
Rexburg
Soda Springs

YELLOWSTONE NP
GRAND TETON NP
Jackson
Gannett Peak 13,804 ▲
Cody
Powell
Worland
Thermopolis
Riverton
Lander
Sheridan
Buffalo
Gillette
Newcastle
Casper
Douglas
Torrington
Wheatland
Laramie
Rawlins
Rock Springs
Kemmerer
Green River
Evanston
Cheyenne ★

Fort Peck Lake
Milk R.
Missouri R.
Yellowstone R.
Bighorn R.
Flathead R.
Flathead Lake
Lake Pend Oreille
St. Joe R.
Snake R.
Salmon R.
Clearwater R.
Bear Lake
American Falls Res.
Yellowstone Lake
Green R.
North Platte River
Sweetwater R.
Seminoe Res.

GLACIER NP

200 Miles
300 Kilometers
100
200
100
0
0

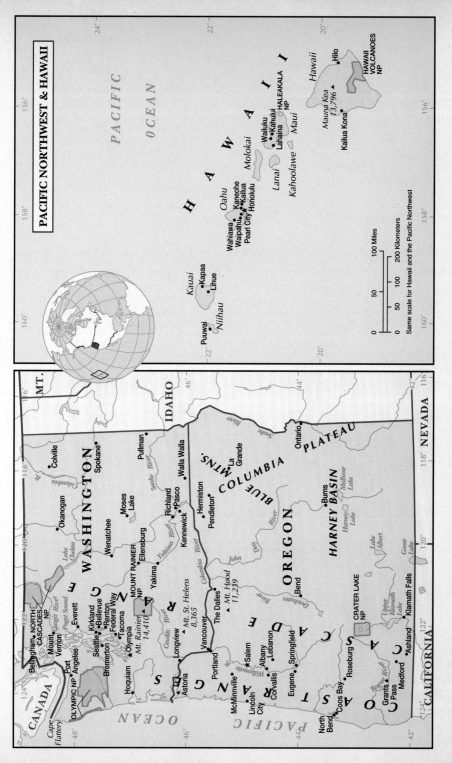

PACIFIC NORTHWEST & HAWAII

PACIFIC OCEAN

H A W A I I

Hawaii

Hilo
HAWAII VOLCANOES NP
Mauna Kea 13,796 ▲
Kailua Kona

Maui
HALEAKALA NP
Wailuku ● Kahului
Lahaina

Molokai
Lanai
Kahoolawe

Oahu
Wahiawa ● Kaneohe
Waipahu ● Kailua
Pearl City ● Honolulu

Kauai
Kapaa
Lihue

Puuwai
Niihau

100 Miles
200 Kilometers
50
100
50
0
0
Same scale for Hawaii and the Pacific Northwest

MT.

IDAHO

Colville
WASHINGTON
Spokane
Okanogan
Wenatchee
Moses Lake
Pullman
Richland
Pasco
Walla Walla
Kennewick
Hermiston
Pendleton
La Grande
Ontario

COLUMBIA PLATEAU
BLUE MTNS.
Snake River

Lake Chelan
Everett
Kirkland ● Bellevue
Seattle ● Renton ● Federal Way
Bremerton ● Tacoma
Olympia
MOUNT RAINIER NP
Mt. Rainier 14,410
Ellensburg
Yakima

NORTH CASCADES NP
Mount Vernon
Bellingham

Port Angeles
OLYMPIC NP
Cape Flattery

CANADA

Hoquiam

Mt. St. Helens 8,365
Longview
Vancouver
The Dalles
Mt. Hood 11,239

Astoria
Portland
McMinnville
Lincoln City
Salem
Albany
Corvallis
Eugene
Lebanon
Springfield

OREGON

Bend

Deschutes River

CRATER LAKE NP

Roseburg
Coos Bay
North Bend
Grants Pass
Medford
Ashland
Klamath Falls

Upper Klamath Lake
Lake Albert
Goose Lake

HARNEY BASIN
Burns
Harney Lake
Malheur Lake

C A S C A D E R A N G E
C O A S T R A N G E S

Rogue River
Willamette
John Day River

CALIFORNIA
NEVADA

PACIFIC OCEAN

255

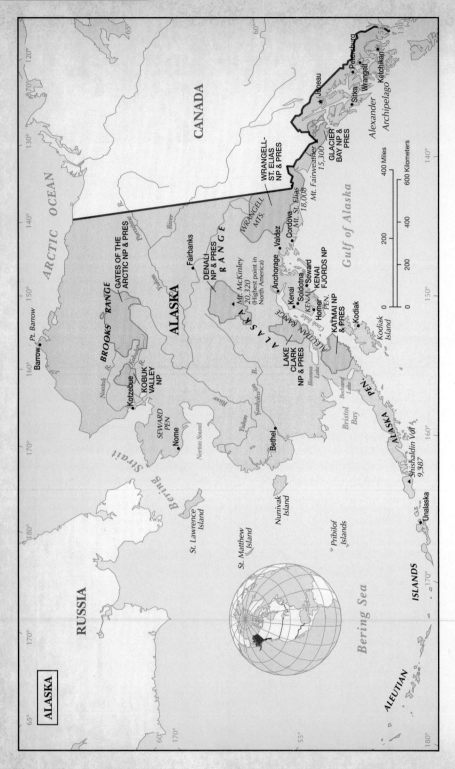

ALASKA

CANADA

ARCTIC OCEAN

RUSSIA

Pt. Barrow
Barrow

BROOKS RANGE

GATES OF THE
ARCTIC NP & PRES

KOBUK
VALLEY
NP

Kotzebue

ALASKA

Fairbanks

DENALI
NP & PRES

Mt. McKinley
20,320
(Highest point in
North America)

WRANGELL-
ST. ELIAS
NP & PRES

WRANGELL
MTS.

Mt. St. Elias
18,008

Cordova

Valdez

Anchorage

Juneau

Petersburg

Wrangell

Sitka

Ketchikan

Alexander
Archipelago

GLACIER
BAY NP &
PRES

Mt. Fairweather
15,300

Gulf of Alaska

Kenai
Soldotna

KENAI
FJORDS NP

Seward

KENAI
PEN.

Homer

KATMAI NP
& PRES

Kodiak

Kodiak
Island

LAKE
CLARK
NP & PRES

SEWARD
PEN

Nome

Norton Sound

Bethel

Yukon

Kuskokwim R.

Iliamna
Lake

Becharof
Lake

Bristol
Bay

ALASKA PEN.

Shishaldin Vol
9,387

Bering Strait

St. Lawrence
Island

Nunivak
Island

St. Matthew
Island

Pribilof
Islands

Bering Sea

ALEUTIAN

ISLANDS

Unalaska

ALASKA

400 Miles
600 Kilometers
400
200
200
0
0

FACTS About the STATES

The Area is the total area, including land and water. It is given in both square miles (sq. mi.) and square kilometers (sq. km.) The numbers in parentheses after Population, Area, and Entered Union show the ranking of the state compared with other U.S. states. For example, Alabama is the 22nd largest state in population, but it is the 30th largest state in area.

ALABAMA

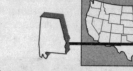

Heart of Dixie, Camellia State

Population (1995): 4,252,982 (22nd)
Area: 52,423 sq. mi. (30th) (135,775 sq. km.)
Entered Union: December 14, 1819 (22nd)
Postal Abbreviation: AL
Flower: Camellia   **Bird:** Yellowhammer
Tree: Southern pine   **Song:** Alabama
Capital: Montgomery
Largest Cities (with population): Birmingham, 264,527; Mobile, 204,490; Montgomery, 195,471; Huntsville, 160,325
Important Products: clothing and textiles, metal products, transportation equipment, paper, industrial machinery, food products, lumber, coal, oil, natural gas, livestock, peanuts, cotton
Places to Visit: Alabama Space and Rocket Center, Huntsville; DeSoto State Park, near Fort Payne

 DID YOU KNOW? Montgomery, Alabama, was the first capital of the Confederate States of America (1861). Alabama is a major center for rocket and space research.

ALASKA

The Last Frontier

Population (1995): 603,617 (48th)
Area: 656,424 sq. mi. (1st) (1,700,139 sq. km.)
Entered Union: January 3, 1959 (49th)
Postal Abbreviation: AK
Flower: Forget-me-not   **Bird:** Willow ptarmigan
Tree: Sitka spruce   **Song:** Alaska's Flag
Capital: Juneau (population, 26,751)
Largest Cities (with population): Anchorage, 253,649; Fairbanks, 30,843
Important Products: oil, natural gas, fish, food products, lumber and wood products, fur
Places to Visit: Glacier Bay and Denali national parks, Mendenhall Glacier, Mount McKinley

DID YOU KNOW? Mount McKinley is the highest mountain in the United States. Alaska is the biggest and coldest state in the United States.

ARIZONA

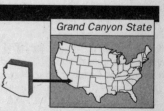

Grand Canyon State

Population (1995): 4,217,940 (23rd)
Area: 114,006 sq. mi. (6th) (295,276 sq. km.)
Entered Union: February 14, 1912 (48th)
Postal Abbreviation: AZ
Flower: Blossom of the Saguaro cactus **Bird:** Cactus wren
Tree: Paloverde   **Song:** Arizona
Capital and Largest City: Phoenix (population, 1,048,949)
Other Large Cities (with population): Tucson, 434,726; Mesa, 313,649; Glendale, 168,439; Scottsdale, 152,439; Tempe, 144,289
Important Products: electronic equipment, transportation and industrial equipment, instruments, printing and publishing, copper and other metals
Places to Visit: Grand Canyon, Painted Desert, Petrified Forest, Hoover Dam

DID YOU KNOW? The Grand Canyon is the largest land gorge in the world and one of the world's natural wonders. It is 217 miles long and 4-18 miles wide at the rim.

ARKANSAS

Land of Opportunity

Population (1995): 2,483,769 (33rd)
Area: 53,182 sq. mi. (29th) (137,742 sq. km.)
Flower: Apple blossom   **Bird:** Mockingbird
Tree: Pine   **Song:** Arkansas
Entered Union: June 15, 1836 (25th)
Postal Abbreviation: AR
Capital and Largest City: Little Rock (population, 178,136)
Other Large Cities (with population): North Little Rock, 61,829; Pine Bluff, 57,140
Important Products: food products, paper, electronic equipment, industrial machinery, metal products, lumber and wood products, livestock, soybeans, rice, cotton, natural gas
Places to Visit: Hot Springs National Park

? DID YOU KNOW? Arkansas has the only working diamond mine on the continent of North America. President Bill Clinton was born in Arkansas and served as one of its governors.

CALIFORNIA

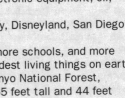

Golden State

Population (1995): 31,589,153 (1st)
Area: 163,707 sq. mi. (3rd) (424,002 sq. km.)
Flower: Golden poppy   **Bird:** California valley quail
Tree: California redwood   **Song:** I Love You, California
Entered Union: September 9, 1850 (31st)
Postal Abbreviation: CA
Capital: Sacramento (population, 373,964)
Largest Cities (with population): Los Angeles, 3,448,613; San Diego, 1,151,977; San Jose, 816,884; San Francisco, 734,676
Important Products: transportation and industrial equipment, electronic equipment, oil, natural gas, motion pictures, milk, cattle, fruit and vegetables
Places to Visit: Yosemite Valley, Lake Tahoe, Palomar Observatory, Disneyland, San Diego Zoo, Hollywood, Sequoia National Park

? DID YOU KNOW? California has more people, more cars, more schools, and more businesses than any other state in the United States. The oldest living things on earth are believed to be the Bristlecone pine trees in California's Inyo National Forest, estimated to be 4,700 years old. The world's tallest tree, 365 feet tall and 44 feet around, is a redwood tree in Humboldt County.

COLORADO

Centennial State

Population (1995): 3,746,585 (25th)
Area: 104,100 sq. mi. (8th) (269,620 sq. km.)
Flower: Rocky Mountain columbine   **Bird:** Lark bunting
Tree: Colorado blue spruce   **Song:** Where the Columbines
Entered Union: August 1, 1876 (38th)   Grow
Postal Abbreviation: CO
Capital and Largest City: Denver (population, 493,559)
Other Large Cities (with population): Colorado Springs, 316,480; Aurora, 250,717; Lakewood, 126,031
Important Products: instruments and industrial machinery, food products, printing and publishing, metal products, electronic equipment, oil, coal, cattle
Places to Visit: Rocky Mountain National Park, Mesa Verde National Park, Dinosaur National Monument, old mining towns

? DID YOU KNOW? The Grand Mesa in Colorado is the world's largest flat-top mountain. The highest bridge in the world (1,053 feet) is in Colorado—it is the suspension bridge over the Royal Gorge of the Arkansas River. Colorado has more mountains over 14,000 feet and more elk than any other state.

CONNECTICUT

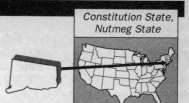

Constitution State,
Nutmeg State

Population (1995): 3,274,662 (28th)
Area: 5,544 sq. mi. (48th) (14,358 sq. km.)
Flower: Mountain laurel   **Bird:** American robin
Tree: White oak   **Song:** Yankee Doodle
Entered Union: January 9, 1788 (5th)
Postal Abbreviation: CT
Capital: Hartford
Largest Cities (with population): Bridgeport, 132,919; Hartford, 124,196; New Haven, 119,604; Waterbury, 103,523; Stamford, 107,199
Important Products: aircraft parts and helicopters, industrial machinery, metals and metal products, electronic equipment, printing and publishing, instruments, chemicals, dairy products, stone
Places to Visit: Mystic Seaport and Marine Life Aquarium, in Mystic; P.T. Barnum circus museum, Bridgeport; Peabody Museum, New Haven

? DID YOU KNOW? The first library for children opened in Salisbury, in 1803, and the first permanent school for the deaf opened in Hartford in 1817. The first woman to receive an American patent was Mary Kies of South Killingly, in 1809, for a machine to weave straw and silk or thread.

DELAWARE

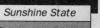

First State,
Diamond State

Population (1995): 717,197 (46th)
Area: 2,489 sq. mi. (49th) (6,447 sq. km.)
Flower: Peach blossom   **Bird:** Blue hen chicken
Tree: American holly   **Song:** Our Delaware
Entered Union: December 7, 1787 (1st)
Postal Abbreviation: DE
Capital: Dover
Largest Cities (with population): Wilmington, 71,529; Dover, 27,630; Newark, 25,098
Important Products: chemicals, food products, instruments, chickens
Places to Visit: Rehoboth Beach, Henry Francis du Pont Winterthur Museum near Wilmington

? DID YOU KNOW? Delaware was the first state to agree to the Constitution and thus became the first state of the United States. Delaware had the first log cabins in America.

FLORIDA

Sunshine State

Population (1995): 14,165,570 (4th)
Area: 65,756 sq. mi. (22nd) (170,308 sq. km.)
Flower: Orange blossom   **Bird:** Mockingbird
Tree: Sabal palmetto palm   **Song:** Old Folks at Home
Entered Union: March 3, 1845 (27th)
Postal Abbreviation: FL
Capital: Tallahassee (population, 133,718)
Largest Cities (with population): Jacksonville, 665,070; Miami, 373,024; Tampa, 285,523; Saint Petersburg, 238,585
Important Products: electronic and transportation equipment, instruments, printing and publishing, food products, citrus fruits, vegetables, livestock, phosphates, fish
Places to Visit: Walt Disney World and Universal Studios, near Orlando; Sea World, Orlando; Busch Gardens, Tampa; Spaceport USA, at Kennedy Space Center, Cape Canaveral; Everglades National Park

? DID YOU KNOW? St. Augustine, Florida, is the oldest city in the United States. Florida grows more citrus fruit than any other state. Also, Florida's warm, sunny climate attracts people from all over the country who are retired from their jobs. One out of every five people there is over the age of 65.

GEORGIA

Empire State of the South, Peach State

Population (1995): 7,200,882 (10th)
Area: 59,441 sq. mi. (24th) (153,953 sq. km.)
Flower: Cherokee rose   **Bird:** Brown thrasher
Tree: Live oak   **Song:** Georgia on My Mind
Entered Union: January 2, 1788 (4th)
Postal Abbreviation: GA
Capital and Largest City: Atlanta (population, 396,052)
Other Large Cities (with population): Columbus, 186,470;
Savannah, 140,597; Macon, 109,191
Important Products: clothing and textiles, transportation equipment, food products, paper, chickens, peanuts, peaches, clay
Places to Visit: Stone Mountain Park, Six Flags Over Georgia, New Echota State Historic Site (eastern Cherokee capital) in Calhoun

? DID YOU KNOW? Georgia is the largest state east of the Mississippi River and has more woods than any other state. The first U.S. gold rush took place in Georgia. The first American Indian newspaper was published in Georgia by a Cherokee in 1828. The first radio station owned and operated by African-Americans started in Atlanta in 1949. Civil rights leader Martin Luther King, Jr. (1929-1968) and baseball player Jackie Robinson (1919-1972) were born in Georgia. Georgia's capital city, Atlanta, hosted the Olympic Games in 1996.

HAWAII

Aloha State

Population (1995): 1,186,815 (40th)
Area: 10,932 sq. mi. (43rd) (28,313 sq. km.)
Flower: Yellow hibiscus   **Bird:** Hawaiian goose
Tree: Kukui   **Song:** Hawaii Ponoi
Entered Union: August 21, 1959 (50th)
Postal Abbreviation: HI
Capital and Largest City: Honolulu (population, 385,881)
Other Large Cities (with population): Hilo, 37,808; Kailua, 36,818; Kaneohe, 35,448
Important Products: food products, pineapples, sugarcane, printing and publishing, fish, stone
Places to Visit: Hawaii Volcanoes National Park; Haleakala National Park, Maui; Iolani Palace, Honolulu; U.S.S. *Arizona* Memorial, Pearl Harbor

? DID YOU KNOW? Hawaii is the only state made up entirely of islands, 122 of them. (People live on 7 of them.) Hawaii's Mauna Loa is the biggest active volcano in the United States.

IDAHO

Gem State

Population (1995): 1,163,261 (41st)
Area: 83,574 sq. mi. (14th) (216,456 sq. km.)
Flower: Syringa   **Bird:** Mountain bluebird
Tree: White pine   **Song:** Here We Have Idaho
Entered Union: July 3, 1890 (43rd)
Postal Abbreviation: ID
Capital and Largest City: Boise (population, 145,987)
Other Large Cities (with population): Pocatello, 46,080; Idaho Falls, 43,929
Important Products: potatoes, hay, wheat, cattle, milk, lumber and wood products, food products
Places to Visit: Sun Valley; Hells Canyon; Craters of the Moon, near Arco; Nez Percé National Historical Park, near Lewiston; ghost towns

? DID YOU KNOW? The first hydroelectric power plant built by the federal government was the Minidoka Dam on the Snake River in Idaho; the first unit started in 1909. Two thirds of all potatoes in the United States are grown in Idaho.

ILLINOIS

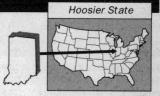

Prairie State

Population (1995): 11,829,940 (6th)
Area: 57,918 sq. mi. (25th) (150,007 sq. km.)
Flower: Native violet   **Bird:** Cardinal
Tree: White oak   **Song:** Illinois
Entered Union: December 3, 1818 (21st)
Postal Abbreviation: IL
Capital: Springfield
Largest Cities (with population): Chicago, 2,731,743; Rockford, 143,263; Peoria, 112,878; Aurora, 112,313; Springfield, 105,938
Important Products: industrial machinery, metals and metal products, printing and publishing, electronic equipment, food products, corn, soybeans, hogs
Places to Visit: Lincoln Park Zoo, Adler Planetarium, Field Museum of Natural History, and Museum of Science and Industry, all in Chicago; Abraham Lincoln's home and tomb, Springfield; New Salem Village

? **DID YOU KNOW?** Illinois has the world's busiest airport (O'Hare) and the tallest building in the U.S. (the Sears Tower in Chicago). The world's first skyscraper was built in Chicago, in 1885. Abraham Lincoln lived and worked in Illinois and is buried there.

INDIANA

Hoosier State

Population (1995): 5,803,471 (14th)
Area: 36,420 sq. mi. (38th) (94,328 sq. km.)
Flower: Peony   **Bird:** Cardinal
Tree: Tulip poplar   **Song:** On the Banks of the Wabash,
                                     Far Away
Entered Union: December 11, 1816 (19th)
Postal Abbreviation: IN
Capital and Largest City: Indianapolis (population, 752,279)
Other Large Cities (with population): Fort Wayne, 183,359; Evansville, 129,452; Gary, 114,256; South Bend, 105,092
Important Products: transportation equipment, electronic equipment, industrial machinery, iron and steel, metal products, corn, soybeans, livestock, coal
Places to Visit: Children's Museum, Indianapolis; Conner Prairie Pioneer Settlement, Noblesville; Lincoln Boyhood Memorial, Lincoln City; Wyandotte Cave

? **DID YOU KNOW?** The first city to be lit with electricity was Wabash. Indiana's Lost River travels 22 miles underground. Indiana is the biggest basketball state and home of the famous Indianapolis 500 auto race.

IOWA

Hawkeye State

Population (1995): 2,841,764 (30th)
Area: 56,276 sq. mi. (26th) (145,754 sq. km.)
Flower: Wild rose   **Bird:** Eastern goldfinch
Tree: Oak   **Song:** The Song of Iowa
Entered Union: December 28, 1846 (29th)
Postal Abbreviation: IA
Capital and Largest City: Des Moines (population, 193,965)
Other Large Cities (with population): Cedar Rapids, 113,438; Davenport, 95,333; Sioux City, 80,505
Important Products: corn, soybeans, hogs, cattle, industrial machinery, food products
Places to Visit: Effigy Mounds National Monument, Marquette; Herbert Hoover Birthplace, West Branch; Living History Farms, Des Moines; Adventureland; the Amana Colonies; Fort Dodge Historical Museum

? **DID YOU KNOW?** The bridge built in 1856 between Davenport and Rock Island was the first bridge to span the Mississippi River. Frontiersman Buffalo Bill Cody (1846-1917) was born in Iowa.

KANSAS

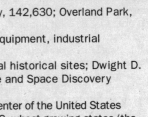
Sunflower State

Population (1995): 2,565,328 (32nd)
Area: 82,282 sq. mi. (15th) (213,110 sq. km.)
Flower: Native sunflower   **Bird:** Western meadowlark
Tree: Cottonwood   **Song:** Home on the Range
Entered Union: January 29, 1861 (34th)
Postal Abbreviation: KS
Capital: Topeka
Largest Cities (with population): Wichita, 310,236; Kansas City, 142,630; Overland Park, 125,225; Topeka, 120,646
Important Products: cattle, aircraft and other transportation equipment, industrial machinery, food products, wheat, corn, hay, oil, natural gas
Places to Visit: Dodge City; Fort Scott and Fort Larned national historical sites; Dwight D. Eisenhower Museum and Home, Abilene; Kansas Cosmosphere and Space Discovery Center, Hutchinson

? DID YOU KNOW? Kansas is located at the geographical center of the United States (excluding Alaska and Hawaii). It is one of the two biggest U.S. wheat-growing states (the other is North Dakota). The carousel with jumping horses was invented in Kansas in 1898.

KENTUCKY

Bluegrass State

Population (1995): 3,860,219 (24th)
Area: 40,411 sq. mi. (37th) (104,665 sq. km.)
Flower: Goldenrod   **Bird:** Cardinal
Tree: Kentucky coffee tree   **Song:** My Old Kentucky Home
Entered Union: June 1, 1792 (15th)
Postal Abbreviation: KY
Capital: Frankfort (population, 25,968)
Largest Cities (with population): Louisville, 270,308; Lexington 237,612
Important Products: coal, industrial machinery, electronic equipment, transportation equipment, metals, tobacco, cattle
Places to Visit: Mammoth Cave National Park; Lincoln Birthplace, Hodgenville; Cumberland Gap National Historical Park, Middlesboro

? DID YOU KNOW? Kentucky has the longest group of caves in the world (Mammoth Caves). Abraham Lincoln was born in Kentucky. Kentucky is also the home of the Kentucky Derby, the most famous horse race in America.

LOUISIANA

Pelican State

Population (1995): 4,342,334 (21st)
Area: 51,844 sq. mi. (31st) (134,275 sq. km.)
Flower: Magnolia   **Bird:** Eastern brown pelican
Tree: Cypress   **Songs:** Give Me Louisiana;
                                You Are My Sunshine
Entered Union: April 30, 1812 (18th)
Postal Abbreviation: LA
Capital: Baton Rouge
Largest Cities (with population): New Orleans, 484,149; Baton Rouge, 227,482; Shreveport, 196,982
Important Products: natural gas, oil, chemicals, transportation equipment, paper, food products, cotton, fish
Places to Visit: French quarter in New Orleans; Jean Lafitte National Historical Park

? DID YOU KNOW? The busiest port in the United States is located in Louisiana. It's the second-biggest mining state (after Alaska). Louisiana is the home of New Orleans, known for its jazz and the colorful Mardi Gras festival.

MAINE

Pine Tree State

Population (1995): 1,241,382 (39th)
Area: 35,387 sq. mi. (39th) (91,653 sq. km.)
Flower: White pine cone and tassel   **Bird:** Chickadee
Tree: Eastern white pine   **Song:** State of Maine
Entered Union: March 15, 1820 (23rd)   Song
Postal Abbreviation: ME
Capital: Augusta (population, 21,325)
Largest Cities (with population): Portland, 64,358; Lewiston, 39,757; Bangor, 33,181
Important Products: paper, transportation equipment, wood and wood products, electronic equipment, footwear, clothing, potatoes, milk, eggs, fish and seafood
Places to Visit: Acadia National Park, Bar Harbor; Booth Bay Railway Museum; Portland Headlight lighthouse, near Portland

? **DID YOU KNOW?** Maine is known for its lobsters, rocky seacoast, fishing villages, and the highest tides in the United States. Mount Katahdin, the highest spot in Maine (5,267 feet), is the first place in the United States where the sun hits in the morning.

MARYLAND

Old Lime State,
Free State

Population (1995): 5,042,438 (19th)
Area: 12,407 sq. mi. (42nd) (32,135 sq. km.)
Flower: Black-eyed susan   **Bird:** Baltimore oriole
Tree: White oak   **Song:** Maryland, My Maryland
Entered Union: April 28, 1788 (7th)
Postal Abbreviation: MD
Capital: Annapolis (population, 33,195)
Largest Cities (with population): Baltimore, 702,979; Rockville, 44,835; Frederick, 40,148; Gaithersburg, 39,452
Important Products: instruments, printing and publishing, food products, transportation equipment, electronic equipment, chickens, milk, corn, stone
Places to Visit: Antietam National Battlefield; Fort McHenry National Monument, in Baltimore harbor; U.S. Naval Academy in Annapolis

? **DID YOU KNOW?** Maryland is the narrowest state—near the town of Hancock, Maryland is only about one mile wide. The American flag on Fort McHenry during the War of 1812 inspired Francis Scott Key to write the "Star-Spangled Banner," the national anthem.

MASSACHUSETTS

Bay State, Old Colony

Population (1995): 6,073,550 (13th)
Area: 10,555 sq. mi. (44th) (27,337 sq. km.)
Flower: Mayflower   **Bird:** Chickadee
Tree: American elm   **Song:** All Hail to Massachusetts
Entered Union: February 6, 1788 (6th)
Postal Abbreviation: MA
Capital and Largest City: Boston (population: 547,725)
Other Large Cities (with population): Worcester, 165,387; Springfield, 149,164; Lowell, 96,054
Important Products: industrial machinery, electronic equipment, instruments, printing and publishing, metal products, clothing and textiles, fish, flowers and shrubs, cranberries
Places to Visit: Plymouth Rock, historical sites in Boston, and Minute Man National Historical Park; Children's Museum, Boston; Basketball Hall of Fame, Springfield; Old Sturbridge Village; Martha's Vineyard; Cape Cod

? **DID YOU KNOW?** The Pilgrims settled in Massachusetts in 1620 and celebrated the first Thanksgiving. Massachusetts is known for other American firsts: the first printing press (1639), the first public school paid for by taxes (1639), and the first college (Harvard, 1636). The American Revolution began in Massachusetts.

MICHIGAN

Great Lakes State,
Wolverine State

Population (1995): 9,549,353 (8th)
Area: 96,705 sq. mi. (11th) (250,465 sq. km.)
Flower: Apple blossom   **Bird:** Robin
Tree: White pine   **Song:** Michigan, My Michigan
Entered Union: January 26, 1837 (26th)
Postal Abbreviation: MI
Capital: Lansing (population, 119,590)
Largest Cities (with population): Detroit, 992,038; Grand Rapids,
190,395; Warren, 142,625; Flint, 138,164
Important Products: automobiles, industrial machinery, metal products, printing and publishing,
plastic products, chemicals, food products, milk, corn, natural gas, iron ore
Places to Visit: Greenfield Village and Henry Ford Museum, Dearborn; Detroit's "Art
Center"; Isle Royal National Park; Pictured Rocks and Sleeping Bear Dunes national
lakeshores; Mackinac Island

? DID YOU KNOW? Michigan is known for manufacturing automobiles. Lake Michigan
is the largest lake entirely in the United States.

MINNESOTA

North Star State,
Gopher State

Population (1995): 4,609,548 (20th)
Area: 86,943 sq. mi. (12th) (225,182 sq. km.)
Flower: Pink and white lady's-slipper   **Bird:** Common loon
Tree: Red pine   **Song:** Hail!
Entered Union: May 11, 1858 (32nd)   Minnesota
Postal Abbreviation: MN
Capital: St. Paul
Largest Cities (with population): Minneapolis, 354,590; St. Paul, 262,071
Important Products: industrial machinery, metal products, printing and publishing, food
products, instruments, milk, hogs, cattle, corn, soybeans, iron ore
Places to Visit: Voyageurs National Park; Grand Portage National Monument; Minnesota
Zoo; Fort Snelling; U.S. Hockey Hall of Fame, Eveleth

? DID YOU KNOW? Minnesota is sometimes called the Land of 10,000 Lakes—it
actually has more than 15,000 lakes. Minnesota is the second coldest state (Alaska
is the coldest). The Mall of America, in Bloomington, is the largest shopping mall in
the United States; it has space for 12,750 cars.

MISSISSIPPI

Magnolia State

Population (1995): 2,697,243 (31st)
Area: 48,434 sq. mi. (32nd) (125,443 sq. km.)
Flower: Magnolia   **Bird:** Mockingbird
Tree: Magnolia   **Song:** Go, Mississippi!
Entered Union: December 10, 1817 (20th)
Postal Abbreviation: MS
Capital and Largest City: Jackson (population, 193,097)
Other Large Cities (with population): Biloxi, 46,319; Greenville, 45,226
Important Products: transportation equipment, clothing and textiles, furniture, electronic
equipment, wood and wood products, cotton, chickens, cattle, oil
Places to Visit: Vicksburg National Military Park; Natchez Trace Parkway; Old Capitol,
Jackson; Old Spanish Fort and Museum, Pascagoula

? DID YOU KNOW? Mississippi was the first state to celebrate Memorial Day
(originally called Decoration Day) as a holiday, in 1866. Mississippi opened the first
state-run college for women in Columbus in 1884. Jefferson Davis, president of the
Confederate States of America, was born in Mississippi.

MISSOURI

Show Me State

Population (1995): 5,323,523 (16th)
Area: 69,709 sq. mi. (21st) (180,546 sq. km.)
Flower: Hawthorn   **Bird:** Bluebird
Tree: Dogwood   **Song:** Missouri Waltz
Entered Union: August 10, 1821 (24th)
Postal Abbreviation: MO
Capital: Jefferson City (population, 35,481)
Largest Cities (with population): Kansas City, 443,878; St. Louis, 368,215; Springfield, 149,727; Independence, 111,669
Important Products: transportation equipment, metal products, printing and publishing, food products, cattle, hogs, milk, soybeans, corn, hay, lead
Places to Visit: Gateway Arch, St. Louis; Mark Twain Home and Museum, Hannibal; Harry S. Truman Museum, Independence; George Washington Carver Birthplace, Diamond

? DID YOU KNOW? Missouri is a major center for shipping and railroads. President Harry S. Truman, agricultural scientist George Washington Carver, and poet Langston Hughes were born in Missouri. It has been said that the ice cream cone was first sold at a World's Fair in St. Louis, in 1904. Gateway Arch, in St. Louis, is the tallest monument (630 feet high) in the United States.

MONTANA

Treasure State

Population (1995): 870,281 (44th)
Area: 147,046 sq. mi. (4th) (380,850 sq. km.)
Flower: Bitterroot   **Bird:** Western meadowlark
Tree: Ponderosa pine   **Song:** Montana
Entered Union: November 8, 1869 (41st)
Postal Abbreviation: MT
Capital: Helena (population, 24,559)
Largest Cities (with population): Billings, 81,151; Great Falls, 55,097; Missoula, 42,918; Butte, 33,941
Important Products: cattle, coal, oil, gold, wheat, hay, wood and wood products
Places to Visit: Yellowstone and Glacier national parks; Little Bighorn Battlefield National Monument, in Crow Agency; Museum of the Rockies, Bozeman

? DID YOU KNOW? Montana is the fourth-biggest state, after Alaska, Texas, and California. The most famous Indian battle in history took place in Montana, at Little Bighorn in 1876.

NEBRASKA

Cornhusker State

Population (1995): 1,637,112 (37th)
Area: 77,358 sq. mi. (16th) (200,358 sq. km.)
Flower: Goldenrod   **Bird:** Western meadowlark
Tree: Cottonwood   **Song:** Beautiful Nebraska
Entered Union: March 1, 1867 (37th)
Postal Abbreviation: NE
Capital: Lincoln
Largest Cities (with population): Omaha, 345,033; Lincoln, 203,076
Important Products: cattle, hogs, milk, corn, soybeans, hay, wheat, sorghum, food products, industrial machinery
Places to Visit: Oregon Trail landmarks; Stuhr Museum of the Prairie Pioneer, Grand Island; Agate Fossil Beds National Monument; Boys Town, near Omaha

? DID YOU KNOW? Nebraska is not only a cattle state; it is the biggest meat-packing center in the world. It is also a farm state. Nebraska is the only state whose nickname comes from a college football team—the popular University of Nebraska Cornhuskers.

NEVADA

Sagebrush State,
Battle Born State,
Silver State

Population (1995): 1,530,108 (38th)
Area: 110,567 sq. mi. (7th) (286,368 sq. km.)
Flower: Sagebrush   **Bird:** Mountain bluebird
Trees: Single-leaf piñon, bristlecone pine   **Song:** Home Means
Entered Union: October 31, 1864 (36th)   Nevada
Postal Abbreviation: NV
Capital: Carson City (population, 40,443)
Largest Cities (with population): Las Vegas, 327,878;
Reno, 145,029; Henderson, 101,997
Important Products: gold, silver, cattle, hay, metals and metal products, printing and publishing
Places to Visit: Great Basin National Park; Nevada State Museum, Carson City; Lake Mead
National Recreation Area; ghost towns
? DID YOU KNOW? It usually rains less in Nevada than in any other state. Between
1980 and 1990 the population of Nevada increased by more than one half, making it
the fastest-growing state. It also has the most wild horses.

NEW HAMPSHIRE

Granite State

Population (1995): 1,148,253 (42nd)
Area: 9,351 sq. mi. (46th) (24,219 sq. km.)
Flower: Purple lilac   **Bird:** Purple finch
Tree: White birch   **Song:** Old New Hampshire
Entered Union: June 21, 1788 (9th)
Postal Abbreviation: NH
Capital: Concord
Largest Cities (with population): Manchester, 99,567; Nashua, 79,662; Concord, 36,006
Important Products: industrial machinery, instruments, electronic equipment, metals and
metal products, rubber and plastic products, printing and publishing, paper, milk
Places to Visit: White Mountain National Forest; Mount Washington; Fort at Number 4
Living History Museum, Charlestown; Old Man in the Mountain, Franconia Notch;
Canterbury Shaker Village
? DID YOU KNOW? Mount Washington is the highest mountain in the northeast. Its
peak is said to be the windiest spot on Earth. The first town-supported, free public
library in the United States opened in New Hampshire in 1833.

NEW JERSEY

Garden State

Population (1995): 7,945,298 (9th)
Area: 8,722 sq. mi. (47th) (22,590 sq. km.)
Flower: Purple violet   **Bird:** Eastern goldfinch
Tree: Red oak   **Song:** none
Entered Union: December 18, 1787 (3rd)
Postal Abbreviation: NJ
Capital: Trenton (population, 88,675)
Largest Cities (with population): Newark, 258,751; Jersey City, 226,022;
Paterson, 138,290; Elizabeth, 106,298
Important Products: chemicals, industrial machinery, instruments, electronic equipment,
metal products, stone, clothing and textiles, nursery and greenhouse products, food
products, milk, tomatoes and vegetables
Places to Visit: ocean beaches; Edison National Historical Site, West Orange; Liberty State
Park; Pine Barrens wilderness area; Great Adventure amusement park
? DID YOU KNOW? The electric light bulb was invented in New Jersey by Thomas
Edison in 1879. The first ferryboat just for cars was built in New Jersey and placed in
service in 1926. New Jersey manufactures more flags than any other state.

NEW MEXICO

Population (1995): 1,685,401 (36th)
Area: 121,598 sq. mi. (5th) (314,939 sq. km.)
Flower: Yucca   **Bird:** Roadrunner
Tree: Piñon   **Song:** O, Fair New Mexico
Entered Union: January 6, 1912 (47th)
Postal Abbreviation: NM
Capital: Santa Fe

Land of Enchantment

Largest Cities (with population): Albuquerque, 411,994; Las Cruces, 62,126; Santa Fe, 55,859
Important Products: natural gas, oil, copper, coal, potash, cattle, milk, hay, cotton, electronic equipment, instruments
Places to Visit: Carlsbad Caverns National Park; Palace of the Governors and Mission of San Miguel, Santa Fe; Chaco Canyon National Monument; cliff dwellings

? **DID YOU KNOW?** The oldest capital city in the United States is Santa Fe, New Mexico. Pueblo Indians had an advanced civilization in New Mexico a thousand years ago. The deepest cave in the United States is in New Mexico's Carlsbad Caverns. The first atom bomb was exploded in New Mexico, in a test on July 16, 1945.

NEW YORK

Population (1995): 18,136,081 (3rd)
Area: 54,471 sq. mi. (27th) (141,079 sq. km.)
Flower: Rose   **Bird:** Bluebird
Tree: Sugar maple   **Song:** I Love New York
Entered Union: July 26, 1788 (11th)
Postal Abbreviation: NY
Capital: Albany (population, 104,828)

Empire State

Largest Cities (with population): New York, 7,333,253; Buffalo, 312,965; Rochester, 231,170; Yonkers, 183,490
Important Products: printing and publishing, instruments, electronic equipment, industrial machinery, clothing and textiles, transportation equipment, metal products, milk, cattle, hay, stone
Places to Visit: In New York City, museums, Empire State Building, United Nations, Bronx Zoo, Statue of Liberty and Ellis Island; Niagara Falls; National Baseball Hall of Fame, Cooperstown; Fort Ticonderoga; Franklin D. Roosevelt National Historical Site, Hyde Park

? **DID YOU KNOW?** New York City is the largest city in the United States. New York City was the first capital of the United States. The first pizza restaurant in the United States opened in New York City in 1895. The first children's museum opened in Brooklyn in 1899.

NORTH CAROLINA

Population (1995): 7,195,138 (11th)
Area: 53,821 sq. mi. (28th) (139,397 sq. km.)
Flower: Dogwood   **Bird:** Cardinal
Tree: Pine   **Song:** The Old North State
Entered Union: November 21, 1789 (12th)
Postal Abbreviation: NC
Capital: Raleigh

Tar Heel State, Old North State

Largest Cities (with population): Charlotte, 437,797; Raleigh, 236,707; Greensboro, 196,167; Winston-Salem, 155,128; Durham, 143,439
Important Products: clothing and textiles, tobacco and tobacco products, industrial machinery, electronic equipment, furniture, chemicals, foods, chickens, hogs, stone
Places to Visit: Great Smoky Mountains National Park; Cape Hatteras National Seashore; Wright Brothers National Memorial, at Kitty Hawk

? **DID YOU KNOW?** The Wright Brothers took the first airplane ride in history in North Carolina. The first U.S. school of forestry was opened in North Carolina.

NORTH DAKOTA

Peace Garden State

Population (1995): 641,367 (47th)
Area: 70,704 sq. mi. (19th) (183,123 sq. km.)
Flower: Wild prairie rose   **Bird:** Western meadowlark
Tree: American elm   **Song:** North Dakota Hymn
Entered Union: November 2, 1889 (39th)
Postal Abbreviation: ND
Capital: Bismarck
Largest Cities (with population): Fargo, 74,711; Grand Forks, 49,425; Bismarck, 49,256; Minot, 34,544
Important Products: wheat, barley, hay, sunflowers, sugar beets, cattle, milk, oil, coal, industrial machinery, food products
Places to Visit: Theodore Roosevelt National Park; Bonanzaville, near Fargo; Dakota Dinosaur Museum, Dickinson; International Peace Garden

? DID YOU KNOW? North Dakota is one of the two biggest wheat-growing states in the United States (the other is Kansas). Theodore Roosevelt was a rancher here before he became president.

OHIO

Buckeye State

Population (1995): 11,150,506 (7th)
Area: 44,828 sq. mi. (34th) (116,103 sq. km.)
Flower: Scarlet carnation   **Bird:** Cardinal
Tree: Buckeye   **Song:** Beautiful Ohio
Entered Union: March 1, 1803 (17th)
Postal Abbreviation: OH
Capital and Largest City: Columbus (population, 635,913)
Other Large Cities (with population): Cleveland, 492,901; Cincinnati, 358,170; Toledo, 322,550; Akron, 221,886; Dayton, 178,540
Important Products: metal and metal products, transportation equipment, industrial machinery, rubber and plastic products, electronic equipment, printing and publishing, chemicals, food products, coal, corn, soybeans, livestock, milk
Places to Visit: Mound City Group National Monuments, Indian burial mounds; Neil Armstrong Air and Space Museum; Cedar Point and King's Island amusement parks

? DID YOU KNOW? Ohio was the birthplace of seven American presidents (Garfield, Grant, Harding, B. Harrison, Hayes, McKinley, Taft). Ohio was the home of the first professional baseball team, the Cincinnati Red Stockings. Ohio was the birthplace of the hot dog.

OKLAHOMA

Sooner State

Population (1995): 3,277,687 (27th)
Area: 69,903 sq. mi. (20th) (181,049 sq. km.)
Flower: Mistletoe   **Bird:** Scissor-tailed flycatcher
Tree: Redbud   **Song:** Oklahoma!
Entered Union: November 16, 1907 (46th)
Postal Abbreviation: OK
Capital and Largest City: Oklahoma City (population, 463,201)
Other Large Cities (with population): Tulsa, 374,851; Lawton, 80,561; Norman, 80,071
Important Products: natural gas, oil, cattle, industrial machinery, transportation equipment, metal products, electronic equipment, rubber and plastic products, wheat, hay
Places to Visit: Indian City U.S.A., near Anadarko; Fort Gibson Stockade; National Cowboy Hall of Fame; White Water Bay and Frontier City theme parks; Cherokee Heritage Center

? DID YOU KNOW? The American Indian nations called The Five Civilized Tribes (Cherokee, Chickasaw, Choctaw, Creek, and Seminole) settled in Oklahoma. Today, more Native Americans live in Oklahoma than in any other state.

OREGON

Beaver State

Population (1995): 3,140,585 (29th)
Area: 98,386 sq. mi. (9th) (254,819 sq. km.)
Flower: Oregon grape   **Bird:** Western meadowlark
Tree: Douglas fir   **Song:** Oregon, My Oregon
Entered Union: February 14, 1859 (33rd)
Postal Abbreviation: OR
Capital: Salem
Largest Cities (with population): Portland, 450,777; Eugene, 118,122; Salem, 115,912
Important Products: wood and wood products, industrial machinery, food products, instruments, cattle, milk, hay, vegetables
Places to Visit: Crater Lake National Park; Oregon Caves National Monument; Astoria Column and Fort Clatsop National Memorial, Astoria

? **DID YOU KNOW?** Oregon produces more timber than any other state. Oregon's Hells Canyon, 7,900 feet deep at its maximum, is one of the deepest canyons in the world, and Crater Lake, which gets as deep as 1,932 feet, is the deepest lake in the United States.

PENNSYLVANIA

Keystone State

Population (1995): 12,071,842 (5th)
Area: 46,058 sq. mi. (33rd) (119,291 sq. km.)
Flower: Mountain laurel   **Bird:** Ruffled grouse
Tree: Hemlock   **Song:** Pennsylvania
Entered Union: December 12, 1787 (2nd)
Postal Abbreviation: PA
Capital: Harrisburg (population, 52,376)
Largest Cities (with population): Philadelphia, 1,524,249; Pittsburgh, 358,883; Erie, 108,398; Allentown, 105,339
Important Products: iron and steel, coal, industrial machinery, printing and publishing, food products, electronic equipment, clothing and textiles, transportation equipment, milk, hay
Places to Visit: Independence Hall and other historic sites in Philadelphia; Franklin Institute Science Museum, Philadelphia; Valley Forge; Gettysburg; Hershey; Pennsylvania Dutch country, Lancaster County

? **DID YOU KNOW?** Pennsylvania is known for the Liberty Bell in Philadelphia, which first rang after the signing of the Declaration of Independence. Philadelphia was also the U.S. capital for 10 years, from 1790 to 1800. The first hospital in the United States was established in Philadelphia in 1752.

RHODE ISLAND

Little Rhody, Ocean State

Population (1995): 989,794 (43rd)
Area: 1,545 sq. mi. (50th) (4,002 sq. km.)
Flower: Violet   **Bird:** Rhode Island red
Tree: Red maple   **Song:** Rhode Island
Entered Union: May 29, 1790 (13th)
Postal Abbreviation: RI
Capital and Largest City: Providence (population, 150,639)
Other Large Cities (with population): Warwick, 85,427; Cranston, 76,060; Pawtucket, 72,644
Important Products: metals and metal products, instruments, clothing and textiles, printing and publishing, rubber and plastic products, industrial machinery, electronic equipment, fish
Places to Visit: Block Island; mansions, old buildings, and harbor in Newport; International Tennis Hall of Fame, Newport

? **DID YOU KNOW?** Rhode Island is the smallest state. The bluffs and islands of Rhode Island attract many tourists who like fishing and swimming. The oldest synagogue in the United States (Touro Synagogue, 1763) is in Newport.

SOUTH CAROLINA

Palmetto State

Population (1995): 3,673,287 (26th)
Area: 32,007 sq. mi. (40th) (82,898 sq. km.)
Flower: Yellow jessamine   **Bird:** Carolina wren
Tree: Palmetto   **Song:** Carolina
Entered Union: May 23, 1788 (8th)
Postal Abbreviation: SC
Capital and Largest City: Columbia (population, 104,101)
Other Large Cities (with population): Charleston, 80,414; North Charleston, 70,218; Greenville, 58,282
Important Products: clothing and textiles, chemicals, industrial machinery, rubber and plastic products, electronic equipment, paper, metal products, livestock, tobacco, stone
Places to Visit: Grand Strand and Hilton Head Island beaches; Revolutionary War battlefields; historic sites in Charleston; Fort Sumter; Historic Camden

? DID YOU KNOW? More battles of the American Revolution took place in South Carolina than in any other state. The first shots of the Civil War were fired in South Carolina. Charleston Museum, established in 1773, is the oldest museum in the United States.

SOUTH DAKOTA

Mt. Rushmore State, Coyote State

Population (1995): 729,034 (45th)
Area: 77,121 sq. mi. (17th) (199,743 sq. km.)
Flower: Pasqueflower   **Bird:** Ring-necked pheasant
Tree: Black Hills spruce   **Song:** Hail, South Dakota
Entered Union: November 2, 1889 (40th)
Postal Abbreviation: SD
Capital: Pierre (population, 12,906)
Largest Cities (with population): Sioux Falls, 109,174; Rapid City, 54,523
Important Products: cattle, hogs, milk, corn, hay, wheat, soybeans, food products, gold
Places to Visit: Mount Rushmore National Memorial; Crazy Horse Memorial; Jewel Cave; Badlands and Wind Caves national parks; Wounded Knee battlefield; Homestake Gold Mine

? DID YOU KNOW? South Dakota is best known for the faces of presidents carved on Mount Rushmore (Presidents Washington, Jefferson, Lincoln, and T. Roosevelt). Famous South Dakotans include Crazy Horse, Sitting Bull, and Wild Bill Hickok.

TENNESSEE

Volunteer State

Population (1995): 5,256,051 (17th)
Area: 42,146 sq. mi. (36th) (109,158 sq. km.)
Flower: Iris   **Bird:** Mockingbird
Tree: Tulip poplar   **Song:** The Tennessee Waltz
Entered Union: June 1, 1796 (16th)
Postal Abbreviation: TN
Capital: Nashville
Largest Cities (with population): Memphis, 614,289; Nashville, 504,505; Knoxville, 169,311; Chattanooga, 152,259
Important Products: chemicals, clothing and textiles, industrial machinery, motor vehicles, food products, metal products, printing and publishing, electronic equipment, wood products and furniture, livestock, milk, soybeans, tobacco, stone
Places to Visit: Great Smoky Mountains National Park; the Hermitage, home of President Andrew Jackson near Nashville; Civil War battle sites; Grand Old Opry and Opryland, USA, theme park, Nashville; Graceland, home of Elvis Presley in Memphis

? DID YOU KNOW? Tennessee can claim Nashville as country music capital of the world. Frontiersman Davy Crockett was born in Tennessee. Elvis Presley and President Andrew Jackson are among the famous people who lived in Tennessee.

TEXAS

Lone Star State

Population (1995): 18,723,991 (2nd)
Area: 268,601 sq. mi. (2nd) (695,676 sq. km.)
Flower: Bluebonnet **Bird:** Mockingbird
Tree: Pecan **Song:** Texas, Our Texas
Entered Union: December 29, 1845 (28th)
Postal Abbreviation: TX
Capital: Austin
Largest Cities (with population): Houston, 1,702,0806; Dallas, 1,022,830; San Antonio, 998,905; El Paso, 579,307; Austin, 514,013; Fort Worth, 451,814
Important Products: oil, natural gas, cattle, milk, transportation equipment, chemicals, industrial machinery, electronic equipment, cotton, hay
Places to Visit: Guadalupe and Big Bend national parks; the Alamo, in San Antonio; Lyndon Johnson National Historic Site, near Johnson City; Six Flags Over Texas amusement park, Arlington

? DID YOU KNOW? Texas is the largest of the contiguous 48 states (the 48 states that border each other) and is second in size only to Alaska. One of the richest states in natural resources, Texas has more oil and natural gas than any other state and the most farmland. Texas is the only state with five major ports.

UTAH

Beehive State

Population (1995): 1,951,408 (34th)
Area: 84,904 sq. mi. (13th) (219,902 sq. km.)
Flower: Sego lily **Bird:** Seagull
Tree: Blue spruce **Song:** Utah, We Love Thee
Entered Union: January 4, 1896 (45th)
Postal Abbreviation: UT
Capital and Largest City: Salt Lake City (population, 171,849)
Other Large Cities (with population): West Valley City, 86,976; Provo, 86,835
Important Products: transportation equipment, industrial machinery, instruments, food products, copper, cattle, corn, hay
Places to Visit: Arches, Canyonlands, Bryce Canyon, Zion, and Capitol Reef national parks; Great Salt Lake; Temple Square (Mormon Church headquarters) in Salt Lake City, Indian cliff dwellings

? DID YOU KNOW? Utah's Great Salt Lake, which contains 6 billion tons of salt, is the largest lake in the United States outside of the Great Lakes. Rainbow Bridge in Utah is the largest natural arch or rock bridge in the world; it is 200 feet high and 270 feet wide.

VERMONT

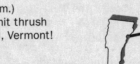
Green Mountain State

Population (1995): 584,771 (49th)
Area: 9,615 sq. mi. (45th) (24,903 sq. km.)
Flower: Red clover **Bird:** Hermit thrush
Tree: Sugar maple **Song:** Hail, Vermont!
Entered Union: March 4, 1791 (14th)
Postal Abbreviation: VT
Capital: Montpelier (population, 8,247)
Largest Cities (with population): Burlington, 39,127; Rutland, 18,230
Important Products: electronic equipment, industrial machinery, printing and publishing, metal products, wood and stone products, milk, hay, maple syrup, granite, marble
Places to Visit: Green Mountain National Forest; Shelburne Museum

? DID YOU KNOW? Vermont is famous for its granite, marble, scenery, and maple syrup. Vermont passed the first constitution (1777) to prohibit slavery and to allow all men to vote. The first ski tow in the United States was established in Vermont in 1934.

VIRGINIA

Old Dominion

Population (1995): 6,618,358 (12th)
Area: 42,777 sq. mi. (35th) (110,792 sq. km.)
Flower: Dogwood **Bird:** Cardinal
Tree: Dogwood **Song:** Carry Me Back to Old Virginia
Entered Union: June 25, 1788 (10th)
Postal Abbreviation: VA
Capital: Richmond
Largest Cities (with population): Virginia Beach, 430,295; Norfolk, 241,426; Richmond, 201,108; Chesapeake, 180,577; Newport News, 179,127
Important Products: transportation equipment, clothing and textiles, chemicals, printing and publishing, electronic equipment, food products, coal, livestock, milk, hay, tobacco
Places to Visit: Colonial Williamsburg; Busch Gardens, Williamsburg; Arlington National Cemetery; Mount Vernon (George Washington's home); Monticello (Thomas Jefferson's home); Shenandoah National Park

? DID YOU KNOW? Virginia was the birthplace of eight presidents (Presidents W. H. Harrison, Jefferson, Madison, Monroe, Taylor, Tyler, Washington, Wilson), more than any other state. The first permanent English settlement in the New World was in Virginia.

WASHINGTON

Evergreen State

Population (1995): 5,430,940 (15th)
Area: 71,302 sq. mi. (18th) (184,672 sq. km.)
Flower: Western rhododendron **Bird:** Willow goldfinch
Tree: Western hemlock **Song:** Washington, My Home
Entered Union: November 11, 1889 (42nd)
Postal Abbreviation: WA
Capital: Olympia (population, 33,840)
Largest Cities (with population): Seattle, 520,947; Spokane, 192,781; Tacoma, 183,060
Important Products: aircraft and aerospace equipment, lumber and wood products, food products, paper, industrial machinery, apples, wheat, cattle, milk, coal, fish
Places to Visit: Mount Rainier, Olympic, and North Cascades national parks; Mount St. Helens; Seattle Center, with Space Needle and monorail

? DID YOU KNOW? Washington's Grand Coulee Dam, on the Columbia River, is the world's largest concrete dam. Mount St. Helens is the tallest volcano in the contiguous 48 states and the only active one. Washington is known for its apples, timber, and fishing fleets.

WEST VIRGINIA

Mountain State

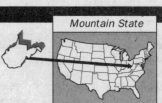

Population (1995): 1,828,140 (35th)
Area: 24,231 sq. mi. (41st) (62,759 sq. km.)
Flower: Big rhododendron **Bird:** Cardinal
Tree: Sugar maple **Songs:** The West Virginia Hills, This Is My West Virginia; West Virginia, My Home Sweet Home
Entered Union: June 20, 1863 (35th)
Postal Abbreviation: WV
Capital and Largest City: Charleston (population, 57,287)
Other Large Cities (with population): Huntington, 54,844; Wheeling, 34,882
Important Products: coal, natural gas, metal and metal products, chemicals, stone, clay, and glass products, industrial machinery, cattle, hay
Places to Visit: Harpers Ferry National Historic Park; Grave Creek Mound, Moundsville; Monongahela National Forest

? DID YOU KNOW? West Virginia's mountain scenery and mineral springs attract many tourists. The state is one of the biggest coal states. West Virginia was part of Virginia until West Virginians decided to break away, in 1861.

WISCONSIN

Badger State

Population (1995): 5,122,871 (18th)
Area: 65,499 sq. mi. (23rd) (169,642 sq. km.)
Flower: Wood violet   **Bird:** Robin
Tree: Sugar maple   **Song:** On, Wisconsin!
Entered Union: May 29, 1848 (30th)
Postal Abbreviation: WI
Capital: Madison
Largest Cities (with population): Milwaukee, 617,044; Madison, 194,586; Green Bay, 102,708; Racine, 84,298; Kenosha, 80,352
Important Products: industrial machinery; paper; metal products; milk, cheese, packed meat, and other foods; printing and publishing; corn, hay, and vegetables
Places to Visit: Dells of the Wisconsin; Cave of the Mounds, near Blue Mounds; Milwaukee Public Museum; Circus World Museum, Baraboo; National Railroad Museum, Green Bay

? DID YOU KNOW? Wisconsin is known as America's Dairyland; more recently it has also become a major manufacturing state. The first kindergarten in America was opened in Wisconsin in 1865.

WYOMING

Equality State

Population (1995): 480,184 (51st)
Area: 97,818 sq. mi. (10th) (253,349 sq. km.)
Flower: Indian paintbrush   **Bird:** Meadowlark
Tree: Cottonwood   **Song:** Wyoming
Entered Union: July 10, 1890 (44th)
Postal Abbreviation: WY
Capital and Largest City: Cheyenne (population, 50,008)
Other Large Cities (with population): Casper, 46,742; Laramie, 26,687
Important Products: oil, coal, natural gas, clays, oil and coal products, cattle, hay
Places to Visit: Yellowstone and Grand Teton national parks; Fort Laramie; Buffalo Bill Historical Center, Cody

? DID YOU KNOW? Wyoming is the home of the first U.S. national park (Yellowstone). Established in 1872, Yellowstone has 10,000 geysers, including the world's tallest active geyser (Steamboat Geyser).

PUERTO RICO

Puerto Rico

History: Christopher Columbus landed in Puerto Rico in 1493. Puerto Rico was a Spanish colony for centuries, then fell to the United States in 1898 after the Spanish-American War. In 1952, still associated with the United States, Puerto Rico became a commonwealth with its own constitution.
Population estimate: 3,801,977
Area: 3,492 sq. mi. (9,044 sq. km.)
National Anthem: La Borinqueña
Became a Self-Governing Commonwealth: July 25, 1952
Postal Abbreviation: PR
Capital and Largest City: San Juan (population, 426,832)
Other Large Cities (with population): Bayamón, 202,103; Carolina, 162,404; Ponce, 159,151
Important Products: chemicals, food products, electronic equipment, clothing and textiles, industrial machinery, coffee, vegetables, sugarcane, dairy products
Places to Visit: San Juan National Historic Site; beaches and resorts

? DID YOU KNOW? Puerto Ricans have most of the rights of American citizens, but they cannot vote in U.S. presidential elections and do not pay federal income tax.

NAME THE STATE PUZZLE

Below are clues to 25 of the states of the United States. Following each clue is the name of the state written in code. Each letter of the state is one letter of the alphabet after the letter of the code (the letter following Z would be A). If the state is TSZG, T = U, S = T, Z = A, and G = H; so, TSZG = UTAH. How many of the states below can you decode? (Answers are on page 305.)

1. The biggest and coldest state: **ZKZRJZ**
2. Mount St. Helens is here: **VZRGHMFSNM**
3. This state is made up entirely of islands: **GZVZHH**
4. The state with 15,000 lakes: **LHMMDRNSZ**
5. The state known as America's Dairyland: **VHRBNMRHM**
6. The biggest basketball state: **HMCHZMZ**
7. Home of the first professional baseball team: **NGHN**
8. The first pizza restaurant opened here in 1895: **MDV XNQJ**
9. Birthplace of eight U.S. presidents: **UHQFHMHZ**
10. The first shots of the Civil War were fired here: **RNTSG BZQNKHMZ**
11. The world's highest bridge is located here: **BNKNQZCN**
12. This state grows more citrus fruit than any other: **EKNQHCZ**
13. The first state-run college for women opened here: **LHRRHRRHOOH**
14. Where you would go to celebrate Mardi Gras: **KNTHRHZMZ**
15. State with the most oil, natural gas, and farmland: **SDWZR**
16. The deepest cave in the United States is found here: **MDV LDWHBN**
17. State with the most people, cars, and schools: **BZKHENQMHZ**
18. The state that usually gets the least amount of rain: **MDUZCZ**
19. World's biggest meat-packing center: **MDAQZRJZ**
20. The 1996 Summer Olympics took place in this state: **FDNQFHZ**
21. First state of the United States: **CDKZVZQD**
22. The state located at the geographical center of the United States: **JZMRZR**
23. In the morning, the sun hits this state first: **LZHMD**
24. The electric light bulb was invented in this state: **MDV IDQRDX**
25. Faces of four presidents are carved on a mountain here: **RNTSG CZJNSZ**

PUZZLE: THE ABC's OF CAPITAL CITIES

Can you match the U.S. capital cities that begin with A, B, or C with their states? (Answers are on page 305.)

Albany	Georgia
Annapolis	Idaho
Atlanta	Louisiana
Augusta	Maine
Austin	Maryland
Baton Rouge	Massachusetts
Bismarck	Nevada
Boise	New Hampshire
Boston	New York
Carson City	North Dakota
Charleston	Ohio
Cheyenne	South Carolina
Columbia	Texas
Columbus	West Virginia
Concord	Wyoming

WASHINGTON, D.C.:
The Capital of the United States

Area: 69 square miles
Population: (1995): 554,256

Flower: American beauty rose
Bird: Wood thrush

HISTORY. Washington, D.C., became the capital of the United States in 1800, when the U.S. government moved there from Philadelphia. The city of Washington was especially designed and built to be the capital. It was named after George Washington, the first president of the United States. Today, Washington is a city of wide, tree-lined boulevards and impressive buildings. Many of its major sights are located on the Mall, an open grassy area that runs from the Capitol to the Potomac River.

Capitol, which houses the United States Congress, is at the east end of the Mall, on Capitol Hill. The dome of the Capitol's rotunda can be seen from many parts of the city.

Jefferson Memorial, a circular marble building located near the Potomac River. At night, it is floodlit and very impressive.

Lincoln Memorial, at the west end of the Mall, is built of white marble and styled like a Greek temple. Inside is a large, seated statue of Abraham Lincoln, whose Gettysburg Address is carved on one wall. From the Lincoln Memorial, you can look down the Mall to the Washington Monument and the Capitol.

National Archives, on Constitution Avenue, is the place to see the Declaration of Independence, the Constitution, and the Bill of Rights.

National Gallery of Art, on the Mall, is one of the world's great art museums. Older paintings and sculptures are housed in the West Building, while 20th-century art is housed in the newer East Building.

Smithsonian Institution has 14 museums, including the National Air and Space Museum and the Museum of Natural History. The Smithsonian Information Center, located in "the Castle" on the Mall, is a good place to start a visit.

U.S. Holocaust Memorial Museum presents the history of the Nazis' murder of over six million Jews and millions of other people from 1933 to 1945. Through old photographs, toys, clothes, and furniture, the exhibit *Daniel's Story: Remember the Children* tells the story of the Holocaust from a child's point of view. It is for eight-year-olds and older. The other exhibits are for visitors eleven years old or older.

Vietnam Veterans Memorial has a black-granite wall shaped like a V. The names of the more than 58,000 Americans who lost their lives in the Vietnam War are inscribed on the wall.

Washington Monument, a white marble pillar, or obelisk, standing on the Mall and rising to over 555 feet. From the top, there are wonderful views of the city.

White House, at 1600 Pennsylvania Avenue, has been the home of every U.S. president except George Washington, who chose its site in 1790 and supervised its construction. Only the public rooms can be visited.

How the STATES

Alabama comes from *Alibamu*, which was the name of the town of a Creek Indian tribe.

Alaska comes from *alakshak*, the Aleutian (Eskimo) word meaning "mainland" or "land that is not an island."

Arizona comes from an American Indian word meaning "little spring" or "little spring place."

Arkansas is a variation of *Quapaw*, the name of a Sioux Indian tribe. *Quapaw* means "downstream people."

California is the name of an imaginary island in a Spanish story. It was named by Spanish explorers of Baja California, a part of Mexico.

Colorado comes from a Spanish word meaning "reddish." It was first given to the Colorado river because of its reddish color.

Connecticut comes from an Algonquin Indian word meaning "beside the long tidal river."

Delaware is named after Lord De La Warr, the English governor of Virginia in colonial times.

Florida, which means "flowery" in Spanish, was named by the explorer Ponce de Leon, who landed there during the Spanish flower festival.

Georgia was named after King George II of England, who granted the right to create a colony there in 1732.

Hawaii probably comes from *Hawaiki,* or *Owhyhee,* the native Polynesians' name for their homeland.

Idaho's name is of uncertain origin, but it may come from an Apache name for the Comanche Indians.

Illinois is the French version of *Illini,* an Algonquin Indian word meaning "men" or "warriors."

Indiana means "land of the Indians."

Iowa comes from the name of an American Indian tribe that lived on the land that is now the state.

Kansas comes from a Sioux Indian word that possibly meant "people of the south wind."

Kentucky comes from an Iroquois Indian word, possibly meaning "meadowland."

Louisiana, which was first settled by French explorers, was named after King Louis XIV of France.

Maine means "the mainland." English explorers called it that to distinguish it from islands nearby.

Maryland was named after Queen Henrietta Maria, wife of King Charles I of England, who granted the right to establish an English colony there.

Massachusetts comes from an Algonquin Indian word meaning "at the big hill."

Michigan comes from the Chippewa Indian words *mici gama*, meaning "great water" (referring to Lake Michigan).

Minnesota got its name from a Sioux Indian word meaning "cloudy water" or "sky-tinted water."

Mississippi is probably derived from two Chippewa Indian words meaning "great river" or "father of the waters," or from an Algonquin word.

Missouri comes from an Algonquin Indian term meaning "people of the big canoes."

Montana comes from a Spanish word meaning "mountainous."

Got Their NAMES

Nebraska comes from "flat water," an Omaha or Otos Indian name for the Platte River.

Nevada means "snowy or "snow-covered" in Spanish. Spanish explorers gave the name to the Sierra Nevada Mountains.

New Hampshire was named by an early settler after his home county of Hampshire, in England.

New Jersey was named for the English Channel island of Jersey.

New Mexico was given its name by a Spanish explorer in Mexico.

New York, first called New Netherland, was renamed for the Duke of York and Albany after the English took it from Dutch settlers.

North Carolina, the northern part of the English colony of Carolana, was named for King Charles I.

North Dakota comes from a Sioux Indian word meaning "allied tribes."

Ohio is the Iroquois Indian word for "fine or good river."

Oklahoma comes from a Choctaw Indian word meaning "red people."

Oregon may have come from *Ouaricon-sint,* a name on a French map for the Wisconsin River, and mistakenly given to the Columbia River. The name of the Columbia River was changed, but the state kept the name.

Pennsylvania, meaning "Penn's woods," was the name given to the colony founded by William Penn.

Rhode Island may have come from the Dutch Roode Eylandt (red island) or may have been named after the Greek island of Rhodes.

South Carolina, the southern part of the English colony of Carolana, was named for King Charles I.

South Dakota comes from a Sioux Indian word meaning "allied tribes."

Tennessee comes from the name the Cherokee Indians gave to their ancient capital. The name was given to the Tennessee River. The state was named after the river.

Texas comes from a word meaning "friends" or "allies," used by the Spanish to describe some of the American Indians living there.

Utah comes from Ute, the name of a Shoshone Indian tribe.

Vermont comes from two French words, *vert* (green) and *mont* (mountain).

Virginia was named in honor of Queen Elizabeth I of England, who was known as the Virgin Queen because she never married.

Washington was named after George Washington, the first president of the United States.

West Virginia got its name from the people of western Virginia, who formed their own government during the Civil War.

Wisconsin comes from an Algonquin Indian name for the state's principal river. The word, meaning "the place where the waters come together," was once spelled *Ouisconsin*.

Wyoming comes from an Algonquin Indian word meaning "at the big plains" or "large prairie place."

NATIONAL PARKS

Most national parks are large and naturally beautiful and have a wide variety of scenery. They are visited by millions of people each year. The world's first national park was Yellowstone, which was established in 1872 in the northwestern United States. Since then, the American government has set aside a total of 54 national parks. Fifty-two of the parks in the United States are listed below. Two outside the United States are in the Virgin Islands and American Samoa. The National Park Service oversees the national parks and tries to keep them unspoiled.

Acadia (Maine)
41,819 acres; established 1929
Rugged coast and granite cliffs; seals, whales, and porpoises; highest land along the East Coast of the U.S.

Arches (Utah)
73,379 acres; established 1971
Giant natural sandstone arches, including Landscape Arch, over 100 feet high and 291 feet long

Badlands (South Dakota)
242,756 acres; established 1978
A prairie where, over centuries, the land has been formed into many odd shapes with a variety of colors

Big Bend (Texas)
801,163 acres; established 1935
Desert land and rugged mountains, on the Rio Grande River; dinosaur fossils

Biscayne (Florida)
172,924 acres; established 1980
A water-park on a chain of islands in the Atlantic Ocean, south of Miami, with beautiful coral reefs

Bryce Canyon (Utah)
35,835 acres; established 1928
Odd and very colorful rock formations carved by centuries of erosion

Canyonlands (Utah)
337,570 acres; established 1964
Sandstone cliffs above the Colorado River; rock carvings from an ancient American Indian civilization

Capitol Reef (Utah),
241,904 acres; established 1971
Sandstone cliffs cut into by gorges with high walls; old American Indian storage huts

Carlsbad Caverns (New Mexico)
46,766 acres; established 1930
A huge cave system, not fully explored, with the world's largest underground chamber, called "the Big Room"

Channel Islands (California)
249,354 acres; established 1980
Islands off the California coast, with sea lions, seals, and sea birds

Crater Lake (Oregon)
183,224 acres; established 1902
The deepest lake in the United States, carved in the crater of an inactive volcano; lava walls up to 2,000 feet high

Death Valley (California)
3,367,627 acres; established 1994
Largest national park outside Alaska. Vast hot desert, rocky slopes and gorges, huge sand dunes; hundreds of species of plants, some unique to the area; variety of wildlife, including desert foxes, bobcats, coyotes

Denali (Alaska)
4,741,910 acres; established 1980
Huge park, containing America's tallest mountain, plus caribou, moose, sheep

Dry Tortugas (Florida)
64,700 acres; established 1992
Colorful birds and fish; a 19th-century
fort, Fort Jefferson

Everglades (Florida)
1,507,850 acres; established 1934
The largest subtropical wilderness
within the U.S.; swamps with
mangrove trees, rare birds, alligators

Gates of the Arctic (Alaska)
7,523,888 acres; established 1984
One of the largest national parks;
huge tundra wilderness, with rugged
peaks and steep valleys

Glacier (Montana)
1,013,572 acres; established 1910
Rugged mountains, with glaciers,
lakes, sheep, bears, and bald eagles

Glacier Bay (Alaska)
3,225,284 acres; established 1986
Glaciers moving down mountainsides to
the sea; seals, whales, bears, eagles

Grand Canyon (Arizona)
1,217,158 acres; established 1919
Mile-deep expanse of multicolored
layered rock, a national wonder

Grand Teton (Wyoming)
309,994 acres; established 1929
Set in the Teton Mountains; a winter
feeding ground for elks

Great Basin (Nevada)
77,180 acres; established 1986
From deserts to meadows to tundra;
caves; ancient pine trees

Great Smoky Mountains
(North Carolina, Tennessee)
521,053 acres; established 1926
Forests, with deer, fox, and black
bears, and streams with trout and bass

Guadalupe Mountains (Texas)
86,416 acres; established 1966
Remains of a fossil reef formed 225
million years ago

Haleakala (Hawaii)
28,099 acres; established 1960
The largest crater of any inactive
volcano in the world

Hawaii Volcanoes (Hawaii)
209,695 acres; established 1961
Home of two large active volcanoes,
Mauna Loa and Kilauea, along with a
desert and a tree fern forest

Hot Springs (Arkansas)
5,549 acres; established 1921
47 hot springs that provide warm
waters for drinking and bathing

Isle Royale (Michigan)
571,790 acres; established 1931
On an island in Lake Superior; woods,
lakes, many kinds of animals—and
no roads

Joshua Tree (California)
792,749 acres; established 1994
Large desert with rock
formations and
unusual desert
plants, including
many Joshua
trees; fossils
from pre-
historic
times;
wildlife,
including
desert bighorn

Katmai (Alaska)
3,674,541 acres; established 1980
Contains the Valley of Ten Thousand
Smokes, which was filled with ash
when Katmai Volcano erupted in 1912

Kenai Fjords (Alaska)
670,643 acres; established 1980
Fjords, rain forests, the Harding
Icefield; sea otters, seals; a breeding
place for many birds

Kings Canyon (California)
461,901 acres; established 1940
Mountains and woods and the highest
canyon wall in the U.S.

Kobuk Valley (Alaska)
1,750,736 acres; established 1980
Located north of the Arctic Circle, with
caribou and black bears; archeological
sites indicate that humans have lived
there for over 10,000 years

Lake Clark (Alaska)
2,636,839 acres; established 1980
Lakes, waterfalls, glaciers,
volcanoes, fish and wildlife

Lassen Volcanic (California)
106,372 acres; established 1916
Contains Lassen Peak, a volcano that
began erupting in 1914, after being
dormant for 400 years

Mammoth Cave (Kentucky)
52,830 acres; established 1941
The world's longest known cave
network, with over 300 miles of
mapped passages

Mesa Verde (Colorado)
52,122 acres; established 1906
A plateau covered by woods and
canyons; the best preserved ancient
cliff dwellings in the U.S.

Mount Rainier (Washington)
235,613 acres; established 1899
Home of Mount Rainier, a volcano dormant since 1870; thick forests, glaciers

North Cascades (Washington)
504,781 acres; established 1968
Rugged mountains and valleys, with
deep canyons, lakes and glaciers

Olympic (Washington)
922,651 acres; established 1938
Rain forest, with woods and
mountains, glaciers, and rare elk

Petrified Forest (Arizona)
93,533 acres; established 1962
A large area of woods turned into
stone; American Indian pueblos and
rock carvings

Redwood (California)
110,232 acres; established 1968
Groves of ancient redwood trees, the
world's tallest trees

Rocky Mountain (Colorado)
265,727 acres; established 1915
Located in the Rockies, with gorges,
alpine lakes, and mountain peaks

Saguaro (Arizona)
91,116 acres; established 1994
Forests of saguaro cacti, some 50
feet tall and 200 years old

Sequoia (California)
402,482 acres; established 1890
Groves of giant sequoia trees; Mount
Whitney (14,494 feet)

Shenandoah (Virginia)
196,466 acres; established 1926
Located in the Blue Ridge Mountains,
overlooking the Shenandoah Valley

Theodore Roosevelt (North Dakota)
70,447 acres; established 1978
Scenic badlands and a part of the old
Elkhorn Ranch that belonged to
Theodore Roosevelt

Voyageurs (Minnesota)
218,035 acres; established 1971
Forests with wildlife and many scenic
lakes for canoeing and boating

Wind Cave (South Dakota)
28,295 acres; established 1903
Limestone caverns in the Black Hills;
a prairie with colonies of prairie dogs

Wrangell-Saint Elias (Alaska)
8,323,618 acres; established 1980
The biggest national park, with
mountain peaks over 16,000 feet high

Yellowstone (Idaho, Montana, Wyoming)
2,219,791 acres; established 1872
The first national park and world's
greatest geysers; bears and moose

Yosemite (California)
761,236 acres; established 1890
Yosemite Valley; highest waterfall in
North America; mountain scenery

Zion (Utah)
146,598 acres; established 1919
Deep, narrow Zion Canyon and other
canyons in different colors; Indian
cliff dwellings over 1,000 years old

Naming HURRICANES

For many years, violent storms have been given names. Until early in the 20th century, people named storms after saints. Then, in 1953, the U.S. government began to use women's names for hurricanes. Men's names began to be used in 1978. Today, there are six sets of names for both Atlantic and Pacific hurricanes. These lists of names are used again every six years (1997 names will be used again in 2003). Representatives of countries that often have hurricanes agree upon hurricane names at meetings of the World Meteorological Organization, an agency of the United Nations.

HURRICANE NAMES FOR 1997	In the North Atlantic:	In the Eastern Pacific:
	Ana, Bill, Claudette, Danny, Erika, Fabian, Grace, Henri, Isabel, Juan, Kata, Larry, Mindy, Nicholas, Odette, Peter, Rose, Sam, Teresa, Victor, and Wanda.	Andres, Blanca, Carlos, Dolores, Enrique, Felicia, Guillermo, Hilda, Ignacio, Jimena, Kevin, Linda, Marty, Nora, Olaf, Pauline, Rick, Sandra, Terry, Vivian, Waldo, Xina, York, and Zelda.

The SPEED of WIND

In 1805, Sir Francis Beaufort, an admiral in the British Navy, developed a system for describing wind speeds at sea. Later the scale was adapted for use on land. Called the Beaufort Scale, it uses the numbers 0 to 12. The numbers get higher as the winds increase in speed.

0 Calm

4 Moderate Breeze

0	Calm	(under 1 mph)
1	Light Air	(1-3 mph)
2	Light Breeze	(4-7 mph)
3	Gentle Breeze	(8-12 mph)
4	Moderate Breeze	(13-18 mph)
5	Fresh Breeze	(19-24 mph)
6	Strong Breeze	(25-31 mph)
7	Near Gale	(32-38 mph)
8	Gale	(39-46 mph)
9	Strong Gale	(47-54 mph)
10	Storm	(55-63 mph)
11	Violent Storm	(64-72 mph)
12	Hurricane	(over 72 mph)

8 Gale

12 Hurricane

The U.S. Weather Service also uses the numbers 13 to 17 for winds of hurricane speed.

WEATHER WORDS

air mass
A large amount of air at a certain temperature and humidity.

atmospheric pressure
Pressure on the surface of the Earth from the weight of the atmosphere. Rising atmospheric pressure usually means calm, clear weather. Falling pressure usually leads to storms.

A **low** or **cyclone** or **depression** is an area of low atmospheric pressure.

A **high** is an area of high atmospheric pressure.

climate
Average weather conditions for an area over a long time period.

front
Boundary, or dividing line, between two air masses.

humidity
Amount of water vapor (water in the form of a gas) in the air.

meteorologist
A person who studies the atmosphere, weather, and weather forecasting.

PRECIPITATION

precipitation
The word for the different forms of water that fall from clouds—like rain, snow, hail, and sleet.

rain
Liquid water falling in drops that measure more than two hundredths of an inch across.

freezing rain
Liquid water that freezes as it hits the ground and other surfaces at temperatures below freezing.

sleet
Drops of water that freeze in cold air and reach the ground as ice.

hail
Frozen raindrops that are kept in the air by upward-blowing air currents. Water keeps freezing on the surface of the hailstone until the hailstone is so heavy that it falls to the ground.

snow
Ice crystals that form in clouds and fall to the ground.

blizzard
A powerful snowstorm with winds of 35 miles per hour or higher and temperatures of 20 degrees Fahrenheit or lower.

STORMS

cyclone
General word for a circulating storm that forms over warm tropical oceans. It is also the name for a hurricane in the Indian Ocean.

hurricane
A circulating storm with wind speeds of 73 miles per hour or more. This type of storm is called a *hurricane* when it occurs in the Atlantic Ocean, a *typhoon* when it occurs in the Pacific Ocean, and a *cyclone* when it occurs in the Indian Ocean.

monsoon
A system of winds that changes direction between seasons.

thunderstorm
A storm with thunder and lightning.

tropical storm
A circulating storm with wind speeds from 39 to72 mph; can develop into a hurricane.

tornado
Violently circulating winds of more than 200 miles per hour form a dark funnel reaching from the cloud to the ground.

? DID YOU KNOW? A snowstorm that drops 2 feet of snow at 20 degrees Fahrenheit would leave 6 feet of snow if the temperature was zero. Snowflakes fall in different shapes at different temperatures, and the colder the air, the fluffier the snowflakes. Fluffier snowflakes create deeper snow.

Taking TEMPERATURES

HOW TO MEASURE TEMPERATURE

Two systems for measuring temperature are commonly used in weather forecasting. One is Fahrenheit (abbreviated F). The other is Celsius (abbreviated C). Another word for Celsius is Centigrade. Zero degrees (0°) Celsius is equal to 32 degrees (32°) Fahrenheit. Temperatures can be easily converted from one system to the other by following these steps:

To Convert Fahrenheit to Celsius:

1. Subtract 32 from the Fahrenheit temperature value.
2. Then multiply by 5.
3. Then divide the result by 9.

   Example: To convert 75 degrees Fahrenheit to Celsius, 75 − 32 = 43; 43 x 5 = 215; 215 ÷ 9 = 23.9, or 24

To Convert Celsius to Fahrenheit:

1. Multiply the Celsius temperature by 9.
2. Then divide by 5.
3. Then add 32 to the result.

   Example: To convert 24 degrees Celsius to Fahrenheit, 24 x 9 = 216; 216 ÷ 5 = 43.2 or 43; 43 + 32 = 75

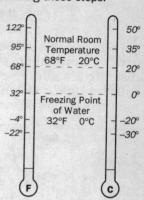

THE HOTTEST AND COLDEST PLACES IN THE WORLD

Below are the highest and lowest temperatures recorded on each continent.

CONTINENT	HIGHEST RECORDED TEMPERATURE	LOWEST RECORDED TEMPERATURE
Africa	Azizia, Libya, 136°F (58°C)	Ifrane, Morocco, −11°F (−24°C)
Antarctica	Vanda Station, 59°F (15°C)	Vostok, −129°F (−89°C)
Asia	Tirat Zevi, Israel, 129°F (54°C)	Oymyakon and Verkhoyansk, Russia, −90°F (−68°C)
Australia	Cloncurry, Queensland, 128°F (53°C)	Charlotte Pass, New South Wales, −8°F (−22°C)
Europe	Sevilla, Spain, 122°F (50°C)	Ust Shchugor, Russia, −67°F (−55°C)
North America	Death Valley, California, 134°F (57°C)	Northice, Greenland, −87°F (−66°C)
South America	Rivadavia, Argentina, 120°F (49°C)	Sarmiento, Argentina, −27°F (−33°C)

HOTTEST PLACES ON RECORD IN THE U.S.			COLDEST PLACES ON RECORD IN THE U.S.		
State	**Temperature**	**Year**	**State**	**Temperature**	**Year**
California	134°F	(1913)	Alaska	−80°F	(1971)
Arizona	128°F	(1994)*	Montana	−70°F	(1954)
Nevada	125°F	(1994)*	Utah	−69°F	(1985)
* Tied with a record set earlier					

The Earliest MEASUREMENTS

We use weights and measures all the time—you can measure how tall you are, or how much gasoline a car needs. Ancient people developed measurements to describe the amounts or sizes of things. These units are called **weights** and **measures**. The first measurements were based on the human body and on activities.

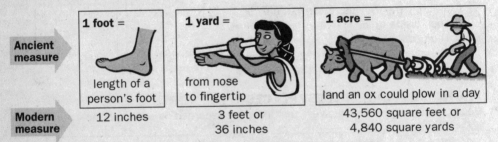

Ancient measure

1 foot =	1 yard =	1 acre =
length of a person's foot	from nose to fingertip	land an ox could plow in a day

Modern measure

| 12 inches | 3 feet or 36 inches | 43,560 square feet or 4,840 square yards |

Measurements Used in the United States

The system of measurement used in the United States is called the **U.S. Customary System**. Most countries use a system called the **metric system**. A few metric measurements are also used in the United States, such as for soda, which comes in 1-liter and 2-liter bottles. In the tables below, when a unit has an abbreviation, the abbreviation appears in parentheses the first time the unit is mentioned.

LENGTH, HEIGHT, and DISTANCE	AREA
The basic unit of **length** in the U.S. System is the **inch**. Length, width, depth, thickness, and the distance between two points all use the inch or larger related units.	**Area** is used to measure a section of a flat surface like the floor or the ground. Most area measurements are given in **square units**. Land is measured in **acres**.
1 foot (ft.) = 12 inches (in.) 1 yard (yd.) = 3 feet or 36 inches 1 rod (rd.) = 5 ½ yards 1 furlong (fur.) = 40 rods or 220 yards or 660 feet 1 mile (mi.) (also called statute mile) = 8 furlongs or 1,760 yards or 5,280 feet 1 league = 3 miles	1 square foot (sq. ft.) = 144 square inches (sq. in.) 1 square yard (sq. yd.) = 9 square feet or 1,296 square inches 1 square rod (sq. rd.) = 30 ¼ square yards 1 acre = 160 square rods or 4,840 square yards or 43,560 square feet 1 square mile (sq. mi.) = 640 acres

CAPACITY

Units of **capacity** are used to measure how much of something will fit into a container. **Liquid measure** is used to measure liquids, such as water or gasoline. **Dry measure** is used with large amounts of solid materials, like grain or fruit.

Dry Measure. Although both liquid and dry measures use the terms "pint" and "quart," they mean different amounts and should not be confused. Look at the lists below for examples.

> 1 quart (qt.) = 2 pints (pt.)
> 1 peck (pk.) = 8 quarts
> 1 bushel (bu.) = 4 pecks

Liquid Measure. Although the basic unit in liquid measure is the **gill** (4 fluid ounces), you are more likely to find liquids measured in pints or larger units.

> 1 gill = 4 fluid ounces
> 1 pint (pt.) = 4 gills or 16 ounces
> 1 quart (qt.) = 2 pints or 32 ounces
> 1 gallon (gal.) = 4 quarts = 128 ounces

☑ For measuring most U.S. liquids,
1 barrel (bbl.) = $31\frac{1}{2}$ gallons

☑ For measuring oil,
1 barrel (bbl.) = 42 gallons

Cooking measurements. Cooking measure is used to measure amounts of solid and liquid foods used in cooking. The measurements used in cooking are based on the **fluid ounce**.

> 1 teaspoon (tsp.) = $\frac{1}{6}$ fluid ounce (fl. oz.)
> 1 tablespoon (tbsp.) = 3 teaspoons or $\frac{1}{2}$ fluid ounce
> 1 cup = 16 tablespoons or 8 fluid ounces
> 1 pint = 2 cups
> 1 quart = 2 pints
> 1 gallon = 4 quarts

VOLUME

The amount of space taken up by an object (or the amount of space available within an object) is measured in **volume**. Volume is usually expressed in **cubic units**. If you wanted to buy a room air conditioner and needed to know how much space there was to be cooled, you could measure the room in cubic feet.

> 1 cubic foot (cu. ft.) = 1,728 cubic inches (cu. in.)
> 1 cubic yard (cu. yd.) = 27 cubic feet

DEPTH

Some measurements of length are used to measure ocean depth and distance.

> 1 fathom = 6 feet
> 1 cable = 120 fathoms or 720 feet
> 1 nautical mile = 6,076.1 feet or 1.15 statute miles

WEIGHT

Although 1 cubic foot of popcorn and 1 cubic foot of rock take up the same amount of space, they wouldn't feel the same if you tried to lift them. We measure heaviness as **weight.** Most objects are measured in **avoirdupois weight** (pronounced a-ver-de-POIZ), although precious metals and medicines use different systems.

> 1 dram (dr.) = 27.344 grains (gr.)
> 1 ounce (oz.) = 16 drams or 437.5 grains
> 1 pound (lb.) = 16 ounces
> 1 hundredweight (cwt.) = 100 pounds
> 1 ton = 2,000 pounds (also called short ton)

Rock ▶
▲ Popcorn

The METRIC System

Do you ever wonder how much soda you are getting when you buy a bottle that holds 1 liter? Or do you wonder how long a 50-meter swimming pool is? Or how far from Montreal, Canada, you would be when a map says "8 kilometers"?

Every system of measurement uses a basic unit for measuring. In the U.S. Customary System, the basic unit for length is the inch. In the metric system, the basic unit for length is the **meter**. The metric system also uses **liter** as a basic unit of volume or capacity and the **gram** as a basic unit of mass. The related units are made by adding a prefix to the basic unit. The prefixes and their meanings are:

milli- = $^1/_{1,000}$	deci- = $^1/_{10}$	hecto- = 100
centi- = $^1/_{100}$	deka- = 10	kilo- = 1,000

For example:

millimeter (mm) = $^1/_{1,000}$ of a meter	milligram (mg) = $^1/_{1,000}$ of a gram
centimeter (cm) = $^1/_{100}$ of a meter	centigram (cg) = $^1/_{100}$ of a gram
decimeter (dm) = $^1/_{10}$ of a meter	decigram (dg) = $^1/_{10}$ of a gram
dekameter (dm) = 10 meters	dekagram (dg) = 10 gram
hectometer (hm) = 100 meters	hectogram (hg) = 100 gram
kilometer (km) = 1,000 meters	kilogram (kg) = 1,000 grams

To get a rough idea of what measurements equal in the metric system, it helps to know that a liter is a little more than a quart. A meter is a little over a yard. And a kilometer is less than a mile.

- ☑ A bottle of soda that holds 2 liters holds a little more than two quarts (2.1 quarts to be exact).
- ☑ A football field is 100 yards long. It is a little more than 90 meters (91.4 meters to be exact).

? **DID YOU KNOW?** Did you know that the metric system is used for measurements in the Olympic Games? Here are a few Olympic Game measurements and what they are equal to in U.S. Customary units.

- ☑ A 50-meter swimming pool is 54.7 yards long. A 400-meter freestyle swimming race is 437 yards.
- ☑ A 10-kilometer relay race is 6.2 miles. A 50-kilometer relay race is 31.1 miles.
- ☑ A 1,000-meter speed-skating race is six-tenths of a mile, or a little over half a mile. A 5,000-meter race is a little more than 3 miles. (Remember that 1,000 meters = 1 kilometer, so a 1,000-meter race would be the same as a 1-kilometer race, and a 5,000-meter race would be the same as a 5-kilometer race.)

You can check these numbers by using the conversion charts on the following page. A calculator will be a big help with this. For example, if you multiply 50 meters (the length of an Olympic swimming pool) by 1.0936, you get 54.68 yards. When rounded off, that becomes 54.7 yards.

Converting U.S. Measurements to Metrics and Metrics to U.S. Measurements

If you want to convert feet to meters or miles to kilometers, you need to know how many meters there are in one foot or how many kilometers there are in one mile. The tables below show how to convert units in the U.S. Customary System to units in the metric system and how to convert metric units to U.S. Customary units. If you want to convert numbers from one system to the other, you may want to use a calculator to help you with the multiplication.

CONVERTING U.S. CUSTOMARY UNITS TO METRIC UNITS			CONVERTING METRIC UNITS TO U.S. CUSTOMARY UNITS		
If you know the number of	Multiply by	To get the number of	If you know the number of	Multiply by	To get the number of
inches	2.5400	centimeters	centimeters	.3937	inches
inches	.0254	meters	centimeters	.0328	feet
feet	30.4800	centimeters	meters	39.3701	inches
feet	.3048	meters	meters	3.2808	feet
yards	.9144	meters	meters	1.0936	yards
miles	1.6093	kilometers	kilometers	.621	miles
square inches	6.4516	square centimeters	square centimeters	.1550	square inches
square feet	.0929	square meters	square meters	10.7639	square feet
square yards	.8361	square meters	square meters	1.1960	square yards
acres	.4047	hectares	hectares	2.4710	acres
cubic inches	16.3871	cubic centimeters	cubic centimeters	.0610	cubic inches
cubic feet	.0283	cubic meters	cubic meters	35.3147	cubic feet
cubic yards	.7646	cubic meters	cubic meters	1.3080	cubic yards
quarts (liquid)	.9464	liters	liters	1.0567	quarts (liquid)
ounces	28.3495	grams	grams	.0353	ounces
pounds	.4536	kilograms	kilograms	2.2046	pounds

Highlights of WORLD HISTORY

The section on World History is divided into five parts. Each part is a major region of the world: the Middle East, Africa, Asia, Europe, and the Americas. Major historical events from ancient times to the present are found under the headings for each region.

THE ANCIENT MIDDLE EAST 4000 B.C. – 1 B.C.

4000-3000 B.C.
1. The world's first cities are built by the Sumerian peoples in Mesopotamia, southern Iraq.
2. Egyptians develop a kind of writing called hieroglyphics.
3. Sumerians develop a kind of writing called cuneiform.

2700 B.C.
Egyptians begin building the great pyramids in the desert. The pharaohs' (kings') bodies are mummified (preserved), and they are buried in the pyramids.

1792 B.C.
First written laws are created in Babylonia. They are called the Code of Hammurabi.

Some Achievements of Peoples of the Ancient Middle East
The early peoples of the Middle East are responsible for many great achievements. They:
1. Studied the stars (astronomy).
2. Invented the wheel.
3. Created alphabets from picture drawings (hieroglyphics and cuneiform).
4. Established the 24-hour day.
5. Studied medicine and mathematics.

1200 B.C.
Hebrew people settle in Canaan in Palestine after escaping from slavery in Egypt. They are led by the prophet Moses.

The Ten Commandments
Unlike most early peoples in the Middle East, the Hebrews believed in only one God (monotheism). They believed their faith was given to Moses in the Ten Commandments on Mount Sinai when they fled Egypt.

1000 B.C.
King David unites the Hebrews in one strong kingdom.

Ancient Palestine
Palestine was invaded by many different peoples after 1000 B.C., including the Babylonians, the Egyptians, the Persians, and the Romans. It came under Arab Muslim control in the 600s and remained mainly under Muslim control until the 1900s.

336 B.C.
Alexander the Great, King of Macedonia, builds an empire from Egypt to India.

around 4 B.C.
Jesus Christ, the founder of the Christian religion, is born in Bethlehem. He is crucified about A.D. 29.

THE MIDDLE EAST A.D. 1 – 1940s

Islam: A New Religion Develops in the Middle East

570

The prophet Muhammad is born in Mecca in Arabia. Muhammad creates a new religion called Islam, which spreads from Arabia to North Africa. Its followers are called Muslims.

The Koran

The holy book of Islam is called the Koran. It was dictated by Muhammad beginning in 611. The Koran gives rules that Muslims must follow. For example, it tells how many times a day they must pray.

661-900

Islam begins to spread to the west into Africa and Spain under the Arab rulers known as the Omayyads.

The Spread of Islam

The Arab armies that went across North Africa brought great change:

1. The people who lived there were converted to Islam.
2. The Arab language replaced many local languages that had been spoken before. North Africa is still an Arab region today, and Islam is the major faith.

Achievements of Arab Muslims

The Muslim Arab empire that stretched across Africa and the Middle East is known for many great achievements. Arab Muslims:

1. Studied math and medicine.
2. Translated the works of other peoples, including the Greeks and Persians.
3. Created governments throughout the empire.
4. Wrote great works on religion and philosophy.

632

Muhammad dies. By now, Islam is accepted in Arabia as a religion.

641

Arab Muslims conquer the Persians.

1071

The Muslim Seljuk Turks conquer the city of Jerusalem. Europeans try to take back Jerusalem for Christians during the Crusades (campaigns by European Christians to take the Middle East from the Muslims).

The Ottoman Empire: 1300-1900s

The Ottoman Turks, who were Muslims, created a huge empire beginning in 1300, covering the Middle East, North Africa, and part of Eastern Europe. The Ottoman Empire fell apart gradually, and European countries took over portions of it beginning in the 1800s.

1914-1918

World War I begins in 1914. By its end, the Ottoman Empire has been broken apart. Most of the Middle East falls under British and French control.

1921

Two new Arab kingdoms are created: Transjordan and Iraq. The French take control of Syria and Lebanon.

1922

Egypt becomes independent from Britain.

Jews Migrate to Palestine

Jewish settlers from Europe began migrating to Palestine in the 1880s. They wanted to return to the historic homeland of the Hebrew people. In 1945, after World War II, many Jews who survived the Holocaust migrated to Palestine. Arabs living in the region opposed the Jewish immigration. In 1948, after the British left, war broke out between the Jews and the Arabs.

THE MIDDLE EAST
1948 – the 1990s

1948
The state of Israel is created.

The Arab-Israeli Wars
Israel's Arab neigbors (Egypt, Jordan, and Syria) attack the new country in 1948 but fail to destroy it. Israel and its neighbors fight wars again in 1956, 1967, and 1973. Israel wins each war. In the 1967 war, Israel captures the Sinai Desert from Egypt and the area known as the West Bank from Jordan.

1979
Egypt and Israel sign a peace treaty. Israel gradually returns the Sinai to Egypt.

The Middle East and Oil
Much of the oil we use to drive our cars, heat our homes, and run our machines comes from the Arabian peninsula in the Middle East. For a brief time in 1973-1974, Arab nations would not let their oil be sold to the United States because of its support of Israel. The U.S. has tried to reduce the amount by drilling for more oil at home and by buying more oil from other regions.

The 1990s
1. In 1991, the United States and its allies go to war with Iraq. Iraq had invaded neighboring Kuwait in 1990. The conflict, known as the Persian Gulf War, lasts only a few weeks. Iraq's army is defeated and is forced to withdraw from Kuwait.
2. After many years of conflict, Israel and the Palestine Liberation Organization (PLO) agree to work toward peace in the area in 1993. Jordan and Israel sign a peace treaty in 1994. In 1995 Prime Minister Yitzhak Rabin of Israel is assassinated by an Israeli opposed to the peace agreement with the PLO.

ANCIENT AFRICA
3500 B.C.– A.D. 900

Ancient Africa
In ancient times, especially from 3500 B.C. to A.D. 100, northern Africa was dominated by the Egyptians, Greeks, and Romans. However, we know very little about the lives of ancient people in Africa south of the Sahara Desert (sub-Saharan Africa). The people of Africa south of the Sahara did not have written languages in ancient times. What we learn about them comes from such things as weapons, tools, and other items that have been found in the earth.

500 B.C.
The Nok culture becomes strong in Nigeria, in West Africa. The Nok use iron for tools and weapons. They are also known for their fine terra-cotta sculptures of heads.

300 B.C.
Bantu-speaking peoples in West Africa begin to move into eastern and southern Africa.

A.D. 100
The Kingdom of Axum in northern Ethiopia is founded by traders from Arabia and becomes a wealthy trade center for ivory.

400
Ghana, the first known state south of the Sahara Desert, rules the upper Senegal and Niger river region. It controls the trade in gold being sent from the southern parts of Africa north to the Mediterranean Sea.

660s-900
The Islamic religion begins to spread across North Africa and into Spain. The Arabic language takes root in North Africa, replacing local languages.

AFRICA 900s – the 1990s

900
Arab Muslims begin to settle along the coast of East Africa. Their contact with Bantu people produces the Swahili language, which is still spoken today.

1050
The Almoravid Kingdom in Morocco, North Africa, is powerful from Ghana as far north as Spain.

1230
The beginning of the Mali Kingdom in North Africa. Timbuktu, a center for trade and learning, is its main city.

1464
The Songhai Empire becomes strong in West Africa. By 1530, it has destroyed Mali. The Songhai are remembered for their bronze sculptures.

1505-1575
The beginning of Portuguese settlement in Africa. Portuguese people settle in Angola and Mozambique.

The African Slave Trade
Once Europeans began settling in the New World, they needed people to harvest their sugar. The first African slaves were taken to the Caribbean. Later, slaves were taken to South America and the United States. The slaves were crowded on to ships and many died during the long journey. Shipping of African slaves to the United States lasted until the early 1800s.

1770-1835
1. Dutch settlers arrive in southern Africa. The Dutch in South Africa are known as the Boers.
2. Shaka the Great forms a Zulu Empire in eastern Africa. The Zulus are warriors.
3. The "Great Trek" (march) of the Boers north. They defeat the Zulus at the Battle of Bloody River.

1880s: European Colonies in Africa
European settlers start moving into the interior of Africa and forming colonies in the mid-1800s. The major European countries with colonies in Africa were:

1. **Great Britain:** East and central Africa, from Egypt to South Africa.
2. **France:** Most of West Africa and North Africa.
3. **Spain:** Parts of Northwest Africa.
4. **Portugal:** Mozambique (East Africa) and Angola (West Africa).
5. **Italy:** Libya (North Africa) and Somalia (East Africa).
6. **Germany:** East Africa, Southwest Africa.

1899: Boer War
The beginning of the South African War between Great Britain and the Boers. It is also called the Boer War. The Boers accept British rule but are allowed a role in government.

1948
The white South African government creates the policy of apartheid, the total separation of blacks and whites.

1950s: African Independence
African colonies begin to receive their independence in the 1950s. European countries could no longer afford to keep colonies, and the peoples of Africa demanded their independence.

1983
Droughts (water shortages) lead to starvation over much of Africa.

The 1990s
During the 1990s many African countries struggle with poverty and political unrest. The South African government officially ends apartheid. Nelson Mandela, a black freedom fighter, becomes South Africa's first black president.

ANCIENT ASIA 4000 B.C. – I B.C.

4000 B.C.
Communities of people settle in the Indus River Valley of India and Pakistan and the Yellow River Valley of China.

2500 B.C.
Cities of Mohenjo-Daro and Harappa in Pakistan become centers of trade and farming.

1600 B.C.
Shang peoples in China build walled towns and use a kind of writing based on pictures. This writing develops into the writing Chinese people use today.

1500 B.C.
The Hindu religion (Hinduism) begins to spread throughout India.

1027 B.C.
Chou peoples in China overthrow the Shang and control large territories.

700 B.C.
Beginning of a 500-year period in China in which many warring states fight each other.

563 B.C.
The birth of Prince Siddhartha Gautama in India. He becomes known as the Buddha—which means the "Enlightened One"—and is the founder of the Buddhist religion (Buddhism).

551 B.C.
Birth of the Chinese philosopher Confucius. His teachings— especially the rules and morals about how people should treat each other and get along—spread throughout China and are still followed today.

Two Important Asian Religions
Many of the world's religions began in Asia. Two of the most important were:
1. **Hinduism.** Hinduism began in India and has spread to other parts of southern Asia and to parts of the Pacific region.
2. **Buddhism.** Buddhism also began in India and spread to China, Japan, and Southeast Asia.

Today, both religions have millions of followers all over the world.

320-264 B.C.: India
1. Northern India is united under the emperor Chandragupta Maurya.
2. Asoka, emperor of India, begins to send Buddhist missionaries throughout southern Asia to spread the Buddhist religion.

221 B.C.
The Chinese ruler Shih Huang Ti makes the Chinese language the same throughout the country.

215 B.C.
Chinese begin building the Great Wall of China. It is 1,500 miles long and was meant to keep invading peoples from the north out of China. The Great Wall is still visited by people today.

202 B.C.
The Han people in China overthrow Shih Huang Ti.

What the Chinese Did During the Rule of the Han
1. Invented paper.
2. Invented gunpowder.
3. Studied astronomy.
4. Studied engineering.
5. Invented acupuncture to treat illnesses.

ASIA A.D. 1 – 1700s

320
The Gupta Empire controls northern India. The Guptas are Hindus. They drive the Buddhist religion out of India. The Guptas are well known for their advances in the study of mathematics and medicine.

618
The beginning of the Tang dynasty in China. The Tang are famous for inventing the compass and for advances in surgery and the arts. They trade silk, spices, and ivory as far away as Africa.

932
The Chinese begin to make books in large numbers by using wood blocks for printing.

960
The Northern Sung Dynasty in China is known for advances in banking and paper money.

1000
The Samurai, a warrior people, become powerful in Japan. They live by a code of honor called bushido.

1180
Angkor Empire is powerful in Cambodia. The empire is known for its beautiful temples.

1215
The Mongol people of Asia are united under the ruler Genghis Khan. He builds a huge army and creates an empire that stretches all the way from China to India, Russia, and Eastern Europe.

1264
Kublai Khan, the grandson of Genghis Khan, rules China as emperor from his new capital at Beijing.

1368
The Ming Dynasty comes to power in China. The Ming drive the Mongols out of China.

1467-1603: War and Peace in Japan
1. Civil war breaks out in Japan. The conflicts last more than 100 years.
2. Peace comes to Japan under the military leader Hideyoshi.
3. Beginning of the Shogun period in Japan, which lasts until 1868. Europeans are driven out of the country and Christians are persecuted.

1526-1556: The Moguls in India
1. Beginning of the Mogul Empire in India under Babur. The Moguls are Muslims who invade and conquer India.
2. Akbar, the grandson of Babur, becomes Mogul emperor of India. He attempts to unite Hindus and Muslims but is unsuccessful.

1644
The Ming Dynasty in China is overthrown by the Manchu peoples. They allow more Europeans to trade in China.

1739
Nadir Shah, a Persian warrior, conquers parts of western India and captures the city of Delhi.

What Indian Civilizations Did
Many civilizations grew in India over thousands of years of history. Among their achievements were:

1. Great literature, especially Sanskrit literature and language.
2. Great architecture, for example, the Taj Mahal, a mausoleum (tomb) built in 1629 under the Moguls.
3. Great world religions, including Hinduism and Buddhism.

MODERN ASIA 1800s – 1990s

1839
The Opium War in China between the Chinese and the British. The British and other Western powers want to control trade in Asia. The Chinese want the British to stop selling opium to the Chinese. Britain wins the war.

1858
The French begin to take control of Indochina (Southeast Asia).

1868
The end of the Shogunate dynasty in Japan. The new ruler is Prince Meiji. Western ideas begin to influence the Japanese.

The Japanese in Asia
Japan became a powerful country during the early 20th century. It was a small country with few raw materials. For example, Japan had to buy oil from other countries. The Japanese army and navy took control of the government during the 1930s. Japan soon began to invade some of its neighbors. In 1941 the two nations went to war after Japan attacked the U.S. Navy at Pearl Harbor, Hawaii.

1945
Japan is defeated in World War II after the U.S. drops atomic bombs on the Japanese cities of Hiroshima and Nagasaki.

1947
India and Pakistan become independent from Great Britain, which had ruled them as colonies since the mid-1800s.

1949
China comes under the rule of the Communists led by Mao Zedong.

China Under the Communists
The Communists brought great changes to China. Private property was abolished, and the government took over all businesses and farms. China became more isolated from other countries.

1950-1953: The Korean War
The Communist country North Korea invades South Korea. The U.S. and other nations join to fight the invasion. China joins North Korea. The Korean War ends in 1953. Neither side wins, but the North Korean army is forced out of South Korea.

1954-1975: The Vietnam War
The French are defeated in Indochina in 1954 by the Vietminh. The Vietminh are Vietnamese fighters under the leadership of the Communists headed by Ho Chi Minh. The U.S. sends troops to fight in the Vietnam War in 1965 on the side of South Vietnam against Ho Chi Minh and Communist North Vietnam. The U.S. withdraws from the war in 1973. In 1975, South Vietnam is defeated and taken over by North Vietnam.

1972
President Richard Nixon visits Communist China. A new period of better relations between China and the United States begins.

1989
Chinese students protest for more democracy but the protests are crushed by the army.

The 1990s
By the 1990s many nations in Asia have become economically strong. Japan is a major economic power, producing a large amount of the world's automobiles and electronic equipment. South Korea, Taiwan, and China also become important trading nations, producing many different products sold around the world.

ANCIENT EUROPE 4000 B.C. – 300 B.C.

4000 B.C.
People in many parts of Europe start building large stone tombs called megaliths. Examples of megaliths can still be seen today.

The Minoans and the Mycenaeans 2500 B.C.-1200 B.C.
1. People on island of Crete (Minoans) in the Mediterranean Sea built great palaces and became sailors and traders.
2. People in the city of Mycenae in Greece built stone walls and a great palace.
3. Mycenaean people invaded Crete and destroyed the power of the Minoans.

The Trojan War
The Trojan War was a conflict between invading Greeks and the people of Troas (Troy) in Southwestern Turkey in 1200 B.C. Although little is known today about the real war, it has become a part of Greek mythology. According to the Greek poet Homer, the Greek soldiers hid inside a huge wooden horse. The horse was pulled into the city of Troy. Then the soldiers jumped out of the horse and conquered Troy.

1200 B.C.
Celtic peoples in Northern Europe settle in farms and villages and learn to mine for iron ore.

Some Achievements of the Greeks
The early Greeks were responsible for:
1. The first governments that were elected by people. Greeks invented democratic government.
2. Great writers such as the poet Homer, who wrote the Iliad, a long poem about the Trojan War.
3. Great philosophers such as Socrates, Plato, and Aristotle.
4. Great architecture, like the Parthenon in Athens, which can still be seen (see below).

700 B.C.
Etruscan peoples rule most of Italy until 400 B.C. They build many cities and become traders.

431 B.C.
Beginning of the Peloponnesian Wars between the Greek cities of Athens and Sparta. The wars end in 404 B.C. when Sparta wins.

338 B.C.
King Philip II of Macedonia in northern Greece unites the cities of Greece and defeats Sparta.

336 B.C.
Philip's son Alexander becomes king. He conquers lands and makes an empire from the Mediterranean Sea to India. He is known as Alexander the Great.
For the next 300 years, Greek culture dominates this vast area.

EUROPE 300 B.C. – A.D. 800s

264 B.C.- A.D. 476: Roman Empire

The city of Rome in Italy begins to expand and captures surrounding lands. The Romans gradually build a great empire and control all of the Mediterranean region. At its height, the Roman Empire includes Western Europe, Greece, Egypt, and much of the Middle East. The Roman Empire lasts until A.D. 476.

Some Achievements of the Romans

1. Roman law. Many of our laws are based on Roman law. Romans had the first independent judges and protected the rights of women and children.
2. Great roads to connect their huge empire. The Appian Way, south of Rome, is a Roman road that is still in use today.
3. Aqueducts to bring water to the people in large cities.
4. Great sculpture. Roman statues can still be seen in Europe.
5. Great architecture. The Colosseum, which still stands in Rome today, is an example of great Roman architecture (see below).

45 B.C.

Julius Caesar becomes the leader of Rome but is murdered one year later by rivals in the Roman army.

29 B.C.

Octavian becomes the first emperor of Rome. He takes the name Caesar Augustus. A peaceful period of almost 200 years begins.

The Christian Faith

Christians believe that Jesus Christ is the Son of God. The history and beliefs of Christianity are found in the New Testament of the Bible. Christianity spread slowly throughout the Roman empire. The Romans tried to stop the new religion and persecuted the Christians. They were forced to hold their services in hiding, and some were crucified. Eventually, more and more Romans became Christian.

337

The Roman Emperor Constantine the Great becomes a Christian. He is the first Roman emperor to be a Christian.

410

The Visigoths and other barbarian tribes from northern Europe invade the Roman Empire and begin to take over its vast territories.

476

The last Roman emperor is overthrown.

The Byzantine Empire, centered in modern-day Turkey, was made up of the eastern half of the old Roman empire. Byzantine rulers extended their power into western Europe. The great Byzantine Emperor Justinian ruled parts of Spain, North Africa, and Italy. Constantinople (now Istanbul, Turkey) became the capital of the Byzantine Empire in 520.

768

Charlemagne becomes king of the Franks in northern Europe. He rules a kingdom that includes parts of France, Germany and northern Italy.

800

Feudalism becomes important in Europe. Feudalism means that poor farmers are allowed to farm a lord's land in return for certain services to the lord.

898

Magyar peoples from lands east of Russia found Hungary.

900

Viking warriors and traders from Scandinavia begin to move into the British Isles, France, and parts of the Mediterranean. They remain for 200 years.

Viking ship ▶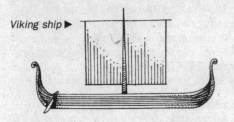

989

The Russian state of Kiev becomes Christian.

1066

William of Normandy, in France, successfully invades England and makes himself king. He is known as William the Conqueror.

The Crusades: 1095-1291

In 1095 Christian European kings and nobles sent armies to the Middle East to try to capture the city of Jerusalem from the Muslims. Between 1095 and 1291 there were about ten Crusades. The Europeans briefly captured Jerusalem. But in the end, the Crusades did not succeed. One of the most important results of the Crusades was that trade increased between the Middle East and Europe.

The Magna Carta: 1215

The Magna Carta is a document signed by King John of England and the English nobility. The English king agreed that he did not have absolute power and had to obey the laws of the land. The Magna Carter was an important step toward democracy.

1290

The beginning of the Ottoman Empire. It is controlled by the Muslims who conquer lands in the eastern Mediterranean and Middle East.

War and Plague in Europe
1337-1453

1. The start of the Hundred Years' War (1337) in Europe between France and England. The war ends in 1453 when France wins.
2. The beginning of the plague in Europe in 1348. This also called the Black Death, a deadly disease caused by the infected fleas. Perhaps as much a third of the people of Europe died of the plague.

1453

The Ottoman Turks capture Constantinople and rename it Istanbul.

The Reformation: 1517

The Reformation led to the breakup of the Christian church into Protestant and Roman Catholic branches in Europe. It started when the German priest Martin Luther opposed some teachings of the Church. He broke away from the pope (the leader of the Catholic church) and said that people should read the Bible themselves.

1534

King Henry VIII of England breaks away from the Catholic church. He names himself head of the English (Anglican) church.

1558

The beginning of the reign of King Henry's daughter Elizabeth I in England. During her long reign, England's power grows.

1588

The Spanish Armada (fleet of warships) is defeated by the English navy as Spain tries to invade England.

1600
The Ottoman Turks a... ...entral Europe.
They take control of ...es in the
Balkans region of s... ...ern Europe.

1618
The beginning of t... ...y Years' War in
Europe. The war ... over religious
issues. Much of ... ...s destroyed in
the conflict, w... ...in 1648.

1642
The English ... ... king Charles I fights
against the ar... ...t (legislature). The
king's orc... a... ...ated and he is
execued ;1... ...t his son, Charles II
returs a...in... ...C1.

176...
Ca...eri... th... ...t becomes the
Epre...of ... ...a She allows religious
fed... and ... ...ds the Russian empire.

The French ...volution: 1789
T...Fren... ...olution ended the rule
...ings ...ace and led to
...nocr... ...here. At first, however,
...ere w...wars, much bloodshed, and
...mes ... ...ictators took control.
... king L...VI and Queen Marie
A...ntoi... ...were overthrown and later
exec... n 1793.

1804
Na...on Bonaparte, an army officer,
dec...es himself Emperor of France.
Un... his rule, France conquers most of
Eu...pe by 1812.

18...
...apoleon's forces are defeated by the
...ritish and German armies at Waterloo
(in Belgium). Napoleon is exiled.

184...
Revolutions break out in countries of
Europe. People force their rulers to
make more democratic changes.

World War I in Europe: 1914-1918
The start of World War I in Europe
(1914). Germany and Austria-Hungary
opposed England, France, and Russia
(the Allies). The United States joined
the war in 1917 on the side of the
Allies. The Allies won in 1918.

1917
The Russian Revolution. The czar
(emperor) is overthrown. The Bolsheviks
(communists) under Vladimir Lenin take
control of the government. The country is
now called the Soviet Union. After Lenin's
death, Josef Stalin becomes dictator.

1933
Adolph Hitler becomes the dictator of
Germany. He persecutes Jews and tries to
take the territory of neighboring countries.

World War II in Europe: 1939-1945
Germany and Italy fought against
England, France, the Soviet Union, and
the United States (the Allies) in
Europe. Germany surrendered in May
1945. During the war, the Germans
killed almost 6 million Jews (the
Holocaust).

1945
The beginning of the Cold War. The Cold
War is a 45-year period of tension
between the United States the Soviet
Union. Both countries build up their
armies and make thousands of nuclear
weapons but never go to war.

The 1990s
Europe in the 1990s experiences great
changes. Communist governments in
Eastern Europe are replaced by
democratic governments. In 1991 the
Soviet Union itself breaks apart into
different countries. The biggest, Russia,
holds democratic elections. In 1995
peace-keeping forces of the North Atlantic
Treaty Organization (NATO) are sent to
Bosnia, to try to preserve a peace
agreement to end a war in that area.

THE AMERICAS 4000 B.C. – A.D. 1600s

4000 B.C.
People in North America gather plants for food and hunt animals using stone-pointed spears.

3000 B.C.
People in Central America begin growing corn and beans for food.

1500 B.C.
Mayan people in Central America begin to live in small villages.

500 B.C.
People in North America begin to hunt buffalo for meat and skin for clothing.

100 B.C.
City of Teotihuacán founded in Mexico. It becomes the center of a huge empire extending from central Mexico to Guatemala. Teotihuacán contains many large pyramids and temples.

A.D. 150
Mayan people in Guatemala build many centers for religious ceremonies. They create a calendar and learn mathematics and astronomy.

900
Toltec warriors in Mexico begin to invade lands of Mayan people. Mayans leave their old cities and move to Yucatan Peninsula of Mexico.

1000
Native Americans in Southwestern United States begin to live in settlements called pueblos. They learn to farm.

1325
Mexican Indians known as Aztecs create huge city of Tenochtitlán and rule a large empire in Mexico. They are warriors who practice human sacrifice.

Europeans Arrive in the New World
(See page 300 for map of American Indians from 1500 to 1800.)

1492
Christopher Columbus sails from Europe across the Atlantic Ocean and lands in the Bahamas, in the Caribbean. This is the first step toward European settlements in the Americas.

1510
The first Africans are brought to the Americas as slaves.

1519
The Spanish conqueror Hernán Cortes travels into the Aztec empire in search of gold. The Aztecs are defeated in 1521 by Cortes. The Spanish take control of Mexico.

Why Did the Spanish Win?
How did the Spanish defeat the powerful Aztec empire in such a short time? One reason is that they had better weapons. Another is that the Aztecs became sick and died from diseases brought by the Spanish. Because the Aztecs never had these illnesses before, they became sick from contact with Europeans.

1532
Portuguese explorers first settle in Brazil. The Portuguese establish colonies in this part of South America.

1534
Jacques Cartier of France explores Canada.

1583
The first English colony in North America is set up in Newfoundland, Canada.

1607
English colonists led by Captain John Smith settle in Jamestown, Virginia.

1682
The French explorer Robert La Salle sails down the Mississippi River. The area is named Louisiana after the French King Louis XIV.

THE AMERICAS 1700s

European Colonies in the Americas

By 1700, most of the Americas are under the control of Europeans:

Spain: Florida, southwestern United States, Mexico, Central America, western South America.
Portugal: eastern South America.
France: central United States, parts of Canada.
England: eastern United States, parts of Canada.
Holland: New York.

1700

European colonies in North and South America begin to grow in population and wealth.

1775-1783: American Revolution

The American Revolution begins in 1775 when the first shot is fired in Lexington, Massachusetts. The thirteen British colonies in North America become independent under the Treaty of Paris in 1783.

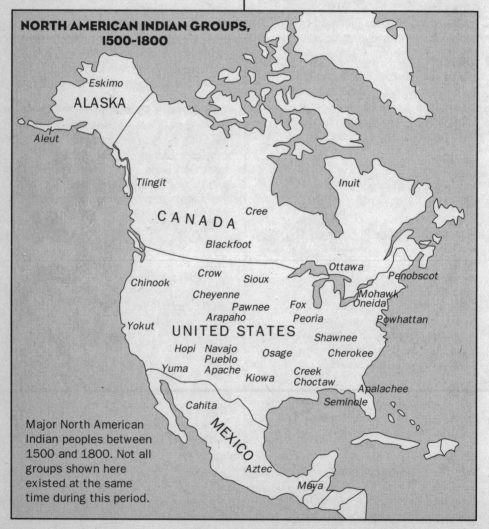

NORTH AMERICAN INDIAN GROUPS, 1500-1800

Eskimo
ALASKA
Aleut
Tlingit
Inuit
Cree
CANADA
Blackfoot
Crow
Sioux
Ottawa
Penobscot
Chinook
Cheyenne
Mohawk
Oneida
Pawnee
Fox
Arapaho
Peoria
Powhattan
Yokut
UNITED STATES
Shawnee
Hopi Navajo
Pueblo
Osage
Cherokee
Yuma
Apache
Kiowa
Creek
Choctaw
Apalachee
Cahita
Seminole
MEXICO
Aztec
Maya

Major North American Indian peoples between 1500 and 1800. Not all groups shown here existed at the same time during this period.

THE AMERICAS 1800s – 1990s

Simón Bolívar: Liberator of South America

Simón Bolívar led a revolt against the Spanish starting in 1810. He fought for more than 10 years against the Spanish and became president of the independent country of Greater Colombia in 1824.

As a result of his leadership, 10 South American countries had become independent by 1830. Simón Bolívar is honored today as a great hero.

South American Colonies Become Independent

Most countries of South America became independent in the early 1800s. Here are the dates each country became independent of European control:

Argentina	1816
Bolivia	1825
Brazil	1822
Chile	1818
Colombia	1819
Ecuador	1830
French Guiana[1]	
Guyana	1966[2]
Paraguay	1811
Peru	1824
Suriname	1973[3]
Uruguay	1825
Venezuela	1821

1. French Guiana is an overseas territory governed by France.
2. Guyana was a British colony until it became independent in 1966.
3. Suriname was governed by the Netherlands until it became independent in 1973.

1810-1910: Mexico's Independence and Revolution

Mexico first revolts against Spanish rule in 1810 and finally wins independence in 1821. In 1846, Mexico and the United States go to war. Mexico is defeated and loses parts of the Southwest and California to the Americans. A revolution in 1910 overthrows Porfirio Diaz.

1867

The Canadian provinces are united as the Dominion of Canada.

1898: The Spanish-American War

Spain and the United States fight a brief war in 1898. The U.S. victory results in Spain losing its colonies of Cuba and Puerto Rico in the Caribbean and the Philippines in the western Pacific.

U.S. Power in the America in the 1900s

During the 1900s the United States was a powerful influence in the affairs of countries in Central America and the Caribbean. For example, troops were sent to Mexico (1916-1917), Nicaragua (1912- 1925), Haiti (1915-1934; 1994-1995), Dominican Republic (1965), Grenada (1983), and Panama (1989). In 1962, the United States nearly went to war with the Soviet Union because that country had put missiles on the island of Cuba, only 90 miles from American territory. The U.S. wanted to remain powerful in the Americas, but it also wanted to bring democratic reforms to the region.

The 1990s: Economic Cooperation

In 1994 the United States, Canada, and Mexico become partners in the North American Free Trade Agreement (NAFTA), which makes it easier for these countries to trade with each other.

ANIMALS

Page 20: **PET PUZZLE**

CATS	DOGS	FISH	BIRDS	RABBITS
HAMSTERS	SNAKES	FERRETS	TURTLES	GUINEA PIGS

Page 26: **SEARCHING FOR DINOSAURS**

```
K S A U R O P O D W T Y U I D S A F G
A T G C B X N H I C O R V B O T P O B
S E N D V A S A P A T O S A U R U S T
D G C Z X C V B L L P L K J H I F G H
F O M N B V C X O L S A D F G C V B N
G S T R E W Q U D O V C X Z A E M H G
K A T Y R A N N O S A U R U S R U Y T
L U H G F D S A C A N N O B X A W E U
I R K J H G F D U U I U Y T R T R E W
P U Q W E R T Y S R S D F G H O K J H
H S V B N M J K L U G E O R A P T O R
Q L T K Y R G F R S X D S W G S J K L
```

COMPUTERS

Page 40: **BINARY SYSTEM**

MOUSE

Page 41: **SMILEY PUZZLE**

First row: Smile, Unhappy, Laughing, Crying
Second row: Shouting, Kiss, Wink, Tongue-tied

COUNTRIES

Page 64: **COUNTRY PUZZLE**

```
T H A I L A N D F T U J D F R E S T B V C D A
K A L A H F Z X C V N M I S R A E L P O L Y M
E J I K L G A D S F G N K I F D S A L K J U G
T Y P W E H S W E R Y T H N J Y J O R D A N T
R E W Y A A Q U Y T H G F G A S L S O U P A Y S
L O R Y I N A S D J F E Q A T A R G Y H A J S
K I T R S I N D I A Z A C P V B N M U R K G A Y
M U W D A S L W E P Q W E O R T Y U L P I T Y
G E S A S T J O M A N A S R P O L J H G S A Y T E
F R D Y D A H Y T N E N T E A M T R E N T A W E
J V I E T N A M Q Z A S D F G Y T E P R A Y E T S
D Y A U F Y G A W A I L P H I L I P P I N E S A
R H S I G U F L E S R Y U P R T R Y W A C S M E
T N D O H M Y A N M A R L K A J H G A C H E A D K
S F E P J I D Y R A N N B V Q C X Z R A H A N K
Y D H P K P A S T P O I L U H K U W A I T O H F A
W L J L A L T I Y T R E W S H I B C E N L H A L
M O N G O L I A P M H N C A M B O D I A S A L
```

COUNTRIES
Page 64: CAPITAL CITY PUZZLE

Bogotá, Colombia; Brasília, Brazil; Buenos Aires, Argentina; Caracas, Venezuela; La Paz, Bolivia; Lima, Peru; Montevideo, Uruguay; Paramaribo, Suriname; Quito, Ecuador; Santiago, Chile.

ENVIRONMENT
Page 97: ENVIRONMENT CROSSWORD PUZZLE

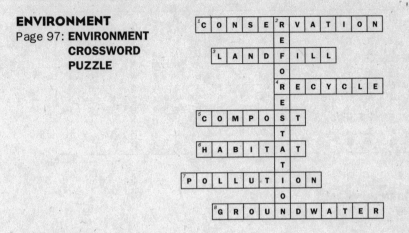

GEOGRAPHY
Page 105: A's in GEOGRAPHY

Continents: 1. ASIA, 2. AFRICA, 3. AUSTRALIA, 4. ANTARCTICA
Countries: 1. ALBANIA, 2. ALGERIA, 3. ANDORRA, 4. ANGOLA, 5. ARGENTINA, 6. ARMENIA, 7. AUSTRALIA, 8. AUSTRIA
States: 1. ALABAMA, 2. ALASKA, 3. ARIZONA

HEALTH
Page 109: TOOTHACHE PUZZLE

3-letter words: ace, act, ate, cat, coo, cot, eat, hat, hoe, hot, oat, tat, tea, the, toe, too, tot
4-letter words: ache, chat, coat, coot, each, hate, heat, hoot, oath, tact, that, toot, tote
5-letter words: cheat, hatch, heath, teach, tooth
6-letter word: thatch
7-letter word: hatchet

LANGUAGE
Page 120: HIDDEN STATE ABBREVIATIONS

When address**IN**g an envelope, we use two-letter postal abbre**VI**ations f**OR** the U.S. States. When writ**IN**g to a frie**ND** in Kentucky, you would w**RI**te **KY IN**stead of the whole state na**ME** and follow it **WI**th the ZIP **CO DE**.

Page 122: PALINDROME PUZZLE

Race car
Was it a cat I saw?
Step on no pets
No lemons, no melon
Enid and Edna dine

LANGUAGE

Page 123: BODY LANGUAGE PUZZLE

1. d. 2. a. 3. e. 4. b. 5. c.

Page 125: "C" FOOD SEARCH PUZZLE

Q	U	I	N	R	E	W	C	H	O	W	D	E	R	D	C	B	N	C
A	S	D	F	C	H	O	H	I	U	C	Y	T	R	E	A	W	E	R
Z	X	C	V	R	G	F	I	S	A	W	R	G	H	J	M	E	N	B
Y	T	C	H	O	C	O	L	A	T	E	F	O	L	K	S	J	U	Y
S	D	F	G	I	L	K	I	H	J	V	C	X	U	M	E	C	V	N
P	O	I	U	S	Y	T	R	E	W	Q	S	D	F	T	R	H	G	F
B	C	O	U	S	C	O	U	S	V	X	Z	A	S	W	O	Q	R	T
L	O	K	J	A	G	H	F	D	S	T	R	E	W	Y	L	N	I	Y
Z	C	X	C	N	V	B	O	N	M	L	C	R	E	P	E	T	S	H
J	O	I	S	T	B	V	F	W	R	E	W	Q	P	O	I	U	L	K
M	A	V	F	G	H	U	Y	T	D	R	T	Y	U	I	P	L	J	H
O	G	F	R	T	C	H	O	W	M	E	I	N	S	A	D	F	G	Y

NUMBERS

Page 150: ROMAN NUMERALS

The year 1997 in Roman numerals is: MCMXCVII

Page 153: HOW HIGH IS THE HIGHEST MOUNTAIN IN THE WORLD?

Number of miles from the Earth to the moon = 238,900
Divide the number by 10 OR cross off the last zero
    = 23,890
Add the number of feet in a mile = + 5,280
    = 29,170
Subtract the number of countries in the United Nations = – 185
    = 28,985
Add the number of states in the United States = + 50
    = 29,035
Subtract the number of days in a week = – 7
The height of the tallest mountain in the world in feet = 29,028

Page 153: WHAT IS THE NAME OF THE HIGHEST MOUNTAIN?

The name of the highest mountain in the world is M O U N T E V E R E S T

Page 153: MAGIC SQUARE

12	7	8
5	9	13
10	11	6

PLANETS
Page 163: **PLANETS PUZZLE**

```
V E N U S
    M A R S
  P L U T O
    J U P I T E R
    E A R T H
N E P T U N E
```

Planet closest to Earth
Planet with the largest volcano
Smallest planet
Largest planet
Third planet from the sun
Planet with the coldest moon

SIGNS AND SYMBOLS
Page 193: **NUMBERS FOR LETTERS**
Greetings from The World Almanac for Kids

Page 193: **SECRET MESSAGE PUZZLE**
You are a good detective.

SPORTS
Page 209: **SPORTS MATCHING PUZZLE**

Monica Seles—tennis
Mario Lemieux—hockey
Mary Lou Retton—gymnastics
Jim Harbaugh—football

Kristi Yamaguchi—figure skating
Dennis Rodman—basketball
Greg Maddux—baseball
Janet Evans—swimming

UNITED STATES
Page 274: **NAME THE STATE PUZZLE**
1. Alaska, 2. Washington, 3. Hawaii, 4. Minnesota, 5. Wisconsin, 6. Indiana, 7. Ohio, 8. New York, 9. Virginia, 10. South Carolina, 11. Colorado, 12. Florida, 13. Mississippi, 14. Louisiana, 15. Texas, 16. New Mexico, 17. California, 18. Nevada, 19. Nebraska, 20. Georgia, 21. Delaware, 22. Kansas, 23. Maine, 24. New Jersey, 25. South Dakota

Page 274: **THE ABC's OF CAPITAL CITIES**

Albany, New York
Annapolis, Maryland
Atlanta, Georgia
Augusta, Maine
Austin, Texas

Baton Rouge, Louisiana
Bismarck, North Dakota
Boise, Idaho
Boston, Massachusetts
Carson City, Nevada

Charleston, West Virginia
Cheyenne, Wyoming
Columbia, South Carolina
Columbus, Ohio
Concord, New Hampshire

The names of the sections are in boldface.

——————— A ———————
Abbreviations, 120
  puzzle, 120
Academy Awards, 14, 174
Accidents prevention of, 114
Acid rain, 92
Acronyms, 120
Adams, Abigail, 233
Adams, John, 226, 227, 233, 237
Adams, John Quincy, 226, 227
Afghanistan, 44-45
  map, 72; flag, 77
Africa
  facts about, 99
  history, 106, 290-291
  map, 74-75
African-Americans
  ethnic museums, 142
  Million Man March, 16
  Spingarn Medal, 176
  population of, 170
AIDS, 113, 199
Air pollution, 92-93
Alabama
  facts about, 257
  maps, 245, 249
  origin of name, 276
Alaska
  facts about, 257
  maps, 248, 256
  national parks, 278-280
  origin of name, 276
Albania, 44-45
  map, 71; flag, 77
Alcohol, 113
Algeria, 44-45
  map, 74; flag, 77
Almanac, 34
Amendments to U.S. Constitution, 217
American Indians. See Native Americans
American Revolution, 236-237, 300
Ancient civilizations
  Africa, 290
  Americas, 299
  Asia, 292
  calendars of, 211
  and constellations, 158
  Europe, 295-296
  Middle East, 288
  money of, 128
  numbers in, 150

  seven wonders of, 35
  weights and measures of, 284
Andorra, 44-45
  map, 70; flag, 77
Angola, 44-45
  map, 75; flag, 77
Animals, 18-27
  and biodiversity, 89
  classifying of, 21
  endangered species, 23
  fastest and largest, 18
  fossils of, 24-25
  habitats of, 24
  life span of, 19
  as money, 128
  museums, 26
  pet shopping, 20
  puzzles, 20, 26
  time line for, 22
  zoos, 27
Anniversaries, in 1996 and 1997, 13
Antarctica, 99
Antigua and Barbuda, 44-45
  map, 67; flag, 77
Arbor Day, 116
Arctic Ocean, 99
Argentina, 44-45
  map, 69; flag, 77
Arizona
  facts about, 257
  maps, 248, 253
  national parks, 279-280
  origin of name, 276
Arkansas
  facts about, 258
  maps, 245, 249
  national parks, 279
  origin of name, 276
Armenia, 44-45
  earthquake, 103
  map, 72; flag, 77
Art, 28-30
  museums, 30, 142
Arthur, Chester A., 226, 230
Asia
  facts about, 99
  map, 72-73
  history, 106, 292-294
Asian-Americans, population of, 170
Asteroids, 157
Atlantic Ocean, 99

Atlas, 34, 65-76, 241-256
Australia
    biggest rock, 81
    facts about, 44-45, 99
    map, 65; flag, 77
Austria, 44-45
    map, 70; flag, 77
Awards. *See* Prizes, awards,
        and contests
Azerbaijan, 44-45
    map, 72; flag, 77

——— **B** ———

Bahamas, 46-47
    map, 67; flag, 77
Bahrain, 46-47
    map, 72; flag, 77
Balkans, 70-71, 100
Ballet, 148, 149
Bangladesh, 46-47
    map, 73; flag, 77
Barbados, 46-47
    map, 67; flag, 77
Baseball, 196-197
    Hall of Fame, 197
    Little League, 13, 197
    Olympics, 195
    standings for 1995, 196
    World Series, 13, 196
Basketball, 198-200
    college basketball, 15, 200
    Hall of Fame, 199
    highlights of season, 199
    NBA champions, 15
    Olympics, 195
    standings for 1995-1996, 198
Belarus, 46-47
    map, 71; flag, 77
Belgium, 46-47
    map, 70; flag, 77
Belize, 46-47
    map, 67; flag, 77
Benin, 46-47
    map, 74; flag, 77
Bhagavad Ghita, 181
Bhutan, 46-47
    map, 73; flag, 77
Bible, 181, 296
Big bang theory, 160
Bill of Rights, U.S., 127, 217
Binary code, 40
Biodiversity, 89
Birthstones, 211
Black Americans. *See*
        African-Americans
Black hole, 160
Blues (music), 145
Bolivia, 46-47
    map, 68; flag, 77

Books, 31-34
    all-time best, 32
    awards, 31
    best of 1995, 32
Bosnia and Herzegovina, 46-47
    map, 70; flag, 77
    peace agreement, 17
Botswana, 46-47
    map, 75; flag, 77
Braille, 192
Brandy (singer), 14
Brazil, 46-47
    biggest swamp, 105
    map, 68; flag, 77
Bridges, 36
    longest in the United States, 214
    longest in world, 36
Brunei, 46-47
    map, 73; flag, 77
Buchanan, James, 226, 229
Buddhism, 180, 292
Budgets, 132-133
Buildings, bridges, and tunnels, 35-36
    seven wonders of ancient world, 35
    tallest buildings in United States, 36
Bulgaria, 46-47
    map, 71; flag, 77
Burkina Faso, 46-47
    map, 74; flag, 77
Burma. *See* Myanmar
Burundi, 46-47
    map, 75; flag, 77
Bush, George, 226, 232
Business. *See* Money and business

——— **C** ———

Cabinet of the United States, 218
Calendars, 211
California
    facts about, 258
    maps, 248, 252
    national parks, 278-280
    origin of name, 276
Calories, 112
Cambodia, 46-47
    map, 73; flag, 77
Camby, Marcus, 200
Cameroon, 46-47
    map, 74; flag, 77
Canada, 46-47
    map, 66; flag, 77
    Niagara Falls, 81
    tallest structure, 36, 81
Cape Verde, 46-47
    flag, 77
Capitals
    of countries, 44-64
    of states, 257-273
    puzzles, 64, 274

Capitol, U.S., 275
Caribbean, 67, 100
Carter, Jimmy (James Earl), 226, 232
Caspian Sea, 105
Cavities (teeth), 109
CD-ROMs, 39, 120
Celsius (centigrade) temperature, 283
Census, U.S., 170
Central African Republic, 48-49
    map, 74; flag, 77
Central America, 67, 100, 299
Chad, 48-49
    map, 74; flag, 77
Chamber music, 144
Chemical elements, 183-184
Chess, 17
Children, rights of, 127
Children's museums, 141
Chile, 48-49
    earthquakes, 103
    map, 69; flag, 77
China, 48-49
    earthquakes, 103
    Great Wall, 81
    map, 73; flag, 77
Cholesterol, 112
Christianity
    facts about, 179, 288, 296
    holy days, 182
    religious text of, 181
    U.S. membership, 181
Christmas, 115, 116
Circulatory system, 108
Cities
    busiest ports, 137
    as capitals of countries, 44-64
    as capitals of states, 257-273
    largest in United States, 169, 214,
        257-273
    largest in world, 168
    with tallest buildings, 36, 214
Citizenship, U.S., 173
Civil War, U.S., 238
Classical music, 144
Cleveland, Grover, 226, 230
Clinton, Bill (William Jefferson), 226, 232,
    233, 240
Clinton, Hillary Rodham, 233
Colombia, 48-49
    map, 68; flag, 77
    volcanic eruption, 101
Colorado
    facts about, 258
    maps, 248, 250
    national parks, 280
    origin of name, 276
Columbus Day, 115, 116
Comets, 157
Comoros, 48-49
    map, 75; flag, 77

Composers, 144
Computers, 37-43
    abbreviations, 120
    binary codes, 40
    and chess, 17
    facts about, 37-39, 41
    imports and exports, 136
    Internet and World Wide Web, 43
    museums about, 41
    programming language, 40
    puzzle, 41
Congo, 48-49
    map, 75; flag, 77
Congress, U.S., 220-222
Congressional Medal of Honor, 176
Connecticut
    facts about, 259
    maps, 241, 249
    origin of name, 276
Constellations, 158
Constitution, U.S., 127, 216-217, 219,
    237
Constitutional Convention, 237
Contests, 178
Continents
    facts about, 99
    hottest and coldest places, 283
    maps, 45, 65-76
Coolidge, Calvin, 226, 231
Costa Rica, 48-49
    map, 67; flag, 77
Cost of living, 129
Côte d'Ivoire (Ivory Coast), 48-49
    map, 74; flag, 77
Countries, 44-82
    currency and exchange rates, 45-63,
        131, 137
    energy producers and users, 86
    facts about, 44-63, 81-82
    flags, 77-80
    immigration, 172
    imports and exports, 136
    languages of world, 124
    largest and smallest in population, 168
    maps, 65-76, 248-249
    puzzle, 64
Country music, 142, 145
Crater, volcanic, 101
Croatia, 48-49
    map, 70; flag, 77
    peace agreement, 17
Crusades (1095-1291), 297
Cryptography, 193
Cuba, 48-49
    map, 67; flag, 77
Currency. See Money and business
Cyprus, 48-49
    map, 72; flag, 77
Czech Republic, 48-49
    map, 70; flag, 77

—————D—————

Dance, 148-149
Declaration of Independence, 236
Delaware
    facts about, 259
    maps, 242, 249
    origin of name, 276
Denmark, 48-49
    map, 70; flag, 77
    Tivoli Gardens, 81
Depression, economic, 129, 239
Deserts, 24, 105, 167
Dictionary, 34
Digestive system, 108
Dinosaurs, 17, 22, 25, 26
Djibouti, 48-49
    map, 74; flag, 77
Doctors, types of, 109
Dominica, 48-49
    map, 67; flag, 77
Dominican Republic, 48-49
    map, 67; flag, 77
Drugs, 113
Dyes, from plants, 167

—————E—————

Earth
    crust of, 102, 183
    facts about, 155
    hemispheres of, 98
    latitude and longitude, 98
    plates of, 102, 103
Earthquakes, 102-103
Eastern Europe, 70-71, 100
Eclipse, 157
Ecosystem, 96
Ecuador, 48-49
    map, 68; flag, 77
    Galapagos Islands, 81
Education
    jobs in, 135
    U.S. spending on, 134
Egypt, 48-49
    calendar, 211
    Great Sphinx, 81
    longest river, 105
    map, 74; flag, 78
    pyramids, 35, 81
Eisenhower, Dwight D., 226, 231
Election Day, 115, 116, 224
Elections, 224-225
Electoral College, 224
Elements, chemical, 183-184
Ellis Island (New York), 173
El Salvador, 48-49
    map, 67; flag, 78
E-mail (electronic mail), 41, 42, 121
Emergencies, what to do in, 114
Emmy Awards, 175

Encyclopedia, 34
Endangered species, 23
Endocrine system, 108
Energy and natural resources, 83-87
    production and use of energy, 86
    renewable resources, 87
    sources and types of energy, 83-85
England. See Great Britain
Entertainment
    awards, 174
    inventions, 118
    movies, videos, and television, 138-140
    museums, 142
    stars of today, 14
Environment, 88-97
    air pollution, 92-93
    biodiversity, 89
    forests and, 95
    garbage and recycling, 90-91, 96, 97
    puzzle, 97
    water pollution, 94
Equator, 98
Equatorial Guinea, 48-49
    map, 75; flag, 78
Eritrea, 50-51
    map, 74; flag, 78
Estonia, 50-51
    map, 71; flag, 78
Ethiopia, 50-51
    map, 74; flag, 78
Europe
    facts about, 99
    history, 295-298
    map, 70-71
Exchange rates, 137
    currency of countries, 45-63
Executive branch, U.S., 216
Exercise, 110
Explorers, 106
Exports, 136

—————F—————

Fahrenheit temperature, 283
Fat, dietary, 112
Figure skating. See Ice skating
Fiji, 50-51
    map, 76; flag, 78
Fillmore, Millard, 226, 228
Films. See Movies
Finland, 50-51
    map, 71; flag, 78
First ladies, 227-232, 233
Flags
    of countries of world, 77-80
    of Olympic Games, 194
    of United States, 80, 215
Florida
    facts about, 259
    maps, 243, 249

national parks, 278-279
origin of name, 276
Folk dance, 149
Food
food pyramid, 111
nutrients, calories, and fat, 112
puzzle, 125
recycling, 90, 91
U.S. spending on, 134
word origins, 125
Football, 201-203
college football, 203
Halls of Fame, 202, 203
standings for 1995, 201
Super Bowl, 15, 201
top performers, 202, 203
Ford, Gerald R., 226, 232
Forests, 95, 166
Fossil fuels, 84-85
Fossils, 24
France, 50-51
Eiffel Tower, 81
map, 70; flag, 78
Franklin, Benjamin, 130, 236

———— G ————

Gabon, 50-51
map, 75; flag, 78
Galapagos Islands, 76, 81
Galaxy, 160
Gambia, The, 50-51
map, 74; flag, 78
Garfield, James A., 226, 229
Gems, 187
General Assembly, UN, 212
Geography, 98-106
continents and oceans, 99
earthquakes, 102-103
explorers, 106
globe, 98
puzzle, 105
reading a map, 104
regions of world, 100
volcanoes, 101
George, Eddie, 203
Georgia (country), 50-51
map, 72; flag, 78
Georgia (state)
facts about, 260
maps, 245, 249
origin of name, 276
Geothermal energy, 87
Germany, 50-51
map, 70; flag, 78
Neuschwanstein Castle, 81
Ghana, 50-51
map, 74; flag, 78
Global warming, 92, 93, 96
Globe, 98
Government of United States, 216-223

Grammy Awards, 14, 175
Grand Canyon, 279
Grant, Ulysses S., 130, 226, 229
Grassland, plants of, 167
Great Britain, 50-51
Buckingham Palace, 82
longest bridge, 36
map, 70; flag, 80
Great Depression, 239
Great Seal of United States, 215
Great Wall of China, 81, 292
Greece, 50-51
Acropolis, 82
map, 71; flag, 78
Statue of Zeus, 35
Greenhouse effect, 93, 96
Greenland, 66, 105
Greenwich meridian, 98
Grenada, 50-51
map, 67; flag, 78
Gross Domestic Product (GDP), 129
Guatemala, 50-51
earthquakes, 103
map, 67; flag, 78
Guinea, 50-51
map, 74; flag, 78
Guinea-Bissau, 50-51
map, 74; flag, 78
Guyana, 50-51
map, 68; flag, 78
Gymnastics, 195, 204

———— H ————

Habitats, 23, 24, 96
Haiti, 50-51
map, 67; flag, 78
Halley's Comet, 157
Halloween, 116
Halls of Fame
band and choral directors, 177
baseball, 197
basketball, 199
conservation, 177
cowboys, 177
football, 202, 203
great Americans, 177
hockey, 205
inventors, 119
rock and roll, 17, 177
women, 177
Hamilton, Alexander, 130
Hanging Gardens of Babylon, 135
Harding, Warren G., 226, 231
Harrison, Benjamin, 226, 230
Harrison, William Henry, 226, 228
Hawaii
facts about, 260
map, 76
national parks, 279
origin of name, 276

Hayes, Rutherford B., 226, 229
Health, 107-114
    accident prevention, 114
    AIDS, 113
    drugs and alcohol, 113
    exercise, 110
    human body, 107-108
    inventions, 117
    nutrition, 111-112
    puzzle, 109
    teeth, 109
Heisman Trophy, 203
Hemispheres of Earth, 98
Hinduism, 180, 181, 292
Hispanic-Americans, population of, 170
Historic restorations, 143
Hockey. *See* Ice hockey
Holidays, 115-116
    legal U.S. holidays, 115-116
    religious holy days, 182
Holocaust Memorial Museum, U.S., 275
Honduras, 50-51
    map, 67; flag, 78
Hootie and the Blowfish, 14, 145, 175
Hoover, Herbert, 226, 231
House of Representatives, U.S., 220-221,
    222
Hubble telescope, 162
Human body, 107-108, 110
Hungary, 52-53
    map, 70; flag, 78
Hurricanes, 281, 282

——— **I** ———

Ice hockey, 195, 205
Iceland, 52-53
    map, 70; flag, 78
Ice skating, 15, 206
Idaho
    facts about, 260
    maps, 248, 254
    national park, 280
    origin of name, 276
Idioms, 123
Illinois
    facts about, 261
    maps, 244, 249
    origin of name, 276
Immigration, 172, 173
Impeachment, 220
Imports, 136
Independence Day, 115, 116
India, 52-53
    earthquakes, 103
    map, 72; flag, 78
    Taj Mahal, 82
Indiana
    facts about, 261
    maps, 244, 249
    origin of name, 276

Indian Ocean, 99
Indonesia, 52-53
    earthquakes, 103
    map, 73; flag, 78
    volcanic eruptions, 101
Instruments, musical, 146
Internet, 43
Inventions, 117-119
    Hall of Fame, 119
Invertebrates, types of, 21
Iowa
    facts about, 261
    maps, 244, 249
    origin of name, 276
Iran, 52-53
    earthquakes, 103
    map, 72; flag, 78
Iraq, 52-53
    map, 72; flag, 78
Ireland, 52-53
    Blarney Stone, 82
    map, 70; flag, 78
Islam
    facts about, 180, 289
    holy days, 182
    religious text of, 181, 289
    U.S. membership, 181
Islands, biggest, 105
Israel, 52-53
    Jerusalem, 82
    map, 72; flag, 78
    Rabin, Yitzhak, 16
Italy, 52-53
    map, 70; flag, 78
    language, 125
    volcanic eruptions, 101

——— **J** ———

Jackson, Andrew, 130, 226, 228
Jamaica, 52-53
    map, 67; flag, 78
Japan, 52-53
    earthquakes, 103
    longest tunnel, 36
    map, 73; flag, 78
    volcanic eruption, 101
Jazz (music), 145
Jefferson, Thomas, 130, 226, 227, 237
Jefferson Memorial, 275
Jerusalem, 82, 297
Jobs of Americans, 135
Johnson, Andrew, 226, 229
Johnson, Earvin "Magic," 199
Johnson, Lyndon Baines, 226, 232
Jordan, 52-53
    map, 72; flag, 78
Jordan, Michael, 15, 199
Judaism
    calendar, 211
    facts about, 179

holy days, 182
museums, 142, 275
religious text of, 181
U.S. membership, 181
Judicial branch, U.S., 216, 219
Jupiter, facts about, 155

———— **K** ————

Kansas.
facts about, 262
maps, 247, 248
origin of name, 276
Kasparov, Gary, 17
Kazakstan, 52-53
map, 72; flag, 78
Kennedy, Jacqueline, 233
Kennedy, John Fitzgerald, 161, 226, 231,
233, 240
Kentucky
facts about, 262
maps, 244, 249
national park, 280
origin of name, 276
Kenya, 52-53
map, 75; flag, 78
Kiribati, 52-53
map, 76; flag, 78
Koran, 181, 289
Korean War, 294
Kuwait, 52-53
map, 72; flag, 78
Kwan, Michelle, 15, 206
Kwanza, 116
Kyrgyzstan, 52-53
map, 72; flag, 78

———— **L** ————

Labor Day, 115, 116
Lakes, biggest and deepest, 105, 214
Landfills, 90
Language, 120-125
abbreviations and acronyms, 120
early writing, 288
idioms, 123
letter writing, 121
palindromes, 122
puzzles, 120, 122, 123, 125
spoken in United States, 124
words from other cultures, 125
of world, 124
Laos, 52-53
map, 73; flag, 78
Latitude, 98
Latvia, 54-55
map, 71; flag, 78
Law, 126-127
and Bill of Rights, 127
first written, 288
lawbreakers, punishment of, 126

law-making process, 222
and rights for children, 127
and Supreme Court, 219
Lebanon, 54-55
map, 72; flag, 78
Legislative branch, U.S., 220-222
Lemieux, Mario, 205
Lesotho, 54-55
map, 75; flag, 78
Liberia, 54-55
map, 74; flag, 78
Libya, 54-55
map, 74; flag, 78
Liechtenstein, 54-55
map, 70; flag, 78
Light, facts about, 186
Lincoln, Abraham, 130, 226, 229, 238
Lincoln Memorial, 275
Literature. See Books
Lithuania, 54-55
map, 71; flag, 78
Little League, 13, 197
Longitude, 98
Louisiana, 262
maps, 245, 249
origin of name, 276
Louisiana Purchase, 237
Lucid, Dr. Shannon, 16
Lunar eclipse, 157
Luxembourg, 54-55
map, 70; flag, 78

———— **M** ————

Macedonia, 54-55
map, 71; flag, 79
Madagascar, 54-55
map, 75; flag, 79
Maddux, Greg, 197
Madison, Dolley, 233
Madison, James, 226, 227, 233, 237
Magma, 101
Magnets, 185
Maine
facts about, 263
maps, 241, 249
national park, 278
origin of name, 276
Malawi, 54-55
map, 75; flag, 79
Malaysia, 54-55
map, 73; flag, 79
Maldives, 54-55
map, 72; flag, 79
Mali, 54-55
map, 74; flag, 79
Malta, 54-55
map, 70; flag, 79
Maps
of continents and countries, 65-76

plates of Earth, 103
reading of, 104
of United States, 67, 241-256
Mars, facts about, 155
Marshall Islands, 54-55
map, 76; flag, 79
Martin Luther King, Jr., Day, 115, 116
Maryland
facts about, 263
maps, 242, 249
origin of name, 276
Massachusetts
facts about, 263
maps, 241, 249
origin of name, 276
Mauritania, 54-55
map, 74; flag, 79
Mauritius, 54-55
flag, 79
McKinley, William, 226, 230
Measurements. See Weights and measures
Medal of Honor, 176
Memorial Day, 115, 116
Meola, Tony, 207
Mercury, facts about, 154
Meridians of Earth, 98
Mesozoic era, 25
Meteors, 160
Metric system, 284, 286-287
Mexico, 54-55
Chichén Itza, 82
earthquakes, 103
map, 67; flag, 79
Michigan
facts about, 264
maps, 246, 249
national park, 279
origin of name, 276
Micronesia, 54-55
map, 76; flag, 79
Middle East
facts about, 100
map, 72
history, 288-290
Miller, Shannon, 204
Million Man March, 16
Minerals, 112, 187
Minnesota
facts about, 264
maps, 246, 249
national park, 280
origin of name, 276
Mir (space station), 16
Mississippi
facts about, 264
maps, 245, 249
origin of name, 276
Missouri
facts about, 265
maps, 244, 249
origin of name, 276

Modern art, 29
Modern dance, 149
Moldova, 54-55
map, 71; flag, 79
Monaco, 56-57
map, 70; flag, 79
Money and business, 128-137
budgets, 132-133
businesses in United States, 134
currency of countries, 45-63, 131
exchange rates, 137
history of money, 128
jobs of Americans, 135
money circulated in United States, 131
spending of Americans, 134
trade, 136-137
U.S. Mint, 130
Mongolia, 56-57
map, 73; flag, 79
Monroe, James, 226, 227
Montana
facts about, 265
maps, 248, 254
national parks, 279, 280
origin of name, 276
Moon
facts about, 156
lunar eclipse, 157
space travel, 161
Morocco, 56-57
map, 74; flag, 79
Mountains, tallest, 105, 214
Mount Everest, 105
Movies, videos, and television, 138-140
Academy Awards (Oscars), 14, 174
best-selling videos, 140
Emmy Awards, 175
movie hits of 1995, 139
popular movies for kids, 138
popular TV shows, 140
stars of today, 14
words about movies, 139
Mozambique, 56-57
map, 75; flag, 79
Muscular system, 108
Museums, 141-143
art, 30, 142
children's, 141
computer, 41
entertainment, 142
ethnic, 142
historic restorations, 143
holocaust, 275
music, 17, 142, 177
natural history, 26
science, 189
Music and dance, 144-149
Grammys, 14, 175
halls of fame, 17, 177
instruments of orchestra, 146

museums, 17, 142, 177
musical notation, 144
musical theater, 147
stars of today, 14
top albums of 1995, 145
types of dance, 148-149
types of music, 144-146
Myanmar (Burma), 56-57
map, 73; flag, 79

—— **N** ——

Namibia, 56-57
map, 75; flag, 79
National anthem, United States, 215
National parks, U.S., 214, 278-280
Native Americans (American Indians)
facts about, 171, 234, 238, 299
museums, 142
in North America, 300
U.S. census, 170
Naturalization, 173
Natural resources. *See* Energy
Nauru, 56-57
map, 76; flag, 79
Nebraska
facts about, 265
maps, 247, 248
origin of name, 277
Nepal, 56-57
map, 72; flag, 79
tallest mountain, 105
Neptune, facts about, 156
Nervous system, 108
Netherlands, The, 56-57
map, 70; flag, 79
Nevada
facts about, 266
maps, 248, 252
national park, 279
origin of name, 277
New Hampshire
facts about, 266
maps, 241, 249
origin of name, 277
New Jersey
facts about, 266
maps, 242, 249
origin of name, 277
New Mexico
facts about, 267
maps, 248, 250
national park, 278
origin of name, 277
News, people and places in, 13-17
New Year (holiday), 115, 116, 182
New York (state)
facts about, 267
maps, 241, 249
musical theater in, 147
origin of name, 277

New Zealand, 56-57
map, 76; flag, 79
Nicaragua, 56-57
map, 67; flag, 79
Niger, 56-57
map, 74; flag, 79
Nigeria, 56-57
map, 74; flag, 79
Nile River, 105
Nixon, Richard Milhous, 13, 226, 232, 240, 294
Nobel Prizes, 176
North America
facts about, 99
map, 66-67
history, 106, 234, 299-301
North Carolina
facts about, 267
maps, 242, 249
origin of name, 277
North Dakota
facts about, 268
maps, 247, 248
national park, 280
origin of name, 277
North Korea, 52-53
map, 73; flag, 78
North Star (Polaris), 158
Norway, 56-57
map, 70; flag, 79
Norwood, Brandy, 14
Nuclear energy, 85
Numbers, 150-153
in ancient civilizations, 150
binary system, 40
large numbers, 151
prefixes used to form words, 151
puzzles, 153
Roman numerals, 150
solid and plane figures, 152
Nutrition, 111-112

—— **O** ——

Oceans, 24, 65-76, 99
Ohio
facts about, 268
maps, 244, 249
origin of name, 277
Oil (fuel), 290
Oklahoma
facts about 268
maps, 248, 251
origin of name, 277
Olympics, 194-195
mascot for 1996, 194
measurements for, 286
Special Olympics, 209
summer/winter sports, 195
Oman, 56-57
map, 72; flag, 79

Opera, 144
Orchestra, instruments of, 146
Oregon
 facts about, 269
 maps, 248, 255
 national park, 278
 origin of name, 277
Outer space. *See* Planets, stars, and
 space travel
Ozone layer, 92, 93

P

Pacific Islands, 76
Pacific Ocean, 99
Painting, 28-29
Pakistan, 56-57
 map, 72; flag, 79
Palau, 56-57
 map, 76; flag, 79
Palestine, 288, 289
Panama, 56-57
 map, 67; flag, 79
Papua New Guinea, 56-57
 map, 76; flag, 79
Paraguay, 56-57
 map, 69; flag, 79
Paralympic Games, 195
Pennsylvania
 facts about, 269
 maps, 241, 249
 origin of name, 277
People and places in the news, 13-17
 anniversaries, 13
 in the headlines, 16-17
 sports highlights, 15
 stars of today, 14
Peru, 58-59
 earthquakes, 103
 map, 68; flag, 79
Pets, 20
Philippines, 58-59
 map, 73; flag, 79
Pierce, Franklin, 226, 229
Planets, stars, and space travel, 54-3
 asteroids, 157
 black hole, 160
 comets, 157
 constellations, 158
 eclipse, 157
 galaxy, 160
 meteors and meteorites, 160
 moon, 156
 planets, 16, 154-156
 puzzle, 163
 satellites, 157
 solar system, 154-156
 space probes, 163
 space shuttles, 162
 space travel, 17, 161-162, 240
 zodiac, 159

Plants, 164-167
 oldest and tallest, 164
 where plants grow, 166-167
Pledge of Allegiance, 215
Pluto, facts about, 156
Poland, 58-59
 map, 71; flag, 79
Polk, James Knox, 226, 228
Polygons and polyhedrons, 152
Polynesia, 76, 100
Pop music, 145
Population, 168-173
 census, 170, 171
 of cities, 168, 169
 of countries, 44-63, 168
 immigration, 172
 of United States, 169
Ports, busiest in United States, 137
Portugal, 58-59
 map, 70; flag, 79
Postal abbreviations, 120, 257-273
Precipitation, types of, 282
President's Day, 115, 116
Presidents of United States
 and cabinet, 218
 death and succession, 218
 election of, 224
 facts about, 227-232
 impeachment of, 220
 list of, 226
 portraits on money, 130
 signing bills into law, 222
 term of office, 218
Prizes, awards, and contests, 174-178
 Academy Awards (Oscars), 14, 174
 book awards, 31
 Congressional Medal of Honor, 176
 contests, 178
 Emmys, 175
 Grammys, 14, 175
 Halls of Fame, 119, 177, 197, 199,
 202, 203, 205
 Heisman Trophy, 203
 in musical theater, 147
 Nobel Prizes, 176
 ulitzer Prizes, 176
 arn Medal, 176
 ports, 15, 194-209
 ony Awards, 175
Programming language, 40
Puerto Rico, 67, 273
Puzzles
 animals, 20, 26
 answers to, 302-305
 computers, 41
 countries and capitals, 64
 environment, 97
 geography, 105
 health, 109
 language, 120, 122, 123, 125
 numbers, 153

s, 163
...nd symbols, 193
sports, 209
states and capitals, 120, 274

———— **Q** ————

Qatar, 58-59
  map, 72; flag, 79

———— **R** ————

Rabin, Yitzhak, 16
Rainbow, 186
Rain forests, 166
Rap music, 145
Reagan, Ronald, 226, 232
Recycling, 90-91, 96, 97
Regions of world, 100
Religion, 179-182
  major holy days, 182
  major religions, 179-180
  religious texts, 181
  U.S. membership, 181
Renewable energy resources,
    types of, 87
Reproductive system, 108
Respiratory system, 108
Rhode Island
  facts about, 269
  maps, 241, 249
  origin of name, 277
Richter scale, 102
Ring of Fire, 101
Ripken, Cal, Jr., 15, 197
Rivers, longest, 105, 214
Rock music, 17, 145, 177
Rocks, 187
Romania, 58-59
  map, 71; flag, 79
Roman numerals, 150
Roosevelt, Eleanor, 231, 233
Roosevelt, Franklin Delano, 130, 226, 231,
    233, 239
Roosevelt, Theodore, 176, 226, 230
Russia, 58-59
  earthquakes, 103
  Kremlin, 82
  map, 71, 72-73; flag, 79
  space travel, 16, 161, 162
Rwanda, 58-59
  map, 75; flag, 79

———— **S** ————

Sahara (Africa), 105
Saint Kitts and Nevis, 58-59
  map, 67; flag, 79
Saint Lucia, 58-59
  map, 67; flag, 79
Saint Vincent and the Grenadines, 58-59
  map, 67; flag, 79

San Marino, 58-59
  map, 70; flag, 79
São Tomé, and Príncipe, 58-59
  map, 75; flag, 79
Satellites, 157, 163
Saturn, facts about, 155
Saudi Arabia, 58-59
  map, 72; flag, 79
Scandinavia, 70-71, 100
Science, 183-189
  chemical elements, 183-184
  famous scientists, 188
  light and sound, 186
  minerals, rocks, and gems, 187
  museums, 26, 189
Sculpture, 30
Seles, Monica, 208
Senate, U.S., 220, 222
Senegal, 58-59
  map, 74; flag, 79
Seven Wonders of the Ancient World, 35
Seychelles
  facts about, 58-59
  flag, 79
Sierra Leone, 58-59
  map, 74; flag, 79
Sign language, 192
Signs and symbols, 190-193
  Braille, 192
  chemical elements, 183-184
  common signs, 190
  cryptography, 193
  on maps, 104
  musical notation, 144
  puzzle, 193
  road signs, 191
  sign language, 192
  U.S. symbols, 215
Simpson, O.J., 16
Singapore, 58-59
  map, 73; flag, 80
Skating. *See* Ice skating
Skeletal system, 108
Ski... ...01
S... ...an, 58-59
  ...na, 70 flag, 80
  ...ein, 60-61
  ...na, 0; flag, 80
  ...ith, ...mitt, 202
  ...nian Institution, 275
  ...or, 207
  ...pics, 195
Soil e...ion, 96
Solar e...lipse, 157
Solomon Islands, 60-61
  map, 76; flag, 80
Somalia, 60-61
  map, 74; flag, 80
Sound, facts about, 186
South Africa, 60-61
  map, 75; flag, 80

INDEX

South America, 99
map, 68-69
history, 106, 299-301
South Carolina
facts about, 270
maps, 242, 249
origin of name, 277
South Dakota
facts about, 270
maps, 247, 248
national parks, 278, 280
origin of name, 277
Southeast Asia, 73, 100
South Korea, 52-53
map, 73; flag, 78
Soviet Union. *See* Russia
Space probes, 163
Space shuttles and space stations, 16, 162
Space travel, 161-163, 240
Spain, 60-61
map, 70; flag, 80
Special Olympics, 209
Spelling
contest, 178
words that sound alike, 122
Spingarn Medal, 176
Sports, 194-209
baseball, 15, 196-197
basketball, 15, 198-200
football, 15, 201-203
gymnastics, 204
ice hockey, 205
ice skating, 15, 206
Olympics, 194-195, 204, 206, 207
puzzle, 209
soccer, 207
Special Olympics, 209
swimming, 207
tennis, 208
Sri Lanka, 60-61
map, 72; flag, 80
Stars
black hole, 160
constellations, 158
galaxy, 160
sun as, 154
"Star-Spangled Banner," 215, 237
States of United States
Electoral College votes, 224
facts about, 169, 214, 257-273
national parks, 278-280
origins of names, 276-277
puzzles, 274
representatives in U.S. House, 221
Statue of Liberty (New York), 173
Stonehenge (Great Britain), 211
Storms, types of, 282
Sudan, 60-61
longest river, 105
map, 74; flag, 80

Sun
distance from planets, 154-156
energy from, 84
solar eclipse, 157
solar power, 87
as star, 154
Super Bowl, 15, 201
Supreme Court, U.S., 219
Suriname, 60-61
map, 68; flag, 80
Swamps, biggest, 105
Swaziland, 60-61
map, 75; flag, 80
Sweden, 60-61
map, 70; flag, 80
Swimming, 207
Olympics, 195
Switzerland, 60-61
longest tunnel, 36
map, 70; flag, 80
Symbols. *See* Signs and symbols
Symphony, 144
Syria, 60-61
map, 72; flag, 80

——— **T** ———

Taft, William Howard, 226, 230
Taiwan, 60-61
map, 73; flag, 80
Tajikistan, 60-61
map, 72; flag, 80
Tanzania, 60-61
map, 75; flag, 80
Taylor, Zachary, 226, 228
Teeth, 109
Television
Emmy Awards, 175
most popular shows in 1995-1996 season, 140
museum of, 142
stars of today, 14
Temperature, 283
Ten Commandments, 288
Tennessee
facts about, 270
maps, 245, 249
national park, 279
origin of name, 277
Tennis, 195, 208
Texas
facts about, 271
maps, 248, 251
national parks, 278, 279
origin of name, 277
Thailand, 60-61
map, 73; flag, 80
Thanksgiving, 115, 116
Theater, 147, 175
Thomas, Jonathan Taylor, 14
Tibet, 72, 105

Time and calendars, 210-211
Time zones, 210
Togo, 60-61
    map, 74; flag, 80
Tonga, 60-61
    map, 76; flag, 80
Tony Awards, 147, 175
Trade, 136-137
"Trail of Tears," 238
Transportation
    inventions in, 117
    road signs, 191
    travel time, 210
Trees, 95, 164
Trinidad and Tobago, 60-61
    map, 68; flag, 80
Truman, Harry S., 226, 231
Tunisia, 60-61
    map, 74; flag, 80
Tunnels, 36
Turkey, 35, 62-63
    map, 72; flag, 80
Turkmenistan, 62-63
    map, 72; flag, 80
Tuvalu, 62-63
    map, 76; flag, 80
Tyler, John, 226, 228

───── U ─────

Uganda, 62-63
    map, 75; flag, 80
Ukraine, 62-63
    map, 71; flag, 80
United Arab Emirates, 62-63
    map, 72; flag, 80
United Kingdom. See Great Britain
United Nations, 212-213
    countries in, 44-63
    goals of, 212
    organization of, 212-213
    rights of children, 127
    secretaries-general, 213
United States, 214-280
    budget, 133
    buildings, bridges, and tunnels, 36
    busiest ports, 137
    capital of, 275
    census, 170
    Constitution, 216-217
    earthquakes, 103
    elections, 224-225
    energy sources, 86, 87
    facts about, 62-63, 214
    government, 216-223
    history time line, 234-240
    hottest and coldest places, 283
    immigrants, 172-173
    jobs, 135
    languages spoken, 124
    largest cities, 169

leading businesses, 134
legal holidays, 115-116
maps, 67, 248-249; flag, 80, 215
money and exchange rates, 130-131,
    137
motto, 215
national anthem, 215
national parks, 82, 278-280
national symbols, 215
population, 169, 170, 214
presidents, 226-233
religious membership, 181
space travel, 161-163
spending patterns, 134
states, facts about, 257-273, 276-277
time zones, 210
trading partners, 136
vice presidents, 226
volcanic eruption, 101
water use, 94
weights and measurements, 284-285
Universe, beginning of, 160
Uranus, facts about, 156
Urinary system, 108
Uruguay, 62-63
    map, 69; flag, 80
    independence, 301
Utah
    facts about, 271
    maps, 248, 253
    national parks, 278, 280
    origin of name, 277
Uzbekistan, 62-63
    map, 72

───── V ─────

Valentine's Day, 116
Van Buren, Martin, 226, 228
Vanuatu, 62-63
    map, 76; flag, 80
Vatican City, 62-63
    map, 70; flag, 80
Venezuela, 62-63
    highest waterfall, 105
    map, 68; flag, 80
Venus, facts about, 154
Vermont
    facts about, 271
    maps, 241, 249
    origin of name, 277
Vertebrates, types of, 21
Veterans Day, 115, 116
Vice presidents of the United States
    election of, 224
    list of, 226
    as presidential successor, 218
Videos and video games, 140
Vietnam, 62-63
    map, 73; flag, 80
Vietnam Veterans Memorial, 275

Virginia
 facts about, 272
 maps, 242, 249
 national park, 280
 origin of name, 277
Volcanoes, 101
 on Mars, 155
Voting, 224-225

——— **W** ———

Washington, George, 130, 226, 227, 233, 237
Washington, Martha, 233
Washington (state)
 facts about, 272
 maps, 248, 255
 national parks, 280
 origin of name, 277
Washington, D.C., 275
Washington Monument, 275
Water
 energy from, 85, 87
 forms of, 185
 and human body, 112
 pollution, 94
 saving of, 97
 use and overuse, 94
Waterfalls
 highest waterfall, 105
 Niagara Falls, 81
Weather, 281-283
 and endangered species, 23
 hottest and coldest places, 283
 hurricanes, 281
 temperatures, 283
 wind speed, 281
Weights and measures, 284-287
 metric system, 284, 286-287
 U.S. measurements, 284-285
Western Samoa, 62-63
 map, 76; flag, 80
West Virginia
 facts about, 272
  maps, 242, 249
 origin of name, 277
What kids are saying, 9-12
White House, 218, 275
Wilson, Woodrow, 176, 226, 230
Wisconsin
 facts about, 273
 maps, 246, 249
 origin of name, 277
World Cup, 207
World history, 288-301
 Africa, 290-291
 Americas, 299-301
 Asia, 292-294
 Europe, 295-298
 Middle East, 288-290
World Series, 13, 196
World War I (1914-1918), 239
World War II (1939-1945), 239, 294
World Wide Web, 43
Wyoming
 facts about, 273
 maps, 248, 254
 national parks, 279, 280
 origin of name, 277

——— **Y** ———

Yellowstone National Park, 82, 280
Yemen, 62-63
 map, 72; flag, 80
Yugoslavia, 62-63
 map, 71; flag, 80

——— **Z** ———

Zaire, 62-63
 map, 75; flag, 80
Zambia, 62-63
 map, 75; flag, 80
Zimbabwe, 62-63
 map, 75; flag, 80
Zodiac, signs of, 159
Zoos, 27

ILLUSTRATION AND PHOTO CREDITS

ILLUSTRATION
Bernard Adnet; Janice Edelman-Lee; Arthur Friedman; Ann Iosa;
Image Club Graphics, Inc., 800-387-9193; Sophia Lato; George Ulrich.

PHOTOGRAPHY
13: Chuck Yeager, © UPI/Bettmann Newsphotos. **14:** Brandy Norwood, © UPN/Courtesy
The Kobal Collection; Jonathan Taylor Thomas, © ABC Television/Courtesy The Kobal Collection.
15: Michael Jordan, © Andrew D. Bernstein/NBA Photos. **16:** Dr. Shannon Lucid, © AP/
Wide World Photos. **17:** Skull of the Carcharodontosaurus, © Courtesy The Kobal Collection;
Elvis Presley, © David Skull/NYT Pictures. **19:** Horses, © Corel. **27:** Animals, © Corel. **31:**
Cover, from *The Midwife's Apprentice* by Karen Cushman. Jacket illustration copyright © 1995
by Trina Schart Hyman. Reprinted by permission of Clarion Books/Houghton Mifflin Company.
All rights reserved. **32:** Cover from *The Horror at Camp Jellyjam* by R.L. Stine. Reproduced by
permission of Scholastic Inc. and Parachute Press. **139:** Scene from *Toy Story*, © Walt Disney
Studio/Courtesy The Kobal Collection. **140:** Cast from *Friends*, © Warner Bros. All Rights Reserved.
145: Hootie and the Blowfish, © Ethan Hill/Atlantic Records. **147:** *The Fantasticks* poster,
Courtesy of *The Fantasticks*. **174:** Scene from *Babe*, © Universal Studios, Inc./Courtesy The
Kobal Collection. **175:** The Tony Award, Courtesy of Tony Awards Productions ®; photo courtesy
of Keith Sherman & Associates, Inc., New York. **194:** 1996 Olympic Mascot, © 1993 ACOG.
196: Major League Baseball logo, courtesy of MLB Properties. **197:** Greg Maddux, © 1996
Scott Cunningham/MLB Photos. **199:** NBA logo, Courtesy of NBA Properties, Inc; Magic Johnson,
Courtesy of Firsteam Marketing, Inc. and © Wen Roberts/Photography Ink. **200:** Marcus Camby,
Courtesy of the University of Massachusetts at Amherst. **201:** AFC and NFC logos, Courtesy of
NFL Properties, Inc. **202:** Emmitt Smith, Courtesy of the Dallas Cowboys Football Club.
203: Eddie George, Courtesy of The Ohio State University at Columbus. **204:** Shannon Miller,
© Dave Black/USA Gymnastics Federation. **205:** Mario Lemieux, © Denny Cavanaugh/Pittsburgh
Penguins. **206:** Michelle Kwan, © Doug Pensinger/Allsport USA. **207:** Tony Meola, Courtesy of
Integrated Sports Intl. **208:** Monica Seles, Courtesy of International Management Group and
© Michael Baz Photography. **211:** Stonehenge, © Corel. **218:** The White House, © Corel. **219:**
Supreme Court Justices, Courtesy of the Supreme Court Historical Society. **221:** Capitol Building,
PhotoDisc Inc. **227-232:** United States Presidents 1-36, © 1967 by Dover Publications, Inc. **232:**
President Nixon, Courtesy of Richard Nixon Library; President Ford, Courtesy of the Gerald R. Ford
Museum; President Carter, Courtesy of the Jimmy Carter Library; President Reagan, Courtesy
of the Ronald Reagan Library; President Bush, Courtesy of Bush Presidential Materials Project;
President Bill Clinton, Courtesy of the White House. **233:** Martha Washington, Abigail Adams,
Dolley Madison, Eleanor Roosevelt, Jacqueline Kennedy, © 1967 by Dover Publications, Inc.;
Hillary Rodham Clinton, Courtesy of the White House. **276-277:** Landscapes, © Corel.

FRONT COVER
Illustration: Dinosaur, Todd Cooper.
Photography: Globe, Courtesy of NASA; Computer, © PhotoDisc Inc; Soccer Player,
© Scott Halleran; Virtual Reality, Courtesy of NASA; Space Shuttle, © Corel;
Totem Pole, © Art Montes de Oca, FPG International Corp.

BACK COVER
Illustration: Money and Inventions, Todd Cooper.
Photography: Gymnast, Elephants, Stonehenge, © Corel; Sandwich, © PhotoDisc Inc.